Gehlen

SPY OF THE CENTURY

By the same author

SECRETS OF THE BRITISH SECRET SERVICE

SOVIET SPY NET

THE NET THAT COVERS THE WORLD

SISTERS OF DELILAH

TRAITOR BETRAYED

THEY CAME FROM THE SKY

FROM BATTENBERG TO MOUNTBATTEN

INSIDE S.O.E.

SET EUROPE ABLAZE!

THE THIRD MAN (*The Truth about Kim Philby*)

GEORGE BLAKE—DOUBLE AGENT

SPY TRADE

To be published by Hodder and Stoughton in 1972:

BRITISH SECRET SERVICE

Gehlen

SPY OF THE CENTURY

BY E. H. COOKRIDGE

RANDOM HOUSE
NEW YORK

Contents

vii

Illustrations

Photographs: Associated Press; Jean Béranger; The Daily Telegraph;
Der Spiegel; European Copyright Co.; J. Mader; Militärarchiv,
Frieburg; National Archives And Records Service, Washington, D.C.;
Wolf Pelikan, Munich; Friedrich Rauch, Munich; Suddeütscher
Verlag; Stockholme Police; United Press International; United States
Army.

Glossary

A-2

US Air Force Intelligence department

ABWEHR

(lit. defence.) The espionage and counter-espionage service of the German High Command, revived from the *Nachrichtendienst* (q.v.) in 1920, at first clandestinely because of its prohibition by the Treaty of Versailles; subsequently the intelligence service of the General Staff and the OKW under Admiral Wilhelm Canaris. Disbanded in 1944 and absorbed into the RSHA *Militäramt* (q.v.)

ABWEHR-AST

Abwehr-Aussenstelle, Abwehr branches, particularly in the German-occupied territories.

ABWEHR III/F

Abwehr group and its branches concerned with counter-espionage and counter-sabotage.

AMT BLANK

Federal German office in 1950 preparing the establishing of the new German Army, precursor of the Federal Defence Ministry.

AMT VI

Office VI of RSHA (q.v.), originally its foreign political information department, became the espionage and counter-espionage service of RSHA, eventually its *Militäramt*, absorbing the Abwehr.

BfV

Bundesamt für Verfassungsschutz, Federal Office for the Protection of the Constitution, West German counter-espionage service established in 1950.

BND

Bundesnachrichtendienst, Federal Intelligence Service, established as a Federal German government department in 1956 by the transfer of the Gehlen Organisation to government control.

BUNDESTAG

Parliament of the Federal Republic of Germany elected for a term of four years.

CHEKA

Chrezvychainaya Komissya po Borbe s Kontrrevoluts-yeyi, Extraordinary Commission for the fight of counter-revolution, set up on December 20, 1917, became GPU (q.v.) on February 6, 1922.

CIA	United States Central Intelligence Agency.
CIC	US Army Counter-Intelligence Corps.
COMINFORM	Communist Information Bureau, an organisation set up in 1947 by the principal communist parties under the aegis of the Communist Party of the USSR.
COMINTERN	Communist (or Third) International, the organisation of the world's communist parties, set up in Moscow in 1920, dissolved in 1943.
DDR	*Deutsche Demokratische Republik*, the East German Democratic Republic.
D-Fing	Direction finding (of radio transmissions by wireless beam).
DP	Displaced Person, description of foreign nationals mainly from Eastern Europe found in Germany after Allied occupation who refused to return to their countries of origin.
FBI	United States Federal Bureau of Investigation, concerned with inter-state crime investigations and counter-espionage within the United States of America.
FHO	*Fremde Heere Ost* department of OKW, engaged on evaluating war intelligence in the East; after Gehlen became its chief in 1942, he arrogated to FHO active espionage and counter-espionage activities.
FHW	*Fremde Heere West* department of the OKW, engaged on evaluating war intelligence in the West.
FREIKORPS	"Free Corps", illegal armed units in Germany after the First World War composed of former officers and men of the Imperial army and navy, opposed to the Weimar Republic and engaged in fighting communists and socialists.
FUNKSPIEL	(lit. radio game.) The use of captured enemy radio operators and transmitters for maintaining a fake radio link with enemy intelligence.
G-2	United States Army Intelligence Department.
GEHEIM	Secret. *Geheime Reichssache*, Secret State Matter; *Geheime Kommandosache*, Secret High Command Matter.

GESTAPO	*Geheime Staats Polizei*, Secret State Police of the Hitler regime, i.e. Amt IV of RSHA (q.v.)
GPU	*Gosudarstvennoye Politicheskoye Upravlenye*, State Political Directorate, Soviet political security, espionage and counter-espionage department, successor to CHEKA, 1922-23, renamed OGPU, until 1934. See NKVD.
HITLER YOUTH	*Hitler Jugend*, para-military formation of the Nazi Party, compulsory for young Germans between 14 and 21; children from 10 to 14 belonged to the "Young Folk" organisation; girls after the age of 14 had to join the *Bund Deutscher Mädel*, German Girls' League, the opposite number of the Hitler Youth.
HIWI	*Hilfswillige*, (lit. willing to help); description of the so-called volunteers from amongst prisoners of war who joined the special units of the German Army composed of East Europeans and Asiatics.
HVA	*Hauptverwaltung Aufklärung*, head office for reconnaissance, counter-espionage department of MfSS (q.v.)
HV-Man	See V-man
IMT	International Military Tribunal at Nuremberg.
ISH	*Internationaler Verband der Seeleute und Hafenarbeiter*, International Union of Seamen and Dockers, the Wollweber organisation.
JAGDKOMMANDO	also *JAGDVERBÄNDE*, the SS sabotage and subversion units in occupied countries, often employed on punitive operations. Skorzeny was head of the RSHA department which controlled them.
K-5	*Kommissariat 5*, the Soviet-controlled espionage and counter-espionage office in the Soviet zone of Germany, precursor of the East German Ministry for State Security.
KAPO	(lit. head, chief, from *capo* Italian.) A foreman in a concentration camp usually selected from criminals detained in the camps.
KGB	*Komitat Gosudarstvennoy Bezopasnosti*, Committee of State Security. Two months after Beria's execution in 1953 the espionage and counter-espionage departments were separated from the Soviet MVD/MGB (q.v.) and were put under this committee, whose chairman has cabinet rank.

KgU	*Kampf gegen Unmenschlichkeit,* "Fight against Inhumanity", an anti-communist organisation in West Berlin.
KRIEGSTAGEBUCH (KT)	(lit. war diary) The official KT of the OKW recorded minutes of Fuhrer conferences, orders issued by OKW and general front operations. KTs were also kept by other Wehrmacht commands, the Abwehr, and other departments.
KZ	*Konzentrationslager,* concentration camp. According to an official survey of RSHA of January 15, 1945, there were at that time still 714,211 concentration camp inmates, though several hundred thousand had died or had been put to death during the war.
MAD	*Militärischer Abschirmdienst,* Military Protection Service, the military intelligence service, incl. military counter-espionage, of the Federal German Republic since 1956, emanating from the Military Security Service of Amt Blank (q.v.)
MfSS	*Ministerium für Staats-Sicherheit,* Ministry for State Security of the German Democratic Republic (DDR).
MGB	*Ministerstvo Gosudarstvennoy Bezopasnosti,* Ministry of State Security, the renamed NKGB. In March 1946 all Soviet commissariats were renamed ministries.
MI5	British Military Intelligence Branch 5, originally the counter-espionage department of the War Office, later a separate department subordinated to the Home Office, since 1945 the Directorate-General of Security Service.
MI6	British Military Intelligence Branch 6, later a separate department (Special Intelligence) linked to the Foreign Office, eventually the SIS (q.v.).
MI9	British Military Intelligence Branch 9, concerned with British (and Allied) prisoners of war; it also assisted Allied agents to escape from nazi-occupied territories.
MI14	British Military Intelligence Branch 14, conducted intelligence operations after the occupation of Germany in 1945.
NACHRICHTENDIENST	(lit. Information service) The intelligence service of the German Empire, it became the ABWEHR (q.v.) about 1920.
NATO	North Atlantic Treaty Organisation; a defence treaty "to safeguard the freedom, common heritage and

civilisation of their peoples" and providing that "an armed attack against one or more of them in Europe or North America shall be considered an attack against them all", signed on April 4, 1949, by Belgium, Canada, Denmark, France, Iceland, Italy, Luxembourg, the Netherlands, Norway, Portugal, the United Kingdom and the United States. It was adhered to in 1951 by Greece and Turkey, and in 1955 by the Federal German Republic.

NKGB   *Narodnyi Kommissariat Gosudarstvennoy Bezopastnosti*, People's Commissariat of State Security. On February 3, 1941, the political police, espionage and counter-espionage branches of NKVD became a separate commissariat, but in July, after the German attack on the Soviet Union, they were reunited with NKVD, becoming in April 1943 again a separate government department, renamed in 1946 MGB (q.v.) and eventually transformed in 1953 into KGB (q.v.).

NKVD   *Narodnyi Kommissariat Vniutrennikh Dyel*, People's Commissariat for Internal Affairs. It included the political police and espionage and counter-espionage departments. See NKGB. Renamed in 1946 MVD, Ministry for Internal Affairs.

NTS   *Narodnyi Trudovoy Soyuz*, National Labour Union, also called Alliance of Russian National Solidarists. An anti-communist organisation of Russian political exiles founded in 1920 in Belgrade; later with many branches in Germany and head offices in Frankfurt and Munich.

OKW   *Oberkommando der Wehrmacht*, High Command of the German Armed Forces, Hitler's Supreme Headquarters.

ORG   Familiar name for Organisation Gehlen used by its staff and agents.

ORGANISATION TODT   A semi-military German organisation during the Hitler regime established in 1933 under Fritz Todt, Minister of Armaments. Its main function was the construction of fortifications, strategic roads and military establishments. After Todt's death Albert Speer became its head.

OSS   Office of Strategic Services, American wartime intelligence organisation.

OSTTRUPPEN   Eastern Forces, units recruited from amongst Soviet prisoners of war, deserters and defectors, serving in German uniforms and under German command in the army and the Waffen SS.

OUN	*Organizatsia Ukrainiskikh Nationalistiv*, Organisation of Ukrainian Nationalists, anti-communist emigré organisation; there were also OUNR (revolutionary) and OUNS (military) groups.
PWE	Political Warfare Executive, British wartime propaganda department.
R-NET	*Rück-Netz*, "the net in the rear"; espionage and sabotage networks established by the Germans during the Allied invasion of Germany in 1944/45.
REICHSBANNER	Para-military organisation of the Social Democratic Party and the German trade unions for the defence of the Weimar Republic against the nazis.
REICHSLEITER	Highest ranking Nazi Party officials, most of whom held ministerial posts.
REICHSWEHR	The German armed forces after 1919, limited to 100,000 men by the Treaty of Versailles.
RFE	Radio Free Europe, an American-financed broadcasting network disseminating anti-communist propaganda with head office in Munich.
RIAS	Radio in the American Sector. US radio station in West Berlin.
RSHA	*Reichs-Sicherheits-Hauptamt*, Head Department for the Security of the Reich. It was formed in 1939, combining the GESTAPO (q.v.), the KRIPO (Criminal police) and the SD Security Service (q.v.). Its head was Heinrich Himmler as Reichsfuhrer of the SS. Its *Amt VI* and later its *Militäramt* conducted espionage and counter-espionage, and controlled armed sabotage and subversion units in occupied territories.
SA	*Sturmabteilungen*, the "Brownshirts", originally the shock troops of the Nazi Party founded in 1921 engaged in beer hall and street riots during the Weimar Republic. After the purge in 1934 eclipsed by the SS.
SD	*Sicherheitdienst*, Security Service of RSHA originally the intelligence service of the SS and Nazi Party it formed the espionage and counter-espionage sections of RSHA under Heydrich and Walter Schellenberg.
SDECE	*Service de Documentation Extérieure et de Contre-Espionage*, Service for Foreign Documentation and Counter-espionage; French Intelligence Service.

SHAEF	Supreme Headquarters Allied Expeditionary Forces; General Eisenhower's HQ.
SIS	British Secret Intelligence Service, emanating from the former Special Intelligence and MI6.
SNB	*Sprava Narodni Bespečnosti*, National Security Office; Czechoslovak Intelligence Service.
SOE	British Special Operations Executive which trained and dispatched officers and agents as instructors to Resistance groups in nazi-occupied Europe.
SONDERKOMMANDO	Special commandos, detachments of the SS employed for police tasks and during the war as punitive units in occupied territories.
SS	*Schutzstaffel* (lit. protection detachment.) Formed in 1929 as *Stosstrupp Hitler*, (Assault troop, Hitler's bodyguard) it became the most powerful organisation of the Nazi Party and the uniformed élite of its membership, assuming wide police powers and manning the GESTAPO, SD and other state institutions, particularly the RSHA, whose officials were SS officers. It became a state within the State with its own SS army. Also see Waffen SS.
SSD	*Staats-Sicherheits-Dienst*, the executive (political police) organ of the East German MfSS (q.v.).
STAHLHELM	The nationalist (not nazi) German ex-servicemen's organisation founded in 1918, was absorbed in 1933 into the SA (q.v.).
TASS	*Telegravnoye Agentstvo Sovietskovo Soyuza*, Telegraphic Agency of the Soviet Union, the official news agency, some of whose correspondents abroad act as KGB agents.
TBK	*Toter Brief Kasten*, a deadletter box, a hiding place for secret messages to be collected by agent or couriers.
TREFF	(lit. meeting or date) in the jargon of secret agents a clandestine meeting.
USAF	US Air Force
USIS	US Information Service
V-Mann (V-man)	(lit. *Vertrauesmann*) a trusted person; an informer, a secret agent; often enlisted by a secret service from

among nationals of the country where it illegally operates. In the Gehlen Organisation there were also HV-men, i.e. *Haupt-Vertrauensmänner*, or Head-V-men, and VF, V-men Fuhrer, i.e. V-men leaders, usually the sub-branch managers.

VOLKSDEUTSCHE   Racial Germans; people of German origin in foreign countries, usually in eastern and south-east Europe.

VOPO   *Volkspolizei*, People's Police, the police of the East German DDR.

WAFFEN SS   Fully militarised combat units of the SS. Several of the forty Waffen SS divisions (including tank units) employed during the war were composed of non-Germans, such as Ukrainians, Tartars, Cossacks, etc.

WEHRMACHT   German Armed Forces, i.e. army, navy and air force under the Hitler regime.

Acknowledgments

First I want to express my gratitude to the many former members of the staff of the Gehlen Organisation and the *Bundesnachrichten-dienst* without whose cooperation this book could never have been written. They supplied me with much information and documentary evidence on the understanding that I would withhold their names. Some of them are still in government service, while others were understandably concerned about possible repercussions upon their future prospects. I gave them, therefore, the promise that their information will be treated confidentially. I also received consider-able help from Central Intelligence Agency officials who were involved in General Gehlen's operations, and from officers who served with General Sibert's G-2 Intelligence HQ during the fledgling years of the Gehlen Organisation and later.

For a major part of the wartime documentation in this book I am indebted to Dr. Robert Wolfe, Specialist for Modern European History and one of the custodians of the OKW archives deposited in the National Archives and Record Service of the United States General Services Administration in Washington, D.C. He very kindly guided me through the microfilm collection of documents from Hitler's OKW and the extant *Amt Ausland-Abwehr* and *Fremde Heere Ost* dossiers and arranged for me to obtain the microfilm rolls I required, some of which are still classified as "privileged". I readily accepted the condition that "any direct citation of this privileged material would be at the citer's own liability".

After three years' research I conducted further investigations at the *Bundesarchiv-Militärarchiv* in Freiburg im Breisgau, where classified war documents have been deposited since they were handed over by the United States National Archives to the govern-ment of the Federal Republic of Germany. For assistance with this part of my research I am grateful to the director of the *Bundesar-chiv-Militärarchiv*, Colonel Dr. Stahl and his deputy, Lieutenant-Colonel Forwick. It proved difficult to locate some of the files I sought, but eventually they were produced. For this I am particularly grateful to Herr Amtmann B. Meier, whose cheerful assistance and encyclopaedic knowledge of the records proved invaluable.

My research has involved contacts with numerous government

departments and institutions in several countries, notably in Germany, the United States and Great Britain, and I should like to thank all the officials and archivists upon whose time and patience I have cruelly imposed. I can here single out only a few: Dr. Seeberg-Elverfeldt, archives director of the *Informationsamt* of the German Federal Government in Bonn; *Regierungs-Direktor* F.von Bebber of the Federal Ministry for the Interior in Bonn; Dr. A. Hoch of the *Institut für Zeitgeschichte* in Munich; Colonel Dr. Schottelius of the *Militärgeschichtliches Forschungsamt*; Mrs. Agnes F. Peterson of the Central and Western European Collection of the Hoover Institution, Stanford University, Stanford, California; Federal Judge Dr. Rinck of the *Bundesgerichtshof* in Karlsruhe for advising me on sources of transcripts of espionage trials; officials of the Supreme Court of the DDR and the editors of *Neue Justiz* in Leipzig for permission to use documents on trials; Mr. David Gitlin, assistant director and Mr. R. Rockingham Gill of Radio Free Europe; the archivists of the Central State Archives (CGAOR) in Moscow.

I wish to express my thanks to the authors and publishers who have given me permission to use copyright material from their publications, all of which are mentioned with appropriate details in the Notes and in Documentation and Select Bibliography in this book, and to Dr. Julius Mader for letting me see his work in manuscript form.

Without the unstinted help of my friend John Goulding, who has on many occasions sacrificed a night's sleep to assist me with research and revision, this book would never have seen the light of day. Leslie Mallory gave me valuable advice. Robin Denniston, Jane Osborn and the production staff of Hodder and Stoughton have generously coped with the problem I posed them and I owe them a debt for the speedy and excellent production of this book. I should also like to commend the devotion of Mrs. S. Norris who produced a flawless typescript.

Finally, I must say a word about General Reinhard Gehlen's own memoirs (*Der Dienst*), of which I read a proof copy. If I had been tempted to look therein for any information I might have missed, I must regretfully say that such a search would have been in vain. His memoirs, launched with so much publicity, have proved to be remarkable mainly for the dearth of information conveyed and the almost total absence of names, dates, places or descriptions of the operations in which he was involved over a period of twenty-five years.

E.H.C.

I

Spy Of The Century

"To create an effective intelligence agency we must have in the key positions men who are prepared to make this a life work, not a mere casual occupation. Service in the agency should not be viewed merely as a stepping-stone to promotion in one of the armed services or other branches of the government. The agency should be directed by a relatively small but *élite* corps of men with a passion of anonymity and a willingness to stick at that particular job. They must find their reward primarily in the work itself, and in the service they render the government, rather than in public acclaim."

These words were written by Allen Welsh Dulles in 1947 in a memorandum submitted to President Truman which became the basis for the establishment of the Central Intelligence Agency, the first centralised and institutionalised intelligence service the United States of America had had since the Declaration of Independence.

The high-minded principles it expressed were, of course, nothing new. The creators of the British Secret Service, men like Walsingham and Thurloe, had adopted them centuries before and their successors in modern times had followed their lead. Indeed, the world supremacy maintained by British Intelligence for many generations was to a great extent due to its adherence to the twin ideals of anonymity and of finding a reward in serving the nation. The same principles have always been observed by the chiefs of Soviet Secret Service, prompting an American Intelligence analyst to describe their espionage operators as "a brilliant corps of professionals which has probably not been equalled before or since in the intelligence agencies of the major powers".[1] With the notable exception of Laurenti Beria, who made an attempt to seize political power after Stalin's death but was quickly and forcefully frustrated, Soviet Secret Service chiefs have always been the obedient servants of their government.

It is debatable whether Allen Dulles himself embraced these precepts, however, when four years after their formulation he was called upon to join, and ultimately to preside over, a corps of men

1

charged with their application in practice. During his eleven years at the CIA he gloried in his authority—conferred on him by President Eisenhower through the agency of his brother, John Foster Dulles, the secretary of state, who had become the real fountainhead of American foreign policy.

Allen Dulles accepted the soubriquet of "the third most powerful man in the world" with visible satisfaction, and was never one to shun public acclaim, albeit alternating with criticism and abuse. He was beyond doubt the best intelligencer the United States possessed at the most critical period of the cold war, a secret agent seasoned in two World Wars and a thorough professional. About positive intelligence—in contrast to counter-espionage, which the FBI had effectively pursued for half a century—the Americans learned a great deal in a short time. In 1941, as their chiefs have often acknowledged, they were still "green" and in awe of their British tutors; within a decade they had lifted intelligence work to unheard-of levels of technological perfection.

To General Walter Bedell Smith, who became head of CIA in 1950 with Dulles as his deputy, must go the palm for laying the sound foundations on which the great network of CIA stations throughout the world is built. Dulles succeeded him two years later and was instrumental in the great build-up of the agency. Yet in many of his actions he neglected the basic prerequisites of strategic intelligence in peacetime—the dispassionate assessment of the capabilities, vulnerabilities and intentions of a potential enemy and the provision of the fullest possible information needed to enable the policy-makers to ensure adequate national security.[2] Instead, partly owing to the bad advice of some of the men around him, such as his director of operations,[3] he began to devise policy himself, eschewing his advisory function, and to take the sort of arbitrary action, not infrequently in direct conflict with presidential pronouncements and decisions, of which the Bay of Pigs *débâcle* was to be the most flagrant example. With hindsight, President Truman, obviously in an attempt to absolve himself from the consequences of his earlier association with Dulles in the creation of the CIA, was to write in 1963 that "CIA had been diverted from its original assignment and had become a policy-making arm of the government".[4] The ex-President took pains to stress that he had always been against "the building up of an American Gestapo".[5]

It may seem inappropriate that I should have chosen to preface this book with these remarks about a man who is not its subject. I feel a need to establish my attitude to Allen Dulles at the very outset, however, for a number of reasons, not least because there will be many people who on catching sight of the somewhat romantic

2

title my publishers have chosen for this book may think that if anyone qualifies for the appellation *Spy of the Century* it is he. Secondly and more important, Allen Dulles must be seen in perspective, since it was he who gave to the post-war career of Reinhard Gehlen the initial impetus without which Hitler's former intelligence chief would never have reached the powerful position of *éminence grise* to the free world which makes him, and not Dulles, the proper subject for a book of this title.

Thus, although after his surrender to the Americans at the end of the war US Army Intelligence chiefs were Gehlen's initial sponsors, it was Dulles who took over the fledgling Gehlen Organisation, just as it was Dulles who provided the vast finance needed by Gehlen to turn it into the largest and most efficient espionage machine in Western Europe. It was Dulles who guided and encouraged Gehlen through the almost insuperable difficulties of the early days, protecting him alike from the rivalry and hostility of the chiefs of US Army Intelligence, men like General George V. Strong and Lieutenant-General Arthur G. Trudeau, and from British and French competition. Finally, it was Dulles who eventually enabled Gehlen to become the head of the Federal German Intelligence Service in 1956, which for several years was to provide seventy per cent of the intelligence required by NATO's Military Committee and its Standing Group.

Not long before Dulles wrote his CIA memorandum, the former Lieutenant-General Reinhard Gehlen had put at the disposal of his former American enemies his unrivalled knowledge and experience of the communist world, and of the Soviet Union in particular, for use in the cold war which had just began. Gehlen can hardly have known at that stage of Dulles' ideal formula for successful intelligence leadership. Yet he followed that formula to the letter.

Admittedly, it was easier for him than for Dulles to apply himself to such strict rules. Since his childhood, at his parental home, at school, and as a cadet-ensign in the post-war Reichswehr, he had been conditioned to obey authority unquestioningly, whether represented by his father, his teachers or his military superiors. By 1946 when he began working for the Americans, Gehlen had already given loyal service for a quarter of a century to governments—first the Weimar Republic and then Hitler's Third Reich—for which he had little sympathy. Reared in the tradition of Prussian discipline, he accepted the authority of the State, whatever its political persuasion. In Dulles' words, he had found his reward in the work itself and in the satisfaction of serving his country. Above all, however, he had a predilection which he pursued with obsessive singlemindedness all his life—the vital need to resist communism at all costs. Thus he resolved at the end of the war to change masters once again in order to secure every opportunity in his crusade against Stalinism.

It is perhaps worthwhile to compare further these two men, Dulles and Gehlen, whose secret activities during the cold war period greatly influenced international politics. In perfect accord with the other's idea of a spy-master's image, Gehlen always preserved his anonymity. Indeed, it was second nature to him. He has always been lonely, withdrawn and self-effacing, neither making friends easily nor seeking any; public acclaim meant nothing to him. Dulles, on the other hand, was ebullient, gregarious and charming, a socialite greatly concerned with what other people thought of him; his secretaries scanned every newspaper and book and recorded every broadcast for the slightest reference to him, whether in praise or blame.

In Jungian terms they were introvert and extrovert respectively, and this showed itself in their attitudes to their activities and to their common enemy. Dulles, the extrovert, "thinking, feeling and acting with reference to the object", responded to external facts, usually in a pragmatic and improvised manner. Thus, he reacted strongly and often temperamentally to every communist challenge. To take a specific example: Soviet involvement in Cuba and the Castro regime represented an actual, palpable threat, and as such called for quick action, however poorly devised and prepared. For Gehlen, on the other hand, immediate objects were a secondary consideration; he orientated himself in relation to the subject, communism, and he concerned himself, above all, with the long-term struggle against it as a concept.

To Gehlen positive action was always a means to an end, to be calculated deliberately and planned meticulously and far in advance. Dulles dreamed of the "liberation" of the peoples of the East assuming that, given a modicum of encouragement, they would rise in revolt; to this end he insisted on establishing a secret private army in Germany* and on parachuting infiltrators into the Soviet orbit, most of whom perished before they were able to carry out any action. He usually underestimated the force of Soviet reaction, as shown in the ruthless suppression of the Berlin revolt in 1953 and the Hungarian uprising in 1956, as well as in the Soviet invasion of Czechoslovakia in 1968. So, in the end, the West had to climb down on such occasions, lest any escalation in the direction of Dulles' intentions might turn the cold war into a hot one.

By contrast, Gehlen engaged on methodical, if somewhat theoretical, tackling of his subject. His secret struggle against the Soviet Union and her satellites, especially the East German regime, was a

* See page 239

prolonged warfare of attrition. He accumulated archives on the Soviet Union, its army, its espionage organisation, and its economic and manpower resources until he built up a unique collection of invaluable information. Whilst this was, of course, a very real asset, one cannot entirely discard the suspicion that his subconscious motivation was the preoccupation of an academic mind with his love-hated subject rather than the determination of a bustler thirsting for real action.

Obviously, Hitler's war against the Soviet Union had propelled Gehlen into action, and by sponsoring the "Russian Army of Liberation" in 1942 and arrogating to himself the control of *Frontkommandos* operating behind enemy lines he acted in exactly the manner that Dulles so eagerly advocated in peace time. That Gehlen counselled against rash action was only natural: any "localised" armed conflict between East and West, fought with conventional weapons, would initially have been fought on German soil. As a German patriot he did not want to see his country and people, who had scarcely yet recovered from the last holocaust, again destroyed, this time probably for good.

Moscow never ceased to describe Gehlen as a "fascist criminal", a "revanchist" and a "warmonger". In officially inspired articles and publications in the Soviet Union and East Germany he was described as the biggest single factor in the prevention of a possible East-West *détente*. It is a fact that for twenty years he did exert considerable influence on Allied, and more particularly American policy and strategy towards the Soviet Union and the communist bloc, but, perversely, he more often appeared as a peacemaker rather than a warmonger. This was the case on such critical occasions as the Berlin Blockade in 1948 when the city was cut off from the outside world but saved by the Allied airlift; in 1958, when Khrushchev threatened to send troops into West Berlin; and again in August 1961 after another threat of aggression on West Berlin had prompted President Kennedy to announce on July 25 that he had put half of the B-52 and B-47 bomber fleets on alert "which would send them on their way with 15 minutes' warning" and had ordered partial mobilisation of US Army and Marine Corps reserves.[6]

On all these occasions Gehlen sent urgent reports to Washington stating that, on the reliable information he had, the Soviet bark would not be followed by a bite and that such troop movements as were taking place in East Germany and by Soviet divisions in Poland and annexed East Prussia were window-dressing rather than serious military measures. Indeed, he succeeded in placating Washington and thus prevented a rash action which might have resulted in disaster.

5

The situation in Berlin was such that one inadvertently fired shot might have triggered off a conflagration.

Gehlen proved himself a superb master of planning and plotting, of devising subversion and political intrigue. This alone would make him the spy-master of the twentieth century as it made Walsingham, Thurloe or Fouché the masters of past centuries. Like these giants, he had a penchant for playing up other people who acted in the full limelight of politics and wars, while himself remaining satisfied to be the puppeteer who pulled the wires behind the scenes.

In this he also emulated the tradition of the spy-masters of Germany in the past, who remained almost completely unknown even to their own people. Of August Wilhelm Eichel, who served Frederick the Great for twenty-seven years, the British ambassador Hanbury-Williams recorded that he was such a mysterious person that "one could be at this court seven years without once seeing him or knowing of him". Yet Eichel worked with the king for several hours every day and was his most trusted adviser. Similarly, only a handful of people knew of Wilhelm Stieber, Bismarck's spy-master; yet the vital intelligence Stieber supplied was instrumental in enabling his king to accomplish the conquest of Austria within forty-five days in 1866, and to defeat the seemingly invincible army of Napoleon III in 1871. Colonel Walter Nicolai, the chief of the Kaiser's *Nachrichtendienst* in the First World War, likewise remained a shadowy personality; even the circumstances of his death have never been fully ascertained.[7] Admiral Canaris, whose career in two World Wars was, of course, to be common knowledge, has nevertheless become an almost legendary figure; war historians are still debating whether he did in fact betray Hitler or not.

It is probable that Gehlen deliberately modelled himself on such spy-masters of the past; the aura of mystery was something to which his character was fundamentally sympathetic. There are also startling similarities between this twentieth-century espionage expert and Cromwell's taciturn, puritan intelligence chief John Thurloe, who gave his allegiance unquestioningly to the authority of the State whether represented by Charles I, the Commonwealth or the Restoration. In spite of having been a perfect royal official, Thurloe accepted appointments under the revolutionary regime without any sense of doubt or divided loyalty. He rose to great heights and accumulated a multiplicity of offices, as secretary of state, war minister, home secretary, master of ordnance and postmaster general, besides becoming the Protector's protector and next to Cromwell the mightiest man in the Commonwealth. Yet after the Restoration he had no hesitation in offering his services to General Monk and then to the new king. Charles II did not accept them, but nevertheless

Thurloe was one of the few of Cromwell's henchmen to escape punishment.

Gehlen, likewise, served Hitler with unswerving loyalty until the bitter end, even though he had long realised not only that the war had been lost, but that its loss was at least partly due to the Fuhrer's disregard of the advice of his saner generals and, above all, of his intelligence chief for the operations against the Soviet Union. As a German war historian put it: "While the intelligence reports were read at Hitler's headquarters the Fuhrer was inclined to give more credence to the creations of his own fantasy and wishful thinking than to the facts acquired by the intelligence departments and front-line reconnaissance, and as time went on, his entourage condoned the state of affairs with increasing equanimity, until even his military advisers themselves could not resist the effects of his prophetic utterances."[8]

It is obvious from Gehlen's many reports quoted later on in this book that he was fully aware of Hitler's disastrous war leadership. Yet, so long as Hitler represented the authority of the State, Gehlen was prepared to serve him, even to the extent of engaging on the futile task of creating the suicide squads, the "Werewolves" which, though largely composed of schoolboys, disabled war veterans and elderly men, were supposed to offer last-ditch resistance to the Red Army in 1945.

A few weeks after the abortive "Werewolf" operation Gehlen surrendered to the Americans and offered them his services in return for their help in his obsessive struggle against the "Red menace", thus remaining completely true to his original Jungian "subject". The lavish finance which the CIA provided enabled him to carry on this fight far more successfully than had been possible under Hitler; moreover, he took good care that he should be his own boss. During the war Gehlen had had to tread cautiously; he had seen many of his colleagues put to death once they attracted Hitler's wrath. This is not to deny that some of Gehlen's wartime exploits had hardly been equalled by Allied Intelligence. His agents, for example, had infiltrated Stalin's war council, as well as the front-line headquarters of Marshals Zhukov and Koniev. There were many occasions when his evaluation of intelligence from behind the enemy lines would have been decisive for German strategy had not Hitler been determined to have his own—usually disastrous—way. This is borne out by the comments of General Halder or General Guderian on Gehlen's reports, which often predicted Soviet strategy with amazing accuracy—for instance in regard to Stalingrad, which was to become the turning-point of the war. Yet Hitler rarely made use of them.

As head of his "Organisation" under the aegis of the CIA Gehlen

was much more fortunate. First US Army G-2 Intelligence, and later the CIA chiefs, particularly Dulles, paid great attention to the information he produced. Having nothing but praise for his activities they put up with his constant nagging about security. Indeed, his ceaseless preoccupation with security led him into a number of serious disagreements with the Americans. He took a poor view, and not without justification, of the manner in which his more carefree American colleagues handled classified matters during the initial years of their co-operation. There were several disastrous leaks from US Intelligence headquarters, and in a number of cases Soviet and East German agents penetrated American army offices, where they got hold of top-secret documents, including Gehlen's own reports. He deeply resented this, and in his Pullach headquarters his contemptuous wisecrack circulated amongst his assistants: "In American Intelligence Offices 'secret' means known to all, 'top secret' only to people who ask, and 'cosmic' known only to the opposition."[9] As CIA grew more sophisticated and the military intelligence branches in Germany gained a deeper understanding of communist espionage methods, the security position greatly improved and Gehlen had fewer grounds for his sardonic comments.

For his own organisation he succeeded in devising and maintaining quite extraordinary security arrangements for many years. His headquarters at Pullach near Munich were disguised as the offices of an industrial company, his many offices, interrogation centres, spy schools and training establishments, laboratories and sabotage armouries as the company's business branches and workshops. All his life he deliberately remained a man of mystery, spreading a shroud of almost impenetrable secrecy over his official and private life.

Newspapermen never succeeded in entering his headquarters and he never in his life gave a press interview. When around 1950 stories began to appear in German and American newspapers and magazines about a "secret espionage organisation in Germany under American sponsorship" very few details about its chief could be unearthed. Such snippets as were published were based on guesswork rather than facts; even the most tenacious reporters were unable to discover where he lived, or whether he was married and had any children. The few photographs which were eventually published showed him as a young officer during the war, in uniform and with a major's rank badges.

In the German press he was referred to as "The Man in the Shadow" (*Die Welt*), "The Man of a Thousand Mysteries" (*Die Zeit*), "The Shadow General" (*Westdeutsche Zeitung*), and a newspaper in Stuttgart stated that he was "the spy chief whom nobody knew". Even the so astute *Time* magazine admitted that he was "submerged

in the shadow" whilst the Zurich *Weltwoche* called him "The Faceless Man". During his twenty-one years at Pullach he only once travelled abroad; on Dulles' invitation and after much urging Gehlen paid a brief visit to the United States for an inspection of the CIA's "spy school" at Monterey in California. He was probably the only VIP whom American reporters failed to locate and interview.

For a man so obsessed by the idea of "complete security" the discovery in 1961 that a double agent had penetrated his very own sanctum of Pullach was a body blow from which he never fully recovered. A man whom he had fully trusted and whom he had put in charge of the counter-espionage department was unmasked as a Soviet agent. Gehlen was then sixty years old and almost worn out by forty years' service; yet he refused to retire and worked on for another seven years.

Gradually, as the Opposition in the Bundestag grew increasingly critical of Gehlen's activities and as a few of his agents who defected to the East began to supply information to East German and Soviet Intelligence Services, some details about him and his organisation at last leaked out. Much of what was published about him in the East was, however, inaccurate and fanciful. In 1968, learning of his impending retirement, I approached General Gehlen for an interview and went to Pullach and to his residence at Berg on Lake Starnberg. I must confess I did not get far. He refused to disclose his secrets, indicating that if he permitted anything to be published at all it would not be before twenty-five years after his death.

Gehlen's Bormann Story—A Damp Squib

He changed his mind, however, in 1971, when German and American publishers reputedly offered him a cool million dollars for his memoirs. Their appetite had been whetted by the announcement that the book would contain startling disclosures: Gehlen, it was claimed, had discovered that Martin Bormann, the Fuhrer's deputy, had been a Soviet agent for many years and had conveyed the innermost secrets of Hitler's war strategy to Moscow. He had been rescued by the Russians in 1945 and spent the rest of his life in the Soviet Union, dying there a few years ago.

I have read Gehlen's memoirs in the original German version prior to their publication. His book is remarkable in two respects only: the total absence of detail and documentation, and the papering over of his employment of former SS men. It contains neither descriptions of the espionage operations he was responsible for nor names of his associates and agents.

In a single paragraph on page 48 Gehlen states that Admiral

Canaris, the chief of the Abwehr, imparted to him during the war his suspicion that Bormann was a traitor and was using a secret radio transmitter to send messages to Russia. Gehlen adds that he himself was unable to investigate Bormann's disappearance until 1946, and that two—*unnamed*—informants have told him that Bormann was alive in the 1950's and lived in the Soviet Union until his death.

Not a shred of evidence is offered for this information. Canaris, of course, has been dead since 1945, before the end of the war. What Gehlen does not say, however, is that on Dulles' request he himself made reports to the CIA, whose agents had for many years been scouring the world for Bormann. Gehlen did so on two occasions in 1953 and 1965. Both reports concluded that it must be assumed that Bormann had been killed with two companions in the cross-fire near the Lehrter Station in North Berlin on May 1st, 1945, after his escape from the Chancellery bunker. Indeed, on Gehlen's advice a park near the station was dug up in June 1965 in a search for Bormann's body.

In his memoirs Gehlen claims that he could not risk keeping too close an eye on Bormann during the war, since the Führer's deputy was "the mightiest man in the Nazi hierarchy and any imprudence would have meant our [Gehlen's and Canaris'] downfall". This may have been so, but in that case *why did Gehlen not disclose his [alleged] knowledge after the war*? Why did he mislead Allen Dulles, the CIA, the German government and the Jewish agents searching for Bormann for twenty-five years? Was it because there is no truth in this story, which is now being used as a stunt to publicize his book? Has Gehlen, or whoever is responsible for the stunt, perpetrated a colossal hoax on a gullible world?

Herr Gehlen will have to answer these questions. He will also have to provide some evidence in support of his assertions, lest he stand accused of trying to mislead his publishers and the world's Press.

In Chapter XVI I give the real story of what is generally agreed by eye witnesses to have happened to Bormann after his flight from Hitler's bunker.

Only the conditions which prevailed in Central Europe at the end of the war could have produced a figure such as Reinhard Gehlen. He had emerged unscathed from Hitler's downfall whilst many of the men with whom he had been associated ended at the gallows of Nuremberg and many lesser figures than he were sent to prison as war criminals. During the long era of the cold war he exerted considerable power and influence over the destiny of nations. Perhaps the extent to which Reinhard Gehlen, although unrecognised and unknown, has affected the international scene can never be measured. Certainly his activities had momentous repercussions beyond the shaping of the new Germany. If Gehlen never became a leading world figure, he can without hyperbole be described as the "Spy of the Century".

* * * *

During my four years' research I have assembled a considerable dossier about Reinhard Gehlen and his activities. I was fortunate enough to obtain first hand information from a number of his assistants and former officers of the Gehlen Organisation and the *Bundesnachrichtendienst*, some of whom appeared somewhat disillusioned with it. My investigations included the examination of several thousand hitherto "privileged" documents of his wartime FHO department, which had remained unpublished until I was given access to them at the Federal Archives at Freiburg in 1971.

From time to time various newspapers and magazines have seen fit to publish speculative tittle-tattle about Gehlen. Perhaps at the cost of sacrificing the occasional amusing or sensational but apocryphal story, I have refrained from including material of this sort. Every incident recorded in the following pages is fully authenticated and supported by documentary evidence. At the risk of wearying the reader I have carefully recorded the dockets and numbers of all relevant documents and full references are given for any quotations used.

II

Never Give Up

Reinhard Gehlen was born on April 3, 1902, in Erfurt, the Prussian enclave in Thuringia. He was a child of the Prussian upper middle class, which provided Imperial Germany's public servants, industrial managers, college teachers and officers of line regiments. Paternalism, tradition and nationalism were the keystones of his caste.

His father, Benno Felix Erwin Walter Gehlen, at that time a lieutenant in Field Artillery Regiment No. 19, was himself the son and grandson of career officers. Reinhard's grandfather served with distinction in the war of 1870/71; he fought under the command of Crown Prince Albert of Saxony in the battle of Sedan, which ended with the capture of Napoleon III and the fall of the French Second Empire. Reinhard's mother, Katharine Margarete, came from an old family of Flemish origin, the Van Vaernewycks, who had settled in Prussia several centuries before. Their crest motto was *Laet vaeren nyt!*—"Never give up"— and Gehlen carried it with him through his life as a symbol of tenacity.

His younger brother, Walter, was born in Leipzig in 1903. The two boys were brought up to revere Bismarck and Moltke, the architects of the German Empire, for the Gehlens regarded themselves as pillars of the society upon which the greatness of the Kaiser's Reich was based. Their powerful class was intensely patriotic, god-fearing, and utterly devoted to the preservation of the established social order. While it did not oppose improvements in social welfare, housing conditions and lower education for hardworking artisans, it expected their subservience in return. The working.man was to be kept in his place, which was to supply skilled labour for Germany's surging industry and disciplined recruits for her expanding armed forces. Aspirations to social progress and intellectual emancipation were viewed with suspicion, and the growth of trade unionism with hostile anxiety: they contained the seeds of rebellion against the existing order.

These fears were borne out sooner than Gehlen's father and his friends expected. He had won the Iron Cross in the battlefield of

Flanders and was an artillery major when in the first week of November 1918 the Kiel sailors mutinied and raised the red flag, precipitating the collapse of the fronts and the defeat of Germany. Major Gehlen's military career was shattered; overnight he found himself jobless, one of the hundred thousand Prussian officers who saw everything they had represented crumbling to the ground. The Treaty of Versailles brought the final humiliation.

There had never been much money in the Gehlens' household. Reinhard's birthplace in Erfurt was a modest three-room apartment at 63-64 Loeber Strasse, a gloomy street near the main station, flanked by railway embankments and engine sheds. After his birth the family had moved from one garrison town to another, and during the four war years while her husband was on active service Frau Gehlen and her children shared the hardship imposed on the German people by the Allied blockade.

Major Gehlen found it extremely difficult to adjust himself to the bleak novelty of civilian life in a post-war Germany ruled by socialists and racked by near-famine, inflation and constant rioting. Help came, however, from his younger brother Max, a lawyer and former state official who had married the daughter of a wealthy publisher and was now general manager of the old-established house of Ferdinand Hirt & Son in Leipzig. Max, who had served in the war, was sympathetic to his brother's plight and arranged for him the post of manager of the publishing firm's Breslau branch.

Thus the Gehlens came to the old Prussian city on the Oder. With stability restored to the family if not to the nation, young Reinhard and Walter settled down to complete their studies. By 1919 the future spy-master was sitting for his *Abitur*, the final examinations at the Konig Wilhelm School at Breslau. Throughout his schooldays Reinhard Gehlen had been at the top of his class, passing his exams with brilliant marks. He learned easily, had an omnivorous appetite for work and matched it with an ambition to excel. His teachers' annual reports invariably stressed his ability to grasp and absorb all subjects with great facility; they described him as "highly intelligent, hard working and well-mannered". In one report he was called "a shining example to other pupils". A school photograph of the time shows him sitting next to the head boy in the front row beside the senior masters and the principal.

Undersized Prodigy

He had an analytical mind and showed prowess in mathematics, algebra and geometry; all his life he retained a penchant for statistics. He devoured works on economics, history and geography, but was also well read in the German classics. In languages he was good at

Latin and French, and he acquired a smattering of Polish, which was the tongue spoken by the servants his mother hired from among the Silesian peasant minority. With quick comprehension and retentive memory went a gift for clear thinking and expression, which won him prizes for his compositions. Thumbing through the hundreds of reports, memoranda and minutes he wrote as an intelligence chief for Hitler and later for the CIA, one is surprised at the lucidity and even beauty of the style. There is no trace of the usual heavy German officialese in his papers.

The reason Gehlen did not become head boy of his school was probably his puny physique and his lack of success in physical training. Perfection in gymnastics, handball, pack marching and semi-military drill was a precondition for leadership at a German school. However hard he tried, Gehlen was unable to overcome his handicaps. He was far from being anybody's idea of the Teutonic Siegfried. Narrow-chested and slight, he never grew taller than five feet four. He had a sallow, peaky face, myopic eyes, protruding ears and mousy hair. Despite his brilliance there are indications that he suffered on these grounds from an inferiority complex, for he was very shy and aloof and made few friends. The less brainy of his school mates regarded him as a "swot" and often treated him with disdain. Hence. he shared in neither their company nor their adolescent pranks, which often ended in rough horseplay.

A psychologist might say that this was why Gehlen in later life delighted in working behind the scenes and, self-effacing, in mastering superiors who believed him to be their devoted servant. He had most of the qualities that make an academic and in his final year at school he thought of going on to university and preparing himself for a scholastic career. His father, however, having somewhat reluctantly accepted brother Max's advice to let the younger boy study law, was determined that Reinhard should carry on the family's military tradition. Notwithstanding the humiliation of Germany's defeat and disarmament, and his detestation for the Weimar Republic and its socialist leaders, Major Gehlen ardently desired that one of his sons at least should wear the *bunte Tuch*, the soldier's uniform. To many Germans, even in those dark days, it was still the only honourable symbol of the nation's rebirth.

Thus, straight from school on April 20, 1920, two days before his eighteenth birthday, Reinhard Gehlen joined as an ensign the new German Army, the Reichswehr, limited by the Versailles Treaty to 100,000 men and forbidden to have a General Staff, tanks, armoured vehicles, aircraft, submarines or vessels exceeding 10,000 tons. The defeat of the Kaiser's Germany in 1918 had produced a very different situation from that which followed her unconditional surrender after the collapse of Hitler's Third Reich in 1945. Large parts of the Imperial Army, particularly on the eastern front, remained intact and after the signing of the Armistice still prepared to resist the *Diktat* of Versailles. The first Chancellor of the Weimar Republic, the Social Democrat Philip Scheidemann, decided to resign rather than accept the peace conditions based on President Wilson's Fourteen Points and made even more stringent by Lloyd George and Clemenceau.

Field-Marshal von Hindenburg had moved his headquarters to Pomerania and on June 17, 1919, exchanged secret messages with Fredrich Ebert, the new President of the Republic, with a view to the resumption of hostilities and the reconquest of the eastern territories which the Allies had given to re-born Poland. Hindenburg assured the President that an offensive against the Poles would be victorious, but expressed grave doubts about the prospects in the west "because of the numerical superiority of the *Entente* forces and the massive supplies they were receiving from America". Characteristically, Hindenburg stated that a final defeat in the west might result in the destruction of the German officers corps and that this "must be prevented at all costs".[1]

It must be remembered that at the time of the Armistice not a single Allied soldier stood on German soil; on the contrary German troops were still in occupation of French and Belgian territory.

A new Chancellor, Gustav Bauer, another Social Democrat, signed the Treaty of Versailles on June 20, 1919, in the face of an Allied ultimatum that hostilities would otherwise be resumed on the 24th. At this time Hindenburg was still the Supreme Commander and most of the generals had remained in command of their troops. Only General Erich Ludendorff, the chief of the General Staff, who during the last two years of the war had been the *de facto* ruler of Germany and had imposed his will not only on the conduct of the war but on all foreign affairs and on home administration, had disappeared. He had fled to Sweden, as had the Kaiser, fearing capture by the Allies and prosecution for war crimes.[2]

The New German Army

The officer corps was still very much alive and active. Before the ink had dried on the peace documents at Versailles, the generals went to work at rebuilding the army. President Ebert and his Social Democrat ministers, threatened by communist uprisings in many parts of Germany and, at the same time, by the excesses of the right-wing *Freikorps*, knew full well that they were at the mercy of the generals, who alone could safeguard law and order. They gratefully accepted Hindenburg's Order of the Day to his troops, which read: "Command of the troops must remain firmly in the hands of the military authorities. The High Command intends to cooperate with Chancellor Ebert, hitherto the leader of the moderate Social Democrats, in preventing the expansion of terrorist bolshevism in Germany."[3]

Three generals were given the highest offices when the Weimar Republic came into being: General Wilhelm Groener (who just before the collapse had succeeded Ludendorff as chief of the General Staff) became minister of defence; General Walter Reinhardt was the new Prussian minister of war; and General Hans von Seeckt, former chief of staff in the Balkans and later commander-in-chief of the Turkish army, became chief of the new *Truppenamt*, the successor to the officially disbanded General Staff. Between them they began the formation of the new Reichswehr, scheming from the very outset to flout the restrictions imposed by the Treaty of Versailles. Though Groener and Reinhardt may sincerely have desired to make the new army into an independent—and according to their lights—even democratic factor in Germany's national recovery, many of their officers saw in it a potential instrument of revenge to be used as soon as possible, particularly for the reconquest of the territories in the east, lost to the Poles.

Ensign Reinhard Gehlen was posted to Artillery Regiment No. 6 in garrison at Schweidnitz, not far from the frontiers of the new Poland and Czechoslovakia. He had decided to follow in his father's footsteps and be trained as a gunner. Three weeks after his arrival flocks of pilgrims converged on the little town to commemorate the famous air ace, Baron Manfred von Richthofen, who was born there. A museum was inaugurated to mark the second anniversary of Richthofen's death on the Somme. Gehlen listened in awe to the stories which the fallen hero's brother officers told of his exploits in shooting down eighty British, French and American aircraft and regretted that he could not become a fighter pilot himself.

The celebration was not merely a tribute to Richthofen's memory. It was a massive demonstration to proclaim that Imperial Germany's Army had not been defeated in the field but "had been stabbed in the back by internal treachery and bolshevist agitation". But, if the officers—Gehlen amongst them—and the big crowd who took part in the demonstration expressed thus their hostility to Lenin's revolution and Russian communism, their more violent hatred was directed against the new Poland.

During the same week the Poles had gone to war against Russia, in an attempt to wrest the Ukraine from the bolsheviks. Still embroiled in a civil war and smarting from the Anglo-American-French "Intervention", the Russians initially suffered heavy defeats. Poland received vigorous aid from the French, who supplied her with

16

Reinhard Gehlen
(*sitting, first on the left*)
at the age of 18 at
his school in Breslau.

Gehlen's birth certificate, dated
April 3, 1902.

Title page of a History of the first four years of the Nazi
State by Gehlen's uncle (using the pen name of "Gehl"),
published in 1937 by his family firm.

Haupt-Register.

Nr. 66.

Die Jahre I–IV
des nationalsozialistischen Staates

Grundlagen und Gestaltung
Urkunden des Aufbaus — Reden und Vorträge

Herausgegeben von

Dr. Walther Gehl

Die Schrift wird in der
NS.-Bibliographie geführt
Berlin, den 24. August 1937
Der Vorsitzende der
Parteiamtlichen Prüfungskommission
zum Schutze des NS.-Schrifttums

Ferdinand Hirt in Breslau
Königsplatz 1

General Erich von Manstein

General Franz Halder

General Heinz Guderian

Lieutenant-General Adolf Heusinger

These four generals smoothed Gehlen's way to the top. Manstein recommende[d] him to the General Staff; Halder made him his ADC; Guderian protected him from Hitler's wrath; Heusinger advised him after the end of the war.

(*Left*) As an officer at the Operations Department of Hitler's Supreme Headquarters.

modern weapons and provided a French chief of staff in the person of one of their most famous war leaders, General Maxime Weygand. Helped by Ukrainian nationalists under the Cossack Ataman Petlyura the Polish Army quickly overran the country, taking its capital, Kiev, in May.

The officers of Gehlen's garrison at Schweidnitz watched these events with growing dismay. General von Seeckt circulated a long memorandum to all Reichswehr commanders, which pointedly expressed the sentiments of the officer corps and, undoubtedly, the majority of the German people: "France seeks to gain in Poland the opportunity for a renewed attack on Germany from the east and, together with the British, has driven an intolerable stake into our flesh close to the heart of our existence as a state. Poland is our mortal enemy . . . never can Germany concede that Bromberg, Graudenz, Thorn, Posen should remain in Polish hands."[4]

Strong units of the illegal right-wing *Freikorps,* openly described as the "Black Reichswehr", arrived in Silesia and made forays into Polish territory. They were enthusiastically welcomed by Gehlen's brother-officers and supplied with heavy arms from Reichswehr magazines. The German government assured Warsaw that all this was greatly deprecated. But very little was done to stop it; in any case the government of the Weimar Republic remained powerless vis-à-vis the Reichswehr commanders.

In the summer of 1920, the victories of the Red Army, which had thrown out the Polish troops from the Ukraine and had appeared on the outskirts of Warsaw, were greeted in Germany with almost jubilation. From General von Seeckt's *Truppenamt* came another memorandum: "The present Polish state is a creation of the *Entente.* The fight of Soviet Russia against Poland hits not only the latter but, above all, France and Britain. If Poland collapses the whole edifice of the Versailles Treaty will totter . . . . Germany has no interest in rendering any help to Poland. On the contrary, we can only welcome it if Poland should cease to exist . . . . It is essential for Germany to free herself from the chains of the *Entente.* This can be done with the help of Soviet Russia, without falling a victim to Bolshevism."[5]

Most of the German generals and many right-wing politicians, however great their hatred of bolshevism, agreed with Seeckt's concept of a revival of Bismarck's time-honoured idea of Russo-German friendship and alliance. Earlier, one of Seeckt's friends, Major-General Count Rudiger von der Goltz, wrote to him: "The most important aim for Germany must be to seek a new, strong friend, and this can only be achieved by winning the friendship of Russia. When we have gained a new friend in Russia and when we possess a large united East European economic area, any new

17

blockade, which Britain would then hardly dare to impose, would be immaterial." Seeckt agreed, but he was wary of the effect such a friendship with the bolsheviks might have in strengthening communist agitation within Germany. To this end his *Truppenamt* offered a remedy: "We must take the necessary measures to prevent bolshevism from flooding Germany . . . . In the first place this means disarming hostile elements and strengthening the authority of the state."

General von Seeckt, as we shall see, had opened secret negotiations with bolshevik leaders as early as the summer of 1919, when Karl Radek—later the spirit of the Comintern—was a prisoner in Berlin. His first contact with Leon Trotsky, the Soviet war commissar, was established through Enver Pasha, the former Turkish minister, whom Seeckt knew well when he commanded Turkish troops during the war. These early contacts led to a military cooperation which lasted for many years, and which enabled the Reichswehr to manufacture heavy arms and aircraft in the Soviet Union, to receive Soviet armament supplies and to train its men inside Russia.

First Taste of Secret Service Work

Of all this young Ensign Reinhard Gehlen obviously knew nothing. But his quick mind absorbed the general trend of thoughts from the discussions of his superior officers. General von Seeckt had sent a number of intelligence officers to Schweidnitz to reconnoitre Polish troop movements across the frontier. Tension between Germany and Poland mounted as the date of the plebiscite in Upper Silesia approached. German intelligencers undertook nightly sorties across the border and Gehlen was one of the young officers of the garrison attached to them as scouts. This was his first taste of secret service work in the field. The Schweidnitz garrison, like all Reichswehr units in Eastern Germany, was kept on almost constant alert.

The plebiscite in Upper Silesia, conducted under the control of British and French officers, resulted in a two-thirds majority vote for reunion with Germany. But an armed rising, led by the Polish Commissioner Albert Korfanty, aided by the Warsaw government and connived at by the French commander, whose troops were supposed to maintain order on behalf of the League of Nations, prevented the reunification. Whilst the League debated for more than a year over what should be done with Upper Silesia, there was sporadic heavy fighting there between the Germans and Poles. Thousands of members of the officially disbanded *Freikorps* flocked to Silesia from all over Germany.

The German government had forbidden an intervention by the Reichswehr, but General von Seeckt flouted the order by sending intelligence officers from his *Truppenamt* in mufti to assist the *Freikorps* insurgents; he also ordered that they should be supplied with arms and ammunition. But despite their successes in the field, the Germans were eventually cheated of their victory. The League of Nations decided on a partition of the province, whereby the majority of the population and more than half of the territory was awarded to Germany, but Poland was given all the principal coal mining and industrial districts. The result was an upsurge of extreme nationalism throughout Germany, particularly after the League's decision that Eupen and Malmedy should be ceded to Belgium, although five-sixths of the six hundred thousand inhabitants were Germans. At about the same time the ancient Hanseatic port of Danzig was detached from Germany and declared a free city.

Many Germans had come to regard their own government as traitors to the nation. The Social Democrats lost the next general election and a coalition of the Catholic Centre party and right-wing Conservatives was formed. The year before the frail foundations of the Weimar Republic had been rocked by the right-wing Kapp Putsch. Rebels led by the Reichswehr General Baron Walter von Luttwitz had seized public buildings in Berlin, forcing the government to flee to Stuttgart. General von Seeckt, after much heart-searching, eventually restored order, but refused to arrest von Lut-twitz or to discipline any Reichswehr officers who had made common cause with Kapp and the *Freikorps*. Indeed, the overthrow of the government was only prevented when the *Freikorps* and the Reichswehr turned about to help it put down a communist uprising in the Ruhr. In August 1921, the Catholic leader Matthias Erzberger, who had signed the Armistice in 1918, was assassinated by right-wing extremists; the murder of the foreign minister, Walter Rathenau, followed in June 1922.

It was in this climate of near-revolution, internal strife and continuous skirmishes across the Polish frontier that Reinhard Gehlen gained his first experience of clandestine activities. He had taken part in a number of reconnoitring sorties into Upper Silesia, but otherwise he was not given to dreams of valour. He had met some of the *Freikorps* leaders and he despised their wildly romantic approach to serious matters. He recognised the *Freikorps* leaders for what they were: hard-drinking freebooters, most of them more interested in personal adventure and easy loot than in the destiny of the German nation. To Gehlen's orderly mind that subtle policy of his commander-in-chief, General von Seeckt, must have seemed, in contrast, entirely admirable. Seeckt acted according to the axiom that politics is the art of the possible and that authority must come first. Hence this conservative monarchist steeped in the tradition of

19

Prussian militarism was ready to serve a Socialist government. Gehlen, too, was brought up to respect authority; he remained on the side of authority all his life.

Under the premiership of Stresemann the situation in Germany began somewhat to improve, despite sporadic upheavals, monarchist plots in Bavaria, and communist riots in Saxony. At last the disastrous inflation was brought to a halt. Hjalmar Schacht introduced the new currency and with massive financial aid from the United States and Britain hopes for economic recovery and modest prosperity seemed to be justified.

The Russian Expert

On leave in Breslau and Leipzig, where he moved among his father's and uncle's right-wing friends, Gehlen met politicians, university teachers, writers and former officers. Some were authors of the Hirt publishing house, which had grown into Germany's leading educational book concern with a near-monopoly in school textbooks. One subject of conversation never dried up in this circle: the bolshevist menace. These educated upper-middle-class Germans were alarmed by the two million votes cast for the communists in the 1925 election, the seditious agitation, the rise of Stalin, the spreading might of the OGPU and Soviet espionage in the West. All of these posed threats to the Fatherland and they were convinced, to the world; to fight these dangers was not merely a question of saving the despised Weimar Republic.

Circulating outside barrack life, Gehlen noted the swelling sympathy· for the aims of the newly emergent National Socialist party. The "Beer Hall Putsch" in Munich in 1923, led by General Ludendorff and Adolf Hitler had ended in a ludicrous débâcle. But during the following two or three years the party of nationalist revolution had grown into a formidable factor in Germany's political life. If Gehlen's well-bred and educated friends and acquaintances were contemptuous of the beer-cellar gabble of that loutish ex-corporal Hitler, they agreed with many of his objectives—those concerned with making the German people strong, proud, and feared again. Above all, they were coming to regard Hitler's demands for *Lebensraum* in the East as the only real solution to the economic disaster which had plagued the country since the defeat of 1918.

The school-books published by Gehlen's family firm contained many passages in this vein. In 1928 his father published a history book for high schools, written by his younger son under the thinnish pseudonym of "Dr. Walter Gehl".[6] In it the author described the Germans as "the only people in Europe of whom one third live outside the frontiers of their national state". He described Germany

20

as "a rump with four German states—Austria, Luxembourg, Liechtenstein and Danzig—outside her imposed frontiers, not to mention the inherently Lower-German Netherlands and millions of German *Volksgenossen* under foreign domination in ten other states, Czechoslovakia, Poland, Lithuania, Hungary, Yugoslavia, Denmark, Switzerland, France (Alsace), Belgium and Italy". The author put forward the conclusion that the Germans were a *Volk ohne Raum*, a nation without space to develop, and he propounded a "Greater Germany" in the same manner as Hitler was to propagate the Third Reich.

Another publication from the family firm was a school atlas which showed Austria, Danzig, the Baltic countries, the Sudetenland and large parts of Poland and Yugoslavia as "ethnically parts of Germany". Furthermore, it depicted the Ukraine as "the natural granary of a new Greater Germany".[7]

Reinhard Gehlen became a firm believer in the imperative need for German expansion in the East. His anti-communism, which took root in that period, was not prompted solely by nationalist emotions, it was based on a rational conviction that the Germans had a sociological and economic mission to dominate Eastern Europe. He turned eagerly to the study of that vast part of the Continent. He began to read books on the Soviet Union and, increasingly fascinated by the subject, assembled quite a library on the Soviet government and administration, on the communist experiments with industrialisation, collective farms and the fight against illiteracy. As a soldier he was particularly interested in the organisation of the Red Army, which Trotsky's genius had transformed from a motley revolutionary rabble into the most formidable army in Europe. What, it seems, soon aroused his strongest interest was the world-wide activity of the Comintern, with its avowed aim of propagating world revolution, and the organisation of the CHEKA and its espionage machine, the like of which no country had ever attempted to establish before.[8]

Gehlen was fascinated by Felix Dzershinsky, the Polish aristocrat an old Bolshevik who had created the "Red Inquisition", and by his lesser known successor Vyacheslav Rudolfovich Menshinsky, then head of the renamed OGPU. Devouring scores of books on Russia and digesting every scrap of information from German newspapers and journals, the young artillery lieutenant in sleepy Schweidnitz became something of a self-made expert. He harangued his brother-officers on his favourite subject even though they listened only half-heartedly and could hardly follow his political and economic arguments. But they liked one story, which Gehlen used to tell in the officers' mess and at garrison parties, and which he considered morbidly amusing.

21

One day, so it went, Stalin, then secretary general of the Central Committee, asked Dzershinsky how many counter-revolutionary suspects CHEKA was keeping under detention. Dzershinsky sent him a note saying the number in Moscow was about 1,800. Stalin returned it with a cross on the margin. The following night all the prisoners were shot. Dzershinsky notified Stalin that his order for the executions had been duly carried out—only to be told it was all a misunderstanding. Stalin's secretary wrote: "Josef Visarionovich usually puts a cross on a report to indicate that he has noted the contents . . . . "

For Menshinsky, least known of the OGPU bosses, Gehlen admitted a grudging admiration. The Russian's name was not unfamiliar to him; he remembered that he had been a Soviet consul in Berlin and had headed an early spy net in Germany. Menshinsky was a rare bird among the ruthless OGPU chiefs, an intellectual said to be fluent in twelve foreign languages, including Chinese, Japanese, Arabic and Persian; he wrote poetry, and dabbled in mathematics, astronomy and physics. Gehlen had much to contemplate in a man who could be boss of the world's most tyrannical secret police and still compose verse, a man who exercised limitless power over people's lives while pursuing scholarship in the humanities, who gazed at stars while commanding a global conspiracy of subversion and espionage.

Gehlen's conviction was strengthened that the Soviet brand of Marxism, the new order of communist society proclaimed in a messianic spirit, was based on barbaric foundations of slavery and terror from a bygone age, even though Russia's rulers toyed with the ideas of Western civilisation. It may well be that the quiet, unassuming artillery officer vowed at that time to make his own contribution to the saving of his homeland and even of the world from that tyranny. But he was young, healthy and, however preoccupied with his favourite subject, ambitious to get on in his career and possessed of the natural instinct to enjoy outdoor life. His devotion to barrack duties was rewarded by his colonel; he was made second-in-command of battery No.2. Also, he had acquired a new interest, which at least was to bring him the reward of prowess in sport and wipe out the irritating memory of his unathletic showing at school.

His battery was, of course, mounted and he had trained in riding as part of his drill. But now equitation became almost an obsession with him, and he spent every free hour, if he could tear himself away from his books, on horseback. The little lieutenant became before long the best rider in his regiment. He excelled in the annual Saint Barbara Rides (in tradition she is the patron saint of gunners) and in the autumn *Jagdritte*, to which the garrison commander invited the local landowners and aristocrats for a great point-to-point competition. Gehlen won many trophies, and riding remained his main exercise. Even in retirement, at the age of sixty-nine, he is a first-class horseman, although in later years motoring, usually at break-neck speed, has become his even more absorbing hobby.

In 1926, the year Field-Marshal von Hindenburg was elected President, Gehlen was posted to the Cavalry School at Hanover. There riding was high on the syllabus, but the place was much more than a training establishment for young cavalry officers. It was one of the camouflaged colleges General von Seeckt had set up, in defiance of the peace treaty, to train selected young officers for his officially non-existent General Staff. On completing the course Gehlen was promoted to first lieutenant and returned to garrison duties at Schweidnitz. But now he was posted to *Stabsabteilung* (HQ staff) and in a junior capacity was concerned with military intelligence matters, mainly relating to security along the Polish frontier. Such a staff appointment was a spring-board for promotion to a General Staff post in Berlin.

In his leisure time Gehlen continued his studies of Eastern Europe, but it is extremely doubtful whether at that time he had any inkling of the deep involvement of the Reichswehr High Command with the Soviet *Stavka* (General Staff) and the Kremlin leaders.

Secret Deal Between the Reichswehr and Moscow

The link between the German generals and the Kremlin was of long standing. As we have seen, Seeckt and other Reichswehr commanders had advocated an alliance with the Soviet Union as early as 1920. Soviet leaders reciprocated these sentiments, believing that the two "young nations" together could destroy not only Poland but eventually the imperialism and capitalism of the West. Behind this philosophy was obviously the idea that after victory over the Western adversaries the Germans could be conditioned to accept communism and that a Soviet domination of Europe would be the initial big stride towards world revolution. The Russians needed modern arms and aircraft if they were to resume the war against Poland. The Reichswehr was prepared to procure armament supplies from Germany and elsewhere, but was hampered by the limitation on the production of war material imposed by the Allies. After initial negotiations between General von Seeckt and the Soviet ambassador in Berlin, Nicolai Krestinsky, the chairman of the Soviet Defence Council, Leonid Borisovich Krassin,[9] arrived secretly in the German capital. The pact between Moscow and the Reichswehr High Command eventually came into being in January 1923; it provided for massive reciprocal arms supplies, the establishment of German armament and aircraft factories in Russia, and the training

23

of Reichswehr officers as pilots, navigators and air engineers in special schools built and controlled by the Reichswehr in Soviet territory.

The most remarkable thing about the agreement was that the German government remained entirely unaware of its real purpose. The Russians had approached several ministries and industrial boards offering commercial treaties over the purchase of training aircraft, engines and sporting planes, and suggesting that Reichswehr officers should act as their advisers. Although the German army was still forbidden to have aircraft, a small-scale production had been re-established for export. General von Seeckt set up within his *Truppenamt* a "Special Group R" (the initial stood for "Russia") and several of his officers—some of whose names were later to become household words—acted as "advisers" to the Soviet buying missions. Among them were Colonel Wilhelm Heye, Lieutenant-Colonels Werner von Blomberg and Baron Kurt von Hammerstein-Equord, and youthful Major Kurt von Schleicher.

A close friend of Hindenburg's son, with whom he had served in the Imperial Guard in 1918, Major von Schleicher was the archetype of a politico-military man. Friend and foe agreed that his unfortunate name, which in literal translation means "creep" or "sneak", superbly fitted his nature. At one time he recruited men for the right-wing *Freikorps* and defended the Kapp Putschists, at another he was involved in secret plots with the Social Democrats. Suave, brilliant, with affable manners, he had excellent contacts amongst politicians, captains of industry, rich merchants and bankers. He had become General von Seeckt's confidant, and he busied himself between the defence ministry, the foreign office and the Herren Club, knowing everybody of importance and fully trusted by no one. Schleicher became the prime mover of the Reichswehr-Kremlin pact; most of the secret negotiations took place in his private apartment.

It was Schleicher rather than Seeckt who persuaded Chancellor Wirth to put a secret credit of 150 million marks at the disposal of the "R-Group". The money was partly used to finance the building of a plant to produce an improved model of the famous wartime Albatros D-III in Russia; the Junkers Works at Dessau at first received forty million marks and later, through Schleicher's mediation with Hugo Stinnes, a further 100 million "without obligation of repayment"[10] for the construction of G-24 fighter aircraft. Production began at a new factory at Fili near Moscow. Krupp was contracted to manufacture field guns and ammunition; the Hamburg shipyards of Blohm & Voss began to build submarines for Russia. The pact foresaw, of course, that the Reichswehr would receive a fair share of the arms production, and this led to the establishment of training camps and special schools in which German officers might familiarize themselves with the new weapons.

To this end the Reichswehr—with every help from the Soviet government and General Staff—established an aerodrome at Loetzk, north of Voronetz, to which a flying school was attached. Before sufficient output of aircraft from the Junkers plant in Russia was available, Fokker planes built in Holland were shipped to Russia. At first only 26 German officers were sent there; but their number grew rapidly and during the following years it is estimated that at least 300 completed air training in the Soviet Union. A gunnery and tank school was later set up by the Reichswehr at Kama near Kazan. Red Army officers and NCO's were also trained there, but under the pretext of language difficulties, separate courses were held for the Germans and Russians, though they combined at field exercises. In 1928, Werner von Blomberg, by then a major-general and chief of the *Truppenamt*, visited Moscow with a military mission, conferred with Voroshilov, and inspected the various Reichswehr camps and schools; as a result the training scheme was intensified and from 1929 also included experiments with poison gas. For this research a number of German scientists and technicians were sent to Russia.

The Reichswehr was receiving substantial supplies of infantry weapons and ammunition from the Soviet Union. Within a period of ten months three Soviet ships unloaded 300,000 shells at the ports of Pilau and Stettin; as early as 1927, General Heye (Seeckt's successor) informed the defence ministry that clandestine army depots—in addition to offical ones—had in store 350,000 infantry rifles, 12,000 light and heavy machine guns, 400 mortars, 600 field guns and seventy-five heavy cannons. Indeed, their armament and equipment was by then sufficient for an army three times as strong as that which officially existed.[11]

The Reichswehr generals did not rely entirely on their communist friends. Their emissaries travelled the world to secure arms. Whilst Schleicher used his genius for business negotiations, Major-General Otto Hasse, who in succession occupied all the important posts at the defence ministry and the *Truppenamt*, was the chief organiser of the great rearmament scheme. It was not mere gun-running; frontmen of the *Truppenamt*, such as the former naval captain Lohmann, with the eager assistance of German industrialists and fat undercover subsidies from secret Reichswehr funds and government "loans", established a string of business companies in Holland, Finland, Turkey and Spain. Lohmann himself controlled the *Ingenieurkantoor voor Scheepsbouw* in Rotterdam, which produced motor torpedo boats and Severs seaplanes. In Finland, Captain Bartenback supervised the building of small U-boats at the Sornas yards in Helsinki. In

Turkey, Vice-Admiral Baron von Gaggern was in charge of torpedo and field gun manufacture. Captain Wilhelm Canaris, the future Abwehr chief, supervised the building of several 700-ton U-boats at Cadiz and Bilbao, where also German merchant ships were converted into men-of-war.[12]

There was a constant coming and going of German officers to Russia, and return visits by Soviet officers to Berlin. Notwithstanding the presence of a small army of Soviet spies and Comintern agitators in Germany, and the fact that Moscow financed the German Communist Party, whose avowed aim was the overthrow of the government, there was also a suprisingly close cooperation between the German and Soviet intelligence services.

This unnatural association went on for years. The German nationalists and militarists were still smarting from their defeat in 1918 and complaining about the injustice of the reparations imposed by the Allies, though Britain had long since renounced all claims and German reparations to other countries ravaged during the First World War had been relieved by generous American and British financial aid. These Germans saw in the Soviet Union a country similarly wronged by the West; they believed that Germany would be able to escape the bear's hug should it become too much of a danger.

The French were well aware that they would become the first victims, once again, of a rearmed and belligerent Germany. In addition to the inter-Allied occupation of the Rhineland, the French had in 1923 sent troops into the Ruhr and kept them there for two years. This was the answer to the Rapallo treaty between Germany and the Soviet Union, directed mainly against France's client, Poland. French spies roamed Germany to discover the extent of her secret rearmament. The British were much more complacent. The then chief of German Intelligence, Colonel Ferdinand von Bredow, reported in 1930 to his superiors that "the British did not worry about the military developments in Germany". He had established close personal relations with the Director of British Naval Intelligence, Vice-Admiral Sir Barry Domvile,[13] and after one of his visits to London, where Domvile introduced him to various military leaders, Bredow reported: "The British War Office assure me in strict confidence that they feel no anxiety about German rearmament, nor about the increase in the strength of our army and navy, but that they follow with great interest the developments in the air and the work done at Brunswick, Warnemunde, Staaken and other airfields and in our aviation industry."[14] He added that "Information gathered by the British Secret Service on German actions regarded as infringements of Versailles and existing treaties is usually withheld by British Intelligence departments from their French counterparts."

Pleased with this information from London, Bredow ordered that "particular caution should be taken to avoid leaks about the production and equipment of the Reichswehr with heavy artillery, mobile flak batteries, anti-tank guns and the new gas and flame-throwing mortar devices . . . . " To cement his strange friendship with the British generals he continued on an increased scale to supply the director of Military Intelligence with information about the Soviet Union, thus playing a peculiar double game.

Gehlen at the time knew nothing of these elaborate conspiracies. But he had arrived at the threshold of his career as an intelligence officer, which was to take him to lofty heights. At the age of thirty-one he was one of a handful of regimental officers selected to enter the newly established War Academy. Soon he was to achieve his ambition and could add to his uniform the coveted red braid of a General Staff officer.

III

A Welcome For The Fuhrer

Gehlen's advancement coincided with Hitler's coming to power. At the time of his arrival in Berlin to take up his posting on the General Staff the nazification of Germany was still tentatively getting under way, and many of his new superiors and colleagues at the Bendler Strasse headquarters continued to regard Hitler's chancellorship as merely another passing phase in the turmoil of German politics.

Despite his comparative seclusion Gehlen had followed the developments of the early 1930's with great attention. His intermittent leaves had been spent in Berlin, Leipzig and Breslau; at the homes of his family and relatives he had met people with connections in high places. Some of them had contacts among industrialists such as Alfred Hugenberg, a director of the Krupp concern, and Franz Seldte, chairman of the *Stahlhelm*,[1] who had become leaders of the conservative German National Party. Gehlen's father, by then general manager of the Breslau subsidiary of the Hirt publishing house, maintained a large house in the Koenigsplatz, where his second wife presided over politico-literary parties. Gehlen's mother had died in 1922 and within a year his father had married Frau von Horner, the titled and well-connected widow of a colonel in the Imperial Guards. She took an affectionate interest in her two stepsons and kept reminding Reinhard that, at the age of twenty-eight, it was time he was thinking of choosing a wife and exchanging barrack life for a home of his own. As a captain with good prospects for promotion to the General Staff, and with a modest allowance from his father, Reinhard Gehlen was decidedly an eligible bachelor though extremely shy; it was said that apart from a few fleeting and functional affairs he had as yet experienced no emotional involvement at all.

His stepmother encouraged him to marry into the aristocracy; indeed, it seems that she arranged his betrothal. On September 9, 1931, after a brief engagement, Gehlen led his bride to the altar. She was twenty-seven-year-old Fraulein Herta Charlotte Agnes Helene von Seydlitz-Kurzbach, the daughter of Friedrich Wilhelm Franz von

Seydlitz-Kurzbach, a retired colonel of the Imperial Hussars who could trace back his ancestry over several centuries. His great-grandfather had been one of Frederick the Great's generals, had fought in the Seven Years' War and died as inspector-general of the king's cavalry. Gehlen's father-in-law owned a large country estate at Zukowken near Glogau in Lower Silesia, and although the post-war inflation had diminished his fortune the wedding at the parish church at Glogau and the reception at the manor house were celebrated with all the traditional pomp and circumstance of the landed gentry.

Thus married into the nobility and related to many Junkers families, Gehlen's prospects were set fair; his long wait for a General Staff appointment was soon over. His younger brother Walter and his cousin Arnold—the son of his uncle Max, the publisher—had also been doing well, pursuing their respective careers in close sympathy with the rising nationalist trend. For his degree Walter Gehlen had chosen to write a thesis examining the position and obligations of a member of parliament; he concluded that the duties of a politician were primarily to the State and not to his constituents. Indeed, by inference he advocated a "one-party state"—a recommendation that Hitler was soon to put into practice. His cousin Arnold had chosen an academic career and had written a book on Fichte—the German philosopher who in his *Theory of Politics* described a Utopian state founded on dictatorship; in another work published some years later he extolled the coming "world of German hegemony."[2] Germans of the class to which the Gehlens belonged were in full sympathy with Hitler's declared policy, though they maintained, of course, in the words of Hindenburg after he had met the future Fuhrer for the first time, that "Germany cannot be ruled by a Bohemian corporal". In the presidential elections of 1932 in which Hitler obtained more than 11 million votes to Hindenburg's 18½ million, the Social Democrats and Liberals voted for the senile field-marshal to keep the nazi claimant out.

The coalition of the centre and right-wing parties still hoped that Chancellor Brüning, the leader of the Catholic party, would produce a miracle, eliminate parliament and restore the monarchy with the help of the army. Brüning, a high-minded but irresolute professor, had been proposed to Hindenburg by General von Schleicher, who had exploited his friendship with the President's son, Colonel Oskar von Hindenburg, to further his own rise to power. He hoped to use Brüning, who, lacking a parliamentary majority, governed largely by presidential decrees, as his tool. When Brüning lost his popularity with the army, Schleicher arranged his dismissal and recommended Franz von Papen as his successor. In Papen's

"Ministry of the Barons", all the important posts were given to nominees of the nationalistic leaders of industry and the Junkers. Schleicher himself took the ministry of defence.

One of Papen's first actions was to make a pact with Hitler, which resulted in the lifting of the ban which Brüning had imposed on the nazi stormtroops. Shortly afterwards there took place what amounted to a *coup d'état* in Prussia; the Social Democratic prime minister and his cabinet were ousted and martial law proclaimed "in order to guarantee that the general elections in November 1932 shall be conducted in an atmosphere of law and order". The surprising result of this measure, directed primarily against the communists and left-wing Social Democrats, was that the nazis lost two million votes and thirty-four seats, whilst the communists gained three-quarters of a million votes and increased the number of their seats to one hundred. There was now complete deadlock in the Reichstag: no government could muster a majority against the extreme left and right, and Papen resigned. On December 2, General von Schleicher, the arch-intriguer, persuaded Hindenburg to make him chancellor. Having failed to conciliate the centre and the left, he offered Hitler a coalition, but this was rejected with disdain. Schleicher's government lasted fifty-five days; it was marked by continuous riots and street fighting between nazi stormtroopers and the communist Red Front, to which hundreds of thousands of the hitherto moderate Social Democratic paramilitary group, the *Reichsbanner*, had gone over.

Germany was on the verge of civil war. Schleicher's scheming was at an end, as was the hope of a restoration of the monarchy and, with it, of law and order, nursed by the conservative nationalists and army leaders for so long. Hitler now held all the cards and when Hindenburg offered him the chancellorship, he played them cautiously. He exchanged his crumpled mackintosh and slouch hat for a morning coat and topper, and having assured the generals and conservative politicians that he would govern "strictly in accordance with the constitution", he accepted his appointment from Hindenburg's hands on January 30, 1933.

Hitler was content with only three cabinet posts for his own party; besides himself as chancellor, he appointed Dr. Frick, a former civil servant and a moderate nazi, as minister for the interior and Hermann Goering, the air ace of the First World War, as minister without portfolio. All other posts went to conservatives, including Papen as vice-chancellor, Baron von Neurath as foreign minister and Alfred Hugenberg, the Krupp director, as minister of economics. The army was represented by General Werner von Blomberg.

The Gehlen family welcomed the new government, as did all their friends. The Reichstag Fire, four weeks after Hitler had come to power, seemed only to confirm the "Red conspiracy" from which Hindenburg and Hitler had saved Germany. It was not then known, of course, that Goering, the new president of the Reichstag, had organised the whole sinister operation, sending his SS fire-raisers down an underground passage from his official residence, and arranging that they should leave behind a former inmate of a lunatic asylum with a communist party card in his pocket. Goering had tried to involve the communist leader Ernst Torgler and three Bulgarian communists, Georgi Dimitrov, Tanev and Popov, as alleged master-minds of the arson, but the Supreme Court—not yet entirely packed with nazi judges—acquitted them. Although this and the subsequent exposure of the nazi arson plot in the world's press embarrassed the government—neither Hitler nor his conservative ministers knew of Goering's *coup de théâtre*—it provided a welcome pretext for the immediate suppression of the Communist Party, the mass imprison-ment of its leaders in hurriedly erected concentration camps and in other repressive measures. Many Social Democrats and trade union leaders were also arrested.

Hitler dissolved the Reichstag but in the last democratic general elections in March the nazi party, despite massive intimidation, polled only forty-four per cent of the total vote, while the Centre Party actually increased its support, the Social Democrats polled nearly eight million, and even the forbidden communists still obtain-ed almost five million votes which were declared invalid.

Hitler now proclaimed the National Revolution, introduced the Enabling Act, which gave him dictatorial powers for four years, and replaced the sovereignty of the German states, by nazi *Statthalters* responsible to himself; he thus disposed of the federal structure of the republic and curtailed the prerogatives of President Hindenburg. With amazing speed the notorious nazi measures sprang into opera-tion: all "non-Aryan", i.e. Jewish, public servants, teachers, notaries and lawyers were dismissed or barred from practice; the Social Democratic Party was suppressed; the German National Party, to which most of the cabinet members belonged, "advised" to dissolve itself; the centre and smaller liberal parties obliged to disband. All Protestant churches were ordered to unite in a state-controlled Evangelical Church. The *Stahlhelm* run by Hugenberg and Seldte was incorporated into the nazi party, and the stormtroopers were given police status. A national boycott of all Jewish businesses and professional men was the signal for a ruthless persecution culmi-nating in the introduction of the Nuremberg Laws by which anyone of one-quarter Jewish extraction was deprived of the rights of citizenship. Strikes were forbidden and subsequently all trade unions were dissolved and taken over by the Nazi Labour Front.

31

In November 1933, the new Fuhrer staged a sham election in which there were no opposition candidates; inevitably the nazis won ninety-two per cent of the votes cast. This figure was extremely doubtful; even the government admitted that there had been three million spoiled ballot papers and many more millions of abstentions by people for whom this was the only way to register protest. The result of this "election" also approved Germany's withdrawal from the League of Nations.

The army's support for the Fuhrer, however, was by no means unwavering; its instability remained the only real threat to the new regime. To deal with it, Hitler struck against the radical social-revolutionary wing of his own party, which resented the way he had come to terms with reactionary captains of industry and the generals. In June 1934, the "Night of the Long Knives", seventy-four leaders of the SA, including its commander-in-chief, Ernst Roehm, once Hitler's closest adjutant and the chief organiser of the nazi movement, were lured into a trap at a Bavarian hotel and murdered by SS thugs; at the same time SS men killed General von Schleicher and his wife in Berlin, as well as three personal assistants of Vice-Chancellor von Papen. Many hundreds of other victims were put to death. The massacre was a warning to the deposed politicians and to members of his cabinet that the Fuhrer would not tolerate any attempt at opposition. The Great Blood Purge was, in so far as it eliminated many "left-wing" nazi leaders, greeted with satisfaction by the generals, many of whom saw it as bringing the removal of Hitler himself a step nearer. Like the world at large, they made the cardinal mistake of underestimating the new Fuhrer's determination to corrupt the entire German people and to make himself their unchallenged dictator. Most of his conservative coalition partners were soon ejected and replaced in the cabinet by rabid nazis whilst others like Papen and the "financial wizard" Dr. Hjalmar Schacht saw "the truth and the necessity of the national socialist dogma" and meekly submitted.

Gehlen had greeted the "revival of the Reich"—particularly Hitler's proclamation of rearmament and his withdrawal from the Geneva Conference with enthusiasm—but he soon became disillusioned. Never the less, like the great majority of German officers, he consoled himself with the thought that at least Hitler fully respected the armed forces, and had not only left men such as General von Blomberg, General von Fritsch and Admiral Rader in their positions but had enhanced their status. Moreover, by denouncing the Treaty of Versailles he had voiced the passionate feelings which Gehlen, his family, and all good German patriots had nursed for many years.

Gehlen, above all, was prepared to accept Hitler without demur as Leader of the State, the Fuhrer of the new Germany, who would triumph over the enemies of the German people, destroy communism and expand the Third Reich towards the East, giving Germany the *Lebensraum* of which Gehlen had always dreamed. During the closing years of the war, as has been mentioned, he came to realise Hitler's disastrous mistakes as a war lord; yet he never sided with the conspirators who wanted to eliminate the Fuhrer, and he remained loyal to him to the very end.

At the War Academy

Gehlen's unbridled ambition to excel was to raise him from subaltern in a provincial garrison to the lofty heights of Hitler's wartime intelligence chief against the most deadly enemy: communist Russia. But in 1933, as a newly appointed General Staff officer, he had first to obtain the usual pass at the War Academy. This staff college—its official name was the Armed Forces Academy—was a new creation. Its syllabus was designed to train officers for the proposed OKW—the High Command of the armed forces. The OKW, devised by General von Reichenau, then one of the few nazi sycophants amongst the army leaders, had not yet come into being at that time; violent resistance to its formation was being encountered from the generals who saw in it a dangerous curtailment of their own power—quite rightly, for the eventual establishment of OKW led to just this.

Gehlen passed out from the Academy with distinction; he was one of its most assiduous students at the special seminar on the Soviet Union. His instructors must have found that he knew more about Marxist ideology, the communist regime, the Comintern, the Red Army and the Soviet espionage system than they did. "No wonder Reinhard Gehlen got top marks", one of his brother-officers, now a prosperous hotelier in Frankfurt, told me many years later. "Some of us considered the course a welcome break from barrack routine and garrison drill, and we spent our evenings chasing pretty girls. But Gehlen kept piles of books about Russia in his room and used to go to bed at night with a heavy volume of the statistical yearbook on the Soviet Union."

The middle thirties were a time of political manoeuvring in Europe. The nazi *Putsch* in Vienna in 1934 and the murder of the Austrian Chancellor Dollfuss temporarily lost Hitler the friendship of Mussolini, who regarded semi-fascist Austria as being within his own sphere of influence. The French leaders were alarmed by the *Putsch* and by the reunification of the Saar with Germany, and at the Stresa Conference in April 1935, France, Britain and Italy joined in a shaky agreement to try and limit German rearmament. France also concluded an alliance with the Soviet Union, which greatly disturbed British Conservatives. The British Government was ready to come to an arrangement with Hitler whereby the latter promised to limit the expansion of his navy. Thus in Britain the foundations of appeasement were being laid. Ribbentrop, when ambassador in London, kept assuring British politicians and Tory hostesses of Hitler's peaceful intentions. Conservative cabinet members, such as Sir John Simon and Sir Samuel Hoare, urged a conciliatory policy towards the Reich. With the exception of Churchill and a handful of his friends, the Conservative Party was united in its admiration for Hitler's achievements; Tory politicians particularly resented France's alliance with Stalin, whom they regarded as the main threat to British security and Britain's colonial possessions. They applauded the rebirth of a strong Germany as a bulwark against communism.

The small but growing group of anti-Hitler generals in Germany, were exasperated by the British attitude, but they hoped to turn it to their advantage. If the British would only understand that, could Hitler be ousted, a conservative, monarchist regime based on a strong army leadership would be a much better bulwark against Moscow's plots for a world revolution, then an understanding between Berlin and London might be achieved on a very different basis. The German military attaché in London, Major General Geyr von Schweppenburg, was an anti-nazi associated with the group of generals headed by the new chief of staff, General Ludwig Beck, who were actively plotting against Hitler. Besides sending official reports to Berlin von Schweppenburg despatched secret ones for Beck's eyes only. Whilst officially reporting that "the British War Office is permeated with a spirit of reconciliation towards Germany" and that "Britain's military leaders are prepared to give us a fair chance, agreeing that a conflict between Britain and Germany would only result in a victory for Moscow",[3] he pointed out to Beck and his fellow-conspirators that it was up to them to acquaint the British military leaders with the true intentions of the German generals.

Thus, on the eve of Mussolini's attack on Abyssinia, von Schweppenburg arranged a visit to Berlin by General Sir John Dill, vice-chief of the Imperial General Staff and head of its Operations Department; he was accompanied by Major-General Sir Bernard Paget, the director of Military Intelligence. Officially, they were invited by the German General Staff: unofficially, they met the anti-Hitler conspirators. The details of the already elaborately prepared *coup d'état* were not communicated to them, but they were told that the German army could, in the not too distant future, become the real ruling force in Germany, provided that the British government would give as least tacit support to their plans.

34

To one of the meetings between Dill and Paget and the German generals, Colonel Heinrich von Stulpnagel, then chief of the *Fremde Heere* department (Foreign Armies Intelligence) brought a pale little captain, whom he introduced as "one of our brightest young experts on Russia". This was Gehlen's first meeting with a British general. He kept himself respectfully in the background amidst all the gold braid and crimson; but when asked a few questions, he took from his bulging attaché case a pile of papers crammed with statistics and folders full of maps of the Soviet Union. In his quiet voice he gave them a comprehensive assessment of Stalin's war potential, reeling off from memory details of the strength and armament of the Soviet Army, its deployment, mobilisation plan, High Command, logistics and reserves, never once stumbling over a word or a figure.

Years later, during the war, when Gehlen's name had become familiar to the British war lords, General Paget recalled that meeting. "Gehlen was already a brilliant staff officer", he told me. "I realised at that meeting how little we knew compared with the knowledge the Germans had about Russia." For Gehlen himself it might have been just a routine lecture ordered by his superiors as a polite gesture to the British visitors. He probably hardly suspected that the German and British generals had also discussed matters very far removed from the strategical situation in Eastern Europe. One wonders what would have happened if the British Opposition had come to hear of certain parts of these discussions in Berlin. But there were no leaks; even today this is the first real account of that particular secret episode.

Generals Dill and Paget reported on their talks to Field-Marshal Sir Cyril Deverett, the chief of the Imperial General Staff. While still GOC Eastern Command, Sir Cyril had himself been invited to observe German manoeuvres and had met Beck, Witzleben and also Halder, at that time the head of the Operations Department of the German General Staff. Beck had assured Deverett that Hitler's days were numbered. Once the Fuhrer had been disposed of, a conservative German government, supported by the army, would be only too ready to conclude "a lasting non-aggression pact, or even an alliance, with Britain"; in return they would expect "a free hand against Russia".

After Hitler's re-occupation of the Rhineland and his denunciation of the Locarno Treaty, Deverett and Dill dissuaded the British cabinet from taking the drastic counter-measures demanded by the French. They stressed Britain's unpreparedness for war and expressed the hope, based on their secret information, that the dictator might yet be ousted. Geyr von Schweppenburg could still report from London that "the dead of the Somme and the common sense of the British generals have saved the peace".[4] He added, however, that Dill had expressed horror at Hitler's provocation and been dismayed by the German generals' meek acceptance of his orders to march.

With the arrival of Leslie Hore-Belisha as secretary for war, however, the honeymoon with Berlin came to an abrupt end. General Dill was removed from the Imperial General Staff and put on half-pay; Major-General Paget relinquished his post as director of Military Intelligence and was sent far away to Quetta as officer commanding the Baluchistan district. There were many changes at the top of the German military hierarchy, too. Hitler dismissed his defence minister, Blomberg, on the pretext that his wife had a questionable past; the true reason was that the Fuhrer thought him too lax with the overbearing generals. General von Fritsch, rightly suspected of being one of Hitler's most dangerous adversaries in the army, was accused of homosexuality; the charge was concocted by the promising young Gestapo boss, Reinhard Heydrich. Hitler abolished the office of defence minister altogether, made himself Supreme Commander and appointed the yes-man General Wilhelm Keitel chief of staff of the armed forces.

These measures at the beginning of 1938 heralded Hitler's preparations for war. The Sudetenland crisis and the annexation of Austria followed. Britain's appeasement policy was at its height. Lord Halifax went so far as to assure Hitler that "a peaceful incorporation of Austria and the Sudetenland into the Reich would not be resisted by Great Britain". London's main objection, Halifax explained, would be to "an arbitrary act of violence"[5] —from which one can only infer that the rape of Czechoslovakia was regarded as a kindly gesture.

Planning the War

Whilst after the aggression on Czechoslovakia the Chamberlain government had, at last, realised that Hitler had deceived them, the prime minister still hesitated to condemn it outright and three days passed before he sadly complained that the Fuhrer "had taken the law into his own hands" and warned that while he was "not prepared to engage Great Britain by new and unspecified commitments operating under conditions which cannot be foreseen", it was wrong of Hitler to suppose that "because the British nation believes war to be a senseless and cruel thing, [it] had so lost its fibre that it will not take part . . . in resisting a challenge if it ever were made".[6]

We now know, of course, that Hitler had long since decided to make it and that, though he hoped to keep Britain and France out when attacking Poland, he told his generals: "It is necessary to prepare for the showdown . . . . England is our enemy, and the conflict with England is a matter of life and death." Several times he repeated it: "If England wants to intervene in the Polish War, we must make a lightning attack on Holland . . . establish our new line of defence on Dutch territory as far as the Zuyder Sea and realise that the war with England and France will be a war of life and death."[7]

Many in the West felt angrily certain that Hitler had been allowed to succeed in yet another impudent bluff, and that Germany's real armed strength bore no relation to the impressions he gave to the world. The annexations of Bohemia and Moravia and of Austria had, moreover, added eighteen million people and important industrial areas to his empire.

During these momentous months Gehlen had been kept extremely busy. He had hardly any time for his family; his first child, a daughter named Katharina, was born in 1934 and his only son, Christopher, on February 11, 1937. On this occasion he was allowed only two days' leave to visit his wife and to see the new baby. In 1936 he had been posted to the Operations Department of the Army General Staff where his chief was Colonel Erich von Lewinsky, later better known as Field-Marshal von Manstein, whom Gehlen idolized. During that period Manstein prepared the plans for the annexation of Austria (which took place in March ·1938) and for the invasion of Czechoslovakia a year later.

Gehlen assisted him, and in March 1939 became one of the planners of the working party, headed by General von Rundstedt and Colonel Guenther Blumentritt, which was completing "Plan White", the attack on Poland. A few months later Manstein was appointed to the command of the Eighteenth Division in Silesia, which was to be part of the spearhead of the invasion of Poland in September 1939. Gehlen went to Liegnitz, ostensibly to artillery regiment No. 18, in fact to do some reconnoitring at the border. He then returned to the Operations Department, where Colonel Adolf Heusinger had been appointed Manstein's successor.[8]

During the night of September 2, 1939, Major Reinhard Gehlen, appointed intelligence officer to the 213th Infantry Division, swept in an armoured car from Silesia across the frontier into Poland, with one of the first units to invade that country. But within thirty-three days his front-line service was at the end. On October 10, 1939, he was recalled to the OKW Fortifications Department and then returned to the Operations Department. The declaration of war by Britain and France presaged much greater campaigns; in mounting them the OKW would need planners of Gehlen's kind. For his brief service at the front Gehlen was awarded, on September 11, the Iron Cross Second Class. Maybe this rather modest decoration, usually given to "other ranks" in the field, was regarded as insufficient for the intelligence officer; for within another month he had added to it the more coveted Iron Cross First Class and later a bar.

A decisive period had opened in Gehlen's life. He had spent eighteen years of his military career in comparative oblivion, most of it in garrison postings. He was thirty-seven years old and had achieved a General Staff appointment somewhat late, having been overtaken by many younger, less brilliant and less qualified officers. Now, with the outbreak of another World War and with Hitler striving to dominate all Europe, the remarkable brain of Reinhard Gehlen was, at last, to be afforded its opportunity.

IV

The Russian Expert

Gehlen's rise during the first two years of the war was meteoric. It can be likened to that of a bit player in a theatrical repertory company who, after years of spear-carrying in the provinces, unknown and almost middle-aged, is suddenly "discovered" and soars to stardom overnight. His appointment as section head of the Fortifications Department under General Alfred Jacob came through the recommendation from General von Manstein. But this posting gave Gehlen the opportunity to meet men in the top echelon of the German High Command and from this point on his rapid ascent was entirely due to his own remarkable qualities.

Another man might have spent the rest of his career in a backroom job, one of the score of technical officers, gaining slow, automatic promotion and retiring well satisfied with the rank of a superannuated colonel. But not Gehlen. The Fortifications Department gave him a chance to display his exceptional talents, and they won immediate recognition. Generals were impressed by his incisive grasp of detail, his tenacious tackling of the most complex problems and his ability to explain his solutions with lucidity; soon he had them vying for his services.

This slight, pale major could spend sixteen hours at his desk engrossed in some difficult strategical problem which had baffled his superiors and then appear before a bevy of gold-braided, bemedalled generals and show no trace of anxiety or fatigue while he delivered a two-hour report which transformed the question into a simple common-sense affair capable of easy solution. Without ever raising his thin voice he would expound and elucidate the issues in a manner which, though quietly confident, never permitted his superiors to suspect that he knew better than they or that he, and not they, was the originator of the daring plans he was putting forward. Within a year he was promoted lieutenant-colonel, and a shower of honours followed.

After such conferences the generals would adjourn happily to the mess for much-needed refreshments—usually without troubling to invite the cause of their bonhomie—complacently satisfied that this clever chap Gehlen could be relied upon to finish off the awkward problem about which they had been so perplexed an hour or two before. It was one of Gehlen's supreme assets that he could manipulate powerful men without seeming to do so, that he could impose his own ideas while appearing as an obedient subordinate who simply executed the plans of his superiors.

Within a month of his arrival at General Jacob's office he was asked to inspect the defences of General von Kluge's Fourth Army on the Western Front. His report and suggestions on this occasion were forwarded to the OKW, where they were received with great appreciation. Early in January 1940 he was ordered to supervise the building of new fortifications in the Saar. He made a detailed report within a week. A few days later, on January 20, he was sent back to conduct an inspection of the west wall, where the *Organisation Todt* had been building and enlarging the giant fortification system since 1936. Further work there had lately been proceeding under the supervision of Albert Speer, Hitler's "great architect" and future armaments minister. It is some indication of Gehlen's progress at this time that while still an artillery major without constructional experience he should have been given this task over the heads of scores of higher-ranking officers and qualified engineers.

He was back on January 29 with a voluminous report in which he suggested that special "shock units" equipped with flame-throwers should be assembled to man the other fortifications and deal with enemy reconnaissance troops. Told to draw up a plan for the organisation of these units, he produced it the next morning—in it the proposed shock troops were innocuously referred to as "pioneer service battalions". The memorandum was submitted at a conference attended by General Halder, the chief of staff, to whom Gehlen mentioned almost casually his interest in the development of fortifications along Germany's eastern borders, which by then extended deep into Poland. Halder immediately asked for a summary of his ideas on the subject and Gehlen worked on this throughout February, while not neglecting the West Wall.[1] Halder was much impressed by his work and in a memorandum dated April 8 praised it in fulsome terms.

Later Gehlen sent Halder an astoundingly accurate assessment of the Maginot Line. It would be an overstatement to say that this report influenced the "Plan Yellow" for an attack on France through Belgium, for that scheme had already been prepared and, indeed, repeatedly revised; obviously the OKW possessed a bulky dossier on the French fortifications. Nevertheless Halder later recorded that this note from Gehlen had contributed to his final plans.

On May 9, the eve of the attack on Holland, Halder appointed Gehlen as his special liaison officer to the XVth Panzer Corps of General Hermann Hoth within the XVIth Army of General Ernst Busch. (One of Hoth's divisions, incidentally, was commanded by a daring young brigadier named Erwin Rommel). The *Blitzkrieg* that led to the conquest of the Netherlands within five days took the tanks of the XVth Panzers across the Meuse. On June 1 Gehlen was transferred to the headquarters of General Guderian's XIXth Armoured Corps, which had reached Sedan in the same night that Hoth arrived at Dinant. An order from General Halder dated June 11 described Gehlen as the "spokesman of the chief of staff at General Guderian's headquarters".

Thus within four weeks Gehlen had reached a position in which he rubbed shoulders with men who were to become Hitler's supreme war lords. His acquaintance with Guderian blossomed into a close friendship. Later, when Guderian became chief of staff, he was to rely heavily on Gehlen's advice and to lose his job as a result of his attempts to protect Gehlen from Hitler's wrath.* On July 1, 1941, Gehlen became General Halder's principal ADC; the chief of staff had been greatly impressed by the confidential reports Gehlen had been sending back on what he saw and heard at front-line headquarters. For the next three months he rarely left Halder's side; he had arrived at the very nerve-centre of Hitler's direction of the war.

Barbarossa and Sea Lion

Early in November Halder sent him back to the Operations Department as group chief and deputy to Colonel Adolf Heusinger. From his temporary preoccupation with the West, Gehlen turned to areas which were much more familiar to him—Eastern Europe. One of his first tasks was to draw up plans for a campaign in the Balkans and eastern Mediterranean; this he did in collaboration with the later Field-Marshal Friedrich Paulus, the future commander-in-chief at Stalingrad. On November 14 Gehlen began work on "Operation Marita", the plan for a build-up of German forces in Rumania for an attack on Yugoslavia and Greece which was to be the prelude for "Operation Barbarossa"—the attack on the Soviet Union. On December 7 the Marita plan was ready.

Some of Hitler's generals dreaded the thought of a war against Russia, and not only because they were wary of fighting on two fronts. As Halder put it "the warnings of his military advisers produced the shadows of Napoleon". But there is nothing in contemporary OKW documents nor in the voluminous War Diary

* See pages 92 and 109

that would show that they had tried to oppose it. Although Halder later wrote derisively of Hitler's "adventure in the East", he also stated: "We know today that Hitler was right, even though he had chosen a date for the attack on Russia which found Germany in possibly the most disadvantageous situation, with the conflict in the West becoming active again." [2]

On November 12, 1940, when Gehlen was still working on "Plan Barbarossa", Hitler issued yet another directive (No.18) dealing with enlarging the operations against Britain by attacks on Gibraltar through Spain and on Egypt from Libya. The directive also announced improvements to plans of the invasion of England outlined in his directives No.16 ("Sea Lion") and No.17 for the conduct of air and sea warfare against Britain, which had been issued in July and August.[3] On November 27 Gehlen attended a long conference with Halder and Heusinger. The invasion directives were on the agenda and Gehlen seized the opportunity to make an impassioned plea for the abandonment of the "Sea Lion" proposals. He urged that the idea of an invasion of England be dropped and that Germany's total power should be concentrated against the Soviet Union.

Halder told him not to worry; he pointed out that "Sea Lion" had already been postponed several times and that on October 12 Hitler had told his generals that "preparations for the invasion of England would continue for the sole purpose of maintaining political and military pressure on England", adding that the invasion would be reconsidered in the spring of 1941.[4] Halder, indeed, anticipated the contemptuous judgement that Rundstedt was to make several years later:

> The proposed invasion of England was nonsense because we never had the ships available . . . , we looked upon the whole thing as a sort of game . . . . Our Navy was not in the position to cover a crossing of the Channel or carry reinforcements; nor was the Luftwaffe capable of taking on these functions . . . . I had a feeling that the Fuhrer never really wanted to invade England; he never had sufficient courage . . . and he hoped the English would make peace.[5]

Thus reassured, Gehlen turned to his work on "Plan Barbarossa". At the Operations Department he had been appointed head of a special *Ostgruppe* (Group East). He had also been one of a handful of recipients of Hitler's top secret directive No.21 of December 18, of which only nine copies were distributed and which stipulated that all preparations for the attack on Russia should be concluded by May 15 of the following year. The document formulated the following "general intentions":

42

The bulk of the Russian Army stationed in Western Russia will be destroyed by daring operations led by deeply penetrating armoured spearheads. Russian forces still capable of giving battle will be prevented from withdrawing into the depths of Russia.

The final objective is to erect a barrier against Asiatic Russia on the general .line Volga-Arkhangelsk. The last surviving industrial areas in the Urals can then, if necessary, be eliminated by the Luftwaffe.[6]

Stating that Germany could count on the support of Rumania and Finland, Hitler outlined the main operations as he envisaged them; a thrust to capture Leningrad and destroy all Soviet forces in the Baltic area; an attack by "powerful armoured and motorized formations" from the area north of Warsaw through Byelorussia with the objective of a quick capture of Moscow; a main attack from the direction of Lublin in Poland into the Ukraine for the capture of Kiev, and thence a thrust to the Donets Basin. The directive ended with an order that detailed operational plans should be submitted "on the basis of this directive".

Gehlen worked like a beaver to comply with the Fuhrer's instructions. Heusinger had assembled a special staff for this momentous task; his deputy, Lieutenant-Colonel von Grolmann, exercised overall supervision as a "progress chaser", Major Helmut Stieff [7] was head of the documentation and cartography section, and Major von Frankenberg in charge of all administrative matters. On Gehlen's suggestion, a secret group for the collection and evaluation of intelligence was also set up, under Major Gehrholz, which had the effect of practically excluding the Abwehr—Canaris' Military Intelligence—from their activities. Gehlen himself assembled a very small staff to assist him, selecting young officers of comparatively low rank: Captains Brandt, Philippi and Ziervogel, First Lieutenant Barnewitz and Lieutenant Baron von Fircks. He was wary of having anyone of significance looking over his shoulder; as we shall see, this lone-wolf approach was to be characteristic of all his work in later years.

He produced detailed plans, bulky documents full of maps and diagrams, with incredible speed. From Halder's notes we know that preparatory work was started in the second half of January (the exact date was probably January 20) and by January 28 Gehlen had ready a lengthy plan entitled "Draft of transportation and logistics for Barbarossa", on which Halder made the marginal comment: "Excellent work!" On February 2 Gehlen flew to Bucharest to confer with the Rumanian military authorities. The plans called for the Rumanians to support the German armies which were to operate in the Ukraine by occupying the area across the lower Pruth and eventually linking up with their allies on the river Dnyester. Without taking them into his confidence Gehlen tried to assess the extent to which they could be relied upon. Hardly had he returned to his headquarters before he produced, on February 17, the final draft for the Balkans campaign, an improved "Plan Marita" and a tentative plan for an attack on Turkey.

Through March and April he and his staff joined with the planners of section 12 of the General Staff, concerned with logistics and arms supplies, in putting the final touches to "Plan Barbarossa". Gehlen followed the events in Greece and Yugoslavia that April with controlled excitement; this was the prelude to the attack on Russia for which he had longed. In another *Blitzkrieg* Hitler's Panzer Divisions smashed across Hungary and Rumania into the heart of the Balkans. "Operation Marita" was executed to perfection; Belgrade was reduced to smouldering rubble under which lày seventeen thousand dead civilians. The Greeks still offered resistance—and Gehlen must have felt twinges of grudging admiration—but it was only a matter of time before they, too, would be forced to their knees.

On May 12 the complete and definitive "Operation Barbarossa" was ready for submission to Halder, who would pass it on to Hitler, Keitel and Jodl. Gehlen had not seen his wife and children for many months. Yet even now, when one might have expected him to take a break from his relentless schedule, he had no thought of a holiday. No sooner was the Barbarossa plan out of his hands than he began preliminary work on the project for a combined German-Italian attack on the Suez Canal to coincide with a land offensive from Libya.

Halder told him that the Fuhrer "was greatly pleased" and presented Gehlen with a leather-bound copy of *The Life of Frederick the Great*, inscribed "For your excellent work". And on Gehlen's index card Heusinger wrote: "A General Staff officer as he should be. Personality, knowledge, diligence far above average. Excellent operative qualities, foresight, and percipience. Completely trust-worthy. Future utilisation corps commander or departmental chief."[8]

On June 21 Germany attacked the Soviet Union. Gehlen's dream had come true; the assault on communism had begun. He felt that, at last, he could leave his desk for a day or two to see his family.

The news from the front was exhilarating. Within a week the careering Panzer division had struck deep into Soviet territory, had captured Brest—Litovsk, Vilno, Lvov, Riga and were surging on across the river Beresina towards Moscow. The Finns had gone to war against Russia; the circle around Leningrad was closing. Everything was going according to plan—the plan on which he had spent almost superhuman efforts. Now the guns would decide the issue.

A month after the beginning of the invasion Halder asked Gehlen to accompany him on an inspection tour of the Army Group North of Field-Marshal Fedor von Bock, which had reached Smolensk and was poised for the final attack on Moscow. There was a double surprise for Gehlen on this trip. On July 22 he was presented to the Fuhrer and Halder gave him the Gold Cross of Merit with Swords. Three days later he was summoned to one of the Fuhrer's conferences—a signal honour. After receiving a firm handshake from Hitler, whose glaring blue eyes he found "magnetic and captivating", Gehlen kept himself modestly in the background. He has not recorded what he heard at that conference, but we know that it was on this occasion that Hitler gave to Field-Marshal von Brauchitsch the following order:

> In view of the vast size of the occupied areas in the East, the forces available for establishing security will be sufficient only if all resistance is punished not only by prosecution of the guilty, but by the spreading of such terror by the occupying forces as is alone appropriate to eradicate every inclination to resist amongst the population.[9]

Halder had told Gehlen that he had "certain plans for his future" which he had "discussed with Keitel but which may have to wait a while". He suggested that Gehlen should take things a little easier and sent him off on an inspection tour to Finland and the Leningrad front. Gehlen spent much of August on this tour, returning in the early autumn to continue his work at the Operations Department. There he read with some misgivings the reports which were reaching the General Staff of the atrocities committed in the occupied eastern territories by the SS and nazi commissars. On November 10 he again accompanied Halder to conferences at the Fuhrer's headquarters, where he developed his ideas to remedy the growing problems of transport during the Russian winter. He saw Hitler only once during this period, at Cholm, when the Fuhrer paid a brief visit to the front.

The Terror

Within seven weeks of launching their attack, the Germans had surged six hundred miles deep into Russia, had overrun Byelorussia and occupied most of the Ukraine. Some fifty million Soviet citizens had fallen under nazi rule. The Centre Army Group under Field-Marshal von Bock had established its headquarters at Krasny Bor outside Smolensk. At once they were faced with the enormous problems involved in maintaining even a modicum of public services and in providing supplies for the scores of large towns they had taken. Hitler had left the German military commanders in no doubt as to the manner in which the war in the East was to be conducted. As early as March, three months before the attack, he had expounded his "terror plan" at a meeting of the commanders earmarked to lead the June invasion:

> The war against Russia will be such that it cannot be conducted in a knightly fashion. This struggle is one of ideologies and racial differences and will have to be conducted with unprecedented, merciless and unrelenting harshness. All officers must rid themselves of obsolete ideas of warfare. I know that the necessity of waging war by such means is beyond your comprehension, generals, but I absolutely insist that my orders be executed without contradiction. The Russian commissars and officials are the bearers of an ideology that is directly opposed to national socialism. Therefore they will be all liquidated. German soldiers guilty of breaking international law and other rules . . . will be excused.[10]

Some of the generals, Halder and Manstein among them, protested against this policy of terror to Brauchitsch, who expressed the opinion that most officers would in any case refrain from carrying out the order too strictly, but asserted that it would be futile to ask Hitler to rescind or alter it, "for nothing in the world would change his attitude". Indeed the order for mass executions not only remained in force, but was followed by another issued on May 13 and countersigned by Field-Marshal Keitel, which gave every German officer power over life and death:

> Persons suspected of action against the German Army and administration will be brought before an officer. This officer will decide whether they are to be shot at once. In the case of offences committed by members of the German Wehrmacht against enemy civilians prosecution is not obligatory even where their actions constitute a crime or offence under German military law.[11]

The Germans officers reacted to this *carte blanche* for the wholesale murder of civilians with varying degrees of enthusiasm. The order to "liquidate" Soviet commissars, officials, chairmen and members of town councils and the police was generally carried out; but many officers refused to indulge in the orgy of killing that Hitler had envisaged, while others insisted that persons suspected of

46

resistance should appear before a properly conducted court martial. However, as the Russian winter and Soviet counter-offensives, aggravated by growing partisan resistance, began to inflict ever-increasing hardship on the occupying armies, ill-treatment of the civilian population increased to new peaks of savagery.

In the initial stages of the war, some of the commanders—and particularly Field-Marshal von Bock—had reported to the OKW on the growing difficulty they were encountering in providing food and meeting other primary needs of the population. However, Goering, who had been put in charge of the economic exploitation of the occupied territories, made it quite clear that its produce, and particularly the harvest of the fertile black-earth belt, was not to be diverted for feeding the conquered people, but should be brought to Germany:

> The German administration of the conquered territories may well endeavour to mitigate the famine which will undoubtedly occur . . . . However, such measures as can be taken will not avert the famine. Any attempt to save the population from death by starvation by utilising surpluses from the black-earth zone would be at the expense of supplies to Germany. This would reduce Germany's war potential and undermine Germany's and [German-occupied] Europe's capacity for resistance to the Western blockade.[12]

This attitude of the nazi leaders regarding the population of the conquered territories was, however, at variance with that of some of the more rational German commanders at the front. Intelligence officers at Field-Marshal von Bock's headquarters at Borisov and later at Smolensk recalled Napoleon's disastrous mistakes in 1812. They realised that such harsh and inhuman treatment would only provoke fierce resistance, producing an intolerable situation behind the lines of the advancing German troops. Moreover, starvation and the collapse of all public services would most probably cause epidemics which would endanger the troops.

Bock's ADC, Major Count von Hardenberg, his chief of Intelligence, Colonel Henning von Tresckow, and Tresckow's deputy, Major Baron Rudolf von Gersdorff, in particular, urged that the help of some of the Russian officials and intelligentsia in the towns should be enlisted. They pointed out that many of them were disillusioned with the communist regime. There were, indeed—at least at first—some people among the townsfolk and the collective farmers who could be expected to collaborate with the Germans in return for tolerable conditions. The farmers, in particular, had for years been squeezed dry by oppressive regulations and ruthless commissars. There were even many communists who were opposed to the Stalin regime, among them those who had supported or sympathised with oppositional groups within the Party, such as the "rightists", whose leaders Bukharin, Rykov, Bulanov and many others had been executed in 1937, or the Trotskyites, whose chief spokesmen Pyatakov, Radek, Sokolnikov and Rakovski had fallen victim to the Stalin purges of the following year. There was disaffection, too, among many Red Army officers now prisoners of war in German hands; thousands of their comrades had been put to death or banished to labour camps in the aftermath of the trials of Marshal Tukhachevsky and seven generals, all of whom were shot in June 1937. Indeed, there was scarcely a family of serving officers that had not seen at least one member imprisoned, banished or executed in the purges.

The Pro-Nazi Ukrainians

Bock's officers—Prussian noblemen who subsequently engaged in conspiracies against Hitler—honestly believed that only the excesses of the nazi officials and SS men who had been charged with the administration of the occupied areas prevented them from arriving at an understanding with the Russian intelligentsia in the towns and with millions of the peasants. They cast an envious eye towards the south, where their Abwehr colleagues on the staff of Field-Marshal von List, commander-in-chief of the Army Group South, had succeeded in enlisting tens of thousands of Ukrainians as collaborators and HIWIS (*Hilfs-Willige*—that is, men prepared to assist the Germans).

The situation in the Ukraine, however, differed fundamentally from that which obtained in the Great Russian and Byelorussian areas. The Ukrainians had been intensely nationalistic for centuries, and acted as a constant thorn in the side of the Moscow government. After the Bolshevik Revolution Ukrainian Cossack leaders, such as Skoropatsky and later Simon Petlyura, had established independent regimes in Kiev and Charkov, whence they had fought the communist regime during the Civil War and the Russo-Polish War of 1920-21. Not until 1926 was Moscow able to impose full control over the Ukraine, and even then uprisings and rebellions continued. Now many Ukrainians looked upon the Germans as liberators, and hoped that a victory for them would bring independence to the Ukraine, albeit under German suzerainty. The Ukrainians had something in common with the nazis, too, in their time-honoured hatred of the Jews.

During the Civil War Petlyura's Cossack bands had slaughtered tens of thousands of Jews, committing atrocities so bestial as to defy description: babies had been impaled on lances and borne aloft, their

48

bodies still wriggling; women of all ages had been raped and then burnt at stakes or bayonetted and mutilated beyond recognition. After his defeat by the Red Army, Ataman Petlyura fled to Poland and, when even the semi-fascist Warsaw government found his presence too embarrassing, eventually to Paris. On May 25, 1926, he was shot in the Boulevard Saint-Michel by Samuel Schwarzbarth, a Jewish watchmaker whose entire family had perished in one of the pogroms. Like Petlyura, many Ukrainian nationalist leaders—as well as Russian anti-communists—had gone into exile in the West. Some set up anti-Soviet organisations in Poland, supported by the Polish General Staff. But most of them found refuge in Germany; under the Weimar Republic many had served for General von Seeckt's Reichswehr Intelligence. Amongst these were Andreas Melnik (German agent "Konsul 1") and Stefan Bandera, who at one time also worked for the British Secret Service. Small wonder, then, that the nazis regarded the Ukrainians as their natural allies against the Russians and Poles and, taking their splendid past record in persecution of the Jews into account, were ready to overlook the fact that as members of the Slavonic race they were merely "sub-human".

Under the aegis of various nazi organisations—and with somewhat shamefaced cooperation from the Abwehr—a number of camps had been set up in 1938 for the Ukrainian emigrés of Bandera's OUN groups and their militant associates of the UPA. Several hundred Ukrainians were allowed to join the SS, despite its strictly Aryan rules. The invasion of the Ukraine gave the Germans a chance to use the emigrés to turn sections of the population into willing collaborators, if not into actual allies. Tens of thousands were recruited within a few weeks of the occupation and enrolled into the "Ukrainian Freedom Legion", among whose organisers was Bandera. From the legion emerged the *Nachtigall* and *Roland* regiments, which became notorious for their atrocities against their own compatriots, Poles and Jews. Eventually they were incorporated into the 201st SS division under SS General Erich von dem Bach Zalewski, the man who crushed the Polish Resistance in Warsaw. By 1942 the Ukrainian brigades comprised more than 200,000 men, while their political OUN wing provided many informers and spies. Yet at the same time their atrocities and the reign of terror instituted by Erich Koch, the stupid and hard-drinking gauleiter of the Ukraine, soon turned most of the potential collaborators amongst the civilian population into enemies. In 1942, Goebbels sadly noted in his diary: "The inhabitants of the Ukraine were at first more than inclined to regard the Fuhrer as the saviour of Europe and to welcome the Wehrmacht ... but this attitude has changed completely in the course of months."[13]

The Germans met with even less success in attracting collaborators and traitors from amongst the Great Russian population in the north and in Byelorussia. Bock's staff officers' attempts to prevent the worst excesses of the SS and Gestapo thugs who controlled the administration were unavailing in preventing the alienation of the inhabitants. They were, however, more successful in attracting allies among prisoners of war; the main reason for this was that a prisoner willing to enlist in the HIWI battalions could, at least, hope to get regular rations, be housed under tolerable camp conditions, and exchange his rags for some warm clothing.

The Russian Army of Liberation

Thus the idea of forming units of Soviet prisoners of war and using them as auxiliaries was conceived at Field-Marshal von Bock's headquarters at Smolensk. He had asked a distant cousin to work there first as an interpreter and later as a liaison officer to the Russians who had been enrolled. This man was Wilfried Strik-Strikfeldt, who as Gehlen's assistant was later to play an important part in the creation of the so-called Russian Army of Liberation under General Vlassov. Born in 1896 in the Russian Baltic provinces of German parents, Strik-Strikfeldt had been educated in St. Petersburg and served in the First World War as an officer in the Tsar's army. After the revolution he escaped to Latvia, which had become an independent republic under British sponsorship, but remained partly occupied by German troops for several months after the Armistice in 1918. He joined the British Military Mission under General Sir Hubert Gough, which assisted the new Latvian government in ridding the young republic of the remaining German troops and the *Freikorps* formed from amongst them. Strik-Strikfeldt served as a British Intelligence auxiliary, and helped with the supply and distribution of British arms to the Latvian army.[14] In 1920 he settled in Riga as a representative of British heavy engineering firms.

By 1939, when the Ribbentrop-Molotov pact resulted in the partition of Poland and the Soviet occupation of the three Baltic republics, Strik-Strikfeldt had once again resumed his wanderings; together with other evacuated Germans he had settled in Posen, in the Warthegau region, which had been annexed to the Third Reich from conquered Poland. Then he came to Bock's headquarters and on orders from Colonel von Tresckow he set up the "Smolensk Group" of a handful of Russian collaborators and ex-Red Army officers. The idea behind it was the ultimate establishment of a puppet "national" Russian government against the Stalin regime, after the pattern of Pétain's and Laval's government at Vichy. It never succeeded, partly because the Germans were unable to find enough prominent Soviet citizens willing to become quislings, but mainly because the majority of the nazi leaders were against it.

Tresckow, Gersdorff and, particularly, Strik-Strikfeldt continued their efforts, but they were greatly frustrated by some of the nazi leaders who had very different ideas on how to treat the Soviet people. Rosenberg, who had become Hitler's minister for Eastern affairs, sent two of his officials to Bock's headquarters to present the field-marshal with his proposals for the future of the Soviet Union after her defeat. Byelorussia (with a population of five and a half million and including the cities of Minsk, Mogilev and Vitebsk) was to be incorporated into East Prussia and resettled by Germans; a large area of western Russia was to be annexed to the Third Reich, "colonised" under a top layer of German settlers and administered by German officials; this area, with a total population of over fifty million, was to extend to Moscow and include the Ukraine, the Crimea, the black-earth region and part of the Caucasus, including its oil-fields. The Russians and Ukrainians within this German colony were to be treated, in accordance with Aryan racial principles, as *Untermenschen* (sub-humans); they would receive only basic education and agricultural training with a view to turning them into a nation of slaves. All the Leningrad and Karelian districts would also be incorporated into Greater Germany. What remained of the Soviet Union in the East and in Siberia would be "the steppes", without any industrial or urban life. Rosenberg's memorandum explicitly stated that some forty million Soviet citizens would need to be eliminated in the proposed "colonial" regions; this would be achieved by "natural means", namely famine. Rosenberg's conclusion was that in this way "the steppes would never again become a danger to Germany and German-dominated Europe."[15]

It is interesting to note that this blue-print for Germany's treatment of Russia corresponded in its broad outlines with the policy propounded in the books of Gehlen's brother and in others published by their father's firm,* though they did not advocate wholesale genocide.

Field-Marshal von Bock and his staff officers were stunned by this plan and Strik-Strikfeldt was sent to Berlin to obtain some clarification of it from the minister. Rosenberg did not receive him but an official told Strik-Strikfeldt that this was "a long-term plan", that the ultimate colonisation of Russia was the nazi cabinet's agreed policy. Famine, which could "eliminate many millions of Russians", must be regarded as inevitable. He added that there were differences

* see page 20

51

of opinion amongst Hitler's ministers about the actual implementation of the Rosenberg scheme. But whatever the outcome of these, millions of Russian men and women, prisoners of war and civilians alike, were to be deported to Germany to provide forced labour in industry and agriculture. There were a few nazi leaders who realised that no power could subjugate 200 million people and turn them perpetually into slaves, and that Germany had neither the military nor the economic power even to attempt it. They also recognised that such a scheme could only result in disaster for Germany itself. As Strik-Strikfeldt later put it "oppression, robbery and exploitation of a dismembered Russia" would not have rid Germany of the danger from that quarter. Goebbels, whom he visited, had drawn up a more sensible plan for a "new Russia", aimed at winning over the peoples of the Soviet Union, and particularly her many ethnic minorites, for the idea of a "new Europe based on freedom and equality", though, of course, under German tutelage.

This more enlightened *Ostpolitik* presupposed a more humane treatment of the subjected population, but the nazi leadership was deeply divided on this issue. Himmler had been charged with the maintenance of law and order in the occupied regions and he interpreted this task by sending thousands of his SS thugs and Gestapo men into Russia, where they indulged in a prolonged orgy of slaughter, killing innocent men, women and children, burning whole towns and villages, and looting anything they could lay their hands on. Swaggering SS hooligans of the lowest type were appointed to high offices as district governors and town mayors. The result of their appalling atrocities was that the ranks of the partisans in the forests, swamps and mountains were swelled by hundreds of thousands of homeless, starving and hunted, yet desperately determined, men, who harassed the occupation forces. Goebbels noted in his diary: "The situation in Russia grows more unstable . . . the partisan danger is increasing week by week."

Bock and his officers of the Centre Army, as well as other front commanders, protested against the continuous outrages and eventually Bock sent a long report to Field-Marshal von Brauchitsch. As a result, on December 18, 1941, he was ordered to hand over his command to Field-Marshal von Kluge. Bock's dismissal was announced by the OKW as being "at the field-marshal's own request on grounds of impaired health". Although Kluge was much more subservient to the nazi leaders, the idea of recruiting Soviet prisoners of war into an auxiliary army was not abandoned. Tresckow pursued it only to obtain replacements for the heavy casualties which the Centre Army Group had suffered during the winter offensive of 1941/2 in its relentless but fruitless attempts to take Moscow. Nearly twenty per cent of its strength had been lost in dead, wounded, sick and missing—this was the official figure, the true losses were much higher. The enlisted Russian "auxiliaries" were to be employed on guard duties behind the lines and as sappers and pioneers to build and repair roads, bridges and rail tracks. Tresckow found an ally in Bock's deputy chief of staff, Colonel Count Claus Schenk von Stauffenberg, who on July 20, 1944, was to attempt the assassination of Hitler. They encouraged the plans to transform the "Smolensk Group" into a "Russian National Committee", on the lines of the plan prepared by the former German Ambassador in Moscow, Count Friedrich von Schulenburg. Several national committees were to be set up, including one at Kiev for the Ukraine, in the Crimea and in the Caucasus, with a view to establishing puppet governments whose recognition would be demanded not only by neutral countries but also by the Allies. The plan was stillborn; Hitler forbade it, being determined to remain the overlord of the conquered people.

Gehlen Takes Over

It was at this juncture that Gehlen appeared on the scene. Shortly after Christmas 1941, General Halder had told him that he had persuaded Keitel to make Gehlen head of the *Fremde Heere Ost* (FHO) department of the OKW. This was the eastern, and most important, military intelligence section of the Supreme Command of the Armed Forces. Hitler had began to rely on it to an increasing degree, in direct ratio as his trust in Admiral Canaris' Abwehr was diminishing. There was also a *Fremde Heere West* department; but it never achieved the importance of its eastern counterpart, since the Abwehr had always concentrated its activities in the West, maintaining efficient networks in all the countries of Western Europe but meeting with only modest success in its espionage efforts against the Soviet Union.

The FHO, the eastern department, was headed by Colonel Eberhard Kinzel, an old-school intelligencer who had served during the First World War in the *Nachrichtendienst* of Colonel Nicolai. He was in his mid-fifties, an easy-going man. Hitler and his generals constantly complained about his lack of initiative and the snail's pace at which his reports were produced. Moreover, Canaris had been taking advantages of Kinzel's inadequacy and making great efforts to steal FHO's thunder in the hope of boosting his Abwehr's stock with Hitler. The chief of the Abwehr Group III, Major-General Eccard von Bentivegni, had set up three front reconnaissance groups in the occupied territories of the Soviet Union. They were code-named WALLI, and their intelligence officers were doing good work in infiltrating spies behind Soviet lines, in interrogating and "turning round" prisoners, and in establishing radio outposts inside Russia operated by infiltrated defectors. Already in the spring of 1941 there were three WALLI groups; WALLI I under Major Hermann Baun was at Sulejowek east of Warsaw; WALLI II under Major Seeliger[16] was mainly concerned with sabotage actions, and WALLI III under Lieutenant-Colonel Heinz Schmallschäger was in charge of *Einsatzkommandos*, groups of tough soldiers who operated, often in Russian uniforms, behind the enemy lines.

At the same time Himmler's RSHA had through its *Amt VI*, the intelligence department of the *Sicherheitsdienst* under SS Standartenfuhrer Walter Schellenberg, established its own espionage and reconnaissance units in Russia. Thus poor Kinzel of FHO found his preserves poached upon from two sides.

In the autumn of 1941, Halder had conferred with Gehlen's immediate superior at the Operations Department, Colonel Heusinger, about the deterioration of Kinzel's work and both had agreed that he should be replaced. Their candidate for Kinzel's successor was none other than Lieutenant-Colonel Reinhard Gehlen. There is little doubt that Gehlen had been casting a covetous eye at this post and had kept Halder informed of Kinzel's failings. But he was aware that in the eyes of the OKW he lacked formal intelligence qualifications and experience of the magnitude required of the director of a military intelligence department at the Supreme Headquarters, and he doubted whether his aspirations would be realised. In fact Halder had encountered opposition on just these grounds when he first mooted his proposals to Major-General Bodwin Keitel, chief of the army personnel department and brother of the field-marshal. But Halder and Heusinger continued to pull strings.

On December 26, Halder had a private conversation with Major-General Gerhard Matzky, the quartermaster general—Kinzel's immediate superior—and won him over. Several other hurdles were overcome, Halder succeeded in convincing Field-Marshal Keitel's chief of staff, Colonel von Ziegenberg, and eventually Keitel himself. At last he had his way. On March 14, 1942, General Rodwin Keitel agreed to put his signature to Gehlen's appointment.

Another and the most important stride in Gehlen's career had taken place. On April 1, Kinzel was abruptly told of his dismissal and his posting to a regimental command at the front. After the war he was to meet a tragic end.[17] Kinzel was told to stay at FHO for one more month in order to introduce Gehlen to his new job. In fact, Gehlen, true to his aversion for being overlooked, eased Kinzel out within a week. Almost immediately after taking charge of FHO, he began turning the tables on his two competitors, the Abwehr and

Schellenberg's *Amt VI*. Himmler's RSHA he would need to treat with great caution. Against the Abwehr he could proceed more ruthlessly and he soon achieved preponderance over its WALLI groups.

Gehlen also quickly turned his attention to the resuscitation of the plans for the Russian Army of Liberation. He had followed with great interest the developments at Smolensk, as well as those concerning the formation of Ukrainian units. For a long time he must have been determined to assume as much control as possible over them. Though remaining true to his youthful dreams of the great German *Lebensraum* in the East, he knew that they could never be achieved along the lines of Rosenberg's crazy schemes. Nor did he approve of the atrocities and outrages of the SS against the Soviet people. He envisaged the "new Russia" as Bismarck had done more than half a century before: a country autocratically ruled by a strong conservative, military regime, allied with Germany, its agriculture, mines, oil and other vast mineral resources developed under German guidance. Russia could then provide the abundant supplies of raw materials and food stuffs which the new mighty German industrial empire would require in order to dominate Europe and assume its rightful place as a Great Power, second only, or perhaps even equal to, the United States. Such a Russia, entirely dependent on Germany's industry, would need an army to keep the working masses in control, an army organised and equipped by the Germans and commanded by generals who fought beside those of Germany in the great struggle against communism. To find and win over these generals and officers Gehlen considered his foremost task. Once they could be·enlisted, the formation of a national, anti-communist army from amongst the prisoners of war and deported workers would offer little difficulty.

Gehlen put his ideas to Halder and Matzky and gained their approval. There were several officers at FHO who enthusiastically supported him, particularly Colonel Baron Alexis von Roenne, born in the Baltic province of Curland. With his superiors Gehlen argued that since he was entrusted with the direction of intelligence against the Soviet Union it was only right that he should be given a say in the plans for the Russian auxiliary units. One of FHO's main duties was the collection of information from Soviet prisoners of war; it would have to keep in touch with potential Red Army defectors and "volunteers", to supervise their recruitment and training, and to advise on the appointment of their officers.

Thus almost overnight Gehlen became the overlord of the Russian Army of Liberation. He managed to arrive at a seemingly amicable arrangement with its original sponsors, assuring them that he needed all their help and advice. In fact they soon faded out of the picture. Colonel Tresckow was given a front command and Count von Stauffenberg, horrified by the atrocities in Russia, asked for a posting to North Africa.[18] Within a few weeks Gehlen had achieved his aim. All matters connected with its staff, were referred to the headquarters of FHO at Mauerwald near Angerburg. Captain Strik-Strikfeldt was attached to Group III of FHO, under Baron von Roenne. He joined there several other Balts, such as Arnold Schbert, Captain Kerkovius, the former Pastor Friedrich Eckert, and Werner Bromann, a former journalist in Riga. It may well be that Gehlen saw in these men the future "administrators" of the "new Russia". Special camps were organised, one of which, Dabendorf near Berlin, later became the centre of the Vlassov Army. At Wulheide a training school for propaganda—in cooperation with Goebbels' ministry—was set up, where former Red Army officers were indoctrinated and trained as agents.

The Acquisition of Vlassov

Gehlen had still to prove that he could enlist some important personalities from amongst captured Soviet generals who would be prepared to put themselves at the head of the Liberation Army. Not only the nazi leaders but also the generals sympathetic to the plan were doubtful of success. By a good chance, however, Gehlen found just the man he was looking for. On July 13, 1942, the Soviet Second Shock Army had suffered a crushing defeat in the area of Volkhov in an attempt to throw back the Germans from the approaches to Moscow. Its commander, General Andrey Andreyevich Vlassov, hid with some of his officers in a barn, where they were found by a German tank unit. Eventually, they were taken to the officers' prisoner of war camp at Vinnitza in the Ukraine. Hitler had moved his headquarters from Rastenburg to this area, where he was waiting for his triumphal entry into the Soviet capital.

Vlassov was one of the best-known younger Soviet generals. Born in the Nizhni-Novgorod province, the son of peasant, he was intending to study for the priesthood when he was called up as a private in the Tsar's army during the First World War. In the Civil War he became a company commander fighting the White armies and afterwards stayed on in the Red Army, gaining quick promotion. As a major-general he headed a Soviet military mission to Chiang Kai-Shek. At the outbreak of the war he commanded a division and was later put at the head of the Second Shock Army for the defence of Moscow. As a prisoner of the Germans he had been treated with respect by General Fritz Lindemann, the victor of Volkhov,[19] and this may have conditioned his attitude to Gehlen, Roenne and Strik-Strikfeldt, who interviewed him at Vinnitza.

Gehlen took good care to avoid trouble with the nazi chiefs over his plans with Vlassov. At Vinnitza he talked to Hitler's OKW generals and then went to Himmler's seat at Zhitomir, a former Soviet officers' training college situated in a beautiful park. Between the headquarters of the Fuhrer and the chief of the RSHA a special, straight road was built, a so-called *Rollbahn* fifty miles long, which have heavily guarded and used exclusively by VIP motor traffic and motorized SS bodyguard units. Himmler was a daily visitor to Hitler's lair and amongst other frequent callers were Goering, Goebbels, Bormann, Heydrich and SS Obergruppenfuhrer Heinrich Muller, "Gestapo Muller", whose support Gehlen easily enlisted. Muller was an "old nazi"; he held radical views and regarded most of the nazi leaders as "decadent" and "bourgeois". Schellenberg suspected that "at heart he was a communist rather than a national socialist", but the Gestapo chief was completely devoted and loyal to Hitler.[20]

At Vinnitza Gehlen had long secret talks with Heydrich. (The SD chief was shortly afterwards assassinated in Prague.) They concluded a pact which resulted in a collaboration between FHO and the SD groups—including the later Zeppelin *Sonderkommandos*. Gehlen promised to respect their reconnaissance operations and, in return for obtaining information, to provide evaluation of it by FHO experts. At the same time he persuaded Admiral Canaris, who paid one of his infrequent visits to Hitler's OKW at that time, to agree on a definition of their respective spheres of activity. In a long letter to the Abwehr's group chief, Bentivegni, Gehlen suggested that they should "bury the hatchet" and cooperate in the future.[21] Thus covered against any possible trouble from his competitors, Gehlen instructed Roenne and Strik-Strikfeldt to organise a staff for Vlassov.

Gehlen's men scanned the camps for other possible collaborators and soon assembled quite a party. Roenne took them to Berlin where they were put up in a comfortable house in the Victoria Strasse. Though their windows had bars and they were guarded by military policemen, they were treated respectfully, and smartly saluted by German officers; their meals were brought from a good restaurant on Potsdamer Platz. Gehlen always applied the carrot-and-stick treatment with men he wanted to "turn round". To ensure continued approbation by the nazi leaders he approached Ribbentrop's and Goebbels' ministries. Officials were sent by them to Vlassov's new headquarters—Dr. Gustav Hilger, a former counsellor of the Moscow embassy as political adviser, and Captain von Grote from the Propaganda Department.

Vlassov's entourage was a strange motley. The most intelligent of his officers was Colonel Mileti Zykov, one of the few Jews who had risen to high rank in the Soviet Army. He had been a supporter of the "rightist deviationists" of Bukharin and in 1936 had been banished by Stalin to Siberia, where he spent four years. Another survivor of Stalin's purges was General Vasili Feodorovich Malyshkin, former chief of staff of the Far East Army; he had been imprisoned during the Tukhachevsky affair. A third officer, Major-General Georgi Nicolaievich Zhilenkov, had been a political army commissar. They and many of the officers whom Gehlen recruited had been "rehabilitated" at the beginning of the war in 1941 and given commands when Stalin discovered that the purges had left the Soviet Army deprived of experienced commanders. But they had never forgotten and forgiven the wrongs they had suffered from Stalin's hands. Even the Jew Zykov was ready to cooperate wholeheartedly with the Germans. Gehlen left the Collaboration Staff at Victoria Strasse in the hands of Roenne and Strik-Strikfeldt. He then turned to his main task, the reorganisation of FHO, determined to make it Hitler's foremost intelligence organisation.

V

Chief Of Intelligence

Gehlen wasted no time. As soon as Kinzel had departed he went to work with a will. On his very first day he assembled the entire personnel—group heads, senior officers, assistants, cartographers, radio operators, clerks, secretaries, everyone down to the last orderly—and treated them to a crisp address. He made it quite clear that from now on things were going to be radically different; he expected complete devotion to the job in hand, unremitting effort and, above all, the observance of the strictest secrecy in everything.

Within days he had made sweeping changes in the senior posts, replacing almost all the heads of groups and sections. Colonel Kinzel's team had comprised a number of middle-aged senior officers: men like Lieutenant-Colonel Dr. Erich Nauck, an old *Nachrichtendienst* man who had worked in Paris—ostensibly as a banker—for several years before the war and was an expert on the economic affairs of the Soviet Union; Lieutenant-Colonel Karl von Ogilvie, head of Group II which provided the evaluation of intelligence; or Lieutenant-Colonel Johannes Hoheisel, in charge of the evaluation of information obtained through the interrogation of prisoners.

Very soon all of these and many others had been shunted into less important positions and replaced by younger men who in Gehlen's view possessed greater initiative and drive. Ogilvie, for instance, was given a small group concerned with the Scandinavian countries. He was later to spend much of his time travelling to Sweden in the furtherance of Hitler's abortive plan to attack that country, by which he hoped to gain control of her iron ore resources and use her northern regions for the passage of troops and for Luftwaffe and U-boat bases for attacks on Allied convoys to Russia.

The new heads of groups and sections were young men whom Gehlen had noticed during his time in the Operations Department. One was twenty-seven-year-old Captain Gerhard Wessel, the son of a Holstein parson, who had joined the Reichswehr a year before Hitler came to power and who, like Gehlen, had been trained as a gunner.

He had fought in 1940 in France as an officer of the Artillery Regiment No.5 and Gehlen brought him to FHO fresh from the War Academy. Wessel became head of Group Soviet Union, whose officers sifted and evaluated the daily reports from the front. Soon he became Gehlen's deputy and worked with him for several years after the war under the aegis of CIA, eventually succeeding him as head of the Federal German Intelligence. Another of Gehlen's discoveries was Major Heinz Danko Herre, who had seen front service as an intelligence officer in the 49th Mountain Corps. Herre took over Group I and with his assistants, Captain Horst Hiemenz, Kurt Goelnitz, Gunther Letchert, Wolfgang Dix, Joachim Bausch, Count Adolf von Arnim, Otto Erhardt, and a number of other officers— amongst whom Gehlen posted Lieutenant Peter von Vaernewyck, a nephew of his mother—began to produce the basic evaluation material that Gehlen required for his reports to OKW. The final versions of these reports Gehlen always composed himself.

Front-line intelligence provided, of course, the life blood of the department's activities. Gehlen reorganised Kinzel's original set-up by dividing Group I into three geographical sections corresponding with the German Army Groups on the front, "North", "Centre" and "South". A separate fourth section dealt with intelligence on Soviet "bandits", i.e. the partisans. Wessel's deputy was Captain Albert Schoellner and their chief assistants were Captains Count Karl Heinrich von Rittberg,[1] Fritz Scheibe, Ernst Gunther Stegmann (later transferred to the Balkans group), Jurgen Reme, Hermann Foerster, Hellmuth von Hagen and a large number of younger officers. Most of them later won quick promotion. Their daily *Lage-Bearbeitunge* (a compilation of front-line reports, signals and all material received from advanced commands and WALLI units as well as from agents behind the enemy lines) provided the all-important information on which the evaluation experts could get to work.

Herre's group was also divided into several sections: one was concerned with the actual evaluation of the front-line reports, while officers in the other sections assembled material from Soviet radio broadcasts, newspapers, intercepted mail, and statements by prisoners prepared by the Interrogations Group. Another section within Group II dealt with Soviet economic matters, resources, manpower, production and supplies; yet another scrutinized all relevant reports and sources in order to detect and prognosticate the strategy of Stalin's High Command.

Major Baron Alexis von Roenne,[2] a Balt with a good knowledge of Russia and a fluent Russian speaker, had served under Kinzel, but Gehlen gave him a much more important position. He was made head of Group III, which was enlarged to six or seven sections and became

Major-General Gehlen at his desk at FHO headquarters. The Chinese proverb behind his desk is an unexpected feature in the office of a German officer.

Gehlen at the FHO staff Christmas party in 1943, as always a little distant and aloof.

Lieutenant-General Franz Eccard v
Bentivegni, head of the counter-espiona
department of Admiral Canaris' Abwel

Reichsführer SS Heinrich Himmler and SS General Reinhard
Heydrich, head of the Nazi Security Service, with whom
Gehlen cooperated.

SS Standartenführer Walter Schellenber

SS Sturmbannführer Otto Skorzeny

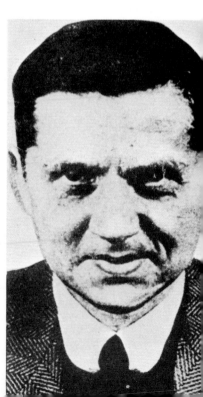

the "brain" of the department. Roenne's tasks were in many respects political. He and his assistants were supposed to produce broader evaluations, surveying the Soviet Union not only in the context of war operations but, above all, with regard to her political and sociological problems, and her global outreach. For instance, Roenne's group paid special attention to Stalin's relations with his allies in the West. Although FHO's field of operations was, of course, officially limited to events in the East, Gehlen was perceptive enough to view these events, whether in the military, political, economic or ideological spheres, in a world perspective. Roenne's assistants scanned all available newspapers, books, pamphlets and other publications, including those published in the West and in neutral countries, for anything germane to Russia and communism; they also monitored radio broadcasts to the same end. Indeed, Gehlen had organised within this group a kind of miniature "foreign office", embracing matters with which, of course, the Abwehr's groups, the intelligence branch of Ribbentrop's foreign ministry, Rosenberg's ministry for Eastern affairs, Himmler's RSHA, various foreign information offices of the nazi party and half a dozen other government departments dealt on a much wider scale. The collection of much of this material at FHO was, one suspects, initiated by Gehlen in order to satisfy his own insatiable curiosity and to enhance his status rather than in the course of his department's normal duties. It was shortly to come in unexpectedly useful, however, when Gehlen was suddenly ordered by Hitler to incorporate into his eastern department intelligence matters concerning the United States.

The evaluations produced by Roenne's group sometimes overlapped with those of Group II. Its output provided enormous quantities of material; Gehlen had ordered that every scrap of information collected was to be filed away in the special archives. Roenne had under him a small army of translators and interpreters and as a result of this it was arranged that he should also supervise the Interrogation Group. His group also maintained liaison with the intelligence staffs of army commands, down to divisional headquarters, and the contact with OKW, the Abwehr, Himmler's RSHA and Schellenberg's *Amt VI*, as well as many government departments. Finally, as we have seen, Roenne was also in charge of all matters connected with the "Smolensk Group", from which Vlassov's "Collaboration Staff" of the Russian Army of Liberation emerged at the Dabendorf camp. Strik-Strikfeldt and the motley fraternity of Balts and Soviet defectors who worked with Vlassov and his generals were under Roenne's command. Thus he also shared with Wessel's Group in the contact with the WALLI front-commandos and their infiltrated agents.

61

The Interrogation Group under Major Kurt Ruthenberg and his deputy Captain Bernard Blossfeld, once manager of the Hôtel de Rome in Riga, had set up a special camp for Soviet prisoners at the old fortress of Boyen near Loetzen in East Prussia. There potential informers were assembled from many other POW camps. Trusted Soviet defectors, such as Major Vasili Sakharov, conducted the initial interrogations. Prisoners, particularly officers with technical training, were squeezed dry and their depositions were then examined by the evaluators at headquarters. Prisoners regarded as potential defectors went through an indoctrination course and, when found suitable for training as agents, received special treatment. Gehlen's interrogators also worked at the Luckenwalde camp for Ukrainians, and at camps where Cossacks, Tartars, Turkmen, Georgians, Kazbeks and members of other ethnic minorities were segregated from Russian prisoners. Many thousands of them were eventually recruited into the HIWI and *Osttruppen* units, commanded by German officers.

The Archives

In his *Sonderkartei*—part of the special archives—Gehlen made a point of assembling every scrap of information that came into his department. Soon the priceless hoard included minute descriptions of every Soviet political and military figure from Stalin down to regional commissars and regimental commanders. A vast amount of topographical material was collected, amounting to a unique and up-to-date survey of Soviet production centres; it listed and described metallurgical plants, munitions and aircraft factories, smelting plants and foundries, power stations and chemical works in places as distant as Perm, Zlatousk, Chelyabin and Sverdlovsk in the Ural region, the newly developed industrial areas of the Kuznetsk Basin, and the Buriat and Mongolian republics bordering on China. Gehlen later took the credit for all this; it is true that only his obsession for keeping everything up to date and as exhaustive as possible made the archives what they were. But much of the earlier material had been accumulated by FHO under Kinzel or came from the Abwehr.

For years before the war, German spies had been swarming through the Soviet Union in the guise of industrial salesmen and technicians employed by German firms which had obtained construction orders from the Soviet government. A few were caught, amongst them technicians of the Froehlich-Dehlman concern, who worked at the industrial centres of the Kuznetsk Basin, and engineers sent by the Ruhr firms for Borsig and Demag to work on Soviet contracts in the Ukraine and Western Siberia.[3] But many returned safely home having passed information to the embassy in Moscow or smuggled it out through couriers. In any case, the German concerns had handed over to the Abwehr copies of every plan and blue-print they had produced for the Soviet authorities. Aware of this, the Soviet government cancelled several contracts and expelled the German technicians, but mostly after the damage had been done.

Nothing was too trivial to merit inclusion in the economic and industrial sections of the archives; textile and paper mills, plants for building material, saw mills and canning factories were treated with the same attention as armament plants. In the hard-worked head of the archives section, Captain Letschert, and his deputy, Franz Wiese-mann, Gehlen had two men completely devoted to the mind-killing work of filing away every scrap of data, including millions of photostats and clippings from newspapers, technical journals and reference books, and of keeping them all constantly up to date by adding information received from agents and POW's, from Luftwaffe air reconnaissance and every other possible source. The special archives were linked to the cartographic section and a drawing office under George Wagner, a well-known artist.

There were several geographical groups and sections at FHO, of which that for the Balkans was the most important. Its head, Major Josef Selmayr, was a former Abwehr officer who after the war rose to high office, first in the Gehlen Organisation and eventually as chief of the Federal German Military Intelligence.

There were, of course, also sections for cryptography, coding and cryptanalysis and a "laboratory" mainly concerned with producing forged documents. The latter achieved such excellent results that the SD and its *Zeppelin* units later regularly turned to FHO whenever they required forgeries of Soviet military papers and other documents, although Himmler's RSHA also had an impressive laboratory run by the Gestapo.

The reorganisation of FHO took many months, although Gehlen worked himself to near-exhaustion—acquiring stomach ulcers and a liver complaint from which he was to suffer ever after—and drove his men extremely hard. To supervise his staff he put a disciplinarian in charge of all administrative matters, and it was not by chance that this was one of the two SS officers whom Gehlen had accepted to please his RSHA friends. He was SS Sturmbannfuhrer Victor von der Marwitz, once a well-known riding champion; at FHO he assumed the more innocuous rank of major.

Hardly had Gehlen settled down to his gargantuan work than he was suddenly given a new and amazing assignment.

Working Against the USA

Since the entry of the United States into the war in December 1941, Hitler had been bombarding Admiral Canaris' Abwehr and the

OKW's *Fremde Heere West* department with demands for detailed reports on America's war potential, the strength of her armed forces and reserves, the extent of mobilisation and, later, of troop transportation to Britain. Neither department was able to satisfy his requirements, however. Eventually the Fuhrer became infuriated with the performance of the FHW chief, Colonel Ulrich Liss, and with typical unpredictability he suddenly asked Halder to arrange for Gehlen's FHO to produce these reports. Perhaps it was not quite unexpected that he should turn to Gehlen. Hitler had read some of his initial evaluations—Gehlen noted in his diary that at Whitsun of 1942 he had worked on a single report for twenty hours at a stretch—and was duly impressed. At that time the Fuhrer had met Gehlen only once, but Halder had given him an efficiency rating of the new head of FHO. It was dated May 1, 1942, and read: "Colonel Gehlen combines extraordinary ability and knowledge with unusual assiduity and a soldier's ardour. He is a born leader and made for high appointment on the General Staff."[4]

Gehlen, however, had only a very vague knowledge of the United States, nor had he any officers at his headquarters who were better informed, with the possible exception of Count Karl-Heinrich von Rittberg, who knew English and had spent some time in America as a student. Yet Gehlen eagerly took on the assignment. He demanded from Colonel Bentivegni that the Abwehr should hand over to him all relevant material. After an exchange of letters with Colonel Liss of FHW, several of the latter's officers were temporarily attached to Gehlen's office. Admiral Canaris fumed, but he had to obey Hitler's order.

The Abwehr was in the doldrums. A few weeks earlier the head of Canaris' Group II, Colonel Lahousen-Vivremont, who looked after espionage against Britain and the United States, and his chief of the "American section", Captain Wilhelm Ahlrichs, better known to US G-2 Army Intelligence and the FBI under his code-name of "Dr. Astor", had mounted an ambitious attempt to infiltrate two teams of spies into the United States. A group of men who had lived in America—some of them born there of German-American parents—had been trained for several months at a secret camp at Quentz near Berlin; from this group ten men were selected for "Operation Pastorius". Their leader was Peter Burger, who had served in the *Freikorps* after the First World War; accused of the murder of several socialists and communists, he was forced to go into hiding and later emigrated to America. There he had become a naturalised American citizen and in 1932 joined the 32nd Division of the National Guard which was used during strike riots in the Mid-West. He returned to Germany soon after Hitler came to power, joined the stormtroops, gained quick promotion and after the outbreak of the war served in Poland. Besides espionage assignments several of the agents had been given explicit instructions for sabotage actions: these were to include blowing up the great aluminium plants at Alcoa, Tennessee, and East St. Louis, Illinois, the Cryolite works at Philadelphia, the river locks on the Ohio from Pittsburg to Louisville, the Pennsylvania railroad at Newark and Altoona, the Chesapeake and Ohio railroad, the Hell Gate rail bridge in New York, and other targets regarded by the Abwehr as important to America's war effort.

On June 14, one team was landed from U-boat 202 at Amagansett, Long Island; three days later the other went ashore at dawn near Ponte Vedra, south of Jacksonville, Florida. Within a few days all the German agents were behind bars and, in addition to their espionage paraphernalia, radio transmitters and explosives, 175,000 dollars were seized on them. They were tried by a military court; seven were sentenced to death and executed, the others were given sentences ranging from twenty-five years to life imprisonment.

When, on June 30, Hitler was told of the disaster which had overtaken "Operation Pastorius", he flew into a rage and summoned Canaris to his headquarters at the Wolfschanze. "What is your intelligence service good for", he yelled, "if it causes such catastrophes?" Canaris replied that the agents had been caught because one of them had betrayed the operation. He calmly added: "This man was an old member of the National Socialist Party and a bearer of the Party's 'Order of the Blood'. He was recommended to me by The Party's foreign department of Reichsleiter Bohle . . . ." This only enraged Hitler even more and he shouted at Canaris: "All right, if you do not like good Party members then you should employ criminals or Jews in the future!" The outcome was Hitler's order that Gehlen should take charge of intelligence work against the United States. The latter got in touch with the unfortunate Dr. Ahlrichs and his deputy, Captain Walter Kappe, but by then they were in disgrace, so Gehlen asked Roenne to prepare reports on America on his own. Eventually, Gehlen decided to get rid of this unwanted assignment which only interfered with his other work; on his suggestion Roenne was later appointed head of the *Fremde Heere West* department, taking over from Colonel Liss, who was given a regimental command on the front.

The Flood of Reports

The enormous output of Gehlen's reports can be judged from the thousands of documents which have been preserved in the salvaged FHO files. Even a brief enumeration of them would produce an interminable catalogue far exceeding the scope of this book. There was a constant flow of the "Daily Evaluations of the Front Situation", the so-called *Lageberichte*, informing OKW of operations of armies, army corps and divisions. In addition there were memoranda concerning small front sectors, limited operations, measures against guerillas, and descriptions of selected Soviet units and their deployment, which Gehlen called *Einzelberichte*, i.e. individual reports. They often conveyed valuable information meant for army commanders and intelligence officers at the front rather than to enlighten Hitler and his OKW generals. Thus, for instance, there are many bulky files preserved with descriptions of Soviet infantry brigades and regiments, tank and artillery and other smaller units, giving details on their strength, armament, equipment and morale. Such individual reports were produced from the summer of 1942 onwards; the first preserved in the FHO files is dated September 7, the last bears the date of March 23, 1945. From the mass of these memoranda Gehlen produced a series of booklets, entitled "Surveys of the Formation, Composition and Distribution of the Red Army", indicating its elements, the time and place at which the units first appeared on the front and where they were presumed to be at the date of the compilation of the original report. To the war historian these booklets are an invaluable source for research. [5]

Among these individual reports were many of great importance; for instance, one dealt in great detail with the construction of defence zones east of Moscow which Stalin, fearing the fall of the capital, had secretly ordered during the winter of 1941. Gehlen watched the construction work with utmost interest and risked the loss of several agents parachuted into the zone in order to obtain more information. But by the late summer of 1942 he did not press the WALLI units for more reports; he had arrived at the conclusion that the Germans would never be able to take Moscow.

Descriptions of Soviet units, large and small, were almost invariably accompanied by often fascinating character sketches of their commanders from marshals and generals to colonels and majors in charge of a battalion. One such biographical collection ran to 453 pages, many bearing annotations and marginal comments in Gehlen's own hand. A bulky folder entitled "Characteristics of Higher Political and Military Leaders of the Soviet Union" was amongst the tens of thousands of microfilmed documents which Gehlen handed to the Americans after the war; it included lucidly written sketches of Stalin, Molotov, Malenkov, Vosnesensky, Khrushchev, Manuilsky and military commanders like Shaposhnikov, Voroshilov, Zhukov, Koniev, Timoshenko, Vassilevsky, Rokossovsky, Malinovsky and many others. There were many pages of rank lists, appointments and promotions, with comments on political commissars attached to army units and on their influence on the morale of the troops.

As mentioned earlier Gehlen did not overlook the problems of economic warfare and the need for finding out and assessing Russia's ability to survive her enormous losses in resources and manpower. Many hundreds of FHO reports and, particularly, its *Grundbücher*— manuals containing economic and statistical surveys—dealt with every facet of Soviet economic and social structure and industrial and agricultural production.[6] Gehlen called in several economic consultants and himself took a hand in the production of a mammoth study (which he later used for a lecture at the War Academy in Berlin on April 16, 1943) entitled "Great Survey and Statistics of the Economy of the USSR". Its many parts had headings such as "Economic Foundations", "Economic Organisation", "Planned Economy", "Agriculture and Collective Farms", "Forestry and Timber Production", "Raw Materials and Industry", "Steel Production", "Armaments Industry", "Electrical Power", "Fuel Transport", "Finance", "Consumption", "Foreign Trade", and so forth. Supported by 214 pages of statistics, these studies went into meticulous detail: the one dealing with steel production had 139 pages with descriptions of 120 steel plants, listing the kind of furnaces they had, their possible maximum output and their fuel requirements. Very little of all this had ever been published before, for such data and figures were strictly classified by the Soviet government before the war and after 1940 no economic and production information was ever released at all.[7]

Throughout 1942 and 1943 Gehlen continued to support OKW's strategical plans with excellent tactical intelligence, until by the end of 1943 he was persuaded that Germany's chances of winning the war, or even of arriving at a negotiated peace settlement, had evaporated. Comparing the official OKW Diary with some of Gehlen's reports one can see how Hitler's and Gehlen's estimates and prognostications were pitted against one another. In his evaluations of the enemy's potential, Gehlen again and again stressed that Soviet reserves in manpower and supplies were far from being exhausted, whilst Hitler told his generals, even in the face of the bitter setbacks of 1942, that "the Russian is dead".

Early in December 1943, in the wake of the Cairo and Teheran Conferences, Gehlen prepared a long analysis of the situation, in which he also summed up several earlier reports, as if to say "I told you so". He regarded the decisions reached by Roosevelt, Churchill and Stalin at Teheran as fatal for Germany. His analysis did not say this in as many words, but he warned OKW that the Soviet offensive early in the New Year on the northern and centre sectors of the front could lead to a breakthrough at many points of the German lines.

During the winter campaign, which had begun with the Soviet attack on the Stalingrad front, the enemy had retaken a large area from Voronezh in the north to Krasnodar and Maikop in the Caucasus.

Gehlen's predictions were once again accurate. The list of German defeats in January 1943 amounted to a débâcle. In mid-January Leningrad was relieved from its seventeen-month siege and the Germans were thrown back on the Moscow front. The Russians subsequently succeeded in retaking Rzhev and Vyazma, thus disposing of further danger to the capital. In February the Soviet forces were back deep in the Ukraine. They crossed the Donetz on a broad front and recaptured Rostov. The Stalingrad disaster was a culminating point; the Germans and their Rumanian, Hungarian and Italian allies had lost 500,000 men killed and captured during the three months' winter campaign. Britain and America had assisted the Soviet offensive with massive arms supplies; despite serious losses in the convoys to Murmansk and Archangel, the United States had shipped 4,100 aircraft and 138,000 tanks, motorized guns and vehicles as well as shiploads of steel and machinery for Soviet armament factories. New supply routes had been opened through Vladivostok and China and via the Persian Gulf and Iran.

The Conspirators

Although Gehlen had concluded that the war was lost and watched with growing anxiety Hitler's plans for yet another spring offensive, he nevertheless refrained from any participation in efforts aimed at extricating Germany from her fate. Gehlen was not unaware that in the spring of 1943 several groups of officers, including some of his own senior assistants and men with whom he collaborated closely in the control of the Vlassov Army, were conspiring to kill Hitler and to stage a revolt in the army against the nazi regime. Once Hitler was dead, they argued, a new German government led by the military could hope to conclude an armistice and obtain tolerable peace terms from Britain and the United States; they nursed the hope that the Western Allies might even give them a free hand against Stalin.

One centre of the conspiracy was the headquarters of Field-Marshal von Kluge's Centre Army Group. In February 1943, at the height of the German retreat on the southern front, Colonel von Tresckow and his ADC, Captain Fabian von Schlabrendorff, embarked on "Operation Flash". It was not the first attempt by Tresckow; he had taken part in the abortive attempt to kidnap Hitler in the autumn of 1941 when the conspirators, headed by General Ludwig Beck and Field-Marshal von Witzleben, had hoped to end the war in its early days. In March 1943 Tresckow and his friends prepared a more ingenious scheme. Hitler was to visit Kluge's

Gehlen at FHO with Lt.-Colonel Gerhard Wessel (*left*) and Lt.-Colonel Josef Selmayr.

Gehlen with his FHO staff. Sitting in the front row are his senior assistants, Lt.-Col. Erich Nauck (*extreme left*), Lt.-Col. Karl von Ogilvie (*fifth*), Lt.-Col. Johannes Hoheisl (*sixth*). In second row: Major Gerhard Wessel (*marked* **X**), next to him Major Count Karl-Heinrich von Rittberg.

General Andrey Vlasov, commander of the Soviet Second Army, who after his capture collaborated with the Germans and created the "Russian Army of Liberation" under German command.

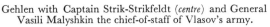

Gehlen with Captain Strik-Strikfeldt (*centre*) and General Vasili Malyshkin the chief-of-staff of Vlasov's army.

Colonel Count von Rittberg, one of Gehlen's officers involved in conspiracies against Hitler. He was executed by the Gestapo.

Colonel Alexis von Roenne, head of Group III of FHO. Arrested after the attempt on Hitler's life on July 20 1944 and executed.

headquarters at Smolensk on March 13 and Tresckow told Kluge that Lieutenant-Colonel Baron von Boeselager, one of his staff officers, had volunteered to shoot the Fuhrer. The field-marshal, however, who had at first supported the conspirators, implored Tresckow not to kill Hitler at his headquarters; when Tresckow ignored this request, Kluge told him that he ordered him to desist. The colonel was a good Prussian officer; he obeyed, but he did not abandon his object, merely altering the method of achieving it. He asked two of his fellow-conspirators in the Abwehr, Colonel Erwin Lahousen-Vivremont, the head of Group II, and Hans von Dohanyi, Canaris' legal adviser, to get hold of two of the many salvaged British bombs dropped to resistance groups in Western Europe by the RAF and collected by Abwehr officers from captured dumps.[8]

Lahousen brought the bombs to Smolensk and Schlabrendorff assembled two explosive packets. After attending a dinner given by Field-Marshal von Kluge in the Fuhrer's honour, Tresckow asked Colonel Heinz Brandt to do him a favour and take the two parcels, which he said, contained two bottles of brandy, to his friend Major-General Helmuth Stieff, head of the OKW Organisation Department, who had remained behind in Hitler's headquarters at Rastenburg. Brandt agreed, and when the Fuhrer's aircraft was ready for take-off on its return flight, Schlabrendorff took the parcels to the airfield. Before giving them to Brandt, he started the time-mechanism of the bombs through a small hole he had left in the wrapping. The bombs were to go off within thirty minutes, when Hitler's plane would be passing Minsk.

Tresckow and his friends were prepared to kill all the men travelling with Hitler in cold blood; they consoled themselves with the thought that all were confirmed nazis. But the bombs never went off. Afraid that the ticking sound might lead to discovery, the conspirators did not use a clockwork mechanism; the spring operating the detonators was to be destroyed by a corrosive liquid, which had begun to drip onto it when Schlabrendorff opened the small bottle. But something went wrong and the spring was never activated. Two hours later came the routine signal from Rastenburg informing Field-Marshal von Kluge that the Fuhrer had landed safely. Tresckow was now afraid that if Brandt handed the parcel to General Stieff the latter might be killed, and there were frantic telephone calls warning Stieff of its deadly contents. Eventually Schlabrendorff flew to Rastenburg where he collected the bombs and defused them.

The conspirators did not give in, however, and during the following twelve months they conceived several other attempts. Within a few days of their first failure, on March 21, Major Rudolf von

Gersdorff volunteered to throw a bomb, which Tresckow gave him, at Hitler during a memorial ceremony at the Berlin *Zeughaus*. It was a suicidal mission: the officer was to put two bombs in the pocket of his greatcoat and, when standing next to Hitler, pull the detonators. But Hitler arrived in a great hurry and his adjutant told Gersdorff that the Fuhrer would spend only eight minutes at the ceremony. He was surrounded by generals and members of his own suite the whole time, and Gersdorff never had a chance to get sufficiently near him. Another attempt was made in September when Tresckow and General Stieff tried to place bombs at Rastenburg. But on the day before the entire stock of their explosives blew up by accident at Stieff's billet. Only by a lucky chance did the conspirators escape discovery when the explosion was investigated by the Gestapo.[9]

In November Tresckow found another willing assassin, twenty-four-year-old Captain Axel von dem Bussche. He was to "model" a new army greatcoat which Hitler wanted to inspect before approving its design. Bussche was to carry two grenades in the pockets of the overcoat; at the inspection he intended to pull the pins and jump at the Fuhrer so that they would be both blown to pieces. This time Hitler was saved by the Allies. An American bomb dropped in an air raid destroyed the store where the overcoat models were kept and the inspection was cancelled. Bussche tried again in December when the Fuhrer was to attend an officers' Christmas party; but Hitler decided to spend the holiday at Berchtesgaden. For the same reason an attempt by Colonel von Stauffenberg failed a few days later, on December 26. He went to the headquarters at Rastenburg for a Fuhrer Conference, but Hitler had remained at his Eagle's Nest for a few days longer than it was expected. On February 11, 1944, Captain Heinrich von Kleist, the son of the famous field-marshal, tried yet another "overcoat attempt", but Hitler did not come because an air raid was in progress.

Eventually, Stauffenberg made his famous attempt on July 20, 1944; Hitler was slightly wounded, his stenographer, Berger, was killed, Colonel Brandt—the man who in March 1943 had carried the gift parcel with the bombs—General Schmundt, the Fuhrer's ADC, and General Korten, Goering's chief of staff, died of their wounds in hospital, and several others were more or less seriously injured.[10] The revolt which was to follow Hitler's death misfired and seven hundred conspirators and suspects were subsequently executed; amongst them were Gehlen's two former close collaborators, Colonel von Roenne and Count von Rittberg. Tresckow committed suicide after escaping arrest.

Gehlen had known of two of these attempts on Hitler's life, and had sensed several others; he had been fully aware of the furtive intrigues that went on at the Centre Army Group headquarters and he had no doubts of Roenne's and Rittberg's involvement. Yet, contrary to some of his own claims made in 1945 after his surrender to the Americans, and to those made in articles he inspired in later years when head of the Federal Intelligence, he had never taken any active part in the conspiracies. He remained loyal to his Fuhrer.

Five months before that last attempt on Hitler's life, which was to be the signal for the *coup d'état*, Gehlen had achieved the greatest triumph of his wartime career. With the elimination of the Abwehr in February and the transfer of most of its functions to Himmler's RSHA and Kaltenbrunner's and Schellenberg's *Militäramt,* Gehlen got rid of his most inconvenient competitors. From then on he wholeheartedly cooperated with Schellenberg's *Zeppelin* enterprise, arrogating to himself the control of the WALLI groups and gaining, through Vlassov's "Collaboration Staff", direction of the recruiting of Soviet defectors until he became Hitler's supreme intelligence chief. If Hitler had not escaped his assassins and the nazi dictatorship had been replaced by a military regime led by men such as Field-Marshal von Witzleben, General Beck and Dr. Goerdeler, Gehlen could hardly have hoped to remain in his powerful position. Nor would he have had much chance, whatever the outcome of the war, to reach yet loftier heights under American sponsorship. We must, however, return to 1942, when Gehlen was still staging some of his most remarkable espionage exploits.

VI

Stalin's Secrets

In some of his early reports to OKW in 1942 Gehlen remarked that he had had to build up his department almost from scratch and that particular efforts had been required to remedy the lack of reports from front-line agents. This was not, however, entirely true. His predecessor at FHO, Colonel Kinzel, had in cooperation with Abwehr's WALLI infiltrated a few agents into the Soviet Union early in the war. If Gehlen's complaints meant that Kinzel had not used FHO's own agents, the explanation is that he was not supposed to do this. Before Gehlen took over, FHO's tasks had been confined to the evaluation of intelligence received through WALLI reconnaissance units and to the scanning of information from other sources. Agents in the field were to be the exclusive preserve of the Abwehr, although the situation changed after the appearance on the scene in February 1942 of the *Zeppelin* commandos of Heydrich's and later Schellenberg's SD *Amt VI*. The *Zeppelin* units were commanded by SS Sturmbannfuhrer Hengelhaupt and reported to Colonel Schild-knecht at OKW, conveying all their information to Himmler's RSHA at the same time. Later the swashbuckling SS Sturmbannfuhrer Otto Skorzeny, an Austrian like Hitler and one of the Fuhrer's few personal favourites, took over temporary control of these commandos in the East—between assignments which ranged from the rescue of Mussolini in September 1943 to his kidnapping of Admiral Horthy in Budapest in October 1944 and his command of the "Skorzeny Gang" of 2,000 SS men in American uniforms who tried to penetrate behind the lines of the US First Army in the Ardennes in December 1944. Whilst the *Zeppelin* units in fact proved useless for the collection of significant information, WALLI I under Major Baun and WALLI II under Lieutenant-Colonel Heinz Schmalschläger worked successfully in placing several agents in sensitive positions and netting a large number of Soviet prisoners who were turned into German agents.

Amongst Kinzel's early agents were Evgeny Rohr, V-540, who had been infiltrated through Finland, and Leif Moordt, who penetrated into the Leningrad area. For a time they worked together and managed to smuggle back detailed drawings of the Yelgava airfields of the Red Air Force and a diagram of a new Russian naphtha-fuelled rocket.[1] Another early agent was a Ukrainian nationalist who appears in the FHO files only under his code name of "Ivar". He worked satisfactorily for Kinzel, but Gehlen was more difficult to please. On one of "Ivar's" reports Gehlen scribbled: *Ivar schickt alte Klamotten* (literally: "Ivar is sending old rags").

However, the same agent put Gehlen to shame when in February 1943, having held down his perilous job for almost two years, he supplied an important report anticipating an offensive by the 33rd Soviet Army under General Yefremov. Gehlen used it in his situation report to OKW dated February 22 and for once Hitler took heed. When Yefremov attacked in the direction of Rzev, the Germans concentrated a strong force at Yachnov on his flank and were able to encircle his army. The Soviet general did not know what had hit him nor why; he blamed himself for the failure of his attack and committed suicide at his headquarters when he saw German tanks approaching.

Ever since the early months of the Russian campaign German Intelligence officers had been combing Soviet prisoners of war for likely informers and men suitable for "turning round" as potential spies. Any they found were dispatched to special interrogation camps; Ukrainians were assembled at Luckenwalde in Brandenburg, south of Berlin. One of Gehlen's first actions on taking charge of FHO was to demand access to these camps. The Abwehr demurred at first, but General Halder ordered them to give Gehlen the facilities he required; in the end FHO took control of Luckenwalde and Gehlen established his own interrogation and training camps.

He had ordered Roenne to send out FHO's own teams of "searchers"; they were led by Captains Kurt Ruthenberg and Bernard Blossfeld and Lieutenant Axel von Melville. The teams netted several thousand "possibles" who were carefully sifted and after careful brainwashing the "probables" transferred to training camps where they enjoyed much better living conditions. Soviet publications after the war claimed that Gehlen had maintained sixty spy schools for training defectors, but this is not accurate; the Soviet war historians lumped together all interrogation camps, transit camps and training camps, as well as spy schools established not only by FHO but by the Abwehr, SD, the German authorities in the occupied territories and the various anti-communist organisations, such as Vlassov's "Collaboration Committee", the Ukrainian OUN and those of many other Soviet ethnic minorities.

Soviet Commissar Becomes Agent 438

At Luckenwalde one of Gehlen's officers made a splendid catch. Amongst the desolated and emaciated prisoners he found Vladimir Minishkiy, who had been captured by a posse of Baun's WALLI I on October 13, 1941. Minishkiy had posed as an army captain and although Baun had arranged that he should be sent to Luckenwalde his real background was not discovered there until the FHO officer arrived. This thirty-eight-year-old Russian was in fact a high official of the Soviet Communist Party who before the war had been one of the seven under-secretaries of the Central Committee. Soon after the German attack in June 1941 he had been appointed political commissar to Marshal Zhukov's Central Army. He had been captured with his driver on a tour of advanced units during the battle of Vyazma.

After eight months in the prison camp Minishkiy was in a state of mind which made the FHO interrogator's job easy. The ex-commissar was deeply depressed by the crushing German victories; moreover he seemed to bear a grudge against his former political superiors. In short, he was ripe for turning round. As soon as the FHO officer discovered his past, he took him to Gehlen's office at Angerburg. Exceptionally, Gehlen undertook his interrogation himself. His quiet manner and soft approach must have touched some spring of thwarted ambition or unconscious abhorrence of the ideology the Russian had followed all his life. Gehlen inquired about Minishkiy's family and learning that he had left his wife and two children in a village west of Moscow, by then occupied by the Germans, he promised him that he would be reunited with them. Gehlen also told him that he would be lavishly rewarded and allowed to live in Germany as a free man, or to become an official in Russia after German victory. In return he was to work as a German agent.

Thus began "Operation Flamingo", which Gehlen staged in cooperation with Baun, who already had a radio operator code-named "Alexander" inside Moscow. Baun's men smuggled Minishkiy across the firing lines and he reported to the nearest Soviet command, where he told of his capture and gave them a story about a daring escape, every detail of which had been concocted by Gehlen's experts. He was taken to Moscow where he was given a hero's welcome and imparted to Soviet Intelligence officers seemingly valuable information on what he had seen during his captivity. As a reward for his courageous exploit he was appointed to a politico-military desk job at the office of GOKO—Stalin's Supreme Headquarters. He soon established contact with "Flamingo's" radio operator and began to send signals, using crystals which he had been given at the FHO office. After a few initial reports, his first big scoop came on July 14, 1942. Gehlen and Herre sat up all night composing from it a report which Gehlen personally presented to General Halder the next morning. It read:

The war council in Moscow concluded its session during the night of July 13. Amongst those present were Shaposhnikov[2], Voroshilov, Molotov and heads of the British, American and Chinese military missions. Shaposhnikov declared that their retreat would be to the Volga, so that the Germans would be forced to spend the winter in that region. During the retreat wholesale destruction was to be carried out; all industries would be evacuated to the Urals and into Siberia.

The British representative demanded Soviet assistance in Egypt, but received the reply that Soviet reserves of mobilised manpower were not as great as her allies assumed. Moreover they lacked sufficient supply of aircraft, tanks and artillery, resulting from the fact that part of the consignment of these armaments earmarked for Russia, which the British were to have delivered through Basra in the Persian Gulf, had been redirected for the defence of Egypt. Offensive operations in two sectors of the front were decided upon: one north of Orel and another north of Voronesh, with the use of large tank forces and air cover. A diversionary attack would be launched at Kalinin. It was essential that Stalingrad, Novo-Rossiysk and the Caucasus should be held.[3]

Gehlen added this comment: "Developments in the general front situation during the past few days make this agent's report fully credible. This is confirmed by the enemy's movements in the sectors of our Army Groups A and B, his evasive actions on the Don front and his retreat to the Volga, whilst holding on to the defence lines in the North Caucasus and to the bridgehead of Stalingrad; in the sector of our Army Group Centre his retreat to the line Tula-Moscow-Kalinin provides additional corroboration. Whether the enemy plans further large-scale retreat moves in case of an offensive by our Army Groups North and Centre cannot at present be discerned with certainty."

Stalingrad

The two Soviet attacks at Orel and Voronesh were mounted, as predicted, in July with considerable tank forces. Halder later noted in his diary: "Lt.-Colonel Gehlen of FHO provided correct information about the enemy forces newly employed since June 28, and of the presumed strength of these units. He also gave an accurate assessment of the enemy's forceful measures to protect Stalingrad."[4]

The report had reached Hitler on the day he moved his head-quarters from East Prussia to the Voronovo estate near Vinnitza in the Ukraine. There, on July 23, he issued his notorious Directive No.45 ordering that Stalingrad and the Caucasus be simultaneously attacked and taken. Two days earlier his Directive No.44 had ordered an all-out attack on Leningrad. In vain did General Halder and the front commanders warn him that the northern flank of the Sixth Army was dangerously exposed along the upper Don. Hitler insisted that the three "satellite" armies, the Second Hungarian, south of Voronesh, the Eighth Italian to the south-east and the Third Rumanian on the Don west of Stalingrad, would be sufficient protection for Field-Marshal Paulus in an attack on Stalingrad. When Halder protested that these foreign troops would never withstand a Red Army counter-attack, and that Stalin could throw a million and a half fresh reserves into the Stalingrad area and some 500,000 troops into the Caucasus, Hitler went for him, in Halder's words, "with froth on his lips and raised fists", yelling that he forebade such "idiotic twaddle". He cried: "The Russian is dead, dead, you understand?"

At first it seemed that Hitler was right and Halder and all the others who had warned him against the offensive wrong. In the Crimea General von Manstein routed the Soviet Army under Koslov and pushed back a Soviet counter-offensive on the Donetz led by Marsha; Timoshenko fell and the Germans took nearly a quarter of a million prisoners, destroying or capturing 1,249 tanks and 2,026 guns. By the end of August the Germans stood deep in Russia in an eastward-curving line from the Lake of Ladoga in the north to Voronezh in the centre and Novorossisk in the south. The most eastern point of their penetration reached Stalingrad.

Yet neither Gehlen nor General Halder felt any reason for optimism. In August Gehlen produced a lengthy report in which he stressed the appearance of 110 new Soviet divisions on the front, of which fifty-six had been identified as armoured divisions abundantly equipped with tanks and self-propelled guns. On August 21 he noted that the Fuhrer was making "impossible demands on his front commanders" and once again emphasised the dangerous situation of the German and allied troops on the Don. But he had already discovered that German strategy was based not on the evaluations of the situation at the front which he was supplying but on the Fuhrer's own chimerical and deceptive calculations. At one conference Hitler swept away all the arguments expounded by Halder and declared that Stalin had lost a hundred million of his population in the occupied territories and ten million on the battle fronts; the Russian leader had exhausted all his reserves, and the hour of total victory was near.

The "Flamingo" operators were still sending reports; but Minishkiy's signals became increasingly gloomy. Early in October Gehlen recalled him, arranging through Baun a rendezvous for him with one of WALLI's advanced units, which whisked the agent back across the lines in the same way as he had been infiltrated. Minishkiy later worked in Gehlen's evaluation section; he remained in Germany and survived the war.

The outcome of the battle of Stalingrad—the turning point of the war in the East—is well known. It raged for five months and ended in disastrous defeat for the Germans. In January 1943 Field-Marshal Friedrich Paulus capitulated with sixteen generals, followed two days later by General Streicher with seven more. The Russians took 91,000 half-starved, frost-bitten prisoners, a large proportion of them wounded. These and the 20,000 wounded who had been evacuated during the course of the battle were all that remained of the once proud army which at the beginning of the offensive had numbered 295,000, including many crack regiments and the flower of Hitler's forces. Of the prisoners only about 5,000 returned to Germany after the war.

The Russians rolled up the Centre and Southern fronts in November 1942 and broke through the German lines on the Don; soon they recaptured all the German gains in the Caucasus. The tide had turned. Gehlen shuddered when examining the reports from the front. His sponsor Halder had been dismissed from his post as chief of staff on September 28. Though he never admitted it, Hitler had realised that Halder had been right and himself wrong; his new chief of staff was General Kurt Zeitzler, a sycophant who never dared to disagree with his Fuhrer's prophecies. As one of the German war historians later put it: "While intelligence reports were read at Hitler's OKW Hitler was inclined to give more credence to the creations of his own fantasies and wishful thinking than to the facts as acquired by the Abwehr and front-line reconnaissance, and as time went on his entourage condoned the state of affairs with increasing equanimity, until even his military advisers themselves could not resist the effects of his prophetic utterances."[5]

If Gehlen could, he made no effort to voice his doubts about Hitler's strategy. He loyally continued his endeavour to obtain as much intelligence from inside the Soviet Union as possible. Bulky FHO folders tell of the many operations he initiated in order to infiltrate WALLI agents. Early in the summer of 1942 through "Operation Graukopf" 350 men in Soviet Army uniforms had already succeeded in crossing enemy lines and carried out widespread sabotage; the main purpose of the enterprise was to leave men behind who would go underground and operate radio posts. The unit was, however, challenged by a strong partisan group and suffered heavy casualties; only a hundred men returned, but with them came several defectors.

In August "Operation Schamil" was staged in the Caucasus. Gehlen had warned OKW that according to information he had collected Stalin had ordered the destruction of the Maikop oil-fields before a withdrawal of Soviet troops to the south. A unit of twenty-five men, fifteen of them Soviet defectors trained at Gehlen's camp at Boyen, was dropped near the Grozny refineries. Their task was to occupy the refineries and prevent their destruction until the arrival of advanced units of the 1st Panzer Army. The operation was successful; the Germans, using silencers on their machine pistols, killed nearly all the Soviet saboteurs left behind by the retreating troops. But a number of the men, led by Sergeant Moritz, were taken for Soviet soldiers by the German troops who had meanwhile arrived, and put up against a wall to be executed by a firing squad. Only at the last moment was Moritz able to save their lives. Eventually, Lange and Moritz brought back a large number of Georgians and Azerbaijani volunteers.

From such Caucasian defectors was recruited a battalion, code-named *Bergmann* (Miner), which grew to comprise three Georgian, one Azerbaijani and one Armenian company under the command of Captain Theodor Oberlander. Some of these men went into action in October 1942 at Terek and Mosdok, collecting 1,600 defectors from a Soviet division whose political commissar was Mikhail Suslov. Gehlen selected some of them for training as agents and several later accomplished remarkable exploits. There were many such combined operations of infiltration, sabotage and netting of defectors. Frequently the infiltrators were landed by parachute; one such operation, code-named "Transcaspian Railway", had the purpose of blowing up railway bridges east of the Caspian Sea and thus preventing British and American armament supplies from being carried from Iran. Early in 1943 "Operation Murmansk" was designed by FHO to achieve the same purpose—depriving the Soviet Army of Allied aircraft, tanks, guns and munitions shipped by the North Atlantic convoys to the northern ports of Murmansk and Archangel.

During the autumn of 1942 Gehlen infiltrated agents into the headquarters of the 46th and 76th Soviet divisions in the Caucasus. Their radio signals directed saboteurs in the area of Kirovograd and Mineralniy Vody to blow up bridges, roads and railway tracks. In October one of his star agents, Rudolf Starkmann, a Balt who had lived for many years in Russia, reached besieged Leningrad, established a clandestine radio post and for many months conveyed valuable information. In April and May 1943 Gehlen's men took part in "Operation Zitadelle", (Citadel), staged in conjunction with the Brandenburg regiment in the area of Kursk-Karatshev. This was part of the great offensive launched in July under General von Manstein's command by an army nearly half a million strong, including no less than seventeen Panzer divisions equipped with the new Tiger tanks. Hitler's object was to entrap the Soviet forces which, after their victory at Stalingrad, had surged westwards, and to make a final desperate attempt at the capture of Moscow. Gehlen made every effort to assist his former boss with all the intelligence FHO could possibly muster. Yet the offensive ended in disaster. Hitler had insisted that Manstein adopt his own strategical concept; Manstein wrote with great bitterness about it in his memoirs.[6]

Early in 1943 Gehlen again conducted several operations designed to frustrate British and American armament deliveries at Murmansk. Agents were sent to this area as pace-makers for saboteurs who attempted to blow up port installations and convoy ships.

On February 22, at the Hotel Regina in Munich, he met with Admiral Canaris and General Bentivegni of the Abwehr and Kaltenbrunner and Schellenberg of *Amt VI* in an attempt to arrive at an agreement for closer cooperation between the three intelligence organisations. The SD leaders, however, while willing to work with Gehlen, were by then determined to eliminate the Abwehr. They did not achieve this until the end of 1943, when Canaris was removed and the Abwehr eventually transformed into the *Militäramt* of RSHA. Gehlen took advantage of the fratricidal struggle between Canaris and the nazi leaders to make off with another slice of the Abwehr's purlieu. One outcome of this conference was that Baun's WALLI I headquarters were moved from Sulejowek near Warsaw to Neuhof-Samland in East Prussia, nearer to Gehlen's own headquarters; subsequently he gained almost exclusive control of all WALLI operations, placating the SD nazis by giving every assistance to their *Zeppelin* groups. Perhaps it was only poetic justice that during the last phase of the war Gehlen slid himself into the situation in which he had put Canaris: his FHO was subordinated to Schellenberg and Skorzeny, the masters of *Zeppelin*.

A few weeks after the conference in Munich the Abwehr offices at 74-76 Tirpitz Ufer in Berlin were destroyed by an Allied air raid and Canaris had to move his staff. He was ordered to transfer most of it to the *Zeppelin* headquarters at Zossen; other sections were allocated cramped accommodation at Eiche near Potsdam. Gehlen then decided to move his headquarters to Zossen too and for the remaining period of the war Zossen became his own little kingdom.

Gehlen Discovers SMERSH

Obviously, FHO paid special attention to all developments concerning Soviet Intelligence and counter-espionage. A vast collection of files from Gehlen's archives has been preserved on these subjects and later stood CIA in good stead, particularly as several of the chiefs of Soviet wartime espionage, such as Abakhunov, Kruglov and Serov, continued in the highest post for several years after the end of the war. Gehlen had instructed Major Schmalschlager's WALLI III and, of course, his own agents, to send him any information, however trifling it might seem, on the Soviet Intelligence organisation. Piecing these scraps together and examining them with his profound knowledge, he carried off a singular scoop: he brought to light the existence of SMERSH.

Many years later the late Ian Fleming was to popularize this organisation as "the official murder organisation of the Soviet. government", adding so much fanciful and absurd extravagance that many of his readers believed that SMERSH was his own invention. In fact it was a very real body, created by Stalin's GOKO Defence Council early in 1943. Six months before, in October 1942, Stalin had abolished the institution of political war commissars, hated by front commanders and troops alike, and replaced it by the *Jedinonatchaliye*, a system whereby commanding officers were to look after the political morale of their troops. Officers of the NKVD, as opposed to military intelligence officers, were thus removed, but the innovation did not work satisfactorily. After the creation of the Russian Army of Liberation under General Vlassov, Gehlen and other German Intelligence officials had redoubled their propaganda efforts to entice Soviet soldiers, and the number of defectors increased by leaps and bounds. Hence Beria created SMERSH—a special counter-espionage and counter-propaganda organisation whose somewhat egregious name was derived from the two first syllables of the words *smert shpionom*—death to the spies. Beria appointed as its head a man who had proved himself an efficient as well as an utterly ruthless NKVD official: Victor Semyonovich Abakhunov. Like Stalin and Beria he was a Georgian and had russianized his real name of Aba Kum. SMERSH officers were attached to every command in place of political commissars; Gehlen's spies soon discovered that there were as many as a hundred of them attached to every army corps headquarters and eventually every unit had its SMERSH men.

When in August 1942 Marshal Voroshilov became the supreme commander of the partisan army, with General Panteleymon Konratyevich Pomarenko as his chief of staff taking actual control of all partisan operations including those behind German lines, Gehlen's

Dienststelle Walli I-Lager   O.U.,den 27. 8. 1943.
Tgb.Nr.2126 /43 geh.

Betr.: russ. Luftlandetruppen.
Quelle: V-Mann "Tumanow", früher Lt. und Komp.-Führer
        im 28. Luftlande-Rgt.
Beurteilung: zuverlässig.

                    An
                        Dienststelle Walli I.

1. Luftlandetruppen. August-September 1941 wurde eine Luftlande-
truppe, gegliedert in 11 Korps, neu aufgestellt. Aufstellungsraum
Gebiet Saratow. Aufgabe der Truppe: Landung und Durchführung grösser
Operationen im Feindrücken.
Da die Verluste der Roten Armee im Sommer und Herbst 1941 sehr hoch
waren, sah sich der Generalstab genötigt, die neu aufgestellten
Korps, halb ausgebildet, nach und nach in selbständige Schützen-
Brigaden aufzuteilen, an die Front zu werfen und rein infanteristisc
einzusetzen.
Im August 1942 wurde mit der Neuaufstellung von Luftlandetruppen
im Raum Moskau begonnen.
I Luftlandekorps. Russ. Bezeichnung: I wosduschno-desantny Korpus.
Aufstellungsort: Ljubercy (ca. 30 km SO Moskau). Kommandeur - Gen.
Major Alexandrow, Chef des Stabes Oberstleutnant i.G. Ksaunko,
Kommissar Kotow, Ia - Major i.G. Gorjatschow. Einheiten des Korps
in gerämten Schulgebäuden und anderen Häusern untergebracht.
Offiziere trafen aus der Schule für Luftlandetruppen (Moskau), aus
Lazaretten (Genesene) und aus aufgelösten Kavallerie-Verbänden ein.
Mannschaften waren zur Roten Armee eingezogene NKWD-Wachtruppen
(Zwangslagerwachleute) aus der Republik Komi, Kolchosbauern, Ar-
beiter und Angestellte des Landwirtschaftskommissariats aus Kasach-
stan.
Alter der Mannschaften 20 - 32 Jahre.
Auf Grund eines Befehls Stalins durften bei Luftlandeeinheiten nur
Mannschaften im Alter von 23 - 30 Jahren eingestellt werden. Dieser
Befehl wurde jedoch beim Aufstellen des Korps, wegen Mangel an
geeigneten Jahrgängen gelockert.

                                                - 2 -

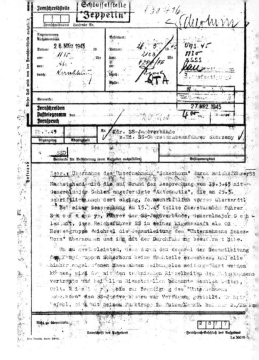

A report from WALLI on the deployment of Soviet parachute units based on information from a Russian V-man.

Gehlen's message to Schellenberg warning that the failure to destroy the Vistula bridges jeopardised the Neisse and Oder fronts.

A memorandum stating that Himmler had ordered Gehlen to hand over control of the "Scherhorn" group to Skorzeny.

Hitler's order to Gehlen to hand over all deception operations to Schellenberg's Nazi Security Service

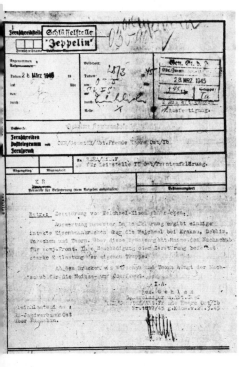

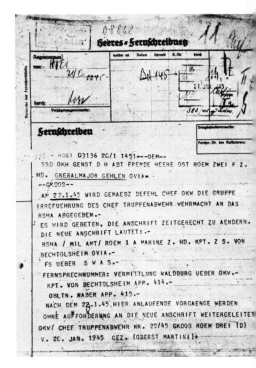

Gehlen addresses his staff shortly before the collapse of the Third Reich and his own surrender to the Americans.

Hitler with some of the "Werewolves", many of them schoolboys, whom Gehlen helped to organise in 1945. The boys have all been awarded the Iron Cross 2nd class.

department became the centre of all counter-operations. An enormous quantity of FHO reports and documents on Soviet guerilla operations is preserved. In addition to his own spies, Gehlen used Major Schmalschlager's WALLI III to deal with the ever-mounting danger of partisan resistance. The very first intimation of the SMERSH organisation reached OKW from Gehlen soon after its inception; subsequent reports covered the period from August 8, 1943, to March 16, 1945. The FHO files of 1943 and 1944 are full of Gehlen's warnings of SMERSH's "terrorist dynamiters and assassins". Hitler and the nazi leaders apparently paid greater attention to Gehlen's reports on this subject than to his more important tactical intelligence evaluations, particularly after partisans had carried out attempts on the lives of Wilhelm Kube, the nazi gauleiter of Minsk, and Otto Bauer, the governor of Lvov. Gehlen's great *coup* was to procure through one of his agents, on July 13, 1943, the secret manual for SMERSH's senior officers; it contained detailed instructions which, it was said, Hitler read avidly from cover to cover in a German translation.[7]

German espionage activities against the Soviet Union were, of course, forcefully reciprocated. On the whole, Soviet Intelligence did not succeed in infiltrating German establishments to any significant extent, although many years later both Colonel Rudolf Abel [8] and Colonel Konon Molody, the so-called "Gordon Lonsdale",[9] claimed that they had served as German officers with Abwehr staffs and had conveyed clandestine radio signals to Moscow from inside the centres of German Intelligence. Regarding networks inside their respective countries, Soviet Intelligence got the better of the Germans every time. In 1942 Gehlen was shocked at the discovery of the "Red Orchestra", the tentacles of which reached into almost every one of Hitler's government offices. Maybe Gehlen felt some satisfaction in that the leader of this vast Soviet espionage network, Harro Schulze-Boysen, a grandson of Admiral von Tirpitz and married to a grand-daughter of Prince Philip von Eulenburg, was an intelligence officer in Goering's Luftwaffe ministry—of all the intelligence bodies with whom Gehlen had to deal his strongest animosity was directed against the intelligence branch of that ministry. Amongst the members of the "Red Orchestra" were government officials such as Higher Counsellor Arvid Harnack of the ministry of economic affairs, Counsellor Rudolf von Scheliha of Ribbentrop's foreign ministry and several other officials, all regarded as loyal nazis.

Moscow was able to set up several successful espionage networks, including in addition to the "Red Orchestra" in Germany the organisations of the "Grand Chief", Leopold Trepper, which spread to Occupied France and Belgium, the Rado-Foote group in Switzerland, Roessler's "Lucy" group—of which Gehlen learned only after the war—the networks of Josef Wenzel, Mikhail Makarov, Konstantin Yefremov and many others. Soviet agents grieved Gehlen deeply. The only consolation for him was that whilst many of these spies had penetrated nazi government and even Party offices his own organisation had not been contaminated. But Gehlen did not rejoice when he heard that on learning of the vast Soviet espionage network uncovered inside Germany, Hitler summed it up in a plaintive wail: "The Bolsheviks are our superiors in one field only—espionage!"

A German war historian echoed this lament: "the Soviet Intelligence had 200 spy schools each producing fifty agents every three months and thus replenishing the cadres of its spy army by ten thousand new operators every quarter." Soviet agents served with partisan units and often harassed the Germans in the occupied territories and deep behind the front lines.[10]

It is interesting to learn the reaction of Soviet authorities, which was not disclosed for many years. In 1965 a summary of German espionage operations as seen through Soviet eyes was at last published. Claiming that in 1940 and during the first half of 1941—that is, prior to the German attack—Soviet counter-espionage had already "smashed sixty-six German spy networks inside the Soviet Union, particularly in the newly acquired Baltic provinces and Russian-annexed Poland—and liquidated 1,596 German spies", the official publication[11] gave a fairly accurate description of the activities of WALLI units, stating that "groups of up to twenty-five spies and saboteurs succeeded in penetrating between fifty and three hundred kilometres behind Soviet front lines". In fact, as we shall see, some of the WALLI groups, such as, for instance, the Scherhorn Group, numbered two hundred and three hundred trained saboteurs. On the other hand, the bulletin exaggerated the number of spy schools and the total of agents trained and infiltrated, stating that between October 1942 and September 1943 "more than 150 groups were destroyed and a total of at least 1,500 spies killed or captured".[12] In Byelorussia alone, according to Moscow, "six thousand spies and saboteurs were trained in thirty-six training camps and twenty-two special spy schools".

The Radio Game

In at least one aspect Gehlen proved himself far superior to Soviet Intelligence. This was in playing the *Funkspiel*—radio game—by using Soviet defectors and captured Soviet radio transmitters to pass fake information to Soviet Intelligence and military commands. If one is to accept German figures of 600,000 Soviet deserters (some German writers claim one million) who served in Vlassov's Army of Liberation, the *Osttruppen* commanded by General Heinz Hellmich and later by General Ernst Koestring which included Ukrainian formations, the Cossack Corps of General Helmuth von Pannwitz, and the various other formations (said to have included 110,000 Uzbeks and Turkmen, 35,000 Tartars, more than 100,000 Caucasians from Georgia, Azerbaijan, Dagestan and Armenia, and thousands of Uzbeks, Kalmyks, Kirghizians and Mongols), then one may conclude that Gehlen must have had little difficulty in enlisting a large number of them as agents.

A report by one of his officers, Captain Ernest Peterson,[13] whom he had made camp commander at Dabendorf, shows that during the period from the 8th to the 25th of September 1943 there were 286 former Soviet army officers and men undergoing a course of training. Taking wastage into account, Dabendorf alone could thus produce some 2,000 potential spies and saboteurs a year. On the syllabus at Dabendorf Peterson reported that during the period mentioned there were 273 hours of instruction, 126 hours of theoretical lectures (including cryptography, wireless telegraphy and photography), 36 hours of practical training (mainly handling of arms and explosives), 68 hours of physical training, 22 of German language lessons, and 20 of miscellaneous tuition.

This applied only to the camp for Vlassov's men, and only a proportion of these became agents; others returned to their units as officers and NCOs. But from many others of his spy schools Gehlen produced a small army of potential spies (many of whom remained in Germany, were enlisted as V-men in his post-war organisation and later worked for BND). Obviously, not all the graduates passed the high requirements Gehlen set for agents; many were never employed, a large number were transferred to sabotage commandos for hit and run raids, and many became casualties in abortive operations.

That such vast numbers of defectors came over to the Germans was to a very large extent due to Gehlen's elaborate schemes to attract them. He devised, for instance, "Operation Silberstreif", in which eighteen million leaflets were dropped from aircraft and distributed in occupied territories, appealing to Soviet soldiers and civilians to defect and promising them good treatment. Gehlen also induced Vlassov to issue an appeal to officers and men of the Soviet Army to join his Army of Liberation. These and other appeals were repeated at intervals and drew an amazing response. Within a few hours of the Silberstreif operation 6,000 Soviet soldiers came running across the lines with their arms raised; for several days the average intake of deserters numbered 2,500 daily.

Soon after his arrival at FHO Gehlen had asked Halder for

permission to conduct his own *Funkspiel*, independent of the Abwehr and RSHA. Although he got Halder's approval it was several months before he could embark on the enterprise. To bamboozle the enemy through fake radio links he needed not only the men but, above all, the Russian radio sets and codes; the transmitters had, of course, to be already tuned to Soviet reception stations. WALLI units which captured such sets invariably handed them over to the Abwehr, which had conducted radio traffic with varied success since the beginning of the Russian campaign.

The first *Spiel* Gehlen was able to begin was on March 5, 1943, after he had got hold of a captured officer plus his transmitter. For technical reasons the fake radio post was set up at Halle in Saxony and was code-named "Trianon". In quick succession more fake stations were established: on April 9 at Moravska Ostrava (*Rotkäp-pchen*); on May 23 at Prague (*Purpur*); the following day in Vienna (*Alpenrose);* on May 31 at Brno *(Kapitän)* and on June 6 in Berlin. This one proved a great disappointment; although the deserter seemed to be cooperative, he inserted warnings into his signals, a fact which was discovered only after many weeks; the Russian was executed. In July and August four more links were established, two from Prague (*Zepter* and *Reichsapfel*), another from Berlin (*Steuer-mann*), served by a Soviet naval officer, and one from Danzig (*Falke*).

The most successful of the radio games was conducted for almost a year by Captain Ivan Markovich Jassineski, a thirty-one-year-old former interpreter at the headquarters of the 86th Soviet Guards division, taken prisoner on August 1, 1943. He was particularly useful as he had fluent German and could produce translations of the signals received. Amongst Jassinski's monitoring notes in FHO files are descriptions of Soviet Intelligence schools at Stavropol and Kuibishev, where SMERSH trained its senior agents.

Many of the signals exchanged between Gehlen's fake stations and receiving stations in the Soviet Union contain a great lot of trivial material. Gehlen's experts provided the texts for the outgoing signals and they had to compose reports supposed to come from Soviet operators, conveying secret information. In some cases the deception seems to have been successful, but from replies and instructions received from the Russians and preserved in Gehlen's files it is clear that Soviet Intelligence played extremely cautiously and appears to have treated most of the received signals with suspicion. There is little doubt that in at least some of the cases the Russians were fully aware that a fake radio game was being conducted. They continued it probably only to find out whether other radio posts were also contaminated.

Gehlen's Agents

Stories of the exploits of Gehlen's agents culled from FHO archives could fill several volumes; only a few of the more remarkable instances can be given here. Amongst these are some which can be corroborated by Soviet documents. For many years after the war the Soviet government was extremely coy about releasing details even of German spies caught. The familiar communist technique was applied of rewriting history and pretending that the Germans had utterly failed to infiltrate any spies at all; in the few instances where espionage had been attempted the spies had been caught immediately and "liquidated". A few individual cases were admitted, however, presumably to demonstrate the vigilance and efficiency of Soviet counter-espionage.

From an official Soviet publication we can supply the sequel to one of Gehlen's successful operations. In the summer of 1942, Gehlen's interrogators spotted in a prisoner of war camp a Soviet officer who, like Minishkiy, had been a political commissar in the army. His name was Piotr Ivanovich Tavrin and he had been captured on May 30, 1942, in the Rzhev area. He informed his captors that he had been awarded the Orders of the Red Banner and of Alexander Nevsky for his service at the front and displayed these medals with pride; but after the usual indoctrination he was prepared to go back as a spy. Gehlen singled him out for specialised training and in September he was smuggled across the enemy lines. Tavrin remained in Russia for two years and was given a succession of important appointments, first at the ministry of defence, then on the staff of the supreme headquarters and eventually, with the rank of colonel, at the headquarters of Marshal Ivan Tchernyakovsky. After the bloody battles on the Dnieper in 1943 he was one of the 306 officers and men who, with their commander-in-chief, were awarded their nation's highest honour—the gold badge of a Hero of the Soviet Union. Throughout this period he produced a spate of reports.

In August 1944, however, Tavrin sent a signal saying that he had fallen under suspicion. Gehlen decided to withdraw him and asked *Zeppelin* to collect him in a Messerschmitt. Aircraft landings behind enemy lines in order to pick up agents were undertaken in exceptional cases and then only to rescue a German. Gehlen therefore concealed Tavrin's identity. What happened next we can learn from the official Soviet version, which is as follows:

On September 5, 1944, a patrol on the road to Karmanovo near Smolensk stopped a man and a woman on a motorcycle. The man wore the uniform of a Soviet Army colonel. He indignantly produced his credentials, but the military policemen took him to a military intelligence post where his hold-all was searched. They found therein a German wireless set, no fewer than seven pistols complete with ammunition and a leather case containing the decorations of a Hero of the Soviet Union, the Orders of Lenin, Red Banner and Red Star and several campaign medals. Sewn into the lining were code pads and notes written in cypher on cigarette paper. Under appropriate interrogations (*sic*) the man, who confessed to being a German spy, admitted that he and his wife were going to meet a German aircraft at a secret landing place in a meadow outside Karmanovo. A military unit was sent there and when the aircraft landed three of its crew were captured, one being killed while offering resistance. Investigations proved that P. I. Tavrin, a former officer who had defected to the Hitlerite fascists in 1942 and later returned to the Motherland, had viciously deceived the Soviet authorities. He had been appointed to positions of trust and awarded high honours, yet while ostensibly serving the Motherland he had committed many acts of treason.

The traitor Tavrin and his woman accomplice paid the deserved penalty for their crimes.[14]

Thus the Soviet report, couched in the familiar jargon of the Party. This was the end of Tavrin, but his work, reflected in several hundred signals preserved in three fat FHO files, could not be undone.

Molotov's Nephew

Amongst the many hundreds of agents infiltrated during these three years were several other determined men of Tavrin's mettle. One of Gehlen's most resourceful agents was twenty-two-year-old Vassili Antonovich Skryabin, a nephew of the then Soviet prime minister and minister for foreign affairs. In the FHO files his personal data were entered thus: "Born May 13, 1920, at Gorki; parents: Piotr Davidovich Skryabin and Maria Josefova, both executed for 'counter-revolutionary activities'; educated at Moscow university; service in the Red Army (lieutenant in 38th Guards Regiment) until August 17, 1941, when defected to German troops and asked for political asylum. Agent's code name: 'Igor'. Has been convinced anti-communist since student days, feeling hatred towards Stalin because of the execution of his parents in the purges. Fully reliable, highly intelligent and energetic; received Afu training, speaks some German."

"Igor" undertook several sorties during 1943, bringing back valuable information from the front and, on two occasions, a number of defecting Soviet soldiers. Eventually Gehlen decided to entrust him with a major mission: the penetration of a Soviet Army headquarters and, if feasible, one of the government offices in Moscow. To this end "Igor" was teamed up with another agent who had years of experience in the spying game. He was agent "Gregor", real name Albert Muller, and his FHO index card tells us that he was born on November 11, 1909, at Leningrad, of a German father, Leo Muller, who had settled in Russia as the representative of various German manufacturing companies, and a Russian mother, Evgenia Pavlova, *née* Stoliar. He was trained as an electrical engineer and after his father's death he emigrated in 1928 to Germany, where he continued his studies at Leipzig University. Some years before the war he was enlisted by the Abwehr and served as an agent at its AST Marienburg in East Prussia under Captain Heinrich Rauch. In 1942 Gehlen enticed him to FHO, where his knowledge of Russian made him very useful as an interrogator.

Gehlen put "Igor" and "Gregor" under Major Otto Schaeffer, who before the war had organised a camouflaged espionage organisation against the Soviet Union and Poland with the sonorous title of the Pan-Germanic Union; he devised "Operation *Drossel*" ("Thrush"). By July 18 the plan was completed; the two agents had received meticulous training, including refresher courses to familiarize them with recent developments in the Soviet Army and the economic and social life of wartime Russia. They were equipped with several sets of forged documents, army pay-books, civilian ration cards and so forth. During the night of August 9 they were taken to Luftwaffe airfield 304, near Vitebsk, and flown over the sector of the Soviet Army commanded by General Kozlov, where they landed safely at 1.55 a.m.

Both wore Russian officers' uniform under their overalls, "Gregor" that of a General Staff major and "Igor" a first lieutenant's with appropriate war decorations. Before they were driven to Vitebsk, Gehlen personally inspected them to ensure that they were properly dressed and equipped. Early next morning, after burying their parachutes and overalls, they made their way to a command post of the 11th Guards Division at Ostrova. "Igor" introduced himself as Major Posyutchin of the General Staff, on an inspection of the front with his ADC, Lieutenant Krassin, and demanded to be taken to General Koslov. He handed the general an envelope containing "sealed orders" from Marshal Alexander Vassilevsky, Stalin's chief of staff. Gehlen's laboratories excelled in producing perfectly forged documents and this order bore all the necessary rubber stamps together with facsimiles of the marshal's signature and the issuing adjutant's counter-signature. Koslov received the two officers most courteously. Indeed the two Germans' stay at the Soviet commander's headquarters was reminiscent of Gogol's famous comedy *The Inspector General*: they were taken on an inspection tour, introduced to several sub-commanders and entertained at a banquet by Kozlov and his staff officers. Two days later they drove to Vitebsk in a car provided by their host, complete with a driver and a batman.

Their amazing adventures are fully recorded in FHO files, side by side with a host of radio signals. At Kozlov's HQ they had been given a secret operational plan; alas, it was in code and they were unable to read it. They duly transmitted it, however, and Gehlen's coding clerks deciphered it in no time. On their further journeys "Gregor" and "Igor" changed their Russian identities at least twice, appearing respectively as Captain Krulov and Major Petrov, and as First Lieutenant Poglyubov and Lieutenant Izmirsky. In Moscow they became civilians for several weeks. Gehlen had asked for the fullest information possible about Russian munitions production, and so "Gregor" produced the papers of a partially disabled soldier and took a job as an electrician in a Gosplan armaments factory. Young Skryabin acquired a pretty girl friend and, though wartime living conditions in the capital were harsh, one can sense from some of his signals that he enjoyed himself.

In order to process the large number of microfilms they had taken at the front and later in defence installations and armament plants around Moscow, they decided to take a rest in the country. Posing as two officers they hired, apparently without much difficulty, a *dacha* outside the capital where they installed an improvised darkroom. Meanwhile Gehlen had arranged for a courier to be sent to them who would try to convey at least some of their written and photographic material back to FHO headquarters. This was a most perilous assignment and it was some time before Major Schaeffer, with the help of Strik-Strikfeldt, found a suitable volunteer among Vlassov's officers. He appears in the FHO files merely under his code name of "Peter" and it seems that on at least one occasion he arrived back safely with his precious burden.

Among the reports which "Gregor" and "Igor" produced were secret operational construction plans and schedules of the wartime rail schedules over 90,000 kilometres of track, regulating the transportation of some 280 million tons of freight, much of it armaments and foodstuffs. Information about the logistical problems of their enemies was particularly important to the German High Command in the late autumn of 1944; for in the north the Soviet troops had reached the Norwegian frontier from Karelia, driving the Germans from what was almost their last foothold in Russian territory until they stood on the outskirts of Warsaw, while in the south they had entered Czechoslovakia and occupied Hungary. Gehlen's only regret with regard to "Operation *Drossel*" was that he had not staged it a year earlier. By October 1944, when he decided to recall the agents, the value of the information they were supplying had declined; now it was of use only in planning the defence of the Third Reich, for offensive action against Russia was a thing of the past.

Whether through humanity or because he wanted to make use of "Gregor" and "Igor" in his final and by then almost quixotic struggle against the Soviet Union, Gehlen spared no pains to bring them back to Germany. Once again an aircraft landed at a prearranged spot, named by the two men in one of their last radio signals—at a meadow not far from the town of Dzershinsk (named, ironically in the circumstances, after the founder of CHEKA) some seventy miles west of Moscow, and by then several hundred miles behind the rapidly advancing front. The aircraft, piloted by one of Colonel Rowehl's special Luftwaffe squadron officers, landed safely, and Gregor-Muller was waiting for it. Igor-Skryabin had implored Gehlen to allow him to bring his girl friend, Marfa, with him and Gehlen had reluctantly agreed. But the couple had not arrived. The pilot, of course, was not prepared to wait; take-off had to be within minutes of landing lest the plane be surrounded or shot at by Soviet patrols. "Igor" and Marfa arrived to see the aircraft a hundred feet above ground and "Gregor" frantically waving from the closing hatch. After his arrival at Gehlen's headquarters at Zossen, Gregor-Muller pleaded for a rescue operation for his friend, who after his misadventures had remained in radio contact with FHO. Incredible as it may sound, Gehlen did, in fact, attempt to bail "Igor" out; in January 1945 he was told to try and reach East Prussia—by then occupied by the Soviet Army—and make contact on the 12th with one of the *Zeppelin* commandos still holding out in the region. But "Igor" never arrived. There is no clue in the FHO files as to his ultimate fate. Considering Lieutenant Skryabin's astuteness, however, one may surmise that Molotov's nephew and his lover may have been swallowed up in the throng of people returning to the liberated territories, and that both survived to live happily ever after.

VII

The Werewolves

In December 1944 Hitler made his last desperate gamble in the West. The US First and Ninth Armies had entered Germany and Charlemagne's ancient city of Aachen had fallen. The British Second and the Canadian First Armies, having liberated Belgium, were poised for the thrust towards the Ruhr. But the Allies had been unable to achieve a breakthrough on the Rhine. Against firm resistance along the West Wall, they had engaged the enemy in battles of attrition. Now, running out of reserves and supplies, Hitler realised that defensive tactics were futile and decided on a bold plan of attack. It was to throw his last crack troops, the Sixth SS Panzer Army, under SS Obergruppenfuhrer Sepp Dietrich, General Manteuffel's Fifth Panzer Army and General Brandenberger's Seventh Army, across the Ardennes. In a single massive strike they were to split asunder the US First and Third Armies, roll up Montgomery's forces in the north, and reach Antwerp. This would deprive Eisenhower of his vital port through which Allied supplies were pouring in.

On December 12 Hitler held his last great war council at Ziegenberg, near Giessen. On entering the bunker the generals were asked to leave their briefcases and revolver holsters in the antechamber. This had become the usual precaution ever since the assassination attempt of July 20. Manteuffel described the Fuhrer as "a stooped figure with a pale, puffy face . . . he was hunched in his chair, his hands trembling, his left arm helplessly twitching, which he did his best to conceal . . . When he walked he dragged his left leg behind him."[1]

But Hitler was still as fervent as ever. He began a long harangue: "The coalition between the ultra-capitalists and the ultra-Marxists is breaking up. Each of the partners has gone into this coalition to realise his own political hopes. America is trying to become England's heir, the heir to a dying Empire; Russia is trying to gain the Balkans. Even now they are at loggerheads . . . their antagonism will grow stronger from hour to hour. If we can now deliver a few more blows this artificially bolstered common front may suddenly collapse with a gigantic clap of thunder . . . but there must be no weakening on the part of Germany. We must deprive the enemy of his belief in victory . . . . "

The generals listened in silence. They knew that Hitler's vision bore no relation to the facts. He had recalled Field-Marshal Rundstedt and reinstated him as commander-in-chief West; within a few months there had been four changes in the command. In July Rundstedt was sent into retirement and replaced by Field-Marshal von Kluge, and Rommel was relieved from the command of his army group. A few weeks later Rommel and Kluge, both accused of treacherous conspiracy, were forced into suicide. Kluge was replaced by Field-Marshal Walter Model,[2] who subsequently, after Rundstedt's recall, took over Rommel's army group. Rundstedt and Model considered Hitler's plan, at least in part, feasible: a sudden and concentrated tank offensive against the thinly held American lines in the Luxembourg-Belgian sector could be successful. But they had grave doubts about what would happen afterwards. They tried to persuade Hitler to change some vital parts of the plan, which required air cover of a strength that was no longer available. But they soon gave up arguing and solemnly promised to carry out his orders.

The Orders of the Day issued on the eve of the Ardennes offensive betrayed the generals' deep pessimism: Rundstedt exhorted his men thus: "Soldiers! I expect you to defend Germany's sacred soil to the very last!", and Model told them: "Soldiers, our homeland, the lives of our wives and children are at stake!" There was no encouraging word in either.

The Battle of the Bulge began on December 16 and lasted until Christmas. The Germans did break through and inflicted heavy casualties on the Americans, but the heroic relief of Bastogne by US 101st Airborne Division halted any further German advance. Hitler, however, kept sending frantic orders to his commanders that Bastogne must be taken at any price, and the attack continued. Then the US 2nd Armoured Division struck from the north and General Patton's Third Army broke through the German lines in the south. On Christmas Eve, Manteuffel came to the conclusion that only a speedy withdrawal could save the German forces from annihilation. But Hitler, as always, knew better: "We shall smash the Americans completely . . . . I do not believe that the enemy will be able to resist forty-five German divisions." Yet these divisions had already been thrown back and decimated and, after desperate counter-attacks, Field-Marshal Model's forces were in danger of being cut off by the British-American counter-offensive. The Germans had suffered grievous losses: 120,000 men killed, wounded and captured, 600 tanks and assault guns destroyed or abandoned, more than 1,500 aircraft—almost the last remnants of the Lutfwaffe—lost. Now the opening of the Allied drive into Germany from the west, and the rapid and powerful Russian thrust from East Prussia, the Vistula and the Danube, fused into a vast assault upon the Third Reich.

On January 8, the day Hitler, cursing his generals, gave his consent to the withdrawal from the Ardennes, Gehlen took his latest *Lage-Beurteilung* to Guderian. It dealt with the desperate plight of the German Army Group Centre which was being subjected to an onslaught by Marshals Rokossovsky's and Chernyakovsky's armies. Gehlen wrote:

> In the face of the offensive by strong Soviet forces the position of the Army Group Centre can no longer be upheld. A decision must be taken as to whether by an orderly withdrawal from the present lines we should hold on to the hinterland of East Prussia, or whether East Prussia should be evacuated in order to gain some respite for our troops. If successfully continued as hitherto, the Soviet offensive will have a decisive bearing on the further conduct of the war. The loss of East Prussia counts less than a final defeat.[3]

Guderian and Gehlen travelled overnight from Zossen in an armoured train to the Fuhrer's redoubt at Ziegenberg. Gehlen was sick with pain from what he called his occupational disease— cholecystitis of the gall-bladder—but he wanted to see Hitler and tell him the truth to his face. Guderian and his ADC, Captain von Freytag-Loringhoven, were shown into Hitler's room. Gehlen, however, was curtly informed that the Fuhrer did not wish to see him, and he returned to the train to wait. An hour later Guderian came back, pale and still quivering, to announce that he had almost come to blows with their master. Hitler had glanced at Gehlen's estimate, swept the papers and maps to the floor, and shouted: "This is completely idiotic! Get rid of this man . . . he ought to be in a lunatic asylum!"

Guderian had lost his own temper and yelled back: "If you want General Gehlen sent to an asylum you had better have me certified as well."[4] Hitler came at him shaking his fists. In the room were Goering, Keitel, Lieutenant-General Paul Winter,[5] General Wilhelm Burgdorf[6] and Hitler's naval aide, Rear-Admiral von Puttkammer. Twice Goering and Winter stepped between the bellowing pair. Hitler then calmed down a little and asserted that "there had never been stronger reserves in the East than at present". Guderian retorted "If you had studied Gehlen's report more closely, my Fuhrer, you would have realised that the Eastern front is a house of cards. If the front is broken at a single point all the rest will collapse." At this Hitler went into another tantrum and was escorted out by Goering. Guderian's comment to Gehlen was: "He has finally gone mad . . . everything is hopeless, but we must carry on." Both of them realised that they were now in personal jeopardy. On January 22 they had another long conference in the Maybach bunker No.5 at Zossen. Guderian asked Gehlen for a fresh situation estimate, as he was due to see Hitler again on the 28th. When Gehlen returned to his office he was given a teleprinter message. It was an order from Hitler transferring *Gruppe Irrefuhrung*, the FHO section for the "deception units", from Gehlen's control to Himmler's RSHA. The order read:

> By order of the Chief OKW the Deception Group is to be transferred to the RSHA on January 22, 1945. Its new station is: RSHA Military Office, ROEM 1 A, c/o Captain von Berchtolsheim. Telephone communications: Waldburg OKW. Capt. von Berchtolsheim, Exchange 414, Naber, Exchange 415. After 22 January 1945 all reports must be sent without further request to this address.[7]

Two days later Gehlen was told that Hitler had put SS Obersturmbannfuhrer Otto Skorzeny in charge of all behind-the-lines operations.

The sacking of Gehlen from the direction of the vast network which he had so laboriously built up in cooperation with the WALLI groups was the direct result of a situation estimate he had sent Hitler on January 17. It dealt with the desperate situation of the Army Group North and accurately predicted the impending opening of yet another Soviet offensive by Marshal Bagramyan's army. Entitled "Enemy Operational Plans against Army Group North", it ran to three closely typed pages, carefully corrected and annotated in his own hand (see illustration). It warned of an all-out Red Army attack from Curland, designed to "destroy decisively the Army Group North and subsequently to carry the thrust deeply into the territory of the Reich". Gehlen's prognostication was extremely pessimistic. Analysing the enemy's strategic plans on the basis of reports from his spies, he expressed grave doubts as to whether the Army Group North, or even its best divisions, could break out of the encirclement which was closing in on them. He warned that the plan for the evacuation of at least some of the troops by sea was doomed. Gehlen had a similar warning to the OKW before Christmas, reporting the intention of the Soviet High Command to make an all-out attack in the north. But Hitler tore it up shouting, "This is the biggest bluff since Genghis Khan! What idiot has dug up this nonsense?"[8]

Gehlen had been told about this by Guderian and, in January, he doubted whether the chief of the General Staff would dare to submit yet another gloomy evaluation. He therefore sent a copy of his January 4 report to Guderian's deputy, General Winter, remarking that "as I am not authorised to pass this report, I should be grateful if you would return it, after taking note of the contents". It was characteristic of Gehlen's determination that his reports should reach the OKW that he risked an action which bordered on insubordination.

Gehlen had, however, underestimated Guderian's nerve. He did show Hitler the reports, one of which contained comments on signals Gehlen had received from his V-men stating that the Soviet First Byelorussian Army had crossed the Oder at Lueben. This information Keitel had apparently withheld from Hitler. Inside a fortnight the Soviet tidal wave had covered almost 250 miles and advance tank units were only 110 miles from Berlin. Hitler, furious that Keitel and Jodl had not dared to tell him the truth, issued Directive No.68 which contained the following paragraph:

Commanders-in-chief, commanding generals, divisional commanders, the chiefs of the Army General Staff, and all individual officers of the General Staff are responsible to me that every report made to me, either directly or through the normal channels, should contain nothing but the unvarnished truth. In future, I shall impose draconian punishment for any attempt at concealment, whether deliberate or arising from carelessness or oversight.[9]

Perhaps emboldened by this order, Gehlen compiled another situation estimate in which he bluntly stated that the Russians were capable of reinforcing their Oder offensive "with four fresh divisions per day". When Guderian took it to Hitler it brought another fit of rage. Hitler roared at Guderian: "This mad Gehlen has been making wrong assessments all the time! He has misled me and my High Command!" Guderian shouted back that this was untrue. Gehlen's estimates had always been correct; the facts proved it. But logic had long been an ineffective lever in dealing with the Fuhrer.

Two weeks later, however, Hitler must have come to realise that the FHO chief had been correct in his evaluations after all. At the end of February he summoned Gehlen to his headquarters. There were good reasons for Hitler's change of attitude towards Gehlen, even if it did not prevail for long.

Gehlen and the Werewolves

Despite the order transferring the direction of the "deception units" operating in the Soviet rear to Himmler's RSHA, Gehlen had not given up his control over the networks and radio outposts he had established in cooperation with *Zeppelin* since 1943. He could bank on his agreeable relations with most of the RSHA chiefs, particularly with Schellenberg, SS Obersturmbannfuhrer Otto Skorzeny, who had become head of RSHA sabotage department VI/S, and SS Sturm-bannfuhrer Dr. Hengelhaupt, chief of *Zeppelin*. As we shall see, Gehlen continued to maintain direct contact with these networks and, indeed, even set up new radio posts during February and March. He transformed them into the R-Net (the 'R' stood for *Rücken*, or rear), which was to serve him well after the war when he resuscitated it for the CIA.

With the rapid deterioration of the situation at the front the existence of these clandestine units inside enemy territory gave rise to the idea of forming a partisan underground army inside Germany itself. The authorship of this plan has been ascribed to several persons—to Himmler, Kaltenbrunner, SS General von dem Bache and SS Lieutenant-General Pflaume (both of whom had fought the maquis Resistance in France) and to Reinhard Gehlen. The name given to this partisan army, the "Werewolves", sprang from Goeb-bels' fertile and romantic mind. In German folklore the *Werewolf* has played an important part since the Middle Ages. Legend has it that there were men capable of changing themselves into ravening wolves; the powers of the Devil rendered such beings invulnerable, except by a weapon consecrated by St. Hubertus, the patron saint of hunters. Hermann Loens, a minor German poet who died in 1914, wrote a Werewolf ballad which the nazis had dug up as "good literature for the young". It was often recited at Hitler Youth rallies.

On September 25, 1944 Hitler issued a decree setting up the *Volkssturm,* a kind of *levée en masse,* proclaiming that "because of the determination of the Jewish-imperialist enemy the mobilisation of every able-bodied German between the ages of fifteen and sixty had become imperative for the defence of the German Fatherland". In fact, all Germans in these age groups had already been drafted, and the pitiful *Volkssturm* battalions consisted of old men, disabled soldiers and under-nourished boys, often no older than fourteen. Some of the units were sent to the shaky front line on the Oder. But by no stretch of imagination could the *Volkssturm* cadres provide the tough men needed for the Werewolves.

The Werewolves were to be centred on the Alpine Redoubt, another last-throw nazi chimera. In July 1944 Goering, when visiting Field-Marshal Kesselring in Italy, had suggested to him that, if the fronts collapsed, they should organise a defence redoubt in southern Bavaria and the Tyrol. There the troops withdrawn from the fronts would hold out until the German leaders—not necessarily with Hitler as the Fuhrer—could come to an agreement with the British and Americans, secure an armistice, and combine with the Western Allies in combat against the Russians. Kesselring showed no enthusiasm for the idea, but Goering succeeded in persuading Hitler to go ahead with it, without disclosing to him his innermost thoughts as to who should lead the Germans in the Redoubt.

The Alpine Redoubt was by no means the myth it has been described as by some military writers in the West since the war. An engineering staff, headed by Major-General von Marcinkiewitz, was assembled in Innsbruck. Frenzied work was begun on the construction of a mountain fortress and other defences, and on accommodation for the troops intended to man them.[10] Some progress was made, but the project was shortly abandoned since the planners had neither the labour nor the material to complete it. Moreover, German Intelligence had got hold of a SHAEF document which revealed finally and unequivocally that the Allies had no intention of bargaining. Captured from an American officer towards the end of the Ardennes battle, the document contained an outline for "Operation Eclipse", the Allied objectives after victory, which included unconditional surrender and the complete occupation of Germany. Hitler and his OKW generals hid this foretaste of doom from all but their closest henchmen. But whether or not Goering, Himmler and Kaltenbrunner shared the knowledge of the document, they knew enough to turn their thoughts away from any prospects of negotiating a settlement on behalf of the nation to betraying their Fuhrer one by one and saving their own necks. They began to send personal representatives to Sweden and Switzerland to seek out Allied emissaries.

Gehlen, who had served in the Fortifications Department of the General Staff before he took over FHO, must have taken a poor view of the Alpine Redoubt plan. The Werewolf project, however, he did consider worthy of his attention. He had long been convinced that the alliance between the West and Stalin could not endure. Once the Red Army had overrun large parts of Germany, a German partisan army fighting the Russians could well commend itself to the British and Americans.

After the heroic Polish Resistance in Warsaw was crushed in October 1944, and the commander of the Polish Underground Army, General Tadeusz Bor-Komorowski, was captured with his staff, Gehlen asked the German commander to send him the papers seized from the Polish headquarters. Professor Hugh Trevor-Roper, who as a

British Intelligence officer interrogated in 1945 several hundred nazi leaders and German generals and officers, has recorded how Gehlen studied the Polish Underground movement and how he "drew up a careful plan for German resistance along similar lines". The professor describes how, when Schellenberg forwarded the Werewolf plans to Himmler, their reception made him tremble for his life. "This is complete madness!", was Himmler's reaction. "If I were to discuss such a plan with Wenck (the general commanding the Twelfth Army, fighting on the river Elbe) I should be denounced as the greatest defeatist in the Third Reich. The fact would be served up to the Fuhrer piping hot."[11] Himmler referred to an OKW circular reminding all leaders and officers of the severe penalties for defeatism; he obviously considered even the thought of a German defeat and an underground resistance an unforgivable crime. Yet, he was mistaken about Hitler's attitude to the Werewolf plan. Hitler did approve of it and he must have discussed it with Gehlen at their meeting on February 27.*

The Werewolf units were formed; SS Obergruppenfuhrer Hans Prutzmann was appointed their commander-in-chief, with Major General Pflaume as his chief of staff. Prutzmann was forty-four, and a seasoned storm-trooper since 1930; he had gained first-hand experience of guerilla warfare as SS and Higher Police Fuhrer in the Ukraine between 1942 and 1944, where he had fought the Soviet partisans with ruthless severity. But if Prutzmann supplied the executive power, the tactical plans for the Werewolves came from Gehlen; they were fashioned on the Polish Resistance organisation. Gehlen had used one of his FHO officers, Captain Friedrich Wilhelm Poppenberger, to work out the details.

The Gehlen plan for the Werewolf organisation foresaw seven main points, some of which incorporated existing WALLI and *Zeppelin* schemes.[12] As Gehlen saw it, all Werewolf operations were to be directed exclusively against the Russians; nothing in his plan concerned underground resistance against the Americans, British and French. The main points were as follows:

(1) The training of saboteurs and guerilla fighters;
(2) The formation of action units of not more than sixty men each;
(3) The preservation of salvaged arms of the German Army and their safe-keeping at secret hideouts;
(4) The setting up of secret radio posts;
(5) Espionage within Soviet military commands and Occupation authorities;

* See pages 94-95

(6) The setting up of "liquidation commandos" against Soviet military leaders and officials in occupied territories in Germany;

(7) The preparation and dissemination of anti-Soviet propaganda by an underground press, leaflets, radio and word of mouth.

Gehlen provided Prutzmann with a detailed blue-print for the organisation of the Werewolves, but he took no part in putting the scheme into effect. Once the plan was approved by Hitler and the nazi leaders need have no fear of being accused of defeatism, Himmler took command of its execution and Goebbels became its most enthusiastic supporter. Indeed, a struggle for the control of the Werewolves ensued among them; at one point Martin Bormann, the Fuhrer's deputy, made a bid to put himself at their head. Goebbels ordered the installation of a special *Werwolf Rundfunk* at the radio station of Konigswusterhausen, and a flood of propaganda was released upon the German people. But they were by now thoroughly tired of the war. With millions of homeless roaming the devastated cities in search of shelter and food, while millions more fled from the advancing Soviet troops, this final attempt to whip up patriotic passions and rekindle the will to resist seemed to have little prospect of success. Goebbels made a number of broadcasts of which the style may be judged from this extract: "We Werewolves consider it our supreme duty and right to kill, to kill and to kill, employing every cunning and wile in the darkness of the night, crawling, groping through towns and villages, like wolves, noiselessly, mysteriously . . ."

Even in the midst of the *Götterdämmerung* which was rapidly descending upon the Reich, the *Werwolf* organisation, at least on paper, was worked out with truly German thoroughness. Some of the middle-aged leaders had served in the illegal *Freikorps* in the early days of the Weimar Republic, others had experience of clandestine nazi cells before 1933. The structure of the Werewolves was built on a similar pattern, based on *Dorfortsgruppe* (village group), *Gemeinde-Ortsgruppe* (rural district group), *Stadtgruppen* (town groups) and so on. Area commanders and *Stabsleiter* (staff officers) were appointed and soon there were more commanders than rank-and-file members. A subsidiary *Werwolf* organisation sprang up in the East German territories already overrun by the Soviet forces, calling itself *Freies Deutschland* (Free Germany).

Every sort of conspiratorial device was introduced, such as recognition signs, passwords, and the *Wolfsangel*, a runic letter which was to be painted on buildings occupied by the foreign intruders and on the houses of German traitors collaborating with the "occupants", marking them for destruction by explosives and arson. Every

98

effort was made by Goebbels' radio propagandists and local *Werwolf* leaders to implant the idea of vengeance in the souls of the children. Young boys and girls of the Hitler Youth were pressed into the auxiliary units, in some districts from the age of nine upwards.

In areas where all these efforts encountered unenthusiastic response and produced poor recruitment figures, Prutzmann and his sub-commanders resorted to enlisting members of the rapidly dissolving units of the Vlassov Army and the Ukrainian UPA; they even sought recruits among Polish forced-labour workers, who were told of alleged atrocities the Soviet Army was committing in their homeland. The nazis tried to gain recruits by spreading fear and also by appealing to religious feelings. "It is as though God had given up his protection of the people in the areas under the Soviet boot and as though Satan now had taken command. Horrible, unmentionable things are happening to our women and children. We must defend ourselves and our dear ones, bravely and secretly, we must creep up like footpads, destroy and get rid of the communist rabble which is ravaging our Fatherland . . . ."

After the liberation of France thousands of former Vichy militiamen of the traitor Joseph Darnand, members of Doriot's French Waffen SS, ex-Cagoulards of Colonel Deloncle and a motley mob of French collaborators and quislings had fled across the Rhine in an attempt to escape the vengeance of the compatriots they had for four long years oppressed more cruelly than the Gestapo. Many of them were recruited into Werewolf units which were to carry out sabotage actions inside France and against the Allied Occupation forces in western Germany. But nearly all of these Frenchmen quickly deserted as soon as they received their paltry bounty. Skorzeny, who for a brief period in 1943 had been in charge of a "special commando" guarding Marshal Pétain and Laval,[13] set up a training centre for French saboteurs at Friedenthal, whilst Darnand with SS Hauptsturmfuhrer Deterding busied himself at Sigmaringen with the organisation of the "white maquis" against General de Gaulle. Attempts at actions behind the Allied lines in France were a total failure. A few of the French SS men dropped by parachute into the Corrèze in December 1944, but they were captured a few hours later and almost torn to pieces by enraged Resistance men.

Skorzeny's only action was during the Battle of the Bulge in the Ardennes, when he organised the "Operation *Greif*" ("Catch"). Hitler had ordered him to assemble a brigade of two thousand English-speaking Germans and Frenchmen, put them into American uniforms and, driving captured American tanks and jeeps, send them towards the Meuse and General Patton's Third Army. This fake "US unit" was supposed to infiltrate American lines, create confusion by killing dispatch riders, misdirect traffic and blow up the Meuse bridges in order to halt or slow down American troops on their drive to relieve Bastogne. Skorzeny had also been given a very special assignment: some of his desperados were to reach Paris and assassinate General Eisenhower. Forty jeeps actually penetrated the American lines, but when one was stopped and a German officer in American uniform unmasked, several copies of the *Greif* plan were found on him. A general alert resulted, rendering harmless most of the infiltrators. By wearing American uniforms they had flouted international conventions of regular warfare, and so they were treated as spies; a number were summarily shot, others were court-martialled and executed by firing squads. However, for a day or two, the infiltrators had succeeded in causing confusion behind the lines and for a week US military police stopped columns of army traffic, checking on the nationality of the officers and men by asking them who had won the last baseball World Series. Skorzeny did not take an active part in the operation and when he was eventually captured by American troops in Bavaria, he was treated leniently.[14]

Some war historians who mention the existence of the Werewolves when describing the last throes of the Third Reich dismiss the organisation as a chimera of Goebbels' propaganda and point out that Germany was the only conquered country in Europe which failed to produce an effective resistance movement against forces of occupation. This is not, however, entirely accurate. It is true that all the nazi leaders who had initiated the Werewolves cowardly deserted them. Himmler, their supreme commander, was secretly negotiating with the Allies through Schellenberg while he was still issuing orders to his Werewolves, and Prutzmann fled in April to Admiral Doenitz' headquarters in Flensburg. After his arrest by the British and facing prosecution for war crimes, Prutzmann committed suicide in a POW camp. Although deserted by their leaders, some Werewolf groups did engage on sabotage actions against both the Western Allies and the Soviet Army. Within a few weeks of the surrender, sabotage and murderous attacks on soldiers occurred in the British zone and thirteen youths, all self-confessed Werewolves, were sentenced to death and executed. In the American zone in March 1946 two Werewolf leaders, Erwin Fisher and Hans Pietsch, were sentenced to seven years' imprisonment for trying to revive their groups in the Frankfurt district. In December 1945, British and American Intelligence officers smashed a widespread neo-Werewolf organisation and arrested eight hundred of its members. Arrests and trials of Werewolves continued for some years during the Allied Occupation; as late as 1960 Federal German police arrested Gunter Welters, a former leader of the Hanover *Werwolf*, who headed his group for five years after the end of the war and later revived its activities by organising a neo-nazi movement. Many of the former *Werwolf* leaders are today among members of the right-wing parties and groups which today plague German politics.

However, *Werwolf* activities against the Western Allies had never been really effective. One reason for this was that on April 25, 1945, Admiral Doenitz, still hoping that Britain and the United States would recognise his "provisional government" in Flensburg and negotiate armistice and peace terms with him, issued an order forbidding all *Werwolf* actions against the West. This did not, however, concern activities against the Russians and, in fact, the Soviet Army encountered during the first months of their occupation of East Germany a series of violent sabotage actions and killings; they were not publicised but were ruthlessly suppressed.

Albert Speer, Hitler's minister of armaments and war production, makes only a fleeting reference to the *Werwolf* in his memoirs, which he published after serving a twenty years' sentence for war crimes. He describes how on April 11 he tried to broadcast "a call to the German Resistance to bluntly forbid any damage to factories, bridges, waterways, railroads and communications . . . . It prohibited *Werwolf* activity and appealed to cities and villages to surrender without a fight." But, he says, "Hitler had censored my speech to such an extent that it was no longer worth giving."[15] He adds that on April 16 he tried to make another appeal from the Konigswusterhausen radio station "which was regularly broadcasting the *Werwolf* messages, and was as its last act supposed to broadcast my speech issuing a ban against *Werwolf* activities". But he never made it; "in spite of all efforts no suitable recording apparatus could be located."

Gehlen had produced the original scheme for the Werewolf, but he watched its futile activities during the last few weeks before the surrender with detachment bordering on contempt. He had never envisaged the use of the Werewolves for underground resistance against the Western Allies. But one feature, and to his mind the only important one, of the *Werwolf* enterprise attracted his serious attention. This was the attempt at setting up clandestine cells, sabotage groups and radio posts inside the territories in Poland, East Prussia, Pomerania and Silesia, from which the German Army was hurriedly retreating behind the Oder and Elbe.

With his R-Net, which he was determined to maintain behind the Soviet lines, these *Werwolf* undertakings could have become extremely useful. Gehlen obtained from SS Obergruppenfuhrer Prutzmann and his staff detailed information about the deployment of their *Werwolf* groups in the East. He was to make some use of this in later years.

VIII

Farewell To Hitler

The closing weeks of the war were a cliff-hanging period for Reinhard Gehlen. He had, of course, long since realised that Hitler was leading the German people to the most terrible disaster that had ever overcome them. But his Prussian officer's code of honour would not permit treachery as long as the Fuhrer represented the authority of the German Reich.

Gehlen was fully aware of the nazi leaders' frantic attempts to save their own necks by trying to establish contact with the Americans and British before it was too late. Through his manifold sources of information he had heard, at first vaguely, of Schellenberg's mysterious visits to Switzerland. In January he learnt that SS General Karl Wolff, Himmler's closest associate and commander-in-chief of the SS troops in Italy, had begun secret negotiations for surrender with Allen Dulles, the chief of the OSS office in Berne, whilst Himmler himself was meeting the Swedish Count Bernadotte at Luebeck. Goering was putting out feelers to the Allies through other Swedish middlemen. Kaltenbrunner, the Gestapo chief, employed SS Sturmbannfuhrer Wilhelm Hoettl as a go-between to the Americans.[1]

Gehlen's contempt for these men was now limitless, although to their faces he still acted as their obedient servant and took their orders. To one of his adjutants he remarked that he felt nausea whenever he met them or heard their names. But neither did he identify himself with the fanatical nazi samurai who were ready to see Germany immolated if they could no longer rule. He began to contemplate ways and means of his surrender to the Allies. It would have to be an honourable surrender, and they would have to allow him to retain the unrivalled weapon he had spent so much effort in forging--his formidable intelligence machine against the Soviet Union. Then they would use it together in a combined espionage offensive against communism and the Soviet rulers. In this way, even if the Red Army were to overrun half of the Reich, his surrender would be meaningful; it would benefit the German people and perhaps in time help to free those in the territories subjected by the Russians. Indeed, in moments of elation Gehlen must have seen himself as a man who could make a vital contribution to saving Europe from the peril of communism.

He was determined not only to preserve his own knowledge and unique dossiers, but also to keep together his experienced staff, and to maintain as long as possible the clandestine cells, radio posts and groups of guerillas and Werewolves in the East. One day they would provide a nucleus from which to penetrate the nerve-centres of the communist bloc. To this end he continued the *Funkspiel* with Soviet Intelligence; it still gave him an insight into Soviet methods of communication. As we have seen, Gehlen had inherited many radio activities from the disbanded Abwehr. Despite constant interference from Schellenberg's *Amt VI* of RSHA, his department had assumed a near-monopoly of secret radio traffic in the East. As has been mentioned before, FHO was also operating fake radio posts tuned to the British Secret Intelligence Service and SOE, and to the American Intelligence headquarters in North Africa and OSS posts.

Even while he was predicting the collapse of the fronts during the winter of 1944/5, Gehlen was still extending his radio net and increasing the *Funkspiel* traffic. His logbook of the "radio games" during that period lists only the short headings of the operations and yet they fill 161 closely typed pages. The extent of this clandestine radio traffic can be measured by the fact that listed signals reached registration number 440,739.

Preparing the R-Net

With hindsight one can grasp the purpose of Gehlen's efforts at a time when they seemed to have none. He was building up his R-Net, and he was particularly anxious to preserve intact such posts as he still had working in East Germany, Austria, Bohemia and Moravia. In addition to the Berlin posts *Meistersinger* and *Steuermann* (Helmsman), he had *Falke* (Falcon), *Hase* (Hare), *Eber* (Boar), *Albatros Krähe* (Crow), *Kiebitz* (Plover) and *Kuckuck* (Cuckoo) in Danzig and East Prussia. He strengthened the installations of the *Watzmann* network at Frankfurt on Oder and Cottbus, and encouraged his men who ran the Austrian stations *Alpenrose*, *Lindwurm* (Dragon), *Rote Mauer* (Red Wall) and *Adam*, all situated either in Vienna or Graz, and *Theiss* on the Austrian-Hungarian border.[2]

Gehlen could foresee the re-emergence of a free Czechoslovakia, which after the incorporation of the Sudetenland into the Reich consisted of the "protectorate" of Bohemia and Moravia. He was, therefore, anxious to preserve his posts *Purpur* (Purple), *Zepter* (Sceptre) *Reichsapfel* (Orb) in Prague—all strangely codenamed after regalia— *Kapitän* and *Löwe* (Lion) at Brunn, and *Rotkäppchen* (Red Riding Hood) in Moravian-Ostrau.

The chaotic situation at Himmler's RSHA during these weeks is illustrated by the fact that, while Gehlen had been ordered to discontinue some of his radio links, he was asked by Schellenberg to take control of new· ones. One such case concerned "Operation *Forstmeister*". On February 20, SS Obersturmfuhrer Naber—who by then shared with Skorzeny the "supervision" of FHO—told Gehlen that the Gestapo was holding a former army colonel, Hans Hoyer, who had been arrested in Austria after his arrival from Russia. Hoyer was under suspicion of being a double agent; he had come to the RSHA office in Vienna with a strange story.

He had commanded an infantry regiment on the eastern front and had been taken prisoner by the Red Army in June 1943 in the battle of Orel. In captivity he had joined the National Committee for Free Germany, headed by the captured defender of Stalingrad, Field-Marshal von Paulus. Hoyer told the RSHA interrogators that he had done so with the express purpose of spying on German traitors, who had agreed to collaborate with the Russians. He went through the usual indoctrination and, having volunteered to work for Soviet military intelligence, was released from the POW camp and given long training. At length he was sent to the German front line in Bessarabia, sneaked into Rumania, and eventually reached Austria. At first Hoyer was treated as a traitor and potential Soviet spy, and might have been summarily executed. But in the end he was sent to the RSHA in Berlin. He was still in custody when Gehlen was told his story.

Hoyer's background was thoroughly investigated by the Gestapo. He was born in 1897, and served in the First World War, leaving the army in 1918 as a sergeant major with the Iron Cross 1st and 2nd class. He became a policeman in Thuringia, joined the nazi party and, when this was discovered, was dismissed in 1932. After the nazis came to power, he rejoined the police, rose to high rank, was transferred in 1936 to the army, fought in Poland, and eventually gained promotion to colonel. He was awarded bars to his Iron Crosses and the Gold Cross for gallantry. When a prisoner of war, Hoyer had told the Russians of his humble background as an NCO, keeping silent about his nazi party membership and police service and posing as an opponent of Hitler's regime. Thus he was sent back to Germany as a Soviet secret agent, with a radio transmitter and detailed instructions for his assignment.[3]

Gehlen realised that Hoyer could be used for yet another *Funkspiel* with Moscow. He accepted Naber's invitation to "take over" the colonel, installed him in Zossen and gave him a Russian radio telegraphist, who had been turned round a year earlier and had worked satisfactorily on other *Funkspiels*. In Gehlen's "radio game" logbook there are a number of entries on Hoyer's successful signal exchanges with Moscow.[4] His unsuspecting Soviet masters tuned to his receiver and bombarded him with queries relating particularly to the possible use of poison gas by the Germans. Gehlen himself and one of his assistants, Captain von Twardowski, who was fluent in Russian, composed many replies to Moscow's anxious requests for information. From Gehlen's logbook one can deduct that he produced some vivid, though obviously entirely misleading, descriptions of German troop movements and defence positions along the Oder.

The deception by *Funkspiel* with Moscow went on almost to the bitter end. On March 22, Gehlen sent Naber a copy of a report which was radioed to Moscow, apparently by the Hoyer link. It gave the Russians a mass of fake information about the imaginary dispatch of fresh German reserves to the East. It contained, for instance, such information as: "The newly reformed XXII Panzer division has left for the front. At Halle a convoy of tanks and armoured vehicles with four hundred men was seen moving in an easterly direction. Two trains, one with thirty-five, the other with forty-seven wagons, loaded with vehicles and a large number of soldiers, left the Berlin-Charlottenburg freight station. A convoy of twelve Panzers and many soldiers in grey and black SS uniforms are moving through Berlin. Inhabitants of Brandenburg and Rathenow say they have observed many troop trains and road transport coming from the south-west and moving in a north-easterly direction."[5]

Gehlen was aware that such vague "information" could hardly impress the Soviet High Command of the effectiveness of these spurious radio posts, even if the Russians still believed that some at least of them were genuine. Moreover, he knew that the Russians, even after the destruction of the "Red Orchestra"[6] had a number of espionage networks and radio posts inside Germany which had escaped detection and which relayed genuine intelligence to Moscow. But even if only some of the fake information was believed by the Russians and their strategic plans or dispositions based on this data, however minor, miscarried, it was sufficient reward for the effort. Besides, Colonel Hoyer, like others of Gehlen's men engaged on deception work, was earmarked as a potential-member of the R-Net.

Gehlen was anxious to let survive as many as possible of the *Jagdkommandos*, ex-Vlassov units, bands of Ukrainian nationalists, and the motley rabble which by then was scattered in small groups behind the advancing Soviet Armies. He knew, of course, that their chance of doing so was extremely small. But if a few could remain alive and undetected, and by good luck held on to their radio receivers, there was hope of restoring contact with them after the end of hostilities. This proved to be no idle speculation. By 1946, when he established his new organisation, Gehlen was able to revive a number of the "sleeper V-men" in East Germany, Poland and Czechoslovakia, and to make contact with anti-communist groups in the Ukraine. In the beginning—until he was able to recruit, train and infiltrate new secret agents—the R-Net was to be the mainstay of his new organisation. During the last weeks of the war he was, therefore, anxious to locate and save these men, who now found themselves in dire danger. Seasoned, tough soldiers of the *Jagdkommandos* were, of course, of particular value to the scheme he was nursing in his mind.

Jagdkommando Scherhorn

Gehlen was particularly concerned about the fate of one large group of "diversants", which operated during the summer of 1944 in the area between Minsk and Mogilev on the Dnieper. It was commanded by Lieutenant-Colonel Scherhorn and originally numbered about 250 men. During that period their main task had been to deal with Soviet partisan bands which harassed the retreating German armies and had in many sectors deeply penetrated their lines.

On April 1, 1944, the OKW issued a pamphlet entitled *Warfare against Bands* which set out the most effective tactics against guerillas. Gehlen had helped to edit it. The Wehrmacht, and much more so the *Jagdkommandos,* controlled by the RSHA *Militaramt*, turned on the partisans with ferocious determination. Colonel Arthur Campbell in his book on guerilla warfare[7] stated that these units "murdered two million defenceless men and women in the rear operational areas and in the hinterland . . . but even these methods were doomed to failure because the psychological battle had already been lost; in the most important aspects of guerilla warfare the Russians defeated the Germans at every stage."[8] The Soviet partisans retaliated by unleashing upon the Germans a warfare without rules; those captured were tortured and killed. Stories of these atrocities spread like wild-fire through the German Army resulting in reprisals of the most violent and indiscriminate nature. This vicious circle grew in scope and effect as the war proceeded.

When the areas in which the Scherhorn group operated were liberated by the armies of Zhukov and Rokossovski, stragglers from many German Army units joined the *Jagdkommandos*. The number of men under Scherhorn's command had grown to nearly two thousand when his group was completely cut off. Gehlen had used Scherhorn to obtain reports about the situation in the Soviet rear and had maintained a regular radio link with the group for many months, even when it was constantly on the move. He must have felt responsible for the ultimate fate of Scherhorn's men, who had tried in vain to break out and rejoin the main body of the retreating army of General Gotthard Henrici. Gehlen tried to advise Scherhorn over the head of RSHA; he also alerted the chief of intelligence staff at the Army Group Centre, Colonel Hans-Heinrich Worgitzky,[9] to secure supplies for the Scherhorn groups, whose dejected and half-starved men were aimlessly roaming the forest during the winter of 1944/5. It speaks for the courage of some of their officers that they were still sending radio signals to Gehlen. His logbook *Unternehmen Scherhorn* contains many entries of such signals up until the beginning of March 1945.[10] By then, however, the situation of the group had become desperate.

After several appeals to the RSHA, Gehlen had a meeting with Skorzeny on March 15 and asked him that something should be done by Himmler to relieve Scherhorn's plight; the Reichsfuhrer SS had been appointed by Hitler "Supreme Commander of the Vistula Army", a purely euphemistic rank since no such army now existed. Gehlen's interference was resented by the SS leaders and the outcome of the meeting was that Skorzeny told Gehlen that "complete control of the Scherhorn operations had been taken over by the RSHA". In a teletype message from *Zeppelin* (N. 030416) Gehlen was ordered to stop all radio contacts with Scherhorn and told that all radio communications would henceforth be handled by the RSHA radio unit Risler from Tutow in Mecklemburg. Gehlen was also told to cease from further contact with *Jagdkommando*, *Rennstrecke,* which according to Skorzeny "was operating with good success".[11]

Two days earlier Gehlen had requested Guderian to promote some of the Scherhorn officers and award them gallantry decorations, if only to keep up their spirits. On March 25, Guderian gave him a backdated order for transmission to Scherhorn. It stated that the Fuhrer had, on March 16, promoted Scherhorn and four of his officers, Lieutenant-Colonels Eckhardt and Michaelis, Major Scholtz and First Lieutenant Vollrath, up a rank and had awarded Colonel Scherhorn the Knight Cross of the Iron Cross. Such as it was, this was a final comfort, for the men had been effectively written off. Although Schellenberg informed Gehlen on April 10 that the Scherhorn group had been located in the area of Naliboki, gleefully adding that it was his *Militaramt* which was organising Scherhorn's rescue, the group was never heard of again; all its two thousand members were either killed or captured, and only a handful of the suvivors returned, years later, to Germany from Soviet prison camps.

All through February Gehlen busied himself with safeguarding the future of his outposts. He remained in contact with Colonel Baun of WALLI I and Colonel Schmalschläger of WALLI III, trying to ascertain the location and preservation of their *Frontkommandos*. He also watched the deployment of the Werewolves, though he refrained from intervening in any of their operations. On February 6 he attended as one of the representatives of the *Führungsgruppen* of the OKW a conference of the *Werwolf* staff and agreed to a directive whereby "all army commanders in whose areas Werewolves operate should support them with supplies of arms, ammunition, explosives and rations".

Last Meeting With Hitler

Gehlen had prepared another lengthy situation report, more gloomy than any he had written previously, and on February 19 he showed the draft to Guderian. They agreed, however, that there was no point in submitting it to Hitler. The draft is preserved among Gehlen's papers. On February 25 Gehlen gave Skorzeny a memorandum which outlined the R-Net plan and stressed the need to equip V-men with Afu radio transmitters. He probably hoped to enlist Schellenberg's help in getting supplies of new transmitters, but Schellenberg was no longer interested. In his post-war memoirs he disclosed that at that time he was engaged, on Himmler's behalf, in negotiations with the former president of the Swiss Confederation to secure a free pardon for the RSHA chief from the Allies, in return for releasing Jews from extermination camps.[12]

On February 26 Gehlen received a summons to Hitler's head-quarters; he was to appear the next morning before the Fuhrer, who had for many weeks refused to see him. Guderian had shown Hitler Gehlen's memoranda referring to the Werewolves and the Fuhrer had expressed a wish to see him. Gehlen must have been shocked by Hitler's appearance, but he noted in his logbook that "the Fuhrer has been most charming", and that they had discussed various topics, including the possibilities of reinforcing the Vistula Army with *Volkssturm* units, Gehlen's evaluation of Soviet tank power, and the plight of German prisoners in Russia. Then Hitler told Gehlen that he should continue to run the "reconnaissance" groups but in cooperation with the RSHA. He then said, obviously as a sop, that he had decided to promote him to the rank of lieutenant-general and would order General Burgdorf to gazette it. In fact, this promotion was never officially announced. Hitler had, however, something much more important to him on his mind, and this was apparently the real reason why he had asked for Gehlen.

He wanted gramophone records with sound effects of combat

108

noise and rolling tanks to be distributed to front-line commands and played from dug-outs as near as possible to the Soviet lines. Gehlen told him that FHO had a record collection and that other discs could probably be obtained from Dr. Goebbels' film propaganda units. But he was shaken by this paranoiac suggestion and he had no intention of getting himself involved in such a hare-brained scheme. He asked Schellenberg to make the RSHA *Militaramt* carry out the Fuhrer's strange order. Gehlen's refusal in this matter, coupled with his intervention in the Scherhorn case, gave his SS adversaries a welcome opportunity to denounce him. On March 9 Skorzeny reported Gehlen's "recalcitrant attitude". There were now several black marks against him at the OKW, and Hitler's seemingly friendlier attitude towards him once again changed to anger. Gehlen knew nothing about this, however, and on March 17 he launched his last major enterprise, Operations "Andressen" and "Atlas", in cooperation with Baun's WALLI I, sending an infiltration group led by Captain Trenk behind the enemy lines.

On March 28 Guderian had his last interview with Hitler, and when he showed him a brief report from Gehlen they had another row. In his memoirs Guderian described several of Hitler's violent outbursts, such as that on February 13: "His fists raised, his cheeks flushed with rage, his whole body trembling, Hitler stood there in front of me, beside himself with fury . . . . After each outburst he would stride up and down the carpet edge, then suddenly stop before me and hurl his next accusation in my face . . . . His eyes seemed to pop out of his head and the veins stood out on his temples."[13]

On this final occasion, Hitler suddenly calmed down, after bellowing at Guderian, and said almost in a whisper: "Herr General Guderian, your state of health makes it imperative that you immediately take six weeks' sick leave". Then he turned on his heel and left the room.

Gehlen heard of Guderian's dismissal the next morning; he realised that his own fate was now in the balance. He had also learned of new SS accusations against him to the effect that he had "disobeyed an order by the Fuhrer" and could no longer be trusted. This referred to a note Gehlen had sent to OKW, stating that an order issued on March 22 about the continuation of deception operations was not transmitted by him to the Army Group Kurland—by then completely cut off—because "unsafe communications made it impossible to safeguard the secrecy of the transmission against possible interception by the enemy".[14]

At last it became clear to Gehlen that the RSHA leaders had decided to finish him off. He devised a neat final act of revenge. On March 28, the day Guderian was dismissed, Gehlen sent to RSHA a teletype signal, making sure that a copy of it went to Hitler's OKW. It read:

> Evaluation of intelligence reports shows that the railway bridges over the Vistula at Cracow, Deblin, Warsaw and Thorn have remained intact. Over these bridges flows the bulk of Soviet reinforcements and supplies. Damage or destruction of the bridges would have meant great relief for our troops. On the bridges at Warsaw and Thorn depends Soviet transport for the Oder and Neisse fronts.[15]

Gehlen knew that the task of blowing up these bridges had been assigned to Skorzeny's *Jagdverband Ost*, which controlled the few remaining squadrons of the SS Air Group. They had failed badly, and as soon as Hitler investigated this the blame was bound to fall squarely on the RSHA bosses. Gehlen's retaliation might be regarded as rash, and it was certainly dangerous at a time when scores of his friends were going before the firing squads—Roenne had already been shot, and Count von Rittberg would soon follow. But, with hindsight, his decision to hurl a last challenge at the SS takes on a significant complexion. He was already pursuing his own plan for his eventual surrender to the Americans. If he succeeded and they demanded proof of his anti-nazi attitude, it would be invaluable to have documentary evidence that he had been at loggerheads with the RSHA. Gehlen carefully put a copy of this teletype message into his personal secret file, marking it in his own hand *PRESERVE! MOST IMPORTANT!* (see illustration).

For some weeks he had been discussing with Wessel and Lieutenant-Colonel Baun the situation that would follow upon the collapse of the Third Reich. Gehlen was convinced that as soon as Germany was defeated a conflict between the Western Allies and the Soviet Union was inevitable, and he expected that this clash would be fought out on German soil. As though to confirm this, two captured Soviet officers of GRU Military Intelligence were brought to him for interrogation. They admitted that they belonged to one of several groups of GRU and NKVD agents who had been ordered to cross Germany and penetrate the American and British lines "to discover Eisenhower's and Montgomery's preparations for an attack on the Soviet Union". Gehlen took this entirely at its face value, and Wessel and Baun agreed with him. From that moment, Gehlen's last-ditch plan blossomed into an active conspiracy.

The bizarre scheme he discussed with Wessel and Baun stemmed from a secret conversation he had had with Guderian on Christmas Eve 1944. He had advised the chief of staff to persuade other army commanders that the only way to save Germany from total disaster was to terminate all hostilities against the West immediately, to withdraw German troops gradually from the countries they still occupied in west and north-west Europe and to throw them against the Soviets, even at the price of Allied occupation of most of Germany. The Germans would then fight on the side of the Western Allies, after the removal of Hitler and the setting up of a German military government, headed perhaps by Guderian or by Gehlen's old idol, Field-Marshal von Manstein. Gehlen seemed confident that Roosevelt and particularly Churchill—whose account of the 1919 intervention against the bolsheviks he had eagerly read—would accept such a solution. His thinking may appear politically naive today; on the other hand Gehlen had not forgotten the secret meetings between German and British generals in 1935 and their common conception of the problems which then faced the world, and which had, in his opinion, hardly changed: nazism and Stalinism.

With this resolve Gehlen began to take stock of what he had to offer to the Western Allies—or, more precisely, what he would have soon, for first he had to steal it, and meanwhile make sure he stayed alive. First of all, he could bring over his own vast experience and his FHO; next, control of the WALLI networks. In March 1945 there were FHO, WALLI and *Zeppelin* outposts still intact near Vologda and Kubinsk, along the railway line from Vologda to Moscow, consisting of groups of up to two hundred men; at Vladimir and Ryasan, north and south of Moscow, were several *Zeppelin* commandos; and near Bryansk and Orel scattered bands of the Vlassov Army, not entirely reliable, but worth taking into account. In the Ukraine, around Kiev and Charkov, and in the former Polish territories around Lvov, Kamentz-Podolski, Luck and Rowno, there were strong groups of armed and disciplined Ukrainian nationalists. An assessment of his own outposts in East Germany, already occupied by the Soviet armies, and in provinces expected to be overrun within the next few weeks rounded up the balance of his assets. His priceless dossiers on the military, economic, industrial and manpower resources of the Soviet Union provided the most important item of all. It was a weighty package, and the Allied leaders would be crazy to refuse it.

Gehlen confided his thoughts to Wessel and Baun, suggesting that they meet in secret to work out the details of the plan. They envisaged moving both the FHO headquarters and Baun's WALLI office, based at Barnekop in Brandenburg, to the Alps. Thus, when the collapse came and the RSHA *Militaramt* disappeared with all its espionage appendages, Gehlen's rearguard would provide the only intact intelligence service for the new Germany.

111

The Pact of Bad Elster

On April 4 the three officers met at the deserted Kurhaus Hotel Quisisana at Bad Elster, in Saxony. Gehlen had driven with Wessel from Zossen, making many detours to avoid possible attention from SD men, who he believed were watching him. He registered as "Dr. Schneider", and Wessel as "Herr West". Baun had already moved his office to nearby Aldorf. When he joined them in one of the hotel bedrooms, Soviet tanks were reported to have reached Vienna, other Red Army units had entered Slovakia, and Zhukov's army was pushing towards the Elbe. The US Third Army was racing across Thuringia and had entered Jena. In fact, on that afternoon the Americans were only sixty miles to the west and Soviet advance units some one hundred miles east of their meeting place. The conspirators could not be sure of getting back safely to Zossen.

In the tense atmosphere of the small hotel room, with Gehlen sitting in the only easy chair, Baun perched on a luggage stool and Wessel lounging on the bed, a pact was concluded that laid the foundation of the vast espionage organisation Gehlen was to control for almost a quarter of a century. He and Wessel were to take care of the FHO archives and their staff, move them to Bavaria and wait for the arrival of the Americans. Baun was to contribute the *Frontaufklärungs-Kommandos*, which he had controlled first for the Abwehr and then under the RSHA. He insisted that he had V-men still working inside Moscow and at the headquarters of Soviet Army commanders. He promised to give orders to the FAK groups scattered in Silesia and between the Oder and Elbe to "disengage" themselves and make for Thuringia. The group leaders would leave some of their men behind, equipped with radio transmitters, and proceed in a south-westerly direction in order to join up with the FHO officers Wessel was to bring to Bavaria. Thus, the combined FHO-WALLI outfit would eventually be assembled and ready for surrender to the Americans.

The operation was planned and mapped out with military pre-cision. Baun's men were to establish dead letter-boxes on their move, to be used for maintaining communications with their com-rades left behind should the radio links fail. They laid down rules for courier traffic and agreed on passwords and on cyphers for each of them: Wessel became "W", Gehlen politely offered "X" to Baun and took "Y" for himself. Not for one moment did they doubt that they would be able to clinch the deal with the Americans. They discussed the enlistment of their staff officers for the new organisation and considered the special qualifications and future employment of the men they selected. The question of who should be the top boss was left open. Gehlen told Baun that they "would, of course, share the command" and they agreed that Wessel was to be their chief deputy.

Gehlen then hurried back to Zossen. Every moment counted now. He had provided for every emergency, even if he should be unable to reach his headquarters south of Berlin. He left orders for Sonder-fuhrer Stange, in charge of the archives administration and his two secretaries, Fräulein Brandt and Fräulein Goede, to supervise the packing and loading of all documents, microfilm, maps, diagrams, photographs, and the huge biographical indices. Marked GEHEIME KOMMANDOSACHE (Secret Command Matter), the instruction read:

In the event of the formation of an advance column and its transfer by *Mot-Marsch* (motorised move) prior to a move of the entire FHO personnel, the Archives and Indices are to be attached to the advance column.

All officers, NCOs and female staff helpers must be ready to leave at the latest within two hours from receipt of the order for evacuation. Within that time the entire contents of the Archives and Indices must be loaded on trucks. Personal baggage, including blankets, must remain with the officers and men and must not be loaded on the trucks provided for the Archives.[16]

To hoodwink the RSHA Gehlen had at the end of February sent Wessel with a part of the FHO archives to Bad Reichenhall, where a sham office of FHO was set up attached to the headquarters of Army Group South, itself in a state of disintegration. Early in March all important documents were microfilmed in triplicate and stored in steel containers. One set was sent to Naumburg in Thuringia, some hundred miles south-west of Zossen, and stored in the wine cellars of one of Gehlen's family friends. Meanwhile Colonel Baun had moved his depleted WALLI office to Baden, out of Russian reach.

After a few days spent in supervising the packing of the documents, burning tons of paper of lesser importance, and arranging for his family's removal to Bavaria, Gehlen received on April 10 a curt order from OKW. It was signed by General Hans Krebs,[17] who had succeeded the "ill" Guderian to become Hitler's last chief of staff. It told Gehlen that he had been relieved from the command of FHO and all posts appertaining to this command, and had been placed on the "retired officers' list". He was ordered to hand over his duties to Colonel Gerhard Wessel.

Gehlen had chosen his hideouts several weeks before. Although he never believed that the Alpine Redoubt would become a reality, he had decided to remove his treasures to the mountains of Bavaria or the Tyrol. He had asked Franz Hofer, the gauleiter of Tyrol, to recommend a safe place where "important secret dossiers of historical value could be deposited in safety from air attacks". Hofer suggested a hut at Wildmoosalm in the wilderness of the Wilder Kaiser mountains, some six miles north of Kufstein.

At Christmas, 1944, after the fateful conference with Guderian at which they had agreed that the war could not last much longer than a few weeks, Gehlen went to Schliersee, which he knew from family holidays in happier times. At the Schlierseer Hotel he registered as "Dr. Wendland", a scientist from Berlin. He made a reconnaisance of the vicinity, finally taking two or three local residents into his confidence over a round of beer. He let them understand that he was looking for a quiet, remote place where he could do some work undisturbed and also store his scientific papers and patent documents. With the cities under bombing attack by day and night, this seemed a sensible enough quest to his listeners. One of them suggested a farmer at Valepp, a hamlet fifteen miles to the south. The farmer, Ludwig Preller, might have the kind of accommodation "Dr. Wendland" was looking for.

Valepp then had a population of about 150, including a few refugee families from Munich. It lies in a deep narrow valley formed by two streams, the Weisse and Rote Valepp, and looming up on either flank are the high peaks of the Stolzenberg and the Kreuzbergerkopf. The road into the valley was a secondary one, bumpy and uninviting. Gehlen liked the look of this spot and later that day it exceeded his best hopes.

The farmer held some sixty acres of pasture on a lease from the state game board, but he was away in the army. His wife, however, was happy to oblige the friendly little Herr Doktor and let him rent a *Senne*, a cottage the Prellers owned up in the mountains. It was not much more than an alpine hut, used from time to time by the farmer's dairyman when he milked the cows. It stood some 450 feet above Valepp, and to reach it it meant climbing a steep path for about two miles along the Elendsgraben.

The dairyman, Rudolf Kreidl, who had come back from the war badly wounded, later recalled how he led "Dr. Wendland" to the cottage for the first time. When the fine gentleman saw it he flushed with excitement and exclaimed "This is just what I was looking for!" Nobody seems to remember Gehlen reacting to anything quite so vivaciously before. Gehlen paid Frau Preller a handsome sum in advance for the rent and returned to Zossen. He was confident that his elaborate scheme would succeed.

114

IX

Surrender At Misery Meadow

Gehlen and his staff began the long haul to the hideout in the Bavarian mountains. The FHO officers were assembled in three groups, each making its way independently. Gehlen, his wife and their four children travelled on a lorry with Major Horst Hiemenz and his wife which also contained part of the archives collected from the wine-cellars at Naunburg. Hitler's "scorched earth" decree, issued on March 20, which ordered the demolition of bridges, rail tracks and transport installations[1] had played havoc on the roads, which were already choked with refugees fleeing from the east. Overhead, US Air Force Lightnings, hunting in pairs, were a deadly menace to anything moving on road and rail.

To all this was added the risk that the convoy might be suspected and held up by roaming SS and Field Police patrols, who had taken to executing stragglers and deserters without ceremony. Four days before the convoy set off, Hitler's penultimate Directive No.73 had appointed Admiral Doenitz commander-in-chief of all German forces in the north, with his headquarters at Flensburg in Slesvig. All military staffs and officers leaving Berlin were ordered to move there. This, of course, applied to the FHO but Gehlen's convoy travelled in the opposite direction; if it was stopped, he would find it difficult to invent a plausible explanation for the journey. As a precautionary bluff Gehlen had, therefore, dispatched Major Fritz Scheibe and Major von Kalkreuth to Doenitz' headquarters in Holstein; they took with them a few steel containers of duplicated low-grade FHO files.

On the journey to Bavaria Gehlen's convoy had a narrow escape from an American air raid. At Hof the lorries were stopped by an SS patrol but eventually made another eighty miles and reached Cham, east of Regensburg. There Gehlen left his family and Frau Hiemenz at an inn and continued the journey with the lorries loaded with containers to Bad Reichenhall, almost a hundred miles further south. From there, with the help of Wessel and the other offices, Gehlen began to distribute the fifty-two containers at three hiding places. One was at Reit-in-Winkel south of Lake Chiem, a second at the

115

Wildermoosalm north of Kufstein, and the bulk of the archives was buried in the mountains above Valepp. An advance party of his FHO officers had gone to Miesbach and Gehlen told them to wait for further orders. Thirty-eight of them had taken lodgings at Miesbach, Schliersee and Fischhausen. The arrangements were completed on April 28, 1945.

But the danger was far from over. Gehlen had chosen Miesbach as the dispersal point, for to send all the trucks up to the mountain hamlet of Valepp at once would have been asking for trouble. The area was full of nazi officials and SS men in search of hideouts in the supposed Redoubt. Miesbach was a notorious nazi town, very proud of its importance as the cradle of the Party's official newspaper, the *Voelkischer Beobachter*.[2] The arrival of a convoy of officers with so many steel containers attracted considerable attention and everyone in the town was asking where they were going. Gehlen decided the faster they were quit of this zealous place the better. Wessel with a few officers went to Bad Reichenhall to make an appearance at his "office". A few officers remained in hotels and private lodgings at Miesbach; others moved to neighbouring Schliersee, Fischhausen and Josefsthal.

Gehlen took only a handful of his most trusted assistants with his treasure trove to Valepp. They had changed into civilian clothes, and at the only hostelry, the Kammerwirt Inn, they bought beer for its robust and interested customers. "Dr. Wendland" and his colleagues explained that secret blue-prints from Ruhr factories and prototype models of technical inventions were being hidden in the mountains to prevent them being stolen by enemy troops. The peasants understood, and kept their mouths shut, proud to be trusted by these important gentlemen.

The heavy containers were dragged on hand barrows up the mountainside to the chalet, which was situated in a pasture called Elends-Alm, in literal translation "Misery Meadow". By nightfall the few men Gehlen had brought with him had buried the containers in ditches six feet deep all around the meadow. He did not want to employ the peasants for this work; no one outside his trusted circle was to know the exact site of the cache. The first part of the operation was over. Gehlen and his men were dead tired but happy. They had stolen the world's most valuable espionage files, and they were still alive.

Looking for the Americans

Every morning Gehlen climbed from his .room at the inn to the chalet. With his binoculars he scanned the mouth of the valley for the first American scout jeep. The US Seventh Army under

Rudolf Kreidl, the farm hand who alerted the Americans.

The chalet at Misery Meadow where Gehlen waited for the Americans.

Miesbach (*arrow at top*), where Gehlen left his officers before burying the FHO archives near Valepp (*arrow at bottom*).

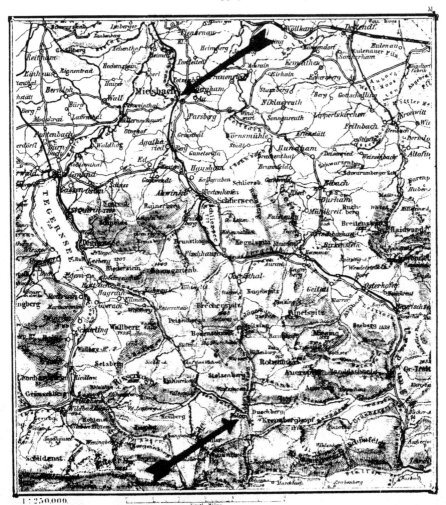

1:250,000.

(*Above*) Lieutenant-General Edwin L. Sibert, G-2 Intelligence head in Germany.
(*Left*) General Lucius D. Clay, US Military Governor in Germany, 1945-49, with General Joseph T. McNarney.

(*Bottom left*) Allen Welsh Dulles.

(*Bottom right*) General Arthur G. Trudeau, US G-2 Intelligence chief, who called Gehlen "a Nazi".

Lieutenant-General Alexander M. Patch was approaching across the upper Danube towards Munich. But its forward elements were in no hurry to roll trustingly into potential ambushes in the side valleys. Patch's G-2 Intelligence officers were still hypnotised by the bugbear of Hitler's impregnable Alpine Fortress. Barely a month earlier SHAEF Intelligence had produced a startling analysis, which foresaw it as being defended by 300,000 men, including all the remaining crack SS divisions.[3] Yet on its rapid sweep the Third Army encountered only disorganised German troops which meekly surrendered in tens of thousands. Some SS units, however, had taken to the mountain forests and offered sporadic resistance. Patch sent his 21st Corps racing to Salzburg and Berchtesgaden, expecting heavy fighting. But when the French Second Armoured Division, attached to this corps, arrived at Berchtesgaden and ascended Hitler's fabled "Eagle's Nest", supposed to be the command centre of the Alpine Redoubt, it was found empty; even the caretaker and his wife had fled. With the capture of Landeck, Innsbruck and the Brenner Pass in the south and Garmisch, Berchtesgaden and Salzburg in the north, the entire area of the "Alpine Fortress" was blanketed by American and French troops.

Gehlen waited restlessly, but the Americans did not come into the valley. On April 28 he had heard on the radio that the Red Army had smashed its way into Berlin. On the same day a workers' revolt had broken out in Munich, the cradle of nazism, and was brutally suppressed in a last orgy of SS violence. A day later a courier arrived at Misery Meadow from Wessel in Reichenhall, with the news that the Americans had entered Munich and liberated 32,000 prisoners from the Dachau concentration camp. On May 1 came the Radio Hamburg announcement of Hitler's death. Admiral Doenitz declared his intention to "negotiate an armistice with the Western Allies".

Gehlen was growing more restive. He had been told of marauding SS men roaming around Valepp and he decided to move on. One of his officers, Lieutenant Weck, a Bavarian gamekeeper before the war, obtained a few tents and they pitched camp high in the mountains above Maroldschneide. Eventually, Gehlen decided that the time had come to contact an American army post and surrender. By then Whitsun had come and on May 19 Gehlen and four of his officers descended into the valley at Fischhausen on Lake Schliersee. One of his officers had told him that his parents had a house there and that they would put him up. Gehlen spent a pleasant if tense few days there exchanging radio signals with the men he had left at Misery Meadow.

While Gehlen still hesitated, the crippled dairyman Rudi Kreidl forced a totally unexpected solution to the problems of the ex-FHO

117

chiefs. Kreidl, a good Catholic, had never been enthusiastic about the nazis, even less so after having been disabled at the battlefront. He suspected that "Dr. Wendland" and his friends had more to do with soldiering or party affairs than with science, and his suspicion grew when he saw one of the "doctor's" companions burying a uniform cap and a nazi gold badge behind the chalet. Kreidl came to the conclusion that it was a group of SS officers who had gone to ground at Valepp; for who but frightened nazis would now need to hide? One day Kreidl went down to Schliersee to collect the weekly food rations. On the road at Neuhaus he met a jeep with a sergeant and two privates of the US 101st Airborne Division in it. With many gestures to assist his mountain dialect, the dairyman managed to explain that some SS men were hiding at Misery Meadow. The sergeant made a note and told him not to worry; they would be picked up soon. He reported the information to his company commander who passed it on to a G-2 officer, Major Leo Schweitzer.

Four days later two American soldiers climbed up to Misery Meadow. They were Sergeant A. Kinghofer, who spoke German, and Corporal H. Hickson. They came out on the grassy plateau and saw a group of men near the house—the officers Gehlen had left behind to guard his buried containers. After a brief interrogation the Germans were told they would be collected a day or two later. Meanwhile Gehlen and his four companions went to the American army post at Fischhausen, which had been set up at the town hall. Gehlen had rehearsed this moment of meeting the first Americans in his mind; he had visualised a solemn exchange of introductions—Wessel had told him that the Americans were treating German generals with great respect. When he entered the US Army office he almost expected that a red carpet would be rolled out. His reception was, however, an anti-climax.

A young lieutenant named Bailin wrote down their names and ranks. Gehlen insisted that he should make a special note that they were officers of the General Staff and that Gehlen and Wessel were chiefs of *Fremde Heere Ost*. "OK, OK, don't get mad," the American remarked, not at all impressed. Then he ordered Gehlen and the rest to be locked up with the several hundred officer prisoners already in the overflowing Miesbach "cage".

Allied soldiers had learnt to be sceptical about the various identities which German prisoners claimed or, more commonly, denied. Most of the officers and men of the 307th CIC unit were easy-going Texans, still relatively green and quite uninformed about German politics and the military hierarchy. The prudent philosophy for the moment was: put those Jerries in first and sort them out later. Consequently, several days elapsed before Gehlen was interrogated again and eventually brought to Wörgl before the CIC unit commander, Captain John C. L. C. Schwarzwalder, a more experienced intelligence officer.

"I am a general and chief of the intelligence department of the High Command of the German Army," Gehlen told him stiffly. "I have information of the highest importance for your Supreme Commander and the American government, and I must be taken immediately to a senior commander, preferably to General Patch."

Schwarzwalder grinned at him and replied: "You *were* a general— you *were*, sir. And please don't tell me what I have to do." He ordered the escort to take Gehlen back to the cage, and the interview was over. A young sergeant, Victor de Guinzbourg, who was taking the notes, told his captain after Gehlen had been marched out that he had heard of the German general; he might really be of some importance. "OK," said the captain, "you deal with this guy and his men. If you think you have a lead on these nazis you are welcome to follow it up."

American Intelligence officers had their hands full handling the thousands of German officers who had been captured, or had surrendered, all over the fabled Alpine Redoubt which had become a mockery of Hitler's defeat. They had netted much bigger and more noteworthy fish than this little fellow who claimed to be so important. In the Seventh Army "cages" were Field-Marshal Wilhelm List, the conqueror of Greece, whom Hitler had sacked because he could not retake Stalingrad in 1943; Field-Marshal Wilhelm Ritter von Leeb, who nearly captured Leningrad; Field-Marshal Albert Kesselring, the ex-overlord of Italy, whom Hitler had made commander-in-chief West in place of Rundstedt three weeks before the surrender, and who had capitulated with his Army Group G, earmarked to defend the "Alpine Fortress".[4] Goering had been caught near Berchtesgaden, and among the nazi prisoners who abounded in the area were Robert Ley, the hard-drinking *Reichsfuhrer* of the German Labour Front, who was responsible for the deportation of millions of forced-labour workers from occupied Europe and who in December 1944 had tried to persuade Hitler to use poison gas, bringing to him a crack-pot inventor who claimed to have discovered a "Death Ray".[5] There were Julius Streicher, the Jew-baiter and editor of the pornographic *Der Sturmer*, and Ernst Kaltenbrunner, chief of the Gestapo, who had tried to disguise himself by shaving off his moustache. When Kaltenbrunner was caught, he had with him his mistress, Countess Gisela von Westrop, and several heavy suitcases. The CIC officers let the woman go, but, inspecting the luggage, found it to be stuffed with stolen jewellery, counterfeited pound and dollar banknotes, manufactured by concentration camp inmates, several revolvers with ammunition, and many packets of candy, chocolate, and liquor bonbons. Skorzeny, the intrepid commander of the "hunting units" and rescuer of Mussolini, had meekly surrendered with his adjutant, SS Hauptsturm-fuhrer Karl Radl, at a US military police post.

Little wonder, therefore, that dealing with Gehlen was left to a young CIC sergeant. Victor de Guinzbourg handled this assignment well; it put him on the road to a brilliant intelligence career in which he later became a lieutenant-colonel. He did not share his comm-anding officer's opinion that Gehlen was "just another nazi guy putting on an act". When he began the interrogations he thought there might be rather more to the pretensions of the little general. The sergeant wrote a comprehensive report, mentioning that the prisoner had told him of some important archives he had salvaged, and suggested that he should be interrogated at US Intelligence headquarters. Gehlen had not, of course, disclosed any details, neither did he tell the American of the hiding place at Misery Meadow. So Guinzbourg, having spotted Gehlen, was soon deprived of him. The Miesbach CIC post was only a transit cage; by virtue of the interest shown in him, Gehlen was advanced in higher CIC eyes from a state of minor significance to one of important mystery. He was transferred to the CIC "special cage" at Augsburg.

There his small figure was lost in a motley mass of Wehrmacht field commanders, Luftwaffe fliers, SS leaders and Gestapo bosses who were being processed with slow attention by the interrogators. Since everybody in the place was assumed to be of a certain prominence, it did Gehlen no good to insist that he was too. On the contrary, the interrogators' deepest interest and suspicions were directed—often quite rightly—at those who alleged they had no importance at all. As Gehlen lapsed into near-despair under the walls of Austria's most spectacular castle, he presented the strange paradox of a spy-master thirsting for recognition by his captors.

He had lost all contact with Wessel, and the FHO officers he had left billeted around the valley had been rounded up by the Ameri-cans. Where they had been taken he had no idea. It was during this period that Gehlen developed his contempt for the CIC's handling of captured intelligence officers; it did not lessen in later years when, under the aegis of the CIA, he operated in competition with G-2 and CIC groups in Germany.

Gehlen's eventual extraction from the "cage" was mainly due to Guinzbourg's report, which had been forwarded to the G-2 head-quarters of the Seventh Army at Augsburg. There, at last, some-body's eyes opened wider on seeing Gehlen's name. Colonel William W. Quinn,[6] the G-2 chief, knew it well. He had contributed to the alarming SHAEF analysis on the Alpine Redoubt. Allen Dulles, when in charge of the OSS European office at Berne, travelled several times from Switzerland in 1944 to meet Quinn in France and brief him on Hitler's plan for the mountain fortress. It was at these meetings that Dulles also told Quinn of the Werewolves and the R-Net preparations, of which OSS knew more than Gehlen had ever imagined. [7]

Colonel Quinn had ordered that Gehlen should be brought to Augsburg and he personally conducted the first real interrogation since his surrender. Quinn was also the first American to whom Gehlen indicated the magnitude of his scheme and whom he told about his staff, by then dispersed at several camps, and of his precious archives, safely hidden.

A number of senior German intelligence officers and SS men from Schellenberg's *Militaramt* were being held at Augsburg; Gehlen saw Obersturmbannfuhrer Skorzeny being led handcuffed through a corridor and he met a few old friends, including Wilfried Strik-Strikfeldt, the Vlassov Army "adviser". His confidence returned when Colonel Quinn told him that most of the FHO officers had been traced and were being brought in from various "cages". He asked Quinn to arrange for him a meeting with General Eisenhower, but was told that this was not possible. However, Quinn handed him over to the chief of G-2 Intelligence at General Omar Bradley's 12th Army Group headquarters. It was a sound piece of protective military reasoning. If Gehlen turned out to be a fake and dished up a cock-and-bull story to the supreme commander, Quinn would have been subjected to Ike's irritation; if Gehlen was sound, Bradley's intelligence chief would present him to Eisenhower, who would soon learn who had initially discouvered the German.

Gehlen Meets His Match

The Army Group's G-2 chief was Major-General Edwin Luther Sibert, then forty-four, an intelligence professional who was to become the decisive catalyst in Gehlen's dealings with the Americans. Although a product of West Point and a former professor at the US War Academy, he did not share the disdain of other senior officers for the OSS. He knew Allen Dulles well. During the summer of 1944 they had worked together on a grand scheme. Dulles had given up hope that Hitler would be overthrown by a German plot at the top. (The events of July 20 had proved him right.) Instead, he pursued with Sibert the idea of turning German front commanders against the Fuhrer and talking them into local truce agreements or capitulation. They also hoped to form a committee of captured German generals on the pattern of that set up by the Russians under Field-Marshal von Paulus, the converted defender of Stalingrad. General Marshall and Eisenhower favoured the idea, but it was overtaken by events. Dulles later demonstrated the efficacy of secret negotiations with German front commanders by his "Operation Sunrise", which led to the German surrender in Italy in April 1945. [8]

Thus Gehlen found himself at 12th Army headquarters at Wiesbaden, talking at last the same language with professional intelligence officers. There is no official record of their conversations, but General Sibert's interest in his fellow-professional was evident; it was based not least on Gehlen's knowledge and experience of unorthodox warfare against the Russians. Sibert asked him to write a précis of his war activities with FHO, and Gehlen's account ran to 129 closely typed pages. Thereafter Sibert assigned Major Philip Russell and German-speaking Captain John Halsted to Gehlen, with whom they had daily conferences. The German developed his great scheme of a secret organisation engaged on intelligence work against the Soviet Union under American aegis but which he would direct. He described the FHO archives to them, but at first did not reveal where he had buried them.

The Americans, too, had something to keep back. They did not tell Gehlen that at that very moment, in virtually identical talks, they were discussing a similar proposition with none other than Colonel Hermann Baun, the former chief of *Frontaufklärungskommando Ost*, WALLI I. Baun was trying to sell them the scheme which he had first devised with Gehlen and Wessel at their conspiratorial meeting at Bad Elster. And Baun had made a better impression on the Americans than had Gehlen.

Baun had returned from the Bad Elster meeting in April to his WALLI office in Baden. When the French Army entered the country, he went into hiding; later he crossed into the American zone of Occupation and surrendered at Rattenberg in Bavaria. He had been luckier in captivity than Gehlen. He had taken with him an attaché case stuffed with secret papers of his command and before long he was taken to General Sibert. He gave Sibert a complete description of the WALLI set-up, of his groups and radio transmitters left behind in eastern Germany, Poland and Russia, and he held nothing back. He offered to recruit a team of his former Abwehr comrades—many of whom Sibert was already holding—and start espionage operations against the Soviet Union without delay. He did not ask that a separate organisation should be set up; he was quite willing to work under the G-2 and CIC officers of Sibert's department. From start to finish, it seems, Baun never mentioned his Bad Elster pact with Gehlen. This does not necessarily mean that he ratted on him. He did not know what had happened to the former FHO chief; for all he knew Gehlen might have been dead.

122

Sibert wisely kept his two would-be trading partners well separated, so neither knew what had become of the other. Baun was kept at the "Blue House", a requisitioned castle in the Taunus, a few miles from the Villa Pagenstecher where Gehlen was held. Things blew up, however, two or three weeks later, when Gehlen learned that Wessel had arrived at Wiesbaden and he asked to be allowed to see his former deputy. Wessel told him that Baun was "somewhere around", that he had seen him and that he was probably negotiating with Sibert. But Wessel could tell nothing more.

A race now ensued between the rival spy chiefs to gain the Americans' sponsorship, like a couple of advertising agents competing for a fat account. Gehlen decided to play his trump card. For though Baun could offer to Sibert the operational structure of such WALLI units as might have survived, Gehlen knew that what he did not have was files: Baun had lost them when he escaped from his last WALLI office in Saxony to Baden. Gehlen asked to see Sibert, sighed, and told him the secret of Misery Meadow.

A CIC search party was hurriedly detailed and sent to Valepp. For three days and nights cursing GI's dug up the rocky earth on the plateau, hauling out one heavy steel container after another. All were safely recovered and this time an American convoy took them north to Oberursel. It required a detachment of G-2 officers, clerks and photographers to help Gehlen and Wessel to sort out the material. A selection of the most important microfilm rolls was made, and prints were produced and shown to General Sibert. He had no doubt of the significance of the material, and he decided the matter must be reported to the Supreme Command.

Sibert went to see General Walter Bedell Smith, Eisenhower's chief of staff. By then SHAEF was already in a state of dissolution. Gehlen was taken to Smith and the outcome of their conference was that Gehlen should put his plan directly to General George V. Strong, chief of the US G-2 Military Intelligence department.

The Russians Search for Gehlen

General Sibert had good reasons of his own for dispatching Gehlen hurriedly to the United States. By July 1945 serious differences had arisen between the Western Allies and Stalin over the treatment of Poland, the scale of German reparations and the administration of the Occupation zones. American and British officers had been barred from the Soviet zone, although Soviet Intelligence missions travelled widely through the US, British and French zones searching for German war criminals with the assistance of their Western colleagues.

A dispute between Allied and Soviet representatives was shaping up at Flensburg, where a Joint Intelligence Commission was sitting at

Admiral Doenitz' former headquarters. The Russians were searching for Gehlen and his FHO staff; obviously they were eager to settle some old accounts. The head of the Soviet mission, Major-General Anatoli Evgenevich Trusov, one of the chiefs of GRU, confronted his American opposite number, General Lowell W. Rooks, almost daily with demands that he find Gehlen and other FHO officers, as well as their archives, and bring them to Flensburg.

Gehlen's office at Zossen had, of course, been occupied by the Soviet Army; its intelligence officers had gone through it with a fine tooth comb, but all they found were empty steel cabinets and piles of waste paper. At Flensburg, Trusov and his men grilled the two officers Gehlen had sent to Doenitz' headquarters in compliance with Hitler's order, and their files were carefully examined. But they contained only a few duplicated reports, maps, pay accounts and clippings from Russian wartime newspapers.

The two unfortunate officers, Major Scheibe and Major von Kalkreuth, convinced their interrogators they were telling the truth: they had no idea what had happened to Gehlen, Wessel and their FHO colleagues, whom they had last seen at Zossen. Neither did they know what had happened to the archives; most likely they had been destroyed; after all even Hitler had been burnt. General Trusov did not believe that they had been destroyed. And where, he wanted to know, were the Abwehr files? Those of RSHA's *Militaramt*, which under Schellenberg had handled espionage against the Soviet Union, were missing as well. Where was Gehlen, where was Schellenberg? [9]
It looked as though the Americans and the British were trying to prevent their Soviet allies from rooting out nazi war criminals, spies and subversives.

Pressed by the Russians, General Rooks got on to 12th Army HQ, asked Sibert whether he knew where the former FHO chiefs were, and requested him to send over any FHO and Abwehr officers he had in custody. Sibert gave an evasive answer. A few, he said, were at a POW camp. but their interrogations had not been completed. The Russians must wait; in any case, why should the Americans be so obliging when the Russians stubbornly refused to allow any of their prisoners—and they were holding such important ones as the deputy chiefs of Canaris' Abwehr, Lieutenant-Generals Franz von Bentivegni and Hans Piekenbrock—to be interrogated by Western Intelligence officers?

Sibert, with Bedell Smith's approval, decided not to give the GRU the chance to examine any of the FHO officers, much less get wind of Gehlen's exhumed hoard. Above all, Gehlen himself had to be quickly removed from Germany. He was told to pick three of his officers who could best assist him in putting all the necessary information before the American Intelligence chiefs; these three were to accompany him to Washington. Gehlen must have spent a few sleepless nights before he was given this good news. Sibert had told him of the furore in Flensburg and, for a while, Gehlen was not at all certain whether the Americans might not give in to Trusov's demand. If this had happened, not only would his great vision have been at an end, but his life would have been at stake. He chose Lieutenant-Colonel Heinz Herre, who had been head of FHO Group II and later liaison officer to the Vlassov Army; Major Albert Schoeller, the successor to Count von Rittberg as head of Group I, who had evaluated the reports of FHO's V-men in the Soviet Union; and Major Hans-Horst von Hiemenz, the expert on Soviet industry, armament production and supplies in Group II.

Top security was ordered for the transport of the four men, GRU spies had been busy around Oberursel for many weeks, and several were caught trying to penetrate the compound. Sibert knew that the Russians had planted informers among German civilian clerks and cleaners. Getting the quartet out unnoticed was a tricky problem. A group of German civilians—it was never suggested that Gehlen and his companions should travel in German uniforms—boarding an US Air Force aeroplane would have attracted unwelcome attention. Major Russell suggested to Sibert that they should go in American uniforms. Gehlen agreed, but characteristically demanded to be given a uniform "according to my rank". The quartermaster's store had nothing for a lieutenant-general in that small size; the best they could provide was a field service uniform, on to which a general's star and badges were sewn on. Gehlen donned it with visible pleasure. The others had to be satisfied with captain's insignia.

Thus attired, the four were driven to a USAF airfield in the middle of the night of August 22, 1945, and put aboard a transport aircraft. A few hours later they crossed the Atlantic.

X

The Deal With The Americans

When Gehlen and his three companions arrived in Washington they were taken to Fort Hunt, not far from the Pentagon on the Virginian side of the Potomac. Although this looked much like any other army camp, it was in fact a maximum-security establishment used by Army G-2 to house a handpicked collection of German, Italian and Japanese prisoners of war pending their interrogation in depth. Apart from the usual huts, Fort Hunt had several well-furnished brick villas, and Gehlen was put in one next to the commandant's house. An NCO "major domo" and white-jacketed orderlies took care of his new quarters. All were attached to the Counter-Intelligence Corps; the villa, like all other accommodation for the high-ranking prisoners, had been wired for sound.

Gehlen was given no hint that he was to be held under tight surveillance. His G-2 guardians encouraged him to believe that he was a free man. But they told him that for his own security and to keep his visit secret he must not leave the camp, or even the house, without escort. Interpreting this as deference, Gehlen appeared to be unaware that all his conversations were being recorded and monitored. Captain Eric Waldman became his chief guardian.

He was politely asked to take off and hand over the American general's uniform. A soberly cut business suit, a few shirts and some underwear were brought from one of the capital's best haberdashers, on F-Street. Standing in his pants on his first day in America, Gehlen had reached the goal he set himself at the start of his perilous journey from the bunker at Zossen. His metamorphosis had begun when he exchanged his Wehrmacht tunic with the embroidered eagle and swastika for the rough *Loden* coat of an alpine villager. It had continued through his masquerade in the olive-drab battledress of an enemy officer; now it was completed as he buttoned his slight figure into the dark grey off-the-peg jacket of an American businessman. The fit was not perfect, but the symbolism was. As he came downstairs, Gehlen was impatient to begin talking business. Washington was sticky with the humid summer heat, but the political climate

126

could not have been more favourable for his negotiations.

At Oberursel, during his talks with General Sibert and the other American officers, Gehlen had come to the conclusion that the great Anglo-American wartime coalition was all but dead. Its military pivot, General Eisenhower's Supreme Headquarters, had been disbanded. Ike had recommended that American and British Intelligence organisations dealing with problems in the Allied occupation of Germany should continue to operate under one head. But the British had turned him down: Field-Marshal Montgomery had chafed too long under Eisenhower's command, and Attlee's new Labour government would brook no hint of continued subordination to American influence. Major-General (later Field-Marshal Sir Gerald) Templer was put in charge of all intelligence matters in the British zone of Germany under Montgomery's deputy military governor, Lieutenant-General Sir Ronald Weeks.[1]

The American generals did not conceal their annoyance at the policies of Attlee and his foreign secretary, Ernest Bevin. General Bedell Smith's reaction was vehement, and it surprised his British friend Major-General Sir Kenneth Strong, the intelligence chief at SHAEF. On the day they parted in 1945 Smith said bluntly that in American eyes "Britain was through". The Soviet Union was "the country of the future" with which the United States would have to ally itself. Soon afterwards Smith went as US ambassador to Moscow—only to return two years later, deeply disillusioned about Stalin, to build up the Central Intelligence Agency.

Though friendship with Moscow was official policy while Gehlen was in Washington, he knew that many American generals, above all General George V. Strong, the chief of G-2 Army Intelligence, and Sibert, were very far from regarding the Soviet Union as a future ally. In fact, a vastly different vision was taking shape at the US Third Army headquarters at Bad Toelz, near where he had buried his FHO files in Misery Meadow. There General Patton was dreaming of rearming a couple of Waffen SS divisions to incorporate them into his US Third Army "and lead them against the Reds".

Patton had put this plan quite seriously to General Joseph T. McNarney, deputy US military governor in Germany, who had relayed Marshal Zhukov's complaint that the Third Army was too slow in disbanding and confining German units in its Bavarian sector. "What do you care what those goddam bolshies think?" said Patton. "We're going to have to fight them sooner or later. Why not now while our army is intact and we can kick the Red Army back into Russia? We can do it with my Germans ... they hate those red bastards."

McNarney, petrified, reported this to his political adviser, Robert

Murphy, who promptly asked Patton to come and see him. Patton was not in the least subdued. "He inquired with a gleam in his eye", Murphy later wrote, "whether there was any chance of going on to Moscow, which he said he could reach in thirty days, instead of waiting for the Russians to attack the United States."[2] The outcome of this and other indiscretions was that Eisenhower relieved Patton of his command on October 2, 1945. Two months later he was fatally injured in a car crash.

Gehlen, during his stay at Oberursel, had heard American officers talking about Patton's attitude. There too he met "Wild Bill' Donovan, the OSS chief, who was deeply disturbed by the expansion of Soviet domination. The German could sense that US Intelligence policies were going into the melting pot and that a showdown for control was looming in the secret councils of his hosts. He had not weathered the conspiratorial storms of Berlin for so long without learning to recognise the signs.

If after his arrival Gehlen felt any pangs of melancholy, his mood soon changed into exhilaration. In the whirl of conferences, discussions and meetings with American Intelligence chiefs he was back in his element. At the initial meeting he found himself opposite men whose names and high positions were well known to him—Fleet Admiral William D. Leahy, chief adviser on security to President Truman, General Strong and Major-General Alex H. Bolling of G-2, Major-General John T. Magruder, Loftus E. Becker, newly in charge of the Strategic Services Unit,[3] Sherman Kent, the brilliant Yale historian and head of the OSS Research and Analysis Branch, and, last but not least, Allen Dulles, who had just returned from Berlin and in his own words as "playing an active role in formulating the basis for the future CIA".[4]

Gehlen's arrival in Washington coincided, however, with a grave crisis which had broken out over the control of future American Intelligence activities. To understand the heavily loaded atmosphere in which the discussions with Gehlen were conducted, I must briefly describe the main events which led to the bitter quarrels among the chiefs of the intelligence departments. For almost two decades, ever since President Coolidge's secretary of state, Henry Stimson, disbanded the intelligence system built up during the First World War—closing the cryptographic office with the classic pronouncement, "Gentlemen don't read other people's mail" the United States had had no centralised, institutionalised intelligence service. There was only the G-2 Army Intelligence, the navy's A-2 Intelligence, and a small "research bureau" within the State Department.

In 1941 the shock of Pearl Harbour drove home the vital need for active espionage. Among the existing bodies there was neither

128

co-ordination nor useful cooperation. When President Roosevelt authorized in 1941 the creation of the Office of Strategic Services, the old departments were united only in one respect: their antagonism to the idea of making OSS the hub of American wartime intelligence.

Roosevelt had made Colonel (later General) "Wild Bill" Donovan head of OSS. The son of a railway worker of Irish Catholic stock, Donovan came from a humble home in Buffalo and was one of nine children. He had worked his way through high school and law college, and while in legal practice had joined the National Guard, in which he rose to the rank of captain. In 1916 he fought Pancho Villa's Mexican raiders along the Texas border, acquiring there the nickname which stuck to him all his life. He served in France as a combat officer in the First World War and during the Anglo-American intervention of 1919-20 he was US liaison officer to the "White Army" of General Koltchak in Siberia. Returning to law, he became assistant attorney general in President Coolidge's administration, remaining in close touch with the FBI and intelligence circles.

After Hitler's rise to power Roosevelt and his secretary of state, Cordell Hull, employed Donovan as an unofficial ambassador-at-large. He travelled widely in Europe, meeting Hitler and Mussolini. Early in 1940 Roosevelt asked Donovan to report on the determination and ability of the European countries, including Britain, to resist the nazis. He was briefed in London by the chief of the Secret Intelligence Service, Major-General Sir Stewart Menzies, and conducted by British Intelligence officers on a tour of France, Belgium, the Netherlands, Yugoslavia and the Balkans. After he set up OSS Donovan admitted that anything he had put into practice he had learnt from the British. He incorporated many ideas drawn from the British Special Operations Executive, and at first he relied on London for sophisticated intelligence.

OSS went through a lot of teething troubles, including much derision from West Point diehards in G-2 who claimed its initials stood for "Oh So Stupid" and "Oh So Slow". (As the organisation absorbed more college bluebloods and took on a tinge of glamour these ribald designations gave way, somewhat in envy, to "Oh So Social" and "Oh So Sexy".) It matured, however, into a formidable clandestine warfare arm, particularly after its fusion with SOE at Eisenhower's headquarters.

Emulating his British counterparts, Donovan enrolled many brilliant people from the universities, industry, the legal profession and journalism. Among them were Allen Dulles, who had wide espionage experience from 1914-18; David Bruce (who was to be US ambassador in London from 1961-68); the historian Arthur Schlesinger, afterwards one of President Kennedy's chief aides; Richard Helms, the present director of CIA; Arthur Goldberg, later a Supreme Court judge and US representative at the United Nations; Loftus Becker, one of the chief prosecutors at the Nuremberg war crimes trials in 1946, and many other first-class brains. The prestige resulting from this calibre of personnel and the exploits OSS achieved during the war raised the hackles of the army and navy intelligence chiefs; in 1945 they could see their whole power base sliding from under their feet. Never the less, they were unable to prevent the movement of intelligence supremacy from the military to the intellectuals. It was a transition that was to pave the way for the rise of the modern politico-military general in America.

Roosevelt's Great Scheme Misfires

The animosity of the generals and admirals towards OSS did not impede Roosevelt in his resolve to pursue the idea of a centralised intelligence organ which would combine all positive espionage in peacetime. Its basis—inevitably, as it had seemed to Donovan—would be OSS. On October 31, 1944, the President called him to the White House and asked him to prepare a draft for the structure of such an agency. Eighteen days later Donovan submitted his memorandum. In his covering letter he wrote: "When the enemies in Europe and the Far East are defeated the need will be equally pressing for information that will aid us in solving the problems of peace." He added that in the work of the proposed agency priority would have to be given to watching the activities of the Soviet Union and communist elements throughout the world.

Donovan assured the President that it was not his intention to arrogate to the new agency the responsibility for military intelligence. "In this plan coordination and centralisation are placed at the policy level", he wrote, "but operational intelligence would remain within the existing agencies concerned. The creation of a central authority thus would not conflict with, or limit, necessary intelligence functions within the Army, the Navy, the Department of State or other agencies."[5]

With the war in Europe still in progress and the prospect of a prolonged campaign against the Japanese by no means ruled out, Donovan was careful not to appear to be provoking dissension at command level. But, with his long experience of governmental in-fighting, he was also hedging his bets. This was not entirely his own idea. I can disclose here that the memorandum was composed with active assistance from Allen Dulles. In order to placate the military leaders, Dulles advised Donovan to include the suggestion that in time of war the centralised agency would automatically be put under the control of the joint chiefs of staff. On the other hand, they wanted a speedy decision from Roosevelt: "There are common-sense reasons why you may desire to lay the keel of the ship at once .... We have now (in OSS) the trained and specialised person-nel needed for such a task, and this talent should not be dispersed," Donovan urged.

It was the President, greatly impressed, who wanted to go further. He asked Donovan for an additional draft which would combine several other existing agencies under the canopy of the new authority. These included the FBI, Army G-2, the Navy's ONI, the Internal Revenue agency, the Secret Service, and the Federal Communications Commission, incorporating the coding and cypher-ing system. Indeed, Roosevelt asked that the draft should be prepared in the form of a Presidential Order to this effect.[6]

The alacrity with which Roosevelt adopted the Donovan-Dulles plan, knowing full well that it envisaged the Soviet Union and its offshoots as priority targets for positive intelligence and counter-espionage operations, is not easy to match to the often-heard assertions that the President was "soft on communism". However, there was soon a sensational move to torpedo the scheme.

On February 9, 1945, two months after Donovan submitted his supplementary draft, the Washington *Times-Herald,* the Chicago *Tribune* and the New York *Daily News* splashed across their front pages beneath headlines five inches high the disclosure: DONOVAN PROPOSES SUPER-SPY SYSTEM FOR POST-WAR NEW DEAL. It was the most complete leak of Donovan's memorandum, the ad-ditional outline and the intended Order.

The article was written by Walter Trohan and simultaneously syndicated in the three newspapers, all of which had been hostile to Roosevelt since New Deal days, Colonel Robert McCormick's *Tri-bune* almost rabidly so. Trohan reported the plan thus: "Creation of an all-powerful intelligence service to spy on the post-war world and to pry into the life of citizens at home is under serious consideration by the New Dealers." There was no lack of partisan sizzle: "The director of the super-spy unit would have tremendous power ... it would be possible for him to determine American foreign policy by weeding out, withholding or coloring information .... The unit would operate under an independent budget and presumably have secret funds for spy work along the lines of bribing and luxury living described in the novels of E. Phillips Oppenheim." Trohan demanded "prompt congressional denunciation of the adoption of Gestapo, nazi secret police, and OGPU Russian secret police methods in the United States ..."

131

How did this extraordinarily detailed and documented leak occur? Its origin has to be attributed to the President himself. Donovan had asked Roosevelt, and received his assurance, that his memorandum and letters should be treated with the utmost secrecy. But FDR, always lacking in perception about security and ambiguous about promises, had shown the file to the joint chiefs of staff. A photostat was made for them in a limited number of copies marked Top Secret. Without the President's knowledge, this was then circulated to the heads of all intelligence departments and agencies, to the State Department and to J. Edgar Hoover of the FBI.

Donovan tried, with the help of his OSS friend Colonel Otto C. Doering, to discover where and how the leakage to the press had happened. Though maximum opposition to the scheme might have been expected in the army and navy departments, Doering was able to report that the leak had occurred in neither. Trohan kept his mouth shut and the source was never identified, or at least never publicly disclosed.

But Donovan now faced a hostile phalanx stretching from the State Department through the Pentagon to the FBI. He knew that not only had his plan aborted, but OSS was finished as well. He went to France, then Germany, where he heard a month later of the death on April 12 of the President in whose personal service he had carried out so many strange missions. Vice-President Harry S. Truman, who had taken over the reins of the nation, did not forget that Roosevelt had denied him the very confidence he had reposed in Donovan. Truman had never been shown top-secret OSS information, nor had he seen the central intelligence plan. On entering the White House he set about rectifying that irritant situation.

The Corpse Is Picked

Shortly after Gehlen's arrival in Washington the new President, without even consulting Donovan, issued his Order terminating the Office of Strategic Services. It was dated September 20, 1945; the shutdown was "as of October 1st". Truman's accompanying letter to Donovan was almost as curt as this notice to quit: "I want to express my thanks for the capable leadership you have brought to the wartime activities of OSS, which will not be needed in time of peace."

Like a flight of vultures the rivals descended on the still warm corpse. The research and analysis branch of OSS was devoured by the State Department. Its Secret Intelligence branch and Counterespionage X-2 branch were swallowed by the War Department and renamed the Strategic Services Unit (SSU). Many OSS outposts overseas were simply closed down and their personnel dispersed on the spot.

132

A fantastic race ensued to tear away one piece after another. Hoover made a determined attempt to get control of the X-2 branch, thus trying to add foreign counter-espionage to the FBI's activities in the United States. But the War Department beat him to it—after the entire X-2 staff threatened to resign in a body if Hoover took over.

The State Department cornered most of the invaluable archives which OSS had amassed during the war. In parts Donovan had built these up through cooperation with SIS and SOE in Britain and with the secret services of the French, Polish, Dutch, Belgian and Yugoslav "free" governments in London; but added to this collection were files assembled in Spain, Switzerland, Sweden, Portugal and other neutral arenas of espionage, and a stack of further high-grade material had been secured from Germany, Austria, Japan and elsewhere in the defeated Axis orbit.

Donovan returned from Europe to the Public Health Service Buildings in Washington, his secret wartime headquarters, to collect his personal papers and take leave of his closest colleagues. Attacked from almost every quarter, he went into retirement, a bitterly disappointed man. Allen Dulles, the only other person who could have saved the remnants of the once proud OSS and shaped them into the new central agency, also withdrew and returned to his law work in New York.[7] For the moment the generals and admirals had regained their ascendancy in the troubled world of American Intelligence—and it was General Strong, the chief of G-2, who now had Gehlen. But the Washington merry-go-round had not yet quite stopped.

The Tug-of-War for Gehlen

Strong, for reasons abundantly evident from the foregoing, was determined to keep exclusive control of Gehlen and his project. At first he trod cautiously. For several weeks, in private talks at the Pentagon and in conferences to which he brought some of his chief G-2 assistants, he encouraged Gehlen to elaborate as fully as possible on his astonishing scheme.

Gehlen's reactions on entering that vast maze of military power, equipped with its own bank, department stores and even a jeweller's shop, confirmed him in the certainty that the United States would be willing to supply the money he needed to start his own secret service. One can imagine his thin, polite smile on being told the standard jokes about the Pentagon, including that of the Western Union boy who enters its concentric corridors to deliver a message and is a full colonel by the time he finds his way out.

In his involuntary seclusion at the Fort Hunt villa, Gehlen had been able to piece together, largely from the newspapers, some idea of the service politics which had reached flashpoint with the Donovan-Dulles exposé. He filled in a good deal more from his discussions with Strong and the G-2 aides. Gehlen was far too experienced in the intrigues of General Staff rivalry not to comprehend the difficulties which all this posed to a quick acceptance of his own proposition. He therefore prepared himself for the likelihood of being kept in America for some time. His hunch proved right.

Before long it became clear to Gehlen—and to a reluctant Strong—that their conferences were not really equipped to estimate the potential of the FHO personnel and files. G-2 had acquired a weapon which it did not know how to work, yet Gehlen was too valuable a bargaining lever to hand over to one of the other departments. Strong decided that the only way to break the impasse in his own favour was to make an alliance with some of the ex-OSS leaders: they knew much more about Gehlen and FHO than he did.

Thus a group was formed to conduct detailed discussions with Gehlen and to examine the material he had handed over. Presiding over it was Rear-Admiral Samuel Frankel (then a captain in the Office of Naval Intelligence). Polish-born, he had specialised in intelligence coverage of the Soviet Union during the war; he and Gehlen found much common ground. Other members were Major-General Magruder, formerly of the OSS, Colonel William Lovell, ex-military attaché in Berlin, and Lieutenant-Colonel John Maury of the Marine Corps, who had been US naval attaché at Murmansk during the war. Allen Dulles was never far away.

They treated Gehlen with great courtesy, wooing him like a wayward lass who can bring a large dowry to offset the blemishes of her past. They accepted his assurances that he had never been a nazi. Some in Washington believed that his personal brand of subtle opposition to Hitler had been more sensible than the idealism of the July 20 conspirators. Many of Gehlen's friends, like Roenne and von Rittberg, who had made the nobler gesture were dead, whereas he had remained alive with his resources intact for a second round against totalitarianism. And so Gehlen bargained his way into the grey dawn of Cold War espionage, conceding or compromising on some points, using pressures near to blackmail to gain others. It says much for his shrewdness, self-assurance and persistence that he was able to take on single-handed such an array of top-ranking American experts.

Gehlen's Conditions

After several weeks of tough negotiating, Gehlen's plan was accepted in principle. He made four basic conditions:

1.   His organisation would not be regarded as part of the American Intelligence services but as an autonomous apparatus under his exclusive management. Liaison with American Intelligence would be maintained by US officers whose selection Gehlen would approve.

2.   The Gehlen Organisation would be used solely to procure intelligence on the Soviet Union and satellite countries of the communist bloc.

3.   On the establishment of a German government, the organisation would be transferred to it and all previous agreements and arrangements cancelled, subject to discussions between the new sovereign authority and the United States.

4.   Nothing detrimental or contrary to German interests must be required or expected from the organisation, nor must it be called upon for security activities against Germans in West Germany.

These were tough and even impertinent terms, coming from a man who was virtually a prisoner of war, and whom the Russians might even consider a war criminal ripe for trial under the terms of the Potsdam agreement. Yet, so powerful was the lure of Gehlen's secret knowledge and expertise that the Washington advisers almost fell over each other to settle for all of them. The confident little German, after his first few weeks in the land of super-salesmen, had closed the deal successfully. In the after-glow of a mutually satisfactory transaction, they got down to crossing the t's and dotting the i's. Gehlen cleared the legal and financial aspects with James Britt Donovan, the former general counsellor to OSS,[8] and Walter Reid Wolff, the Wall Street banker who had been an economic warfare consultant to American Intelligence.

Baun's Rival Secret Service

General Strong's strategy, after the successful conclusion of the deal with Gehlen, did not gain him the commanding heights he had hoped for in his campaign to bring the other American Intelligence departments under his hegemony. He not only failed to reach this objective but, as we shall see, wound up within a few months by losing Gehlen altogether. Never the less, G-2 still had a card up its sleeve. As a longstop, in case anything went wrong with the Gehlen negotiations, it had gone to the fantastic lengths of setting up a rival German Secret Service of its own. The hero of this Florentine acme of cunning was the missing and long silent Colonel Hermann Baun, late of WALLI I.

Strangely enough, while Gehlen was at Fort Hunt the Americans allowed him to receive letters from his former FHO officers, though undoubtedly his mail was carefully screened. Eventually he was able to reopen contact with his ex-deputy, Colonel Wessel, who was still at the US camp near Frankfurt. Wessel's letter, couched in guarded terms, reported that "the gentlemen at Oberursel"—a thinly veiled reference to General Sibert and his G-2 assistants—had been holding long conversations with Baun. Even more dismaying to Gehlen, they had installed him at the Blue House in the Taunus and were preparing him for actual operations.

What had happened was that when Gehlen disappeared from the Oberursel compound Baun assumed that his old chief would be kept in American captivity for a long period, on the principle that the higher the echelon you were passed on to, the longer and more thorough the interrogations became. Baun therefore pursued on his own the scheme they had concocted at Bad Elster. But he had been long enough at Oberursel to learn how to give his proposals the kind of touch that would make G-2 feel good. By October 1945 Baun had submitted to Sibert a detailed plan for mounting an espionage organisation against the Soviet Union. Baun himself would naturally be its head but—and here was the tasty bait—the organisation was envisaged as a section of G-2 in Germany.

Because of the upheavals in the intelligence set-up in Washington, there was a temporary break in communication between Sibert and his G-2 superiors about the Gehlen negotiations. At that juncture, it seemed to Sibert, there was a possibility that the negotiations might go wrong. He therefore decided to play ball with Baun.

The adaptable colonel was, of course, unable to provide material of such scope or magnitude as Gehlen's, nor did he know much about the actual espionage work of FHO. As the WALLI commander, he had been almost exclusively concerned with the infiltration and maintenance of wartime radio links behind the Soviet lines. However, Baun was one up on Gehlen in that he knew where some of his radio agents were to be found, in the East German areas now occupied by the Red Army. He was also able to gather up many of his WALLI officers who had worked with Gehlen at FHO and in the former Abwehr KO's and FAK's. He had, in fact, enough to go into business on his own account.

In March 1946 Sibert put Baun into the Blue House with a handful of these ex-officers. They set up two groups, one for "collection of information" and one for counter-espionage. They were still on the paper work when Wessel's tip-off reached Gehlen and alerted him to this private enterprise.

The ball was back in Gehlen's court. He had been taken up by Dulles and the other OSS veterans—but what if they did not re-emerge as the makers of intelligence policy? It would be wise for Gehlen too to hedge his bets. Refinements that would have made even Machiavelli blink now entered the strategy. Gehlen concluded that, all in all, he must stay on good terms with G-2 in Germany. His next move was to write to Wessel instructing him to tell Baun that if he had really got his spy-firm going Gehlen was prepared to work under him. There is little doubt, however, as to what Gehlen really intended. He knew he was much the better spy-master, and once in Baun's outfit he would soon be running it himself.

Sibert, prompted by General Strong, was anxious to bring a G-2 espionage section to operational readiness without delay, for in the spring of 1946 events in Europe were not waiting for Washington to unravel its feuds. The Red Army was in occupation of all eastern and south-eastern Europe with the exception of Greece, and even there a communist-inspired civil war was raging. The Soviet front line extended a hundred miles west of Berlin. Having taken over half the Continent, Stalin had riddled the Western zones of Germany with thousands of spies and agitators.

While America's leaders were talking of withdrawing US troops and demobilising US war potential Stalin had said at the Red Army's first victory parade: "We are watching the plans of the capitalist reactionaries in London and Washington who are hatching plans for a war . . . against our socialist motherland. Constant vigilance is needed to protect the strength of our armed forces who may be called upon to smash a new . . . imperialist aggression."

First Soviet Networks in Germany

Much of this "vigilance" was exercised by Nicolai Ivanovich Melnikov, an old hand at espionage. He had headed the notorious AMTORG ring in the United States, when the Russians did their spying there under the cover of a trade mission. Melnikov, now promoted to major-general, led the reparations detachments sent into the Western zones of Germany to extract Russia's share of machinery and other industrial equipment. She had already picked her own zone clean but under the Potsdam terms was also entitled to ten or fifteen per cent of available equipment in the other zones, according to category. The reparations parties were large, and not merely because of Moscow's hunger for machine tools: they also provided splendid cover for espionage against the Western Allies.

At the same time the MGB (later to become the KGB) under Lavrenti Beria began to organise "internal security" in the Soviet zone. A huge contingent of secret police arrived in East Berlin, ostensibly to deal with nazi war criminals but in reality to establish a widespread network of spy rings and agitation cells. Its chief was General Ivan Serov, who after Beria was executed in 1953 succeeded him as MGB boss. Serov's top assistants in Berlin were Vladimir Semyonov, then aged thirty-five, a Politburo expert on propaganda and subversion; and Colonel Igor Tulpanov of GRU. Tulpanov was accompanied by a posse of specialists, including armaments advisers and even atomic physicists.

These experts were attached to every "technical reparations commission" which travelled in the British, French or US zones. They were given facilities to inspect German factories, scientific institutes and laboratories, but many seemed more interested in Allied bases and airfields.

One of the main tasks of these Soviet delegations was to recruit informers and organise clandestine radio posts, whose transmitters were tuned to MGB headquarters at Karlshorst in Berlin. It was not until 1949 that the versatile "reparations" parties were barred by the Allies; up to then they had been able to go about their espionage almost unmolested.

Neither the Americans nor the British had any adequate organisation to take effective counter-espionage measures. The CIC had hardly any trained officers, and the US Constabulary under General McNarney was stretched to the limit in preserving law and order among German civilians and the millions of roaming displaced persons. It was more than two years before a proper counter-espionage force was functioning.

British counter-espionage in Germany did rather better. Its small team was run by experienced officers under Brigadier Dick Goldsmith White, who had gone from MI5 to SHAEF after several notable catches; he later became chief of SIS.

On a few occasions Soviet spies were caught in the act, as in the case of the MGB agents Shulkin and Sedov. In an earlier time, their superiors might have avoided embarrassment by the standard device of saying they had never heard of them. A brazen note from the Soviet military commandant, Major-General Kotikov, however, went to the other extreme. It accused the Allies of "trying to persuade two Soviet officers to defect and conduct espionage against the Soviet Union on behalf of the US and British Intelligence". This was indicative of the way relations were worsening between the two Germanies, and between the great powers which controlled them. The board was being set out for the grim espionage battle of the Cold War, and the Americans were ill-prepared to fight it.

With the pressures closing in, G-2 was the department in the hot seat in Germany. Sibert, impatiently watching the preparations at the Blue House, asked again: How soon would Baun be able to start up his agents?

But Gehlen had already recovered the initiative, never to lose it again. In Washington an overdue giant was being born, and it was on his side.

The Coming of CIA

President Truman soon had to suffer the consequences of disbanding OSS in so brusque a fashion. The chickens of chaos came home to roost at the White House. He was complaining that "conflicting intelligence reports flowing across my desk from the various departments left me confused and irritable, and monumentally uninformed".[9] He was learning what all politicians have to learn when they come to power, though some, like Hitler never did—and perished as a result. The decision-making processes of successful government and successful command rest upon high-quality information, i.e., information which is true, relevant, clear and in a quantity appropriate to the decision-maker's "need to know". Collated intelligence meets these requirements. "Raw" intelligence, on the other hand, is as useful as its name implies. Since America had no central intelligence authority, who was to collate it and present it to the President in analysed, comprehensible and significant form? Truman, rather late, saw the point. He announced that he wanted "as soon as possible somebody, some outfit, that can make sense out of all this stuff".

In January 1946 he was driven to issue an Order creating the Central Intelligence Group. This was a pale reflection of the concept proposed in the Donovan plan, but in many ways it was based upon it. The first step was to set up a National Intelligence Authority under Admiral Leahy, who was now seventy-one. Also on this body were the secretaries of state for the army and the navy. It was a messy temporary arrangement pending the passage of the Unification Act which would bring the bureaucracies of all three armed services under a single Department of Defence and provide centralised intelligence. Meanwhile, the members of the NIA were supposed to advise and report to the President, and at the same time they were to control the Central Intelligence Group, whose main task was to keep him informed with intelligence that "made sense". In this situation confusion was richly inherent; it was not the only jumble the Truman administration devised.

When James V. Forrestal moved into the Pentagon as the first secretary of defence, he said: "This office will probably be the biggest cemetery for dead cats in history." Worn out and broken by overwork, Forrestal was to fall victim to the endless problems and conflicts of the period; he committed suicide in May 1949. Among the cats eventually interred was the National Intelligence Authority; it was pretty well stillborn.

To head the Central Intelligence Group the President appointed one of his old poker cronies, Rear-Admiral Sidney W. Souers, who had at one time owned the Piggly Wiggly stores in Memphis and had later gone into the insurance business in St. Louis. Like many businessmen and bankers in the United States as well as in Britain, he was "drafted" into intelligence work during the war, looking after administrative matters and moving up to honorary rank as one of the deputy chiefs of Naval Intelligence. But command of the new CIG proved too much for him; after less than six months on its creaking bridge he gratefully returned to insurance. Because of the implacable hostility of the Army G-2 chiefs, Truman was compelled to find another CIG head outside the army, and he turned to an airman, Lieutenant-General Hoyt S. Vandenberg.*

During his stay in Washington, Gehlen had witnessed only the beginnings of the American Intelligence revolution. On July 1, 1946, accompanied by Captain Eric Waldman, Gehlen and his three officers embarked aboard an old Liberty ship in New York for Le Havre. After a restful passage they were flown from Le Havre to Frankfurt and put up at General Sibert's headquarters at Oberursel. One of Gehlen's first actions on his return was to seek out the inventive Colonel Baun to discover how far he had already managed to build up the worrying spectre of a rival German secret organisation with which the Americans could fight the Cold War.

* See page 148

OCCUPATION ZONES IN GERMANY AND AUSTRIA, AS FINALLY ADOPTED, JULY 1945

XI

Organisation Gehlen

On July 9, 1946, Gehlen and his officers were back at Oberursel. Having concluded his deal with the American Intelligence chiefs and received detailed briefing from his "guardian group", he expected no difficulties from Major-General Edwin L. Sibert who had in the meantime taken over the control of all intelligence and counter-espionage departments under General Lucius D. Clay, the US military governor.[1]

Although confident that he would be able to set up his organisation without delay, Gehlen realised that there were still a few hurdles to be overcome. At their first meeting Sibert told him of the arrangements with Colonel Baun and expressed his hope that Gehlen would cooperate closely with his old colleague. Baun was to stay at the "Blue House" with a number of his WALLI and Abwehr officers. US Signal Corps engineers had installed a radio receiving station there and Baun had established contact with some of his groups in Soviet territory. Gehlen and his assistants would be accommodated at Castle Kransberg and could get to work on the analysis and evaluation of the reports Baun was gathering.

This was not what Gehlen had expected, even though the arrangement was based on the traditional system. During the war, when he had taken over the FHO department, he was supposed to collate and analyse Abwehr reports and evaluate the rating of the information as to its reliability, the trustworthiness of its source, and the probability of the events reported. Then, in the context of the front-line reports, FHO was to digest the intelligence and disseminate it with suitable comments to OKW and the Ic sections of the army, air force and navy. In fact, however, Gehlen had arrogated to himself at FHO a much wider field of activity. His department had not only analysed reports from the WALLI reconnaissance groups, but recruited and sent out its own V-men, maintained direct contacts with the Vlassov Army, the Ukrainian units and with *Jagdkommandos*, turned round deserters, trained defectors, and conducted vast deception and radio-game operations.

142

In Washington Gehlen had suggested that his new organisation should follow the same pattern. He was deeply angered at Sibert's suggestions which, as he told his assistants, "demoted us to American clerks". But he restrained himself and told Sibert that he would discuss the plan with Baun; he was sure, he said, they would arrive at an amicable arrangement. His patience was soon rewarded. Baun had been producing reports for Sibert's deputy, Colonel James Deane, and had claimed success in restoring radio contact with several of his old V-men in the Ukraine, Poland and East Germany. He had also told the Americans that there was every hope of restoring the most important link, with his "Flamingo" group* in Moscow. Weeks had gone by, however, without this promise being fulfilled. Calls to "Flamingo" remained unanswered; all that Baun's receivers were able to pick up were sporadic signals from a few scattered units in the Ukraine and a fair number of reports from Soviet occupied Germany. Some, giving the movements and deployment of Soviet troops and describing the plight of the population under Soviet rule, were interesting; but they did not provoke much excitement among the American Intelligence officers.

From Gehlen's point of view this was good news: the Americans would become disillusioned with Baun and turn to him to provide the goods. Meanwhile he was biding his time. He told Sibert that he needed several weeks, or even months, to assemble his staff, to retrain it for the new tasks, and to organise future work. Many of his officers had been brought to Oberursel from neighbouring camps at Mannheim and Wiesbaden; he had made his final selection, assembling a staff of about fifty. Although most of them had acquired good knowledge of Soviet affairs and the Red Army during the war, few were suitable for the positive espionage tasks Gehlen envisaged. He needed men who had experience as secret agents in the field and instructors to train new recruits whom he could infiltrate into communist territory.

To find, enlist and train such men proved not to be easy. There were, of course, many former Abwehr, RSHA, SD and Gestapo men in special POW camps where they were being interrogated, sorted out, and some of them put on trial for war crimes. Gehlen found out that at the camps at Moosburg and Landshut in Bavaria the Americans were holding several thousand such "possibles"; he compiled a list, which Colonel Deane sent to the camp commanders, requesting the transfer of about forty or fifty to Oberursel. But the interrogators at these camps had been sent from Washington; they were collecting masses of political, military, industrial and scientific

* See page 74

143

information from the prisoners and they were unwilling to part with them.

Neither was General Sibert prepared to allocate the most useful men to Gehlen; the CIC had set up its own groups of V-men and potential spies recruited from among former German intelligencers. Baun had meekly accepted the handful of ex-Abwehr and WALLI officers Sibert had allowed him. Gehlen, of course, envisaged a staff on a much grander scale. A further difficulty was that he had solemnly promised in Washington not to employ SS and Gestapo men. In fact, among his first recruits there were several proscribed men, whom Gehlen enlisted under aliases and with false personal documents. He could always plead that he knew nothing about their true past.

Thus it happened that among the early arrivals at Castle Kransberg were SS Obersturmfuhrers Franz Goring and Hans Sommer, and SS Sturmfuhrer Herbert Steinborn. None was registered by Gehlen under his real name. Goring, then thirty-eight, had been a butcher's assistant in 1930, and had advanced to become a section head at Schellenberg's *Militaramt* by 1942. He arrived at Gehlen's office as a humble ex-infantry sergeant under the alias of Wilhelm Tobias, vetted and released by the Americans. During his long service under Gehlen he was to rise to become head of the Hamburg office, using at least four other aliases.[2] Sommer served during the war at the RSHA Paris office and got into trouble even with his own Gestapo superiors when in October 1941 he organised the firing of seven Jewish synagogues.[3] He later became chief of Gehlen's office in Kiel. Steinborn had been a Hitler Youth leader before the war and then an officer in the SS *Leibstandarte Adolf Hitler*, the Fuhrer's bodyguard. He became one of Gehlen's most astute V-men leaders, and we shall meet him again in these pages.

Generals Serve Under Gehlen

Gehlen could risk employing these, and later many more, SS and Gestapo men because he counter-balanced them with army officers of high rank and with glittering names which greatly impressed the Americans. There were Lieutenant-General Friedrich Wilhelm von Mellethin, ex-chief of staff of the 4th Panzer Army;[4] Major-General Nettke, who had commanded a division in Poland and Russia; Major-General Rudolf Kleinkamp, ex-chief of the OKW personnel office; Lieutenant-Colonel Heinz Guderian, the son of the famous Panzer general, Colonel von Kretschmer, former military attaché in Tokyo, who had helped to unmask the Soviet master spy Sorge; Colonel (or rather SS Standartenfuhrer) Willi Krichbaum, who had been liaison officer at RSHA to Admiral Canaris; Colonel Kurt von Rohrscheidt, an Abwehr chief and liaison officer to Ribbentrop; Colonel Joachim Rohleder, former chief of Abwehr III/F counter-espionage; Colonel Oscar Reile, the amiable head of the Paris Abwehr at the Lutetia Hotel, who had caught many British SOE agents; and Lieutenant-Colonel Hermann Giskes, who held a similar post in the Netherlands and played the famous "Nordpol" radio game, which netted him fifty-seven Dutch agents sent from Britain, all of whom the Gestapo eventually put to death at the Mauthausen concentration camp.

The generals and colonels provided splendid window-dressing, but in charge of the groups, which Gehlen organised at Oberursel on the FHO pattern, he put some of his own officers: Colonel Heinz Herre became the "chief evaluator", Colonel Dr. Nauck presided over investigations of Soviet economic problems, Captain Blossfeld set up an interrogation section—though at first there was no one to interrogate. A small team of instructors was assembled and Gehlen appointed Colonel Reile as their chief.[5] Courses were arranged, and Gehlen himself gave a series of lectures. But they were still working in a vacuum; months of planning and preparations went by without any effective results.

Poor Baun, whenever he met members of Gehlen's exalted staff he instinctively clicked his heels and stood to attention. Yet, in fact, he was doing better than they. His mythical "Flamingo" team in Moscow remained silent, but after weeks of frantic knob-twirling he was, at last, receiving regular signals from some of the Ukrainian and Polish bands, which were up in arms against the Soviet Army and their communist rulers. In Byelorussia and the Ukraine draconian measures had been imposed on Stalin's order against "counter-revolutionary bandits" and anyone suspected of having collaborated with the German invaders during the war.

The remnants of General Vlassov's "Liberation Army", after last-ditch fighting on the Oder, were moved in March 1945 to a line between Prague and Linz in Austria. On his last visit to Gehlen's office at Zossen, Vlassov's "special adviser", Captain Strik-Strikfeldt, had been told by Gehlen that the Vlassov units should take to the Bavarian "redoubt" and then surrender to the Americans; if they were overrun by the Soviet Army they would get short shrift. Most of Vlassov's generals gratefully followed this advice and subsequently found themselves in American POW camps in Bavaria. Vlassor himself, however, bravely or foolishly, remained with some of his units on Czechoslovak territory and was eventually caught by the Russians, probably betrayed by one of his own men. His generals were taken from Bavaria to the American VIP "cage" at Mannheim; for a while they shared captivity with German warlords such as Blomberg, List, Leeb, Weichs and Guderian, and also with their own former supreme commander of the *Ostheer,* General Koestring.

But their fate was sealed. At the Yalta Conference, Roosevelt and Churchill had given Stalin an undertaking whereby any of Hitler's "fascist traitors" found in Allied-occupied Germany after victory would be handed over to the Soviet Army. At the end of April all the Vlassov generals were taken from Mannheim and, with many of their officers and men who had been held in Bavaria, sent under American guard to the Russian lines. On August 12, 1945, Moscow Radio announced that the military tribunal of the Supreme Court of the USSR had sentenced Vlassov, Malyshkin, Zhilenkov, Trukhin and seven other generals to death "for treason, espionage and terrorist activities against the USSR as agents of the German espionage service", and that the sentences had been carried out. Many other Vlassov officers and men shared their fate, while tens of thousands were sent to penal camps "for rehabilitation".

Baun's White Army

Inside the Soviet Union and in Poland, however, large scattered groups of the "Whites" had remained and were putting up a desperate fight. In south-west Ukraine and eastern Poland bands of the nationalist UPA many still with their German SS officers, harassed the Soviet Army, the Polish militia of the communist-dominated Warsaw government and the local authorities set up in the liberated territories. At various times between November 1945 and the spring of 1947 these "counter-revolutionary bandits" were in effective control of many villages and rural districts. Trained in guerilla warfare by the Germans, they ambushed Soviet road convoys, used hit-and-run tactics, and carried out innumerable sabotage actions. Indeed, some of the Ukrainian insurgents held out in the forests of the Carpathian mountains until 1952.

The Soviet authorities also encountered trouble in the former Baltic states; after four years of nazi occupation many German soldiers, particularly of the Curland Army which had been cut off during the winter of 1944, had remained there. Together with Latvian and Estonian patriots they now turned upon the "red liberators". The Russians used ruthless methods to suppress the rebels, resorting to wholesale deportations of the indigenous population. In Moscow's eyes the insurgents were traitors, who had been armed by the nazis to fight against their own country. Today this attitude might appear cruel, especially when taken with the atrocities the Soviet police are known to have committed against often innocent people. Yet it must be remembered that French Resistance members treated nazi collaborators hardly more gently, and that even the British executed traitors after the war for, perhaps, lesser

146

crimes, such as broadcasting anti-British propaganda from Berlin.

Although the Soviet government announced that by the spring of 1947 "all counter-revolutionary fascist bands under German command had been annihilated", in fact this was not so. For years the communists kept silent about the extent of the fighting, which in many areas amounted to a minor civil war. It was not until 1959 that a Polish military writer published some staggering details about the widespread sabotage carried out by anti-communist bands and the heavy casualties suffered on both sides.[6] The Polish communist authorities were more successful in liquidating the insurgents within their smaller territories. Many of them were former members of the *Armja Krajowa*, who had fought bravely in the resistance to the nazis, and now turned against the communists. Some of these Polish units fought side by side with the Ukrainians in the eastern areas by then incorporated into the Soviet Union. When, in the end, they were rounded up, Soviet military courts, for political reasons, treated the Poles much more leniently than their own nationals. Sentences handed out to one of the Polish rebel commanders, General Okulicki, and sixteen of his officers ranged from ten years to six months in prison.

As long as the insurrections continued Colonel Baun at Oberursel was able to establish fairly regular radio links with his "White Armies" which were maintained for several months. In the Ukraine and, particularly, in the Baltic countries, several of his WALLI men had remained with these guerilla units and had kept their transmitters. At Oberursel US Signal Corps engineers had adjusted American receivers by tuning them to the old Afu sets of Baun's *Frontaufklärung*. Baun was thus able to claim that he had succeeded in restoring communication with men inside the Soviet Union; but his reports had hardly any intelligence value besides affording some satisfaction over the troubles the communists had to cope with. Gehlen reported to Sibert that there was little to analyse or evaluate from the material Baun supplied.

The Americans were growing impatient and Baun had to admit that he had raised his hopes too high. Gehlen used this to persuade Colonel Deane that one of his own officers, Lieutenant-Colonel Wilhelm Dienser, should be attached to Baun as his "chief of staff". Meanwhile he sent confidential reports to his "guardians" in Washington, suggesting that he should start dispatching agents into the Soviet territory and engage in both *Tiefenforschung* (deep penetration) and *Nahforschung* (infiltration of agents into the Soviet sector of East Berlin and the Soviet occupied zone of East Germany). Slowly but surely, Gehlen was taking over Baun's original assignment of intelligence collection.

These reports arrived when the reorganisation of the American Intelligence system had reached a decisive stage after a lengthy transition period. Rear-Admiral Souers had thrown in the towel and returned to his more congenial job as chairman of insurance companies in St. Louis. He was replaced as head of the Central Intelligence Group by Lieutenant-General Hoyt S. Vandenberg, who had commanded the Ninth US Air Force in England and North Africa during the war. His first decision was to create a research branch as the basis for a more active pursuit of positive espionage activities than the CIG had planned hitherto. Where the necessary material and information were to come from, however, nobody knew. The State Department, as will be remembered, had carried off the rare booty of the OSS Research and Analysis branch; nor was General Strong of the Army G-2 department going to turn anything over to an outfit which might be here today and gone tomorrow. Indeed, Strong was determined that his G-2 subsidiary under Sibert in Germany should continue as a parallel organisation to anything Vandenberg's CIG might try to set up there.

Nevertheless, Vandenberg went ahead. As Lyman B. Kirkpatrick, later inspector general of CIA, put it, "he was not hampered by having an uncle, Senator Arthur Vandenberg, as the influential chairman of the Senate foreign relations committee."[7] When his assistants submitted a draft for the research branch which proposed a staff of eighty, he sent them away and told them to come back with a plan for a personnel of eight hundred. During these erratic developments in Washington, Gehlen found himself between two stools; on one hand he was under the control of Sibert, who represented the Army G-2, on the other hand he was still responsible to his "guardians", who were supposed to take directives from Vandenberg's CIG.

At his juncture Captain Eric Waldman was given the task of examining the progress, or otherwise, of the activities of both Gehlen's and Baun's groups. A peacetime lecturer on military science, he was better qualified than some of his superiors.[8] Waldman conferred with Sibert and Deane and the outcome was that Gehlen was told that the two groups would be combined under his sole control; this was the creation of "Organisation Gehlen". Gehlen had achieved his aim and he magnanimously accepted the deeply offended Baun as his deputy. Their collaboration lasted for less than two years; Baun was slowly eased out from a succession of posts Gehlen allocated to him.

British and French Competition

One reason why the Americans decided to make a clean sweep and

US army camp at Oberursel near Frankfurt where Gehlen began to work for the
Americans

Castle Kransberg, where General Sibert installed Colonel Baun (*inset*)
in competion with Gehlen.

SS Brigadeführer Franz Six, head of RSHA research group; he was to be Himmler's representative after the invasion of Britain.

Colonel Oscar Reile, head of the Abwehr counter-espionage in Paris; he caught many British SOE agents and French Resistance members.

SS Obersturmführer Franz Goring served at Himmler's RSHA, and after 1946 for the Gehlen "Org" as "Wilhelm Tobias".

Lt.-Colonel Hermann Giskes, wartime chief of the Abwehr in Holland, who caught 50 British and Dutch agents.

combine the two groups was that they had become worried about attempts by British and French Intelligence in Germany to set up similar organisations. As early as the autumn of 1945, officers of MI9 and MI14 of the British War Office had assembled some fifty former Abwehr and OKW officers at a "hush-hush" camp in Ostend, administered by Field-Marshal Montgomery's 21st Army HQ. British interrogators were looking for German Ic officers who had served at army headquarters on the Russian front or in the eastern section of the OKW and, of course, for ex-Abwehr and FHO officers. They had already thoroughly interrogated the handful of officers they had found at Flensburg, including the two Gehlen had sent there before embarking on his convoy to Bavaria.

Beside the many generals who had commanded troops in Russia, the British had made a good catch in Lieutenant-Colonel Adolf Wicht, one of Gehlen's former assistants, who from 1943 until the end of the war had headed the FHO group which evaluated the depositions of Soviet prisoners of war. Early in 1947, Wicht, with a few other Abwehr and FHO officers, was taken to the British Intelligence headquarters at Munster. He had salvaged some of his personal files and hidden them near Brunswick. Soon he was composing for the British a series of reports about his wartime experience. However, any hopes they had had that he might assist them with post-war problems of espionage against the Soviet Union were soon dispelled when SIS officers interrogated him and read his effusions. In the judgement of SIS, Wicht could contribute little to any plans the military intelligence officers might have nursed of making him into their own miniature Gehlen. Maybe it was the traditional rivalry between SIS and the War Office that cut short Wicht's career with the British. He was released early in 1947 and was later received with open arms by Gehlen. Nevertheless, the German section of the Foreign Office, and the various branches of Military Intelligence established in the British zone of Occupation at Munster and Bad Oeynhausen continued to employ German ex-officers for several years. The British were particularly careful to have no truck with former Gestapo and SD men. They set up a Commission for Criminal Organisation, headed by Colonel Airey Neave, formerly in charge of "Room 900" of MI9,[9] which inter-rogated Abwehr, SD and Gestapo prisoners suspected of war crimes. Even so it was inevitable that a few black sheep should slip into the British flock. One of them was ex-SS Sturmbannfuhrer Fritz Schmidt, a former lawyer, born in 1908 at Bochum, who had been Gestapo chief at Kiel. In 1946 he was enlisted by the British under the alias of "Friedrich Schuette", having produced fake credentials. Only much later it was found out that he had been involved in the executions of foreign forced-labour workers at the Friedrich Ott camp near Kiel in 1944. He was put behind bars, but released in 1948, and eventually enrolled by Gehlen.

Such local difficulties as the British experienced with some of their V-men in Germany were nothing compared with the real trouble which was then brewing at the Secret Intelligence Service headquarters in London, but which remained undetected by its chiefs for many more years to come. During the war SIS had strengthened its small Section IX concerned with the Soviet Union. This section had been set up more than twenty years before and subordinated to SIS general counter-espionage branch of Lieutenant-Colonel Felix Henry Cowgill. In the last three years of the war, the Soviet embassy in London had expanded into a complex organisation containing a large military mission under Major General Ivan Sklarov, with a naval department under Rear-Admiral Nicolai Kharlamov and an air force department under Colonel Morozovski, armament supply, technical and shipping departments, and a staff of more than two hundred. Since 1941, after Lord Beaverbrook (then minister of supply) and Averell Harriman had gone to Moscow to confer with Stalin, Britain and the United States had been supplying the Soviet Union with tanks, guns, munitions, aircraft, petrol and raw materials for arms production worth hundreds of millions which were shipped in perilous convoys from British ports to Murmansk and Archangel.

Soviet officers and technicians came to the United States and Britain to be instructed in handling new arms and aircraft; soon they were discovered to be spying on their Allies and trying to ferret out secrets of scientific research and industrial production. SIS and MI5 watched their activities with growing anxiety; several cases of unashamed spying were discovered but hushed up so as not to provide propaganda for Dr. Goebbels.

One of the brightest officials of Section V of SIS was Harold "Kim" Philby, who had been a communist double-agent for at least ten years. By clever intrigue he succeeded in persuading the chief of SIS, Major-General Sir Stewart Menzies, to make him head of the newly enlarged counter-espionage Section V, which took in the "Russian" Section IX. Cowgill was eased out, transferred to the Intelligence Corps and eventually given an irrelevant post in Germany.[10] Thus Kim Philby began to "counter-spy" on his own Soviet masters, passing on to them every scrap of information he gained and warning them beforehand of any measure he was to take against Soviet spies. On at least one occasion he gave his SIS chiefs a report on the clandestine activities of "a certain Boris Krotkov", who was in fact his own "controller" in London; they must have had a good laugh together. It was not until 1961 that Philby was finally

150

unmasked—not without Gehlen's assistance, for the German spy-master was able to provide evidence from Soviet defectors.

The French, too, were busily catching potential agents from among German prisoners of war in their zone. At Bregenz in Austria and at Friedrichshafen on Lake Constance they established two secret camps for ex-Abwehr and SD officers; at Bregenz the star of the French group, headed by Major Maurice Blondel of General de Gaulle's SEDCE, was SS Sturmbannfuhrer Otto Hoettl, who had been chief of Schellenberg's *Amt VI* section for south-east Europe.[11] At Friedrichshafen an Alsatian, Raoul Kaiser, was in charge of the recruiting group of the French Intelligence.

Neither Sibert nor Gehlen had, in fact, anything to fear from the competition of the British and French. The British relied ultimately on their own experienced intelligencers, even though they continued to employ useful German V-men. The French effort, amateurish from the very outset, soon petered out. However for a time the Americans did worry about their Allies' attempts in this field, if only because they were loth to lose some useful men for their own organisation.

The First Infiltrations

Gehlen concentrated his initial efforts on "near-infiltration", that is, on dispatching agents into the Soviet zone of Occupation in East Germany. He had neither the right type of men for "infiltration in depth"—into the Soviet Union itself—nor the means to convey them. He had suggested to General Sibert that some agents should be dropped by parachute into Soviet territory, but Sibert brushed off such plans as "fantastic", although Gehlen proposed the use of unmarked aircraft. Overflying even of Soviet-occupied East Germany to reach West Berlin had become perilous for US Air Force planes. The Soviet *Kommandatura* insisted that in each case a flight plan and exact route must be filed with them before take-off. The Russians later devised flight corridors; American aircraft were buzzed during wholly legitimate flights and in one case a C-47 freighter was shot down with the loss of several lives.

Neither were Sibert and the US Air Force chiefs prepared to accept Gehlen's suggestions of detours by way of Austria and Hungary. An unarmed C-47, which had left Erding near Munich with freight for members of the US embassy in Belgrade, had been intercepted by Soviet fighters over western Hungary and forced to land at a Soviet airfield near Papa. Agents of the MGB searched it and found four ordinary radio sets which the embassy officials had requested for their private use. The pilot, Captain Dave Henderson of Shawnee, Oklahoma, and his crew were declared to be "spies and saboteurs" and subsequently sentenced to long prison terms, to be released only when Washington, after protracted negotiations, submitted to a ransom demand of 120,000 dollars. The aircraft, worth a great deal more than this, was confiscated and never returned.

Overland infiltration into the Soviet Union by way of Austria and Czechoslovakia was no easier. The Czech frontier region was heavily guarded and alive with newly laid minefields; the Hungarian frontier was similarly reinforced. The ideal of communist unity, which Moscow never tired of expounding was belied by the internal barriers it erected within its orbit. No matter how convincingly the agents were disguised and their identity papers forged, those of German nationality had little chance of reaching the Soviet Union. Even if a German agent did manage to get through he would have little prospect of surviving undiscovered in Russia. Hence Gehlen later resorted to the use of V-men of eastern European nationalities, recruited from among displaced persons in German refugee camps. But these were early days.

Better opportunities existed for crossing into East Germany; in particular, it was still relatively easy to enter the Soviet sector of East Berlin from the American, British and French sectors, though Gehlen had first to place suitable agents in the city. He did succeed in dispatching a few men at an early date, among them Gerhard Pinckert and Friedrich Wilhelm Poppenberger. Pinckert was a former lieutenant-colonel of the Brandenburg Regiment, the crack sabotage unit of the Abwehr. An old hand at the game, he had trained secret agents for General Franco during the Spanish Civil War, and had scored some astonishing exploits behind the Soviet lines in 1943. He reached Saxony, and set up several cells there, making contact with some of the R-Net "sleepers" and ex-Werewolves in Leipzig and Dresden; he also worked in Thuringia, establishing a sporadic radio link with Oberursel. At last, apparently betrayed by a stool-pigeon whom he had tried to enlist, he was caught and sentenced by a Soviet military tribunal to twenty-five years in prison, charged with trying to revive a nazi organisation.

More fortunate was Major Poppenberger, a German born in Rumania, who had served under Gehlen in FHO and supervised Russian defectors in the POW camps of Luckenwalde. He, too, was sent to Saxony, where the Red Army had vast establishments of its reserve divisions in East Germany. He succeeded in being accepted as a new convert to communism, became an official of the Party at Erfurt and enlisted several V-men. Eventually, he was caught at Breslau in Silesia, which had become part of Poland. He was kept in prison for two years and might have ended in front of a firing squad, but he managed to escape in 1950 and make his way back to West Germany.

The New CIA

But such infiltrations were, at first, few and far between. Gehlen's efforts were also greatly hampered by far-reaching changes in Oberursel and Washington. General Sibert had been recalled and appointed deputy chief of G-2 Intelligence. Colonel Deane followed him soon afterwards, and Gehlen found himself deprived of his two sponsors. He sorely missed them; Sibert, in particular, had had a knack of snipping red tape. After his and Deane's departure Gehlen had to report, through G-2 officers at the camp, to a remote boss in Washington, Major-General Alexander Bolling, the assistant director of G-2 Intelligence. Sibert was later replaced at Oberursel by Lieutenant-General Lucien Truscott, who had commanded the US Fifth Army in Italy. He favoured the activities of American Intelligence units based on the CIC, or working independently, and soon many such groups began to proliferate in the American-British "Bi-zone", particularly in West Berlin, much to Gehlen's chagrin.

Help came, however, from G-2's rival, the new Central Intelligence Agency. On May 1, 1947, General Vandenberg had made a contented exit after heading the CIG for only one short year to become Air Force chief of staff. His successor was another non-army officer: Rear-Admiral Roscoe H. Hillenkoetter. This time President Truman was more fortunate in his choice; the new CIG chief had an efficient background. A graduate of the Annapolis Naval Academy, he was fluent in three foreign languages, including German, and had served as naval attaché in Paris. Severely wounded in the battleship *West Virginia* at Pearl Harbour, he recovered to form a first-class intelligence staff for Admiral Chestèr W. Nimitz's Pacific fleet in 1943, and headed it until the end of the war against Japan.

Hillenkoetter's value to the White House was the administrative smoothness he introduced. He was aware of the fate Donovan had met in feuds with Strong and the State Department, and he did not believe in rocking the boat. At last the bafflement and quarrelling subsided. But his long Far East service had curtailed his knowledge of post-war European intelligence problems. Awareness of this, perhaps, led him to over-prudence. He was quoted as saying: "I am no fortune teller. I am basing my prognostications on such real information as is available." He seemed to regard CIG as a huge receiving set at which would arrive all the intelligence required. This philosophy, shared by an astounding number of command-level intelligencers on both sides of the Atlantic, was like hoping that gold will come and find you.

153

Intelligence gathered by his staff under this policy of restraint was on the whole a watery and feeble brew.

In July 1947 Congress passed the National Security Act,[12] and on September 8 the CIG became the Central Intelligence Agency (CIA), with a greatly enlarged field of activity. At the same time the National Security Council was created, chaired by the President, with the Vice-President, the Secretary of State, the Secretary of Defence, and the Director of Foreign Operations Administration as its members, and the Director of CIA as its chief adviser.

The National Security Act provided that the CIA director would have power to coordinate the entire intelligence effort of the United States, and that he might be appointed either from the armed services or from civilian life. The CIA was to be specifically protected from pressure or interference by the military departments. This gave Hillenkoetter the opportunity to exercise far greater influence on the activities of the Gehlen Organisation. Above all, the appointment of General Sibert, who had crossed over from the G-2 department, as Hillenkoetter's deputy, augured well for Gehlen. Sibert always referred to the Gehlen Organisation as "my baby".

For many months after Sibert's departure Gehlen felt stifled at Oberursel. He resented having "a bunch of ignorant American junior officers" looking over his shoulder. He was also having to take account of the feelings of his fast-increasing staff. They were none too content to remain isolated in Oberursel, which reminded them of a POW camp. It was distant from their families, most of whom lived in Bavaria; it was also overcrowded and clearly insecure for the sensitive enterprise on which they were engaged. Any communist agent sitting out on the windy hills with a telephoto lens could photograph people entering, leaving and walking around the camp, for all that protected it was a wire-mesh fence.

Gehlen determined to move his organisation to a place where he could work under far tighter security and, above all, could ensure a minimum of interference from his American paymasters. Efforts to find such congenial accommodation went on for many months. His house-hunting was centred on Bavaria, and he sent out Colonel Heinz Herre, accompanied by an American officer, to reconnoitre the land. At last, at the beginning of the winter, Herre could report that he had found the ideal location.

XII

Pullach

The place was a bedraggled ghost from Hitler's Third Reich, one of the SS model housing estates built in many parts of Germany before the war. It was situated outside Pullach, a pretty village some eight miles from Munich. There, in 1938, a large housing development had been built for SS officers and their families and named in honour of the Fuhrer's deputy, *Wohngemeinschaft Rudolf Hess*. In this and other such racial havens the black-uniformed *élite* of the Reich had lived in pure-blooded segregation under their weird and strict rules, siring the Aryan master-stock which was to rule for a thousand years.

Once the estate housed Rudolf Hess' staff; after he made his adventurous flight to England his successor, Martin Bormann, took it over. Officers of the Dachau concentration camp also found pleasant accommodation there. Office buildings, apartment houses and a number of detached villas for the higher ranks, all with small flower gardens, stood in neat rows in 150,000 square yards of parkland. There was a large community centre, a hall with a theatre and cinema, a gymnasium, indoor and outdoor sports areas and a school to which a Hitler Youth annexe was attached.

During the last year of the war it had been turned into improvised barracks for the Wehrmacht. The last ramparts of its tribal sanctity were overthrown after the surrender in 1945, when a few hundred ragged and hungry displaced persons of every nationality took it over. The squatters were chased out in turn by a small army of clerks and accountants of the US Quartermaster Corps and Ordnance units. But this bespectacled garrison could not muster enough rank to resist the landgrabbers of the US G-2 Intelligence. Capping their fountain pens and complaining bitterly, they were driven forth, and the compound was handed over to Gehlen.

Walking round it, he found the houses and the community centre badly dilapidated and the sports grounds and park overgrown with weeds. He was delighted, however, by the privacy and seclusion. On one side a steep embankment led down to the railroad along the river Isar. On the other, along Heilmannstrasse, was a tall grey wall, above which little more than the roofs could be seen from outside. The estate was hidden too from Pullach village itself, which had been a popular spot with weekend parties coming out to picnic in the woods or on the river bank in the shade of the ruined Schwaneck castle. But as the bleak winter of 1948 drew in, with its food and fuel crises, there would be no more picnics for a while.

The Americans were impatient to get the Gehlen Organisation running smoothly, for relations with Stalin were rapidly deteriorating. In the East, he had broken the treaties over Hungary, Rumania and Bulgaria and was preparing for the communist *coup* which would deliver Czechoslovakia into the Soviet maw. In the West, the communist parties, following the strategy dictated by the new Cominform, were trying to foment general strikes and industrial chaos in order to wreck the Marshall Plan and create revolutionary situations, particularly in France and Italy. The Allies, and, in particular, the United States, had been slow to imitate the determined intelligence policy which Stalin had laid down as far back as the 12th Party Congress, when he spoke of perfecting "a number of barometers which will anticipate every change, register and forestall ... all possible storms and misfortunes". Now it was the West which needed the barometers, and obtaining reliable indicators of Soviet plans was the urgent priority of every Allied intelligence organisation.

It cost the Americans three million dollars to convert Pullach into a veritable fortress, working from plans produced by Gehlen's own architects. Very substantial rebuilding took place, and several new structures were added, including a modern communications centre. A row of large underground bunkers was constructed, each three levels deep. Strongrooms were embedded in protective shells of steel and concrete and air-conditioned. Doors and gates were operated by electrical relays, and the latest electronic devices available at the time were installed to increase efficiency and security.

The compound was surrounded with more high walls and an electrified fence, which was hidden behind stout hedges. None of the new buildings was more than two storeys above ground level, so that no curious passer-by had a chance of seeing what went on inside the perimeter. Watch-towers and a guardroom were also provided, and day-and-night patrols of armed men dressed in Bavarian gamekeepers' outfits and leading fierce dogs were a further deterrent to possible intruders. The dwelling houses were modernised and furnished as homes for Gehlen's key staff and their families, and for resident secretaries, clerks, cryptographers, monitors, telephonists and radio operators. The former Hitler Youth centre was spruced up and converted into the training college, where Gehlen, the heads of his groups and a rapidly increasing staff of instructors gave daily lectures. In a well-equipped laboratory new American miniature W/T sets were tested and sabotage equipment and the manifold paraphernalia of the spy craft designed and improved. Rank-and-file agents and V-men, of course, were not trained in Pullach; for them a large number of schools were set up, which are described later.

During the first two years, although the staff quickly grew to four hundred, all Gehlen's personnel were discouraged from leaving the estate except on official business. Families were obliged to send their children to the compound school, and Gehlen's two younger daughters went there as well. In compensation, recreation and entertainment facilities were provided and an excelllent shop was stocked by the American PX. Inside Pullach, the Gehlen families enjoyed luxuries and delicacies which to ordinary Germans would have been utter fantasies. Butter, real coffee, a rich selection of canned goods and unlimited supplies of American cigarettes were available at a fraction of the prices then current on the black market which ruled the shattered economy outside.

For many weeks before Gehlen and his staff moved in (during the second week of December 1947, in good time to combine a warming-up party with Christmas festivities), he had been making meticulous plans to shroud his new headquarters in almost impenetrable secrecy. He had, of course, to reckon with local gossip, which might reach Munich and arouse the interest of the newspapers, after twelve years of nazi censorship burning with zeal to assert the freedom of the press and expose all manner of things. People in the Pullach district were naturally inquisitive about the new residents of the previously derelict SS estate, which had been so intriguingly restored. For several reasons Gehlen contrived a false but acceptable identity for "Fort Pullach".

His stratagem was based on an intelligence principle he invoked several times in his career: if you have to keep a secret, you may often do so successfully by disguising it as a minor and rather boring secret. In a surprising number of cases, this will slake the curiosity of all but the most relentless professionals, whereas an attempt at a wholly innocent explanation may simply increase suspicion. Resorting to the same type of scientific-industrial cover as he had used at Valepp (fooling, it should be remembered, everyone but a peasant dairyman), Gehlen had a brass plate mounted on the main gate in the Burgweg opposite the ruined castle. On it was the name: SÜD-DEUTSCHE INDUSTRIE-VERWERTUNGS GmbH, the South German Industries Utilisation Company.

In this way, Gehlen disguised his headquarters as the head offices of a new corporation concerned with scientific research and the development of new technological inventions. Members of his staff patronised the cafés and beerhouses in Pullach, Grosshessalohe and other neighbouring villages hinting that their company was working on patents which must be kept secret from foreign competitors. As before, this tactic brought out the patriot in their Bavarian listeners. Confidential winks were exchanged in the *Rabenwirt* and the *Bürger-Bräu*, and it was agreed that smart Germans could still hide a thing or two from their trade rivals.

If Gehlen had left it at that, Pullach's cover might have held a little longer. His less credulous neighbours, however, inferred much more from a smaller sign on the gate reading: "No hawkers. Cars must switch off headlamps and switch on internal lights. Beware of fierce dogs." At the guardroom several "gamekeepers" manned the electrically operated steel barriers and double gates, and visitors had to show passes bearing the holders' photographs.[1] The local inns revised and up-graded the original estimate. It was now held in the area that the men and few women behind the walls were working on some new weaponry for export to the United States. This belief grew into certainty when passers-by noticed that the two tall flagpoles were flying the black-red-gold standard of the new Germany next to the Stars and Stripes, and that besides the "gamekeepers", US military policemen guarded the estate and occupied the main gate lodge. Many people believed that the new industrial company had something to do with nuclear research, for atom bombs were much in the news.

The people of Pullach were not entirely wrong, Gehlen was indeed perfecting a powerful weapon and exporting the yield to America. For this the United States had at first allowed him a budget of 600,000 dollars in 1948, having borne all the costs of reconstructing, modernising and equipping his spy base, and provided all PX articles free. Although the dollar could buy a lot in the Germany of those days, these operational funds soon proved inadequate and they were increased substantially from year to year. During the ten years for which Gehlen worked exclusively for the CIA, or, after his organisation officially became the *Bundesnachrichtendienst* of the Federal German government, was subsidised by them, CIA provided about 200,000,000 dollars for his organisation, partly from its funds, and partly by inducing the American business world to contribute large sums of money.[2]

The Venetian Blind Business

The creation of the *Süddeutsche Industrie* company was a stroke of genius, not merely because it provided an excellent cover for the doings at Pullach. It also enabled Gehlen to build up the "Org", as

and masses of paperwork without provoking any suspicion or needing much concealment. Moreover, agents and V-men could come and go almost without limit, calling at the local offices as salesmen and "real" representatives, collecting samples or delivering orders. All this greatly facilitated the local recruitment of potential agents and V-men, upon which by 1948 the "Org" had embarked on an ever-increasing scale, until their number exceeded four thousand.

Operation Hermes

Even in the Oberursel days, Gehlen had begun sending out some of his assistants to the many camps for refugees from the East, for whom the Germans had coined an emotive name: *Heimatvertriebene*—people driven out from their homeland. More than two million of them had come, penniless and often only with the clothes they stood in, from Czechoslovakia, the provinces annexed by Poland and Russia—East Prussia, Pomerania, Posen and Silesia—and from as far away as Transylvania, the Banat and Croatia. Article XII of the Potsdam Agreement provided for the transfer of the German population from the Sudetenland, Poland and Hungary; its three signatories, Truman, Attlee and Stalin, had agreed that "the transfer should be effected in an orderly and humane manner . . . since the influx of a large number of refugees into Germany would increase the burden already resting on the authorities". Indeed, the Potsdam Agreement provided that "all expulsions pending further examination should be meanwhile suspended".

Hundreds of thousands of these German refugees did not, in fact, wait for official expulsion orders. Obviously, after the liberation they had become the target of violent hostility from the peoples their nazi compatriots had subjugated and oppressed for five or six long years. Almost without exception they had been given offical positions by the nazis, and ran the local authorities in towns and areas where they represented only a small minority; many had amassed fortunes as a result of privileged treatment in commerce and industry. Some had managed to flee with the retreating German occupation forces, but most of them flooded into the American zone of West Germany, which was nearest to their former homelands. Only a small proportion of these wretched families could find shelter with relatives, housing conditions in bomb-ravaged West Germany being appalling. Most were put up in camps run by the Allied military governments and a number of official and charitable organisations.

Amongst them Gehlen's recruiting officers searched for potential V-men. Their qualifications were obvious: they and their families, often for many generations, had lived in the territories which had become the main targets of interest for the "Org"; they knew the countries and the customs of their inhabitants and they spoke their language.

Another and even more promising source for V-men was offered by repatriated prisoners of war from the Soviet Union. At least three million were known to be in Soviet camps, but by 1947 only a trickle had begun to return home. The Soviet authorities used the prisoners as cheap labour and did not release them for several years. However, those who did return had brought with them knowledge which could be tapped. Many thousands had spent up to seven years in the Soviet Union, had learned the language and, as trained soldiers often with technical skills, had observed things about which they could provide valuable information.

Gehlen had set up an interrogation group for these people at Castle Kransberg; after the move to Pullach this group was greatly enlarged. In some of the rehabilitation camps for ex-POW's, such as Kornwestheim, Regensburg, Weiden and Bad Langensalza, the American CIC, which independently of Gehlen's "Org" conducted its own interrogations, provided special facilities for Gehlen's men. Many of the ex-prisoners were reluctant to talk, particularly to the Americans, British and French (interrogation centres were also set up in the British and French zones) because their families lived in Soviet-occupied East Germany and they were afraid of possible reprisals.

Gehlen, therefore, organised "Operation Hermes" in such a way as to appear as innocuous as possible. His interrogators presented themselves as social workers, welfare officials or researchers from the "Historical Institute at Weisbaden", an institution existing only in the imagination of the "Org". Although much of the material thus collected was valueless—sheafs of paper were covered with pathetic stories of hardship, hunger and despair—the analysts who for many months ploughed through these reports sometimes found information and data which could be put to good use.

Many of the ex-POWs had worked in Soviet mines, on building or repairing roads and railway tracks, in armament factories, and in the new industrial areas on the Volga and beyond the Urals. In a few cases Gehlen's interrogators pieced together information from technically minded or trained men on new machinery and even on scientific research. Former Luftwaffe officers and aircraftsmen could tell what they had seen when working at airfields or in aviation plants, even though their work had been of the humblest, as labourers, loaders or cleaners; ex-naval men could provide scraps of information about Soviet ports, river shipping and so forth.

In one case a former prisoner showed an interrogator a piece of rock, which he had kept as a souvenir because it could be used as a flint and because the Russians were mining it at a new mine at Takmytsk in the Omsk region, apparently observing great secrecy. The mine, he said, was guarded by soldiers and, when he worked there for a few weeks, he had seen men in "funny leather aprons and masks". The interrogator, who had some knowledge of geology, exchanged the souvenir for a packet of Camel cigarettes, and when the stone was analysed it was found to contain fragments of radioactive uranium pitchblende, which had never been known to occur in the Soviet Union. Thus Gehlen was able to inform his CIA masters that the Russians had found uranium; this was the first intimation that they need no longer depend entirely on the Joachimsthal uranium mines in Czechoslovakia.

Other ex-prisoners reported that they had seen new strange-looking aircraft, or Soviet plants where captured German Panzer tanks were reconditioned and fitted out with long cannons and new turret hatches. The more intelligent and, particularly, those who were able to make a simple drawing or trace a map, were asked to make sketches of the areas around their camps and their workplaces. They were encouraged to remember names of corps or numbers of regiments, as well as those of commanders and higher-ranking officers. Most of the prisoners had brought release documents and other scraps of official papers, passes, travel vouchers and suchlike, and the interrogators made photocopies of them. Facsimiles of Soviet headings, addresses, rubber stamps and signatures were useful for manufacturing fake Soviet documents at the Pullach forgeries laboratory. Above all, the contact with the ex-prisoners and refugees provided the "Org" with an opportunity to enlist a number of promising V-men; after training some of them might be willing to work in Soviet or Soviet-occupied territory.

The "Quellen" System

Even when, at first, only a handful of potential V-men had been enlisted, Gehlen devised an elaborate system of *Quellen*, the sources of information which are the life-blood of any espionage organisation. The structure contained a number of categories, of which the main ones can here be conveniently reduced to six:

P-QUELLE *(Penetrierung)*, the penetration source to produce intelligence from V-men infiltrated into government offices, public service authorities, party and political organisations, industrial and commercial managements, etc.

U-QUELLE *(Überprufung)*, V-men and informers working at, or living near, "target objectives", such as military establishments, armament plants, airfields, telecommunication centres and so on.

163

R-QUELLEN (*Reise*), V-men who by the nature of their work could undertake travel, or were employed as railwaymen, sailors, dockers, transport workers, and besides being able to supply information about their own work, could make observations on their journeys. R-agents also included travelling salesmen, newspaper reporters, tourist guides and visitors to industrial fairs, exhibitions etc.

T-QUELLEN (*Technik*), comprising trained technicians, engineers, and otherwise skilled workers, who could report with a degree of expertise on technical matters, understood or could be trained to understand technical drawings and blue-prints, and to examine machinery and make sketches or photographs of what they had seen.

S-QUELLEN (*Spitze*), represented by "top agents", who could be entrusted with assignments to infiltrate particularly sensitive targets, such as headquarters, barracks and camps of the Soviet Army, the People's Militia in East Germany and the armies and police forces of the satellite countries. Top V-men (*Haupt V-Männer*) would also be required to attempt an occasional burglary or safe-breaking and the procurement of secret documents of special importance.

III/F QUELLEN (this code revived the old Abwehr and FHO label), comprising V-men employed in counter-espionage, who could observe and discover communist agents and contacts, undertake surveillance, and ideally also be employed as double agents, infiltrating the secret services of opponents and handling "spielmaterial", i.e. planting false information on the enemy. These agents were also supposed to uncover enemy schemes to deceive or mislead the "Org".

To find, set up, instruct, tap and maintain this great everglade of sources, Gehlen created a no less elaborate human chain. He modelled it largely on time-honoured patterns of espionage, but he included many innovations which improved the system of classification and the apportioning of tasks. At the end of the complex hierarchy were the *Tippers* (from the English word "tip"). These were the spotters who provided the first information or suggestion which might lead to the recruitment of a new potential informer. The "tip", given maybe by a sympathiser to a friend employed by the "Org" or coming from a V-man, had to be passed to headquarters. Only Pullach decided whether it should be taken up.

The "tip" was examined by a *Forscher*, an investigator, first at headquarters and then, if not discarded, by another attached to a regional or local branch (*General-Vertretung, Bezirks-Vertretung*),

Gatehouse at Pullach before the considerable rebuilding of Gehlen's headquarters.

Main administration building at Pullach.

(*Left*) Gehlen's fortress, guarded by armed "game keepers" round the clock. (*Above*) Back gate used by Gehlen to come and go unseen by his staff.

The high wall and tall trees nearly conceal the Pullach buildings.

disguised as a commercial undertaking. These researchers looked into the background, qualifications and potentialities of the "tipped" source and weighed up the possible benefits and risks of using him. If his report was favourable and Pullach (or one of the chiefs of a main branch office) approved, a *Heranholer*, or collector, took over, approached the potential V-man and handled the actual recruitment. Until then the man or woman to be recruited had no inkling of the elaborate machinery which had been set in motion.

The new recruit then passed to an *Instructeur* for espionage training according to the category which best suited his circumstances and qualifications. This first school for training V-men was set up at the castle of Countess Totenbach at Weidekamp. In quick succession other schools, some in cooperation with CIC and later with CIA (which created its own spy groups in West Berlin) were opened at Buckeburg, at Karlsplatz in Munich, at Weinheim-Bergstrasse north of Mannheim, at Ulm in Wurttemberg, and in Diessen in Bavaria. After some years, when training became much more elaborate and included parachute jumping, handling complex explosives and sabotage gadgets, cryptography and cryptanalysis and technical subjects beyond W/T operation, some sixty schools were—and many still are—producing agents for the "Org".[5]

Under chief instructor Colonel Oscar Reile, who had together with Gehlen devised the general syllabus of the training, were soon working some twenty instructors; their number was subsequently greatly increased and included "travelling instructors", who on occasions ventured into East Germany to improve the knowledge of V-men in the field who might be unable to risk a visit to one of the schools. Among the first instructors were Captain Herbert Bauer and Captain Kaiser, both of whom had been with Gehlen at FHO during the war and had worked on "deep penetration". Another was former SS Standartenfuhrer Rudolf Roeder, who did the same work during the war in RSHA spy schools. His assistant was an RSHA officer, Seibold, who used the alias of Seitz.

The "Org" assembled within a comparatively short period a number of efficient "collectors" or recruiting officers. Upon their skill depended not only the eventual enlistment of the V-man, but also his future usefulness; as a rule, these officers also "conducted" him in his assignment. Amongst Gehlen's maestro conductors were men such as Otto Ritter, nicknamed *Blümchen* (Little Flower). Held, Winkler, Herbert Steinborn, Theiss-Michel, Willi Hochberg, Ahrend and Momber, some of whom we shall meet again in these pages when the exploits or failures of their wards are described.

This was the basic framework of Gehlen's outwards-working espionage machine, operated by the branch offices. Vertically and horizontally, for it closely resembled an industrial management "tree", there were many other departments, most of them in Pullach, but others in Munich, Stuttgart and Frankfurt. At headquarters the system of main groups had been retained, such as the Evaluation Group, at first headed by Colonel Baun after his shaky R-Net radio communication outfit was fused with the Gehlen Organisation, and soon taken over by Colonel Heinz Danko Herre. There were groups for research on military developments in the Soviet Union and the Cominform countries, and for investigations into their political and economic situation and future planning, an ever-growing personnel department, several sections run by experts in clandestine communication, in document forgery, in "black" propaganda, in coding and cryptanalysis. The interrogation group was engaged on such operations as "Hermes" and many others which are described elsewhere. The technical section, which procured and distributed explosives and gadgets for sabotage actions and to which was attached a secret armoury, was, at one time, at Stuttgart. Later an aviation section was added, liaising with the CIA and US Air Force when Gehlen's agents were to be parachuted into the Soviet Union. A separate group was engaged on counter-espionage, including discreet surveillance of West German cabinet ministers, politicians and public figures, after CIA asked Gehlen to provide this additional service in 1950. Administrative, finance, and archives departments—the last mentioned bringing up to date the FHO treasure trove dug up at Misery Meadow and replenishing it with an unending flood of records, data, statistics, biographies and photographs—completed the complex structure.

But as any business company has to rely on its salesmen for its prosperity so the great edifice of the Pullach corporation depended on the efficiency of its V-men, the rank-and-file spies.

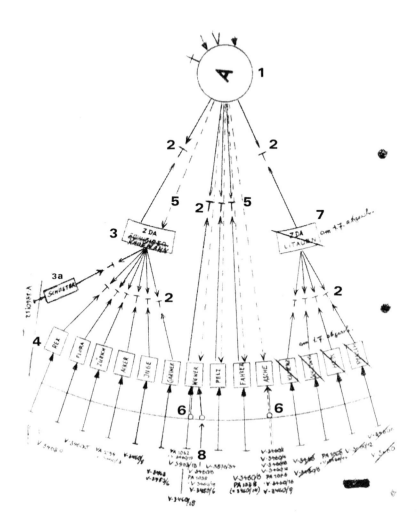

Chart of communication links of one sub-branch of the Gehlen Organisation, including "Who Knows Whom" contacts.

The *HV-Mann*, a Head V-man "A" (1) is in contact through "cut-outs" and couriers (2) with *V-Führer*, V-men leaders (3 and 3a), who convey instructions to, and receive reports from, V-men (4) listed by their code-names ("Rex", "Flora", etc.), gathering information from regular, occasional and potential "sources" and WKW V-men (8) indicated by numbers. Dotted lines show some of the radio links (5) and V-men operating clandestine transmitters (8) indicated by arrows with small circles.

XIII

V-Men

The German abbreviation *V-Mann* stands for *Vertrauens-Mann,* a trusted man. It goes back to the *Nachrichtendienst* of the Prussian king created a century ago by his spy-master Wilhelm Stieber, whose V-men, disguised as pedlars of religious objects, journeymen and waiters, infiltrated every Austrian military establishment and provided sufficient intelligence to make the Prussian conquest of 1866 possible within forty-five days. Stieber's V-men accomplished even more significant exploits before the Franco-German war of 1870-1, providing timely information on the new *chassepôt* rifle and the *mitrailleuse* machine-gun of the French Army, regarded by Napoleon III as invincible.

In the course of time the description "V-men" for hired and paid informers, other than officers serving in intelligence departments, became a misnomer: V-men were used, but they were trusted by no one. In the Gehlen Organisation, which depended on them for its existence, they were a class apart. The officers at Pullach and in charge of the branch offices regarded them as dubious mercenaries, which they were. To one of Gehlen's colonels was ascribed the remark that the "secret service is for gentlemen only", a rather strange axiom, since this is one attribute which spies rarely enjoy.

Directives from Pullach sent to the heads of the *General-Vertretungen* again and again urged them not to permit any familiarity between V-men and their superiors; regional and districts heads were discouraged from dealing with rank-and-file V-men altogether and told to send instructions via and receive reports only from *Filiale-Leiter*—the local branch leaders, or Head V-men (HVM). This was good security policy, but the tone of some of Gehlen's decrees betrays a deeply rooted contempt for his informers. Directive No.568, issued in June 1953 when the "Org" employed at least three thousand full or part-time V-men read: "The V-man is a merchant in information. His leader should maintain with him correct business relations, which should be impersonal and not include social intercourse. An agent must be treated with distrust;

168

only thus will he exert himself to produce fully reliable information."

Gehlen was too old a hand at dealing with informers to assume that he could enlist only brilliant and efficient men. In a directive to "tippers" and recruiting officers, he laid down general rules which did not exclude ordinary men, provided they could be trained; he attached, however, great importance to certain qualities: "As regards a V-man's intelligence quotient, it should be remembered that some may have little formal education and shrewdness, qualities which make them suitable for the service. Quick apprehension and perceptiveness are of the greatest importance. Observation and the ability to describe events and things seen are also very important; so is presence of mind, particularly in couriers. Most important of all, however, is absolute discretion, the V-man must be educated to be uncommunicative to anybody but his V-leader; above all he is required not to ask any questions about the Organisation and not to discuss it with any other V-man or superior."[1]

Whatever Gehlen's patrician attitude to the plebeian V-men, he tried to make their perilous tasks lighter and their lives more secure. Thus, he devised simple mnemonic guides to remind them for what they were supposed to look. For instance, an agent sent out to reconnoitre a Soviet Army camp was told to remember the word AMBOZ (anvil). Its five letters stood for the initials of five words, thus

A	=	*Art* — sort (of troops)
M	=	*Menge* — number
B	=	*Beschaffenheit* — quality
O	=	*Ort* — place, location
Z	=	*Zeit* — time (of observation)

Gehlen also did his utmost to protect V-men in the field. This was not, of course, due to sentimentality or a charitable disposition; a captured agent made to talk would not only endanger his own network and other agents, he could inflict grave harm on the whole Organisation. Many signals from the Pullach telecommunications section contained security instructions and advice on how to behave in an emergency. A simple Morse code of three letters, A, B and C, was devised. If it was felt that an agent was in danger, for instance, because another agent had been caught in the vicinity or because communist counter-espionage was known to use radio-detecting devices in the area, a series of warning signals was repeated, preceded by the agent's code number. Thus 384-A meant "Utmost danger, go into hiding immediately", B meant "Danger ahead, lie low, observe radio silence, hide transmitter, prepare to leave", whilst C was an instruction to seek advice from the Head V-man or conductor, using either a prearranged dead letter-box or a courier.

Over the years radio communication played an increasingly important role in maintaining contact with V-men in the field. The system of "sleepers", operators ordered to observe radio silence and go "into reserve" pending further orders, saved many agents. For instance, Heinz Fink, a former Wehrmacht telegraphist who had served in Rommel's Africa campaign and joined the "Org" after returning from a British POW camp in 1946, operated the radio post "Schaller" at Potsdam near the Soviet barracks for almost ten years, until he was eventually detected in 1962. But often he was put on the "sleeper roster" for months on end. Another operator, Franz Pankraz, alias Ernst Menzel, a former naval radio telegraphist, enlisted for the "Org" in 1950 and was employed at the Soviet radio station at Koepenick. For the astounding period of fifteen years he worked for Gehlen from the lion's den, from time to time being put into suspended animation.

The destination of the early infiltrators was almost exclusively the Soviet-occupied zone of East Germany. In 1948, before the Berlin blockade and Allied airlift* the movement of Germans between the zones and the Berlin sectors was not greatly hampered. Whilst Red Army military police and the newly established "VOPO" tried to impede the streams of refugees to the West, the eastward traffic was hardly hindered. If a German came to a crossing point and said that he wanted to return to the East or to visit relatives, he was admitted. Former prisoners of war released from American, British and French camps who, despite the blandishments of the West, expressed a desire to rejoin their families in Thuringia, Saxony or the Brandenburg province were received with open arms as potential comrades. Such repatriates were usually treated kindly by the communist authorities, and on reaching their destination they were soon enough approached by agents of the MGB or the new Kommissariat V, the precursor of the East German Ministry for State Security. If they seemed to be potential spy material, they were asked to work in the West as communist V-men; their families were used as hostages. Others, particularly technicians and skilled workers of whom there was a great shortage, were offered jobs and then invited to join the Communist Party.

This policy naturally offered welcome possibilities to Gehlen. While it remained well nigh impossible to infiltrate agents into the Soviet Union, penetration of East Germany by trained and plucky

*See page 202

The main gate bears signs with warnings that all cars must switch off headlamps and switch on internal lights.

The new main gate showing several of the new office buildings.

(*Above*) Part of the radio reception station at Pullach which links headquarters with V-men. (*Below*) A four-square-inch miniature tuning condenser of an American-made radio transmitter supplied to Gehlen's agents (1) Converter with inserted crystal container (2) Tuning crystals (3) Battery (4) Plug for earphones.

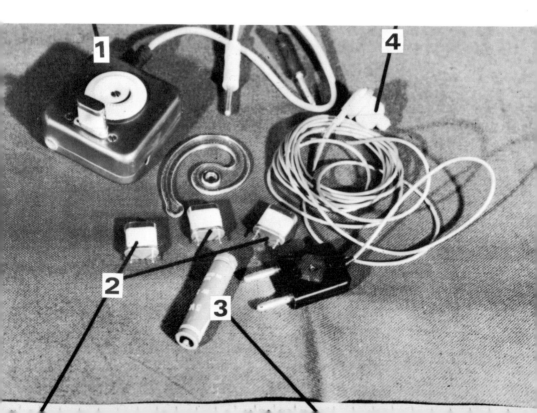

operators presented far smaller problems. He was therefore able to put in a number of his own V-men in quick succession. Some provided valuable information over long periods. From the ample records in the author's possession, a few such cases have been selected. These have been deliberately limited to Gehlen agents who were eventually caught and whose names and activities are already known to the communist security authorities. Others mentioned here returned safely and have now retired from service in German Intelligence. To disclose names and details which remain undetected by the Soviet and East German counter-espionage departments would be to endanger many people still living in East Germany even though several years may have elapsed since they last worked for Gehlen and the *Bundesnachrichtendienst*.

A Gehlen Agent As Party Boss

One of the most successful of the early infiltrators was Captain Kurt Heinz Wallesch. The son of a Leipzig police officer, Wallesch returned to his native city, equipped with a plausible cover story about his sufferings in a British prisoner of war camp, at the end of the war. On Gehlen's instructions, he avoided professing any enthusiasm for communism, but declared that he accepted the new regime in the East as the best solution to Germany's economic troubles. Wallesch joined the so-called National Democratic Party, whose leaders had thrown in their lot with the communists. He soon obtained an important position in the party organisation, was elected to its national committee and became a member of the Leipzig municipal council. He struck up a friendship with Fritz Selbmann, the communist president of Saxony, who later became minister of industry and science in the East German government. Through this connection, Wallesch soon got onto excellent terms with General Timon Dudorov, the Soviet commander of the Leipzig region.

Though communists are initially suspicious of converts, once they believe them trustworthy they take them to their hearts. For some years Wallesch sent back a flood of information culled from the top-secret files of the regional government of Saxony and later from the offices of the East German government itself. At last, in 1952, fate caught up with him. Perhaps his continued success lulled him into relaxing his security, but it is more likely that the efficient direction-finding vehicles of the DDR's counter-espionage apparatus intercepted and traced radio signals from the three powerful transmitters he was using to send out his material. Wallesch was tried and sentenced to life imprisonment. He probably died in prison, but the network he had organised survived for several years after his arrest.

Another planted Gehlen agent who rose to a key appointment in the East German administration was Dr. Hans Jess, but he was not, of course, an ordinary V-man. During the nazi regime, while unconnected with the Gestapo, he had been head of the criminal investigation office of the Mecklenburg police. After the war Jess went to the US zone of Germany. In an exact counterpart of the communist technique with refugees, Gehlen and US intelligence officers asked him to return to the East and to try to obtain a position in which he could usefully work for the Organisation. He was then fifty-six years old, but he willingly agreed to this perilous assignment. The communists were as short of executive civil servants as they were of experienced technicians, and they welcomed the apparent sympathiser gratefully. Jess was put in charge of the transportation department of Schwerin and rose to be a director of the *Reichsbahn*, the railway system. In this high post he worked for Pullach and provided invaluable information. When Jess was in imminent danger of discovery, Gehlen sent him a message telling him to escape and arranging the route. Jess later became police chief in Frankfurt, and eventually held a high post in the Federal German counter-espionage office.[2] There his experience of communist espionage methods and personnel was manna for the security files.

Probably the most durable of all Gehlen's senior V-men was Johann Richter, a former Wehrmacht captain who had served in the railway engineers regiment, having been a railway technician before the war. In 1946 he returned from a British POW camp to his home town of Wittenberg in East Germany and became district manager of the rail network at Wittenberg and later production manager in East Berlin. On a visit to the US sector in the course of his official contact with Western rail authorities, he met an ex-captain named Schroeder who had served with him up to 1945 in the army. Schroeder was one of Gehlen's "collectors", or recruiting officers, and he persuaded Richter to work as an agent. During further duty trips to the West, the railway executive attended training lectures at one of Gehlen's secret schools. Under the code name of "Bucholt" he organised several highly productive cells, maintaining a separate personal cover which prevented his sub-agents from learning his real identity or official position. Richter was to render important service during the 1953 rising in East Berlin. Later, when communication between the East and Western sectors became more difficult, he got his reports out through a number of "dead drops" in Wittenberg cemetery and in the Tiergarten.[3]

He also used couriers, including young women who carried microfilm concealed on their bodies. For several years he kept up a flow of high-grade intelligence. From him Gehlen obtained a detailed report on East German railway construction and projects, as well as on strategic communications projects, not only in the DDR but also in Poland and the Soviet Union. The secret plans for transit lines from Berlin to Naustrelitz, Rostock and Lalendorf, the modernisation of the Genshager and Seddin viaducts, and a host of other details were being analysed at Pullach even before the highest transportation authorities in Warsaw and Moscow had full technical knowledge of them. Moreover, Richter provided microfilmed copies of the plans for the new international harbour in Rostock—and even a film showing work in progress on it. He sent detailed descriptions of Wittenberg harbour, Schonefelde airport, the nuclear power station at Rheinsberg and the new bridges across the Elbe. But these examples cannot convey the massive volume of Richter's intelligence output; the full list of his activities acquired by the writer amounts to a bulky file. Some of his other successes are described in a later chapter.

Heinz Fink spent almost as long in Gehlen's nerve-stretching employ. He was a twenty-three-year-old wireless operator in Rommel's army when the British took him prisoner in North Africa in 1943. Four years later he returned to his native Berlin suburb of Oberschoenweide, only to find that his parents' home had long since disappeared in the rubble of the bomb-sites. Fink worked for a time in a socialised factory which produced accumulators for the vehicles of the Soviet Army. One day in a beer cellar he met a man to whom he talked about the hard work and poor pay at his plant. The listener was sympathetic. He was a Gehlen "collector" named Captain Koehler who was on a trip to East Berlin, under his cover name of "Holbach", on the lookout for likely V-men. Fink and "Holbach" .made a deal. The mechanic was offered a monthly retainer of two hundred Marks and instructed to come to an address in West Berlin. Between 1951 and 1961 Fink managed to make no fewer than two hundred runs to the western part of the city with information, under the cover of his later job as a test driver, in which capacity he seemed to have little difficulty in passing the border guards.

Fink's background was very different from those of the ex-officers mentioned so far. He was an uncomplicated fellow without much education but he had the sharp wit and shrewdness of the true Berliner, and he was good at *Augenerkundung* or "eye-spying". This form of espionage is of particular value in work against military, as distinct from political, targets. A shoulder flash, a collar badge, a divisional sign on an armoured car or a stencil on a munitions crate will often yield more hard intelligence than might be picked up in a year by more sophisticated penetration efforts. Fink became one of Gehlen's brightest and most instructive S-sources, that is, agents concentrating on military matters. His Pullach file was soon thick with accurate and significant details which revealed the deployment and the establishment of the Red Army and Air Force in the Berlin and Brandenburg regions. This agent, on his earlier short trips to West Berlin, had been put through a sandwich course by Gehlen's special instructors and proved a quick pupil.

Most notably, he was the first of Gehlen's spies to discover and report the very beginning of the new "National People's Army" in East Germany, making comprehensive reports on twelve of its bases. He also sent back eleven reports on Soviet Army installations in Berlin, Potsdam, Frankfurt-on-Oder and Halle, in which he described their armament and equipment, new Soviet tanks, artillery, rockets, ammunition depots, and correct unit strengths. Fink worked with another Gehlen *Quelle*, Horst Sterzik, who was infiltrated into the civilian labour force on the Red Air Force field at Brandenburg and later became a senior technician of the East German Air Force. Some of their *coups* on developments in military aviation during their ten-year period of cooperative spying are described elsewhere. Even from these few instances—and there were many others—it can be seen that Gehlen's infiltration tactics were bringing results at an early stage and from a great variety of levels. But the quest of ever more V-men never abated.

"Operation Pfifficus"

In 1949 a handful of West Berlin lawyers, led by Dr. Theo Friedlander and Dr. Walter Linse, founded the League of Free Jurists.[4] Initially the League's main task was to assist the families of prisoners in the Soviet zone with legal advice. It also befriended prisoners of war repatriated from Russia, many of whom were in a poor state of health, crippled, or with serious mental disorders. They turned to the League to claim allowances or housing grants; some had had their property in East Germany confiscated and transferred to deserving Communist Party members. The League was swamped with calls for help against oppressive measures by Soviet and East German authorities, evictions, dispossessions, trumped-up charges of "economic sabotage", followed by confiscations of shops, farms and homes. The League began to investigate such cases, and also the persecution of lawyers, university teachers and students in the Soviet zone; on one occasion fifty-eight professors and students of Jena University were sentenced to prison terms, accused of "sabotaging academic studies" by not toeing the Marxist line. The Free Jurists also intervened against the growing encroachment on religious freedom in East Berlin.

From small beginnings the League grew into a formidable defence organisation against communist tyranny and the Americans were very ready to contribute funds. Soon the League occupied a building in the Lima Strasse and employed about a hundred legal advisers, clerks and typists. Gehlen and the CIA began to take an interest in its activities when they learnt that it was sending researchers and investigators to the eastern zone and to East Berlin. Without engaging in spying, they could, of course, gather interesting information. Moreover, the Free Jurists had assembled archives and a card index, listing thirty thousand Soviet and East German officials by name; it included, as might be expected, many engaged on espionage. Several of the League's members and researchers had been arrested across the border, and two were sentenced to long terms of imprisonment.

What incensed the communists most about the League's activities was the efficacy with which it clandestinely distributed anti-communist literature. Eventually, the MGB chiefs at the Karlshorst HQ decided to retaliate. The counter-stroke was organised by the "special security" section at Karlshorst, a branch of the 9th Section "for Terror and Diversion" of the *Chastny Otdyel* (special division) in Moscow. Supervised by its chief in East Berlin, Major-General Yuri I. Kaverntsev, a major of the East German SSD, known only as "Paul", assembled a posse for a kidnapping operation code-named *Weinmeister*. At least three of the LFJ leaders were to be abducted and taken to East Berlin: Dr. Theo Friedlander, Dr. Walter Linse and Dr. Bernd. Members of the MGB team included criminals released from prison for the kidnapping. Amongst them were twenty-two-year-old Kurt Knobloch, with a record of four convictions for assault and burglary, Karl Bennwitz, serving a life sentence for murder, and Hans Borchardt, a former amateur boxing champion. The team consisted of thirteen men, most of them from the SSD.[5]

The execution of the plot deserves a brief description; it shows the elaborate methods of communist agents, which were characteristic of many other kidnappings. A few days before the date fixed for the attempt, an SSD agent approached a taxi driver in West Berlin and offered him twenty Marks (then worth about five dollars) to drive him to the Soviet sector. As soon as the taxi crossed the border, it was stopped by two men who said they were police officers. They loudly accused him of being an American cigarette racketeer and grabbed a parcel which the passenger had put on the cab's floor. He pretended to be very frightened and was led away. The men told the taxi driver to run home on foot; they retained his cab "for a thorough search". The driver, glad to be treated so leniently, quickly obeyed.

Thus the *Weinmeister* gang came into possession of a West Berlin taxi; they put on it new, fake number-plates. On July 8, 1952, the gang laid an ambush for Dr. Friedlander. But the LFJ chairman, who had escaped three previous kidnapping attempts, used frequently to change his residence and the gangsters went to the wrong address. The taxi was then taken to Gerichts Strasse, where other members of the team were watching the house of Dr. Walter Linse. It was 7.20 a.m. when Linse left his home and Knobloch approached him and asked for a light. Whilst he fumbled for his lighter, Knobloch pounced, but this was only a sham attack to frighten Linse. The lawyer broke free and, seeing a taxi slowly approaching, he ran towards it, shouting "Help!" The taxi driver stopped and opened the door; before Linse realised it was a trap, he was dragged in by two men who had been crouching on the floor of the cab. One of them fired a revolver, and hit Linse in the left leg. The taxi then sped towards the Soviet sector, where VOPO-men immediately lifted the barrier and let it in.

When the kidnapping became known the US military commander in Berlin, Major-General Lemuel Mathewson, fired off protests to the Soviet authorities; at a mass meeting of twenty-five thousand angry West Berliners Mayor Ernst Reuter said: "We appeal to the whole civilised world for help for this victim of inhuman brutality." But the Soviet officials blandly denied all knowledge of the outrage; they declared that no man of Linse's description had ever been in a Soviet prison. When the US High Commissioner, John J. McCloy, was returning to America, he used his farewell call on the chairman of the Soviet Control Commission, General Vasili Chuikov, to protest against the kidnapping and demanded Linse's return; but the Soviet general just shrugged his shoulders.

The Russians probably planned to stage a show-trial of Linse. But the world-wide condemnation of the kidnapping made them change their minds. Linse was taken from the MGB headquarters at Karl-shorst, where despite his injuries he had undergone brutal treatment and constant interrogation, to the Soviet military prison at Lichten-berg and then to the notorious Vladimir prison near Moscow. Months later there was a brief announcement that he "had made a full confession of spying", and had been sentenced to twenty-five years' imprisonment. Nothing was ever heard of Dr. Linse again; his father died of a broken heart soon after the kidnapping, while his wife became ill of mental anguish; parcels of food and clothes for the prisoner sent to the Soviet Kommandatura were returned with a sticker: "Address unknown". But the Russians must have broken Linse completely; they extracted from him the names of twenty-four LFJ agents in East Germany, most of whom were subsequently captured.

Kidnappings of anti-communists and of quite innocent men and women by Soviet and East German agents in West Berlin had become a commonplace in the 1950s; the West Berlin police commissioner Stumm told the author that in a single year 356 persons were abducted by force or lured under some pretext to East Berlin.

Although Gehlen was at first reluctant to cooperate with the League of Free Jurists—for he always maintained that amateurs engaged on secret work constituted a risk to professional agents—he came to realise that in fact the lawyers conducted their business in a thoroughly professional manner. The link which was eventually established proved fruitful; some of the Free Jurists' researchers proved more efficient than Gehlen's V-men. Through the League's agents, Dr. Bernd, Hansen, van Berk and Olsen, the "Org" and later the BND gained much valuable information; more important, Gehlen was able to enlist several good V-men from amongst refugees from East Germany who were being looked after by the League.

The best result of the cooperation between the "Org" and the League was, however, "Operation Pfifficus", which was to continue for several years. Many of the League's protégés were scientists, teachers, engineers, students and skilled craftsmen, who could be turned into useful V-men. Gehlen set up a special section in West Berlin, given the code X-9592, which began sifting and questioning suitable applicants. Thus a number of men with knowledge of one or more Eastern European countries and languages were enrolled, and a small group of university graduates was trained for participation at international congresses and scientific meetings abroad and sent quite openly to the Soviet Union, Poland, Czechoslovakia, Hungary, Rumania and Yugoslavia whenever opportunity occurred. Moreover, through people enrolled by "Operation Pfifficus", the "Org" gained contacts among scientists and technicians in the East. In quite a few cases it succeeded in persuading them to defect to the West.

The exploits of such V-men and women in the field of scientific and industrial espionage may be illustrated by a few cases, all of which can be disclosed because they concern people who have been either captured or identified by communist counter-espionage. As in the case of any agent of Gehlen's who remains unknown to the communist authorities, the author observes here the rule that their names and activities should not be disclosed, lest this might even now endanger them and their families.

Franz Hinrich, who had been a lieutenant in a mechanical engineers' regiment, returned from a POW camp to his home town of Schwerin to work at the local power station, where he gained quick promotion and became chief engineer at Wittenberg. He was a regular secret listener to the Free Jurists' broadcasts and, when approached by two researchers named "Thomas" and "Norbert", agreed to provide information about East German power stations and the two giant Soviet radar stations and radio transmitters at Zippendorf and Gorris, which served Soviet airfields and which he had helped to instal. For more than seven years Hinrich supplied technical reports until in 1957, probably through betrayal, he was caught, tried and sentenced to death.

Another Free Jurists' contact was Albert Junge, a textile technician, who began working for Gehlen in 1950. He had studied at the Karl Marx University, became the leader of the communist students' federation and was trusted to such a degree that he was appointed a municipal councillor of the city of Leipzig. He too remained undetected for seven years, during which he supplied a wealth of information. Arrested in 1957, he was tried and sentenced to death. There was also a student named Kunisch, who began his work for the Free Jurists distributing clandestine leaflets and organising an Underground student movement in West Berlin. He proved himself particularly useful during the June uprising of 1953. Arrested in 1956, he was sentenced to fifteen years' imprisonment.

Communist judges are usually careful not to reveal in too much detail the harm done by agents from the West, if only in order to uphold the myth that communist security is well able to nip "criminal subversion by capitalist spies" in the bud. It was, therefore, surprising that at Junge's trial the prosecutor revealed that the accused had succeeded in recruiting "hundreds of accomplices", though he added that this was done "by threats and intimidation". In fact, industrial and scientific espionage is usually conducted by agents working alone, or in very small teams. It is directed against specific targets—a research laboratory, a scientific institute, an armaments or aircraft factory, a defence establishment—to which the agent has direct access.

This was the case with Dr. Gisela Zurth, employed as a senior researcher in the Berlin-Adlershof Institute of the East German Academy of Science. She obtained permission to attend a congress in West Germany where she made contact with the League. For some eight years she sent back reports on research into chemical and bacteriological weapons, until caught with twenty-nine microfilm rolls of secret documents and blue-prints. As a woman she was spared the death penalty, but she was sent to prison for life. Life imprisonment was also the punishment for Dr. Arnold Kieser, manager of the VEB Radio works at Koepenick. After several years of work for Gehlen, during which his daughter Hannelore, a student at West Berlin University, acted as courier, he was arrested in 1958.

The risks taken by some of these informants in bringing out their material, refusing reward and even expenses, are truly amazing. Manfred Gerlach, in Gehlen's files code-named "Ferdinand", was the technical manager of the aircraft factory at Pirna where parts for Soviet MIGs were manufactured. Twenty-seven times he travelled to Darmstadt—where the "Org" provided him with an imaginary relative, the wife of Professor Gunther B.—thus bringing out six hundred microfilms of technical drawings and of photographs of the assembly products. When in the end he was caught, his highly successful activities so embarrassed the communists that they were never disclosed. He was therefore tried on a trumped-up charge of industrial sabotage, resulting in damage to machinery and production delays. For this his sentence was life imprisonment.

Another aviation technician was Hans Held, who had been employed at the Junkers aircraft works at Dessau from 1934 until the outbreak of the war. He returned there in 1946 and subsequently became supervisor of the engine plant. Later he was manager of construction plant No.5 near East Berlin. In 1951 he was given permission to visit his sister in the American sector and there he got in touch with the League and through it with the "Org". He not only delivered information about developments at Junkers, but obtained from friends who worked as scientists in chemical plants top-secret information about the production of new explosives based on a benzyl-cellulose formula, and of pharmaceutical products, including new streptomycin drugs. He must have been a most versatile man, for among his reports in the "Org" files there are also several descriptions of Soviet airfields and barracks near Dessau, giving many details about the strength of the Soviet Air Force in East Germany.

When Held was eventually caught, he was tried behind locked doors together with another agent, Rudert, who had got into the Gehlen net in 1951. Rudert had a managerial post at the VEB electrical factory at Erfurt and procured information and drawings on the new, classified Gnom valves, which were then being manufactured and exported to the Soviet Union, Poland and China. Rudert was a typical *P-Quelle* agent; he succeeded in gaining the trust not only of his works directors but also of the political "commissars" who were attached to the personnel management, and he became vice-chairman of the trades union council at Erfurt. Besides his technical reports the Pullach files also contain twelve reports on East German trades unions and a plan for emergency measures for safeguarding industrial production and the labour force in the event of a war between the communist countries and the West. Both Held and Rudert were sentenced to death by the Supreme Court of the DDR on January 27, 1956.

Amongst other agents acquired by Gehlen through his contact with the League was Leopold Muller, an engineer at the secret telecommunications centre at Rostock. Muller was also employed at several radio transmitters at Wittenberg, Schwerin and Ludwigslust, and for several years he supplied Pullach with a complete layout of the radio net in East Germany and its communications with the other countries of the Warsaw Pact. From these few examples the extent and richness of the harvest that "Operation Pfifficus" provided for Pullach may be judged. Even today many of its exploits cannot be yet revealed.

Who Knows Whom?

No less important an element in the recruitment of V-men already resident in the target territories was the *Unternehmung Wer Kennt Wen?*—"Operation Who Knows Whom?"—devised by Gehlen and Colonel Otto Wagner, who at one time was chief of the recruitment group at Pullach. Wagner had been a department chief at Admiral Canaris' Abwehr and became one of Canaris' few close friends.[6] In 1941 he took over the Abwehr AST Bulgaria and from his office at Sofia established an espionage network with branch offices in Varna and Burgos on the Black Sea, at Dedegatch and Kavalla on the Aegean, as well as at Karmanli and Svilengrad, thus covering the whole country and northern Greece as well.[7] Gehlen made him, at first, his chief recruiting officer, but Wagner, a staunch anti-nazi who had risked his life during the war when suspected by the Gestapo of conspiring against Hitler, began to raise objections to the employment of former SS and Gestapo men. Gehlen eventually made him head of the Balkans group at Pullach and in this capacity we shall meet him again.

The Pullach "collectors", like the recruiting officers of every intelligence service, had to rely almost entirely on recommendations from people they could trust. The "tippers" were, however, sometimes not fully reliable, and in any case they were unable to provide a sufficient number of leads to meet Gehlen's continual requirements. The "tipping" arrangement also carried with it the risk of enlisting men planted on the "Org" by its opponents. Operation WKW—"Who Knows Whom?"—was, therefore, devised to find V-men on the recommendation of already proven. members of Gehlen's shadow corps.

Inevitably this led to the enlistment of more former nazis. Gehlen tried to explain this, when questioned by an inquiry committee of the Federal Parliament many years later, by stating that one reason for this was that the would-be agents usually belonged to the age group which had served in one capacity or another under the Hitler regime. The other and more plausible reason was that Gehlen expected recruits to have some qualifications for the perilous work they were to do. Military service provided such a qualification. He

(*Left*) A lane in the Archives department at Pullach. Secret dossiers including agents' reports and evaluation are stored in thousands of steel cabinets.

A micro-filmed report containing several hundred words is no bigger than a thumb.

REGIERUNG DER
DEUTSCHEN DEMOKRATISCHEN REPUBLIK
Ministerium für Verkehr
DER STAATSSEKRETÄR

BERLIN W 8, DEN 28.3.1953
Telefon 42943
Tel.: 67 00 15 · 22 08 08
App.: 33 600   50 04

Herrn
G r a m s c h ,
Generaldirektion Schiffahrt,
B e r l i n - NW 7 ,
Clara Zetkinstraße 37.

Der Stellvertreter des Ministerpräsidenten und Leiter der
Koordinierungs- und Kontrollstelle für Industrie und
Verkehr, Herr R a u , hat am 26.3.1953 verfügt, daß
die Transportkommission aufzulösen ist und die Leiter der
Generaldirektionen in ihrem Bereich für den reibungs-
losen Ablauf des Verkehrs voll verantwortlich sind.

Im Auftrage des Stellvertreters des Ministerpräsidenten,
Herrn R a u , spreche ich Ihnen den Dank für Ihre
Tätigkeit in der Transportkommission aus.

gez. Wollweber

Beglaubigt:
(Müller)
Sekretärin.

Gramsch, Walter
Name   Vorname
15.1.1897
Geburtsdatum
2758/49, VPR 28/5
DPA-Nr.   Ausstellende VP-Behörde
Abteilungsleiter
Dienstbezeichnung
Berlin, den   6.5.1953
                        Leiter der Kaderabteilung

A letter from Ernst Wollweber, the East German Minister for State Security, expressing his thanks for the good work of Gehlen's double agent Walter Gramsch ("Brutus") and Gramsch's credentials as an official of the Ministry.

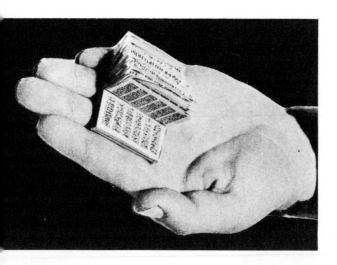

An agent's code book measuring one inch by two. (*Right*) Hans Geyer, alias Henry Troll, the communist double agent who became Gehlen's branch manager and betrayed the telephone sluice operations.

considered it a bonus if the men had specialist training, as radio operators, dispatch runners, drivers, signal corps soldiers, photographers, or rail and transport operatives. If they had served as policemen, field gendarmes, in the Abwehr or in the *Sicherheitsdienst*, this was a distinct advantage, since such men were experienced in security work. He had, however, promised his American sponsors not to employ Gestapo men and Colonel Wagner insisted on keeping this pledge. Thus Wagner selected Abwehr and army officers as "tippers", and hoped that they would exclude ex-Gestapo men from their recommendations.

A few instances may illustrate the success of the WKW system. In 1951, one of Gehlen's "collectors", Hans Leuteritz, recruited a former army officer, Wilhelm von Ackern. This man did subsequently little espionage work himself, but he became an ace of the WKW system because of his wide circle of friends and acquaintances, and perhaps even more so because of what his superior Weller, the branch manager of the *Filiale* 975, called "his sunny nature". Von Ackern was one of those people who make friends easily. After a course at one of Gehlen's special schools, at Backnang on Murr in Wurttemberg, where two of Gehlen's instructors, Willkens and Mertens, trained agents earmarked for infiltration, he became a *V-Mann Führer*.

Within a few months Von Ackern recruited twenty-four new agents, of whom five were trained as *Forscher* (researchers) and nineteen became P- and S-source agents. Some of Von Ackern's friends were also employed as itinerary R-source agents. Two were sent to Poland and one to the Soviet Union. Johann Baumgart and Jan Mszyk, the latter of Polish origin, supplied valuable material about rail communications; Mszyk obtained a temporary job with the Polish State Railroads. Von Ackern worked for almost five years and would have remained an important member of the Organisation—he was paid, in addition to his monthly salary, an expense allowance of 3,600 Marks—had he not become frustrated with his safe office job. He made several trips to the East, and from one, in the spring of 1955, he did not return. Gehlen learnt of Von Ackern's misfortune only when, on June 13, 1955, he stood before the judges of the East German Supreme Court and was sentenced to life imprisonment. With him was tried Johann Baumgart, caught a few weeks earlier; he too, was sent to prison for life.

A large number of agents recruited through the WKW system rarely or never left their home towns in East Germany. Instructed by travelling HV-men and special instructors, they often supplied valuable material over long periods. In some cases, however, the lack of proper training had obvious disadvantages and the V-men did not last very long. A railway worker, for example, named Johannes Goll, had recruited six V-men, including Hans Range, an engineer at the Jena Optical Works of Carl Zeiss. From him Gehlen received important information about the production of instruments for the Soviet Air Force and scientific and aeronautic research institutes in the Soviet Union. But within a year, Goll, Range and several others were arrested and sentenced at Erfurt to long prison terms.

At times the WKW system worked through romantic connections. Although Gehlen had a distinct prejudice against employing female agents, some of his branch managers did employ women, who were sometimes ladies of easy virtue. Fräulein Kathe Feige was a hostess at the *"Fröhliche Insel"* ("Gay Island") nightclub in the Grunewald Strasse in Berlin-Schoneberg. There Ewald Misera, also known as "Eddy Holl", recruited a number of men who became very useful, including Karl Bandelow, who was employed at the East German ministry of communications. Bandelow's output was truly astonishing. Every month he supplied copies of documents and as many as a hundred photographs of rail installations, roads, and bridges, as well as sheafs of military ordnance maps, blue-prints of road building programmes, timetables of military transports and directories and personnel lists of the ministries concerned, which he borrowed from the archives at his office.

The Spies Who Counted the Trains

Material about transport communications was high on Pullach's list of required intelligence. The logistics problems facing the Soviet Army, the new East German People's Army and the armies of the Warsaw Pact countries had to be ascertained to discover how quickly, or otherwise, troops and supplies could be moved. Gehlen had always reckoned with the possibility of an armed conflict between the East and the West, which would begin as conventional warfare on German soil. With the ever-present tension over Berlin and the constant Soviet threats to end Allied control of its western sectors, the city was the natural trigger-point for the "E-Case" (The letter "E" stood for *ernst*, meaning earnest or serious), and.Gehlen devoted much of his attention and labour to producing the E-Plan, which included a voluminous study of the transportation problems of both Soviet and Allied armies.

A large number of "solo V-men" and several teams and networks were, therefore, trained and employed exclusively to gather intelligence about rail, road, waterway and air communications. Several of the Pullach "collectors", particularly Paulberg and Moser, were instrumental in organising R- and S-sources, which stretched into Poland and the Soviet Union. As we shall see, the most valuable material about planning and preparations in this field came from Walter Gramsch, the top official at the East German ministry of communications and chairman of its transport commission. But this unique source dried up in November 1953, when Gramsch had to be hurriedly recalled.

Likewise, another official at the East German ministry of reconstruction and development, Commissioner Walter Schneider, worked for a considerable time for the "Org". He was in contact with one of the few women agents, Frau Christine Heims, who had been infiltrated into the *Bau-Union*, constructions corporation. These two assisted Heinz-Otto Ostereich to organise networks of "on the spot" observers. A proof of how dangerous and damaging their work was considered by the Soviet and East German authorities was the severe sentences meted out after some of these "spotters" were eventually caught. Ostereich's twenty-two-year-old brother Rolf, who had got himself elected as chairman of the Communist Youth League and was a trade union official at Wismar in Mecklemburg, forty-three-year-old Walter Rennert, who specialised in aviation matters, and thirty-eight-year-old Siegfried Altkruger, who became an expert on rail communications from the Soviet Union to East Germany, were all sentenced to life imprisonment.[8]

Although their captures were bitter setbacks, several agents they had recruited carried on, and new "spotter" cells were established. Indeed, the BND and the MAD department of the Federal Army relies on some of these agents for information on strategic communications to this day. Whilst the instances of V-men's activities given above, which ended in the capture and in most cases in executions of the agents, may give the impression that they invariably ended in *débâcles,* it must be remembered that only cases which became known to the Soviet and other communist authorities are here described. A great number of other successful cases remain unsolved puzzles for the KGB chiefs.

XIV

Operation Bohemia

One enterprise, which began by chance and was, at first, regarded by Gehlen as a gamble without much prospect of coming off, was to develop into one of the "Org's" golden windfalls, and endured for many years. After the communist take-over in Prague in February 1948, Gehlen turned his attention to Czechoslovakia and infiltrated a few V-men there, mostly Sudetenland exiles, fluent in Czech and with a good knowledge of the country. But the results of their efforts remained poor. The Czech government had established an efficient secret service and counter-espionage under its fearsome minister of the interior and police, Vaclav Nosek, the most rabid Czech Stalinist, trained in his youth by the Moscow CHEKA. His SNP—the Department of National Security—was staffed by experienced MGB officers, who had come to Prague in the wake of the Red Army in 1945, and nearly all its Czech officials were graduates of Soviet spy schools; some had worked inside Germany during the war, others had been members of the Czech Resistance.

One day in the summer of 1948 a "tipper" mentioned to a Pullach officer that he had met a young girl who had escaped from Czechoslovakia and was staying with an aunt in Passau near the Austrian frontier. The "tipper" suggested the girl might have some useful information since one of her relatives was employed in the Czech security service or police. A *Forscher* was sent out to interrogate the girl. She was a pretty nineteen-year-old student by the name of Rosalie Božena Hayek, and she was quite happy to tell her story. She had been unhappy at home, not because of the political changes, for which she cared little, but because her parents were very strict and forbade her to go out with friends at night. She said she wanted to go to America; she had an uncle in Philadelphia, where he had emigrated before the war. The Pullach man told her this could be arranged and then began delicately to question her about her relatives. The girl mentioned that her older sister was married to an officer who held an important position in the secret service; his name was Captain Vojtech Jeřabek.

The *Forscher* returned to Pullach and made routine enquiries in the archives. Gehlen's unique wartime card index was religiously kept up to date; within minutes the card containing complete data on Captain Jeřabek was produced. It contained a startling entry: Jeřabek, a former teacher who had left Czechoslovakia in 1938 for Russia, had established a remarkable intelligence career by the comparatively early age of thirty-one. He had been trained at the Moscow Institute for International Affairs, the notorious spy academy, and had been one of the few Czechs who had not been pressed into the Red Army but given a desk job at the then NKVB. After his return home he had become head of the SNB station at Karlovy Vary, the once famous spa of Karlsbad. The *Forscher* reported his discovery to Colonel Joachim Rohleder, then in charge of the Pullach III/F group.[1]

At the end of July 1948 Gehlen had a long conference with Rohleder. The agenda was "Penetration of the Czechoslovak SNB". By August 5 a slim folder had reached Gehlen. It contained a single sheet of paper and the cover was labelled OPERATION BOHEMIA. The brief report informed him: "V-man Ondřej left on August 4 at 1700 hours for Prague with orders to contact Staff Captain Vojtech Jeřabek. Assignment: Enrolment of Jeřabek for OG." (OG was the "official" abbreviation for the "Org".)

Soon the folder began to fill up with reports of startling importance. Ondřej was a pre-war intelligence officer in the Czech forces who had fought in the anti-nazi Resistance during the war. Afterwards he found his way into a displaced persons' camp, where he was spotted by a Gehlen interrogator. Following his recruitment, he was trained at the Bad Wiessee school for V-men.

Ondřej arrived in Prague and sought out some of his surviving Resistance comrades. He was warmly welcomed and told the familiar story that he had returned to help build socialism in his liberated homeland. He was given a minor post at the district food ration office at the suburb of Žizhov and he began to look for some old friends who might be serving at the SNB office. Luck was with him; after a week he was sitting opposite Major Vaclav Tyřc, a school-fellow who now had a post in one of the military offices which housed the swelling legions of officialdom. He told Tyřc that he had met a girl in Germany who had run away from home and claimed her brother-in-law, one Captain Jeřabek, was some high-up in the secret service. Tyřc got quite excited about the news: "Yes, I know Jeřabek, that is, if it's Vojtech Jeřabek.... He's got a fine job, spreads himself out at Karlovy Vary and is hand in glove with the Muskovites.... You must go and see him, and tell him all about that silly girl. The family must be terribly worried; it's very

185

unpleasant for Vojtech . . . what will his Russian friends think if they hear that his wife's sister has run off to Germany . . . to the Americans, at that?"

The major appeared none too happy about conditions in Prague, neither did he speak lovingly of the Russian liberators. Ondřej let drop a hint that he might return to Munich where he had been offered an interesting and well-paid job at an American office, which he had foolishly refused because he had felt homesick. The major inquired whether there was another job like that going, and after the third glass of kirsch they understood each other splendidly. The major suggested they should go together to Karlovy Vary and look up Jeřabek. They found the intelligence officer extremely worried. The escapade of his sister-in-law had come to the knowledge of his superiors and he had been questioned about it; apparently there was now a big black mark against his name in the notebook of one of the Soviet MGB supervisors at headquarters.

It did not take Ondřej long to persuade Jeřabek that a discreet exit would solve all his troubles, and that he would get an excellent reception on the other side of the frontier in Bavaria. When Jeřabek told him the next evening that he had decided to accept this advice, Ondřej made a further suggestion: it would be wise to take a few interesting papers with him; they might be worth a small fortune over there.

In Munich Ondřej had arranged with his *Filiale* manager that he would send word if things worked out satisfactorily. The coded note was to be passed to a V-man at Sisice, a village some twenty miles from the frontier. The courier would then use a dead letterbox, from which another courier would collect the message and carry it across the frontier to Furth am Walde, the German frontier post, where the "Org" maintained a permanent *Filiale*. Couriers usually posed as smugglers; they had little difficulty in passing the frontier. A few packets of American cigarettes, or half a pound of second-rate Colombian coffee supplied by the American PX were regarded by some of the frontier guards as a better credential than a passport. This particularly applied to an old and trusted client such as this courier.

After receiving confirmation from Pullach that all necessary arrangements had been made, a little cavalcade set out on a dark and frosty November night in two official SNB cars from Karlovy Vary towards the frontier. Jeřabek had brought his wife and two children, but Major Tyřc was alone; apparently he had taken French leave from his wife. Jeřabek's colleague, Captain Ottokar Fejfar, was also in the party. He had got into trouble with one of the Soviet "commissars" and hurriedly decided to join the others. But he was extremely worried at having left behind his fifteen-year-old daughter, Ludmilla, who had missed the rendezvous for the departure.

The Czech frontier guards saluted smartly when the two motorcars briefly stopped at the barrier. Jeřabek sternly told them that he was going on official business for a few hours to Furth to discuss some official business with the American military police. Maybe the soldiers were puzzled as to why the SNB officer was taking his wife, two children, and a load of passengers to an official meeting, but Jeřabek waved his SNB identity pass in front of their noses and they dared not ask questions. Thus the three Czech officers were taken by Ondřej to his superior in Furth and then brought to the "guest house" of the "Org" at Munich-Straubing where Colonel Rohleder was waiting. Jeřabek handed over the documents he had purloined at his office. They included a list of a score of Czech agents working in Germany. Captain Fejfar was heartbroken; he confessed he had been too frightened to carry his material on him and had left a microfilm roll with his daughter, hoping she could follow the party to the frontier. Colonel Rohleder took pity on him—maybe he also wanted the missing film—and ordered that a V-man resident in Prague should put the girl on the next train. This was arranged by a harmless-sounding telephone call to a commercial office in Prague.

Young Ludmilla arrived the next morning. It was a Sunday, and the disappearance of her father at the weekend had not yet been noticed. Like all members of SNB officers' families, she had a special identy card and had no difficulty in explaining to the frontier police that she was going to visit a school friend for a day or two. All the same, the girl took considerable risks; she carried microfilms of a roster of another Czech network in Germany. The first name on the list was Frantisek Klecka.

The Restaurant Car Waiter

He was one of the busiest Czech spies in the American zone. Though only thirty he had a decade of espionage experience behind him. As a philology student in Vienna before the war, he had worked for the NKVD, narrowly escaped arrest after the 1938 *Anschluss* and fled to Moscow. It was a dangerous time for a foreigner to appear there, for Stalin's bloodbath was at its height. Klecka, however, had earned the confidence of his Soviet bosses, and they sent him to one of the MGB's training schools, whence he emerged as a graduate in secret work. After the 1945 Liberation he returned to his native Prague and was put in control of a spy ring operating inside Bavaria. When direct rail traffic was restored between Munich and Prague the young agent took a job as head-waiter with the International Restaurant Car Company. This enabled him to make snug, well-fed trips twice weekly on the Prague-Paris express and to keep up safe communication between his agents and head office in the Czech capital.

By a typical irony of the trade, Klecka himself was on duty in the restaurant car in which young Miss Fejfar spent most of the journey. At Munich Central Station the friendly head-waiter helped her with her baggage and handed a porter the bag in which was concealed the telling microfilm and the code key of radio signals which he used.

This information Gehlen passed to the American CIC. As a result two Czech rings were smashed. Klecka and several of his accomplices were arrested; others were left temporarily at large in order to keep Moscow and Prague guessing. Klecka was tried by a US military tribunal on February 17, 1949, and was sentenced to twenty years' imprisonment. Prague retaliated by bringing charges of espionage against two American soldiers who had been in their custody since strolling inadvertently across the frontier around Christmastime. They were Sergeant Clarendon Hill and Private George Jones. In order to save them General Clay, the US military governor, reduced Klecka's sentence to five years, indicating that he would be released and deported within a reasonable period. As so often before and since, the communist tactic of "looking after our spies" by bartering them for innocent hostages had been effective. But the Americans hit back: as soon as the two soldiers were freed, the CIC rolled up enough of the remaining rings to produce four further trials, and most of the accused got heavy sentences.

Prague's espionage bosses took every advantage of the sympathetic attitude the Americans showed to refugees from Czechoslovakia. People who wanted to go to the West, particularly Sudetens of German origin, were persuaded to spy for the SNB and MGB. Often they were spurred by the threat that if they refused their relatives would suffer.

Gehlen had many conferences with General Clay, Major-General Ernest N. Harmon, the CIC commander, and Major-General McNarney, commander of US forces in Europe. He warned them of the grave security risks posed by the infiltrators among the refugees. At that time three hundred thousand German civilians and displaced persons were employed in hundreds of offices of the US Army of Occupation, the US military government and the control commission. Gehlen provided proof that these offices had been penetrated by Soviet, Czech, Polish, Hungarian and Yugoslav agents, as well as East German spies. The Americans, however, followed the principle that it was better for ten guilty people to go free than to punish one innocent person by mistake; in the long hard slog of trying to restore democracy and justice in Germany after the years of nazism, such considerations were politically important.

188

Luckily, "Operation Bohemia" solved some of these problems. Jeřabek and Fejfar, besides the lists they had brought, could rattle off dozens of names of other agents and informers supposed to work for the SNB in West Germany. The Pullach III/F officers had their hands full for many months. Besides sifting and analysing the depositions of the defectors, who gave them many personal details about their superiors and colleagues, about the relation of SNB to the Soviet, Polish and Hungarian intelligence services, and a mass of information about political and military subjects, they had to deal with several urgent cases of infiltration by Czech and Polish spies into US Army establishments, about which Jeřabek and Fejfar had enlightened them.[2]

The Spy Who Guarded a US Army Camp

Whilst the CIC was still mopping up the remnants of the betrayed Czech networks, an agent named Andrej Tokarcik was put into Bavaria from Prague. His arrival caused no surprise at Pullach; Jeřabek had expected it. Tokarcik was a trained radio telegraphist and he had slipped across the frontier with a transmitter and a large amount of money. Having hidden his equipment, Tokarcik reported to an International Refugee Organisation camp at Valka, passed an American security check and soon obtained employment in a US Army office at Mannheim. He was not a particularly clever operator, however, and a few months later he was caught copying classified documents. What followed was, from a security point of view, pure farce.

To the military tribunal which tried him, Tokarcik told a hard-luck story so plaintive that his judges could almost hear the gypsy violins: he had been blackmailed into this hateful business in the most cynical manner. Shaking their heads at this tragedy of Central Europe, they let him off with the lenient penalty of one year. Tokarcik was released on the sentimentally appropriate occasion of Christmas week, 1950, and nobody deported him. Instead he went back to Bavaria, made sure his transmitter was all right, got himself some forged papers and was almost immediately accepted into a US Labour Service unit. They gave him a smart blue uniform and a gun and put him on guard duty at a fascinating variety of army establishments, motor pools, an airfield and an army hospital where the patients talked endlessly of what they had seen and done. As help and facilities go, this was spying *de luxe*; and the American pay and rations were not bad either. Tokarcik could have kept it up for years, causing really serious damage, had he not wrecked his own chances. In January 1952 he got into a quarrel with some Germans in a beer cellar, drew his American pistol and wounded one of them.

The German police, being German police, made a routine check of his forged papers with the Gehlen "Org"—and discovered his real identity. Prague's most contented agent was out of business.

The Czech spy was able to play his charade, despite Jeřabek's warning of his impending arrival, becaused he had, of course, used a false name and forged documents and, although Pullach had informed the CIC that his visit was due and had provided a description obtained from the Czech defectors, the CIC apparently let him slip through their fingers.

The Tokarcik case made Gehlen furious. He was already exasperated by a series of similar instances in which lower-level US commands had disregarded even elementary rules of precaution. "It is lost labour to teach Americans security", he told Generals Clay and Harmon. And as events were to demonstrate, where sex was concerned security might never have been devised at all.

Sexual Blackmail

As "Operation Bohemia" continued fruitfully, Gehlen's agents in Czechoslovakia supplied information which led to the obliteration of further communist rings in the US and British zones. One of their reports revealed that Lieutenant-Colonel Jan Salgovič,[3] head of the SNB department running espionage against West Germany, was at his wits' end to find replacements for his continually constantly vanishing spies. He had therefore resorted to recruitment by a technique of sexual blackmail. Salgovič told one of his more personable officers, Captain Ivan Janda, that he would have to become a "professional lover".

Janda decided he would do even better with a woman helper. The suave captain began with the conquest of a pretty Sudeten girl of twenty-five, Edith Dietrich. He had her trained in Prague for a few months, then took her with him into the American zone of Germany. They parcelled out the bedroom battlefield between them. Janda was to "love" young German women employed at US and British headquarters, working in offices of the German regional authorities, or married to civil servants. Edith was to make dates with American officers. She did so and got useful information out of some of them. Janda meanwhile ensnared Maria Heblick, the wife of a Bavarian official. Another of his victims was Elfriede Zierlich, a typist in an American office. He promised her marriage and a well-padded life if she passed him classified papers. Elfriede, whom he code-named "Source Lilian", did so for quite a time.

But eventually Gehlen's ex-SNB men heard of the operation. Janda managed to escape the day before he was due to be arrested, but Edith Dietrich and several of his accomplices were caught. She told her judges how she had fallen "hopelessly in love" with her seducer and been badly used by him; but this time the violins did not sigh, and she got a nine-year sentence. Frau Hablick, who had stolen her husband's secret files to oblige her lover, got seven years, and "Source Lilian" three.

A year later Gehlen's V-men penetrated another Czech spy net through "Operation Bohemia". It had twenty members, including several radio operators, in various parts of Germany and was controlled by on Jaroslav Zajicek, who talked a great deal after his arrest. He was a real stone in the pond—the eddies of what he told the CIC interrogators extended to swamp several other rings, all controlled by Soviet "directors". Zajicek also revealed that the communist spy-masters, in their search for competent agents, were ready to employ former nazis and Gestapo men.

Zajicek, the Americans learnt with some consternation, had been a productive fellow. He had collaborated with the Germans during the war, joined the Waffen SS and served in Italy. The Gestapo brought him back and employed him against the Czech Resistance, which had killed the "Protector" Heydrich by bombing his car in a British-based operation. After the war, using his old Gestapo contacts, Zajicek managed to worm his way into the German administrative offices. He had collected information on the strength of US Air Force formations, the pattern of its air bases, new types of aircraft sent from the United States, details of radar installations, radar-operated gunsights, artillery and missile emplacements and firepower, and chemical warfare depots. To add to this merry pile, he had obtained manuals and secret reports on the state of the training and morale of US troops in Germany which were prepared at Frankfurt headquarters for the eyes of the Pentagon. One of his most worrying disclosures was that he had secured much of this highly professional and sensitive material by using sexual blackmail against American officers. Zajicek, like Janda, had employed several women, and the officers had been threatened with disclosure of their affairs to their wives or superiors.

Some time after this case, a Gehlen V-man met the wife of a man named Georg Paintz, a smuggler engaged in running American cigarettes, tobacco and coffee over the border into Czechoslovakia, where the communist ideology had not quite strangled the appetite for such trivialities—or not, at any rate, in the upper reaches of the Party. Frau Paintz told the V-man that she had been nervous when her husband confided that he had been asked by two men to take a coded letter across on his next run. She did not know the V-man's real business. He reported this to his own station and Paintz was questioned. The smuggler said he had been told to put the letters in "strange hiding places" which were of course dead drops. Among them were hollow trees in the Fichtel forest and disused pipes along the Bayreuth-Marktredwitz railway line. Paintz led Gehlen's V-men and a group of CIC officers to the drops. Inside were several cyphered messages.

The Microfilm Missioner

The trail eventually led to Emil Szwiertna, a Pole who had packed a lifetime of espionage into his thirty-five years. A member of the Polish Communist youth league in the 1930's, he had spent five years in German wartime concentration camps. On being freed in 1945, he became an agent once more, and was sent to London as a member of the first post-war Polish trade mission. His next assignment was in Switzerland, after which he came to Bavaria as head of one of the frontier rings of Polish and Czech spies.

He set up cells in Stuttgart, Ludwigsburg and Munich, where his main target was the headquarters of the US Seventh Army. Szwiertna's network was highly ingenious in the matter of dead-drop communication. Microfilmed copies of purloined documents were placed in jam-jars and buried along the sidewalks bordering the Seventh Army's main compound, where several of Szwiertna's assistants worked as civilian clerks. After his arrest he calmly admitted that some of them even used the G-2 office's photographic darkroom for copying classified files and reports.

This further example of penetration could not be ignored by the CIC, whatever it felt about restoring democratic principles in German life. They were faced with investigating seven hundred civilian employees at army bases in a hunt which lasted over six months and, as a judge remarked at Szwiertna's trial, cost fifty thousand dollars. Even then they were not much wiser. It was not until May 1951, when the energetic Pole had been sentenced to twelve years in prison, that several of his humbler colleagues began to sing in the hope of lighter stretches. In this case, it was the heavy sentence which helped to smash the ring and winkle out the spies in the military's bosom.

The "Org" followed up by breaking another Czech Intelligence operation which this time led most embarrassingly into the CIC itself. Hans Horst Baumgarten, a thirty-nine-year-old interpreter and translator, was employed on confidential work at the CIC office at Freyling in Bavaria, where he was completely trusted by high-ranking officers. His record was clean: he had been mixed up in anti-nazi activities during the war and had spent several years in concentration camps. Baumgarten went to work for the Americans in 1947, was quickly promoted and assisted the CIC in interrogating war criminals and suspected agents. He also had access to restricted documents—a privilege he greatly appreciated, seeing that since 1949 he had been working for the chief of Czech espionage in Frankfurt, a major named Obrich Burda. Burda went under the alias of "Otto Wenzel" and his days were filled with an avalanche of American paper work.

Apart from his good CIC salary, Baumgarten drew the princely sum of one thousand Marks (then about 250 dollars) from the Czechs as a monthly retainer. His chief courier, Peter Harnung, indulged in smuggling tobacco and coffee, a practice regarded as virtually legitimate by everyone except the German frontier guards. When they arrested Harnung they found on him a scrap of paper in code. Being German frontier guards, they did what the policemen had done in the case of the airfield guard; they informed the Pullach III/F, The trail led from Harnung to Baumgarten, and a fuming Gehlen notified the CIC that their well-loved interpreter was more than likely working for the Czechs. Only then did the military sleuths realise what had been going on under their noses.

Baumgarten had not done badly by Major Burda for his monthly stipend. He had sent out photographs and microfilm of material from the CIC and HICOG headquarters, including information on the repercussions of the Korean War on army strength in Germany. Order-of-battle officers in Moscow and Prague, no doubt humming to themselves as they updated their boards, knew which US combat units were being withdrawn from Germany and any reductions in the flow of aircraft, spares, ammunition and equipment arising from the Korean commitments.

This time the trial was conducted behind closed doors. Baumgarten and Harnung were given fifteen years each, and several of their helpers received sentences of up to ten years. A number of CIC officers were recalled to the United States and later dismissed the services.

Gehlen's opinion of American security after that sank even lower. Not only had these penetrations endangered the Allied military defence line in Europe, but they now stood to ruin the patient and intricate infiltrations which were bringing such good results from the East. Indeed Pullach was now convinced that Baumgarten had betrayed four Gehlen agents from inside the CIC office. Two of these, Karl Bartak and Karl Bosak, had been based at Gehlen's "frontier post" at Furth am Walde, the village on the wooded slopes of the Rieseck which was, as has been seen, an important relay point for couriers, *passeurs* and other communications with the "turned" SNB agents in Czechoslovakia. It also kept Pullach in touch with V-men whom Gehlen had placed in Cesky Brod and had infiltrated into the key target of the Skoda armaments plant at Pilsen. The other agents he lost at that time, as well as several couriers, were Jaroslav Vacik and Vaclav Stradal, an official of the Czech ministry of justice, enlisted by Fejfar, who had been a most valuable source. All were tried in Prague and given heavy sentences, Bartak and Bosak receiving life terms.

Stung by these casualties, Gehlen told members of the US military government in Frankfurt that unless security was improved he would be forced to withhold top-secret information. While he was issuing this threat, however, he had no idea that a far more dangerous cuckoo was already rifling his own nest from a key desk inside Pullach itself.

The Intrepid Polish Colonel

The Polish spy rings in West Germany were, if anything, even more daring than their Czech counterparts, and the capture of Szwiertna had by no means drawn their sting. Though Gehlen had set up his special "Polish Section" mainly with positive intelligence in mind, it now found itself increasingly occupied on counter-espionage assignments in close cooperation with his III/F units. He enlisted several ex-officers with long experience in this area. One of these was Dr. Emil Augsburg, a *Volksdeutscher* born in Poland, who had served there on Himmler's wartime staff.* Another of the Polish Section's specialists was Gotthard Gebauer, known at Pullach by his alias "Gellert" (though more often by the unflattering nickname of *Marzipan-Schweinchen*, or "candy pig"). A Silesian, he spent most of the war as an Abwehr officer in Poland and later served under Gehlen at FHO. These two experts afterwards had much to do with arranging the infiltrations of Pullach agents into the country they knew so well.

Gehlen wanted to concentrate on setting up these offensive penetrations. He showed dwindling interest in the Augean chore of helping the Americans to clean spies out of their own offices. However, in several cases he did switch his efforts to breaking Polish rings in the US and British zones, and Augsburg and "Gellert" were largely instrumental in uncovering them.

The first of these cases concerned a former Polish cavalry commander, Colonel Gregor Kowalski. After his homeland was defeated in 1939 he escaped with other Polish soldiers through the Balkans to France and reached England. In London he was appointed adjutant to the Polish leader, General Wladyslaw Sikorski, who went to his mysterious death at Gibraltar in July 1943.[4] After the war Kowalski was one of the very few Polish officers to return home and throw in

*See page 240

194

their lot with the new communist regime in Warsaw—and to be trusted by it. By 1948 Kowalski was in the British zone of Germany, ostensibly as head of a Polish reparations mission. In fact he was there for espionage. He renewed his acquaintance with British officers who remembered the gallant way he had distinguished himself with the Polish brigade on D-day and again at Arnhem. Even though some had the sense to treat him with caution, the dashing colonel was invited to British officers' clubs and was able to pick up many nuggets of careless talk. After a similar tour of the American zone Kowalski returned to his Polish mission headquarters in Berlin to found the most complex and wide-ranging network that Gehlen had yet had to tackle. Code-named the "Kolberg Ring", it operated for three years with brilliant success.

The Kolberg Ring, though it collected an enormous amount of information on military matters, aimed particularly at the highest policy levels of political intelligence. Its web ran from Berlin to Frankfurt and into Cologne. Kowalski recruited as his chief lieutenant a former German officer, Heinko Kunze, who posed as an art historian. They used as their front an antique shop owned by a woman named Marie-Louise Frankenberg in the American sector of Berlin. Kunze introduced his mistress Maria Knuth, an attractive actress, into the ring and she worked in the shop as bait for American and British customers. When friendships which such officers ripened in the intended way, she entertained them in an apartment which Kunze had in Frankfurt; the network also arranged a second love-nest in a luxurious villa on the outskirts of Cologne.

Effective though the system was, it had unforeseen results. Apparently unable to bear the continuing strain of seeing his mistress prostituted under the pressure of Kowalski's blackmail, Kunze committed suicide. But Maria Knuth, whether she mourned him deeply or not, proved tougher; she kept up her espionage and transferred her favours to her Polish boss. A principal target of the Kolberg Ring was the super-sensitive *Amt Blank*, the office newly set up by Dr. Adenauer's cabinet minister, Theodore Blank, to prepare for the formation and equipment of the future Federal German Army[5]. Pressed by Warsaw for details of this German rearmament programme, Kowalski did his utmost to penetrate Blank's department. In his understandable eagerness, however, his *apparat* fell victim to a beautifully conducted counter-penetration which must be rated as one of the classic operations in the annals of that treacherous business.

The BfV at that time had little experience or competence in the battles of Cold War espionage; and, to be fair to it, it had plenty to do keeping track of the more overt dangers posed by both neo-nazi and militant left-wing groups. However, the BfV did have an agent, Ernst Boldt, who had been trained at one of Gehlen's spy schools. Ranged against Kowalski now were American, British, Gehlen and BfV resources; if they were not a coalition, at least they kept in contact, and among them they came up with leads pointing to the existence of the Kolberg Ring. As soon as they had something to go on, Boldt was prepared for his assignment. He assumed the identity of "Dr. Petersen", an official of the *Amt Blank,* and waited for the red fish to rise. They did.

Marie Knuth met "Dr. Petersen" and reported back to Kowalski that he was troubled by the idea of a rearmed Germany. He was willing to supply information—and thought he might even get her a job in his office. The Polish colonel sent a triumphant message to his controllers (which counter-espionage duly intercepted) announcing that he had penetrated the *Amt.* "Petersen" was recruited into the Kolberg Ring as a valued member. Gehlen, with American and British Intelligence experts, had fun concocting "play material" for Boldt to pass on. Kowalski beamed on reading a letter from Dr. Adenauer and "secret" plans for the organisational structure of the *Bundeswehr* and American arms supplies.

Since the colonel's controllers had been even more exercised to produce some inkling of German military intentions for their masters, congratulations passed back down the line. Kowalski was commended and told that his reports were being read with great interest by Marshal Rokossovsky, the Soviet commander-in-chief of the Polish Army. All such deception games, however, must sooner or later end, and Allied Intelligence officers realised from monitored radio signals to "Kolberg" that Warsaw was beginning to get suspicious. It was time to move in. In May 1952 the final trap was laid for Maria Knuth. British officers of MI5 arrested her while she was collecting a *poste-restante* letter from Kowalski in a Cologne post office. German police pounced on other members of the ring. Their catch included Inspector Hermann Westbold of the Frankfurt police, and a middle-aged woman, Marianne Oppelt, who worked in the police passport department. But, thanks to a misunderstanding among the various Allied intelligence groups in the operation, Colonel Kowalski himself ducked out of Berlin on the eve of the round-up and crossed to safety in the East.

The trial of the Kolberg Ring members was the first espionage case dealt with by a German Federal court. The relatively light sentence of three years imposed on Maria Knuth was influenced by the fact that she had cancer (she died after two years in the prison hospital). Neither Pullach nor the Allied intelligence men, however, could see why the "bent" policeman Inspector Westbold should have been given an equally lenient term, and the rest of the ring got off with a few months each, being regarded by the judges as mere dupes.

The destruction of this ambitious network led to the discovery of further Polish rings. One was headed by Captain Wlodek Kamien and another by an old hand with the impenetrable name of Theodore Szczendzielorz. The latter had been trailed for some time by V-men from Gehlen's Polish section at Pullach, which had hopes of "turning" him and playing him back as a double agent. He had served in Polish Military Intelligence before the war, until he was caught by the Gestapo while spying in Germany in 1938 and sentenced to death. Instead of being executed he was sent to a succession of concentration camps. He survived Buchenwald and was freed from the extermination camp at Gross Rosen by the Russians in 1945. He returned to Poland but by 1948 was in Germany again as a communist agent, having apparently retained his taste for dangerous living.

But his Pole's imagination once more outran his skill, and what happened to him made an unpleasant contrast to the light sentences passed on the German nationals of the Kolberg Ring. After his arrest, Gehlen's officers who examined his records were exceedingly amused by the claptrap he had been sending his Warsaw employers. One of his reports was a full and compelling description of a "motorless aircraft" which the Americans were supposed to be supplying to the as yet embryonic German forces. In another he assured them that "the total stockpile of American atom bombs in West Germany is about six hundred". Nevertheless, he had also sent some well drawn maps and accurate figures on locations and strengths of US and British Army units. For the second time this ageing adventurer stood trial for espionage. He was sent to prison for thirty years—which, he told his judges, "will mean my death". His accomplices also received heavy sentences.

The counter-espionage operations of the Gehlen "Org" were crowned with some decided successes, as these few instances show. But Gehlen always regarded this work merely as a minor adjunct to his main function of mounting positive intelligence offensives against the Soviet Union and the satellites of that part of the world known on the maps of Pullach as the *S-Block*. Trapping Russian, Czech and Polish spies in Germany might be of some help in this direction, for information could certainly be gathered from those who were willing to talk or defect. Even so, he knew very well that in the secret arena it seldom pays to take one's eye off the ball for long. His own interests lay in carrying the campaign into the opposition's home camp.

"Operation Bohemia" was by no means finished after the collapse of the Czech rings, which the SNB never managed to revive on the previous scale. In fact, the infiltration of agents into the very heart of the Prague intelligence system went on for many years, resulting in 1968 in Gehlen's final *coup*: obtaining advance information of plans for the Soviet invasion of Czechoslovakia during the short-lived "liberalisation" regime of Alexander Dubček.

XV

War Of The Radio Waves

Although experimental broadcasts of speech and music took place in Britain and the United States only fifty years ago and regular transmissions for the entertainment and edification of listeners two or three years thereafter, "steam radio" appears to us well-nigh archaic in the era of colour television, which can bring into our living-rooms pictures of astronauts straddling the moonscape. Yet its power as a medium of propaganda remains unrivalled. The distribution of newspapers and books can be suppressed; but even the most ingenious attempts at jamming the radio waves have never fully succeeded in stopping the spoken word over the ether.

Radio propaganda in the strict sense began about fifty years ago. The Soviet Union was the first, the United States the last nation to embark on it. Within a few weeks after Hitler came to power in 1933, Dr. Goebbels became its unrivalled master. The British turned to it slowly, but soon achieved mastery, for they succeeded as no other nation in concealing the purpose and aim of propaganda broadcasts behind a civilised and apparently objective style of delivery. In comparison, Goebbels' vulgar and blatantly mendacious use of the radio waves defeated its purpose. In the United States radio propaganda on an international scale developed slowly after the Administration came to an arrangement with the NBC and CBS by which they would broadcast "inspired" material over and above that sent out by government-sponsored World Wide Broadcasting Foundation stations.

The war brought an undreamt of upsurge in propaganda broadcasting; German stations transmitted hardly anything else, using Beethovén's or Richard Wagner's music and Goethe's poetry as side-dishes to sweeten Goebbels' indigestible fare and Hitler's bellowed verbosity. No less enormous was the outflow from Radio Moscow, broadcasting in many languages a mixture of high-flown patriotic oratory and obscene invective against the fascist beasts of Hitler's Germany.

To beleaguered Britain, radio became the most important link with the outside world and the most valuable means for disseminating propaganda, providing nazi-subjugated Europe with, on the whole, truthful and objective news which kept up flagging spirits and encouraged resistance against the oppressor. Though it is, of course, a hyperbole to say that Churchill's broadcasts to the nation "won the war", there is little doubt that they greatly strengthened the determination of the British people to hold out in darkest days and to retain confidence in ultimate victory.

Last but not least, radio had become the most important instrument of intelligence and espionage communications. Already in the First World War wireless telegraphy had made its first appearance in this field, although it could be used over short distances only and mainly to convey signals from the front lines and trenches to command headquarters in the rear and vice versa. None of the 1914-18 spies used radio to communicate with his masters; invisible ink, coded letters, or whenever possible cyphered telegrams to cover addresses in neutral countries were his communication media, which now seem to us as old-fashioned as carrier-pigeons.

During the Second World War the waves were overcrowded with espionage traffic. The *sub rosa* activities of OSS, the dispatch of almost seven thousand British and Allied agents and sabotage instructors by parachute and boat from England to nazi-occupied Europe, the operations of the "Red Orchestra" in Germany,[1] the Rado and Lucy ring in Switzerland,[2] the enterprises of the German Abwehr, *Sicherheitsdienst*, *Zeppelin* and WALLI commandos, the *Funkspiele* and, last but not least, Gehlen's own radio deception achievement at FHO—all these would have been impossible without the use of radio.

The Cold War added new aspects and, if possible, an increased volume of transmissions and clandestine signals flooded the ether. Here the United States, with its enormous electronic industrial potential and financial resources, was first in the field and in West Germany radio propaganda flourished on a scale never attempted before. There a remarkable coalition of US government and private enterprise interests created the most powerful world-wide broadcasting network in history.

Gehlen Gets a Powerful Ally

In the summer of 1948, a man who had been a "black intelligence operator" almost all his adult life had come from Washington to Europe to co-ordinate American Intelligence efforts. He was Frank G. Wisner, a Mississippi-born lawyer who had been involved in American undercover activities before the war in Germany and after 1941 joined OSS under Allen Dulles, to become its chief in Rumania, where he succeeded in stirring up a strong anti-nazi opposition within the Antonescu regime. In a later phase of the war he moved to Turkey where he conducted a battle of wits with Franz von Papen, head of the huge German spy network. When peace came and OSS was broken up, he returned—like his friend Dulles—to his legal practice with the New York firm of Carter, Ledyard and Milburn.

In November 1947, Wisner was called to the State Department on Dulles' recommendation and given the lofty rank of a deputy assistant secretary of state. Soon afterwards the newly established National Security Council produced a secret document (NCS 10/2, later to become notorious as "ten-slash-two") creating a hush-hush body innocuously named the Office of Policy Coordination. It was nothing less than a parallel, if miniature, CIA. President Truman and his first secretary of defence, James V. Forrestal, were becoming increasingly worried about the suspended animation of the CIA under cautious Rear-Admiral Hillenkoetter.

Hillenkoetter, accurately enough described by the expert Kim Philby[3] as "an amiable sailor who did not leave much of a mark on American Intelligence history",[4] seemed satisfied to receive what Gehlen's "Org", at that time just finding its feet at Pullach, was sending—the first modest information from a few V-men, statistics on Soviet military deployment in East Germany, and bits and pieces on political events behind the Iron Curtain. The admiral thought Gehlen was giving good value for the money he was receiving. The daily "get" of intelligence, as it is called in the jargon of the professionals, seemed to contain sound stuff from the mysterious East; it was nicely retyped and laid on President Truman's desk each morning with the CIA report in a large envelope adorned with the agency's new emblem proudly embossed in blue.

The Cominform was making every effort to soften up Western Europe for a pre-revolutionary upheaval. The White House, Congress and the State Department had become alarmed by the *Putsch* in Czechoslovakia, when the communist premier Klement Gottwald decided that it was time to end the unnatural pseudo-democracy based on a coalition with the Social Democrats and Liberals. He ousted Benes from the presidency, and Jan Masaryk, the foreign minister and staunchest friend of the West, was found dead in mysterious circumstances.[5] A totalitarian police state completely subservient to Moscow came into being in Prague. France, despite the outpouring of Marshall Aid, was on the verge of economic collapse; in Italy a communist victory in the forthcoming elections seemed almost certain, possibly followed by a *Putsch* on the Czech pattern.

In Germany relations between the Western Allies and the Russians had gone from bad to worse. In December 1947, Secretary of State

201

Marshall laid bare the imperialist aims of the Soviet Union and her determination to sabotage the rehabilitation not only of Germany but of the whole of Europe, in the hope of extending communist domination over western and southern Europe. In his report he said: "The issue is really clear-cut. Leaders of the Soviet Union and the Communist Parties in Europe openly predict that this restoration will not take place. We, on the other hand, are confident of the rehabilitation of European civilisation . . . . "

To constructive measures taken by the Western Powers in Germany, the Soviet Union responded with a series of aggressive steps which had the declared aim of ousting the Western Allies from Berlin, and of starving the city into submission. The timetable of these events is significant. On March 20, 1948, the Soviet representatives walked out of the Allied Control Council for Germany—a far cry from the day when the first military governors of the United States and the Soviet Union, General Eisenhower and Marshal Zhukov, toasted each other in the same building and sang "Old Man River". On April 1 the Soviet authorities imposed the first rail and road restrictions on Allied military and supply traffic to West Berlin. On June 23, Soviet representatives walked out of the Berlin *Kommandatura*; their obvious intention was to produce chaos in the administration of the city.

Up to that time the movements of population between the Western and the Soviet sectors was fairly free. The municipal council was elected from all four sectors. Despite every effort to produce an impressive number of communist councillors—and there was a great deal of intimidation—the communists and their allies polled less than one fifth of the votes, the non-communist parties gaining eighty-nine seats to their nineteen. The town hall was in the Soviet sector (and occupied by the communist police), and thousands of party members, brought to Berlin in Soviet Army trucks from all over East Germany, now began to stage riots all over the city. The election of mayor Ernst Reuter was prevented by the Soviet commander, General Kotikov. The next morning the Soviet authorities closed all roads and water routes between Berlin and the country, and stopped all rail traffic from West Germany. Marshal Sokolovski, the commander-in-chief of the Soviet Army of Occupation publicly stated: "The Americans, British and French are now in Berlin only on sufferance; soon there will be only one controlling authority in the city, that of the Soviet Union." Russian and German agitators spread rumours that Western troops would soon leave the city. Radio broadcasts from the outside world and from Allied transmitters in West Berlin were jammed. The cold hand of fear descended on the population. This fear was aggravated when the British and French began to evacuate the families of their officials and officers. General Lucius D. Clay, however, stopped similar plans at the American headquarters. The Russians began to cut telephone communications. The East Berlin radio station announced that water supplies to West Berlin, which came from reservoirs in the Soviet sector, would be stopped. Everywhere around the borders of the three Western sectors Soviet tanks and strong units of infantry and artillery took up positions.

At one stage during that momentous week, the Western Allies considered breaking the blockade by military force. This would have meant war. General Clay decided on a different solution: a mass airlift of foodstuffs and coal to the beleaguered city. This at first seemed impossible. To feed the population of two million a daily supply of four thousand tons of food was needed and another five hundred tons to provide rations for the Allied troops and officials and their families. Yet, the airlift was carried through. For eleven months every scrap of food and every lump of coal the people used was transported by air from the West. In a total of 277,728 flights, American, British and a few French airmen brought in 2,343,300 tons of supplies. At the height of the airlift, planes were landing at airports and improvised airstrips at the rate of one every forty-five seconds. The Russians did not dare to shoot down an aircraft, since they knew that the Allies would have regarded that as a belligerent action. But they buzzed the unarmed planes and intercepted radio and radar signals, causing many accidents and crashes in which seventy-one airmen, including thirty-one Americans, lost their lives. Moscow hoped that the winter, with fog, frost and bad visibility would bring the airlift to a halt and force the Allies to abandon the city. They erred in this, however, and in the end they had to admit defeat. By May 1949, after a meeting of Stalin's envoys with Western representatives in New York, all restrictions were lifted.

Wisner arrived in Berlin during the summer of 1948, at the height of the airlift crisis. Gehlen came up from Pullach and they had long conferences. Indeed, Wisner spent more time with Gehlen than with General Clay and officials of the US military government. Gehlen had warned Washington of the Soviet plans to take Berlin either by starving it out, or by a *coup de main*, or by a combination of both. But his reports were not believed. He told Wisner of Soviet plans long before they became apparent; including the intended setting up of the German Democratic Republic, which Moscow would recognise, thus making permanent Germany's division into two states. He also told him of the rapid increase in the strength of the VOPO, the "People's Police". This was in fact, an army with several tank divisions and its own air force, which soon numbered well over 140,000 men, it was followed by the creation of the "National

People's Army", heavily armed with modern Soviet weapons and commanded by Russian officers. The East German Army proper was established more than a year ahead of the first, puny units of the new Federal German defence forces. Within less than three years it had grown to over 250,000 men.

Gehlen and Wisner became firm allies. Wisner's Office of Policy Co-ordination was a hybrid; it was nominally controlled by a triumvirate of the Pentagon, the State Department and the CIA. In fact it was very much a one-man show, and became known to its contemporaries as "the department of dirty tricks". Its speciality was subversion and counter-subversion, and Wisner conducted it with almost unlimited independence. Gehlen must greatly have envied him; he decided to emulate Wisner's enterprise.

Wisner was ready to help. The "ten-slash-two" directive of the National Security Council had provided him with large unvouchered funds. Some of them Wisner used in Italy, with the result that the expected communist election victory was much less formidable then Washington had feared. A large sum went to Gehlen and this enabled him to embark upon many new operations for which he had hitherto had insufficient funds.

Radio Free Europe

The Soviet blockade of Berlin was accompanied by violent and effective propaganda by radio, leaflets and newspapers which was aimed at frightening West Berliners and West Germans and weakening their trust in the Allies. Hitherto the latter had made hardly any answer to this concerted propaganda assault. Wisner, advised by Gehlen and several of his radio experts, immediately went to work to remedy this situation: a powerful radio transmitter was to be established to counteract communist aggression over the ether. Even when the initial plans were still being drafted, Wisner was envisaging a chain of transmitters, broadcasting in all the languages of the many nations within the Soviet orbit, which would fan discontent, and encourage opposition and open rebellion against the communist rulers.

Initially there was only one American medium which could be used. This was RIAS ("Radio in the American Sector"), the official transmitter of the US military commander in Berlin; it limited its transmission to brief bulletins, news talks and a great deal of musical entertainment. Wisner had little difficulty in impressing upon Major-General Frank L. Howley, the sector commandant, that RIAS programmes must be radically revised. Gehlen provided a few experienced broadcasters, which soon brought more zip into the transmissions. But the plan of the great transmitter took some time to come to fruition; above all it required very large funds, which Wisner was unable to obtain from his superiors.

He turned to American business tycoons for help. Allen Dulles, whom President Truman had asked to head a committee of three[6] to investigate the effectiveness of Hillenkoetter's CIA, willingly offered his help. The two company lawyers passed the begging bowl along with splendid success. At that time several private bodies in the United States, such as the Council on Foreign Relations, the Council Against Communist Aggression, Congress for Cultural Freedom, American Friends of Russian Freedom, the Free Asia Committee and a number of "citizens' committees" in several states and cities (some of which were to lend support to Senator Joseph McCarthy), were engaged in fighting communism in their own fashion. Dulles and Wisner enlisted the prestigious help of General Eisenhower, who had retired from his post as US chief of staff to become the president of Columbia University, and assembled the Free Europe Committee,[7] whose list of sponsors read like a Who's Who of American industry and banking.

Headed by Alan Valentine, erstwhile Yale history professor and Rhodes scholar at Oxford who had gone into big business and was a director of the Finance Securities Trust Company, the American Sulphur Corporation and the Buffalo-Rochester-Pittsburg Railroad, they included Clark McAdams Clifford, a director of the National Bank of Washington, C. Rodney Smith, president of American Airlines, Frank Altschul, senior partner in the banking house of Lazard Frères, C. D. Jackson of the Luce Organisation, publisher of *Time, Life* and *Fortune* magazines, A. F. Francis, chairman of the General Food Corporation, the world's largest breakfast cereal manufacturers, Henry Ford II, Edwin H. Land, president of Polaroid, and William O. Baker, vice-president of the Bell Telephones Corporation. There were many more willing donors, amongst them General Motors, General Electric, Westinghouse, Chrysler, United Food and all the oil companies, headed by Esso and Standard Oil.

Early in 1950 Radio Free Europe was installed in a row of prefabricated buildings in the Englischer Garten, a pleasant park in the centre of Munich. Within an amazingly brief period, with an initial budget of ten million dollars, Radio Free Europe began its transmissions from its new, powerful station; it also used existing transmitters in several friendly countries. In the course of time RFE grew into a chain of twenty-nine radio stations, beaming round-the-clock anit-communist propaganda in sixteen languages to East Germany, Poland, Czechoslovakia, Hungary, Rumania, Bulgaria, Yugoslavia and the former Baltic states. Broadcasts in Albanian were eventually discontinued when it was discovered that there were very

205

few radio receivers in that Chinese-oriented country. Today RFE transmitters are also situated in Portugal, Spain, Greece and Turkey and they cooperate with another chain of CIA-sponsored radio stations in Saudi Arabia, Iran, Pakistan, Thailand, Vietnam, Indonesia and Japan, which cover the Middle East, Africa, Asiatic Russia, South East Asia and the Far East.

From Frankfurt the war of the ether was initiated by a kindred foundation, Radio Liberty, which broadcast exclusively to the Soviet Union in a multitude of its languages and dialects, from Russian, Ukrainian, Ruthenian, Finnish and Latvian to Turcomen, Tadzik, Chuvach and the Ural-Altaic dialects of Mongolia. The official *Voice of America* completed the mighty barrage, catering for listeners with sufficient knowledge of English.

Gehlen eagerly cooperated from the very outset with RFE and its supervisors from the Office of Policy Co-ordination, Colonel Kotek and William Griffith. He delegated as his liaison officer ex-SA Bannfuhrer Peter Fischer, who went under the alias of "Major Fiedler". He had become the chief radio expert at Pullach, and could boast excellent credentials. During the war he had served in the SD in the Netherlands under SS Sturmbannfuhrer Joseph Schreieder, who had been instrumental in conducting *Funkspiel* radio deceptions with London, succeeding in catching by the use of fake signals nearly every SOE agent sent to the Dutch Resistance from England, and also the leaders of the Resistance Council.[8]

First Link with Aerial Intelligence

Another important factor in Gehlen's rise was the encouragement he received from Major-General John B. Ackerman, who became chief of US Air Force Intelligence (A-2) in Germany. The Air Force had been freed from army control and placed as an independent service under a new Washington department headed by Secretary W. Stuart Symington. As the defence arm most popular with the American public, and with an appropriation vastly outstripping those for the army and navy put together, it carried decisive weight in the shaping of strategic policy. Hence its intelligence division had moved up mightily in the market for information, and this was reflected in Germany. It was said that Ackerman was personally convinced that war with the Soviet Union was only a question of time. After the outbreak of the Korean War in 1950, he instituted a special intelligence branch in Germany, along the lines of Britain's MI9, to plan an escape organisation for US airmen shot down over Russia and Eastern Europe.

Major-General Ackerman and his aides were alive to the increasing need for photographic surveillance of the Soviet sphere and for the many forms of radio and electronic intelligence, known in espionage jargon as "elint". The employment of spy planes, such as the U-2 and EC-121, was still to come. But meanwhile it was possible to stuff existing aircraft with receivers, recorders, radar scopes and computing equipment and to penetrate at least the edges of communist air space. From even faint signals unscrambled from the "grass"—the background static—an extraordinary amount of technical intelligence could be extracted. Intercepted air-to-air conversations between communist pilots revealed much about the aircraft they were flying. Vectors and landing directions given out by flight controllers helped to locate secret airfields. And overheard radio traffic between ground troops gave clues to their weaponry and procedures, as well as providing material for the American code-breakers to study.

Radio contact with planes on such penetration sorties already occupied the minds of Ackerman and Gehlen. The Soviet military government in Berlin had complained of recurring infringements of East German air space by American aircraft. The A-2 branch had established a number of headquarters in the US zone of Occupation, one of which was the Konigshof Hotel in Munich. With Gehlen just down the road, as it were, and Radio Free Europe round the corner, Ackerman was nicely placed to put together what he had in mind. One of his nominees became a RFE executive; he had an inter-service liaison with CIA—a link which later led to the shared control of the B-36 and RB-47 "weather reconnaissance" flights and eventually to the U-2 long-range penetrations. How Gehlen eventually became closely associated with the US Air Force and A-2 Intelligence, when he initiated the first parachute drops of his agents into Soviet territory—an enterprise which ended in almost unrelieved disaster—is described in another chapter.

Radio communications became the mainstay of the "Org", particularly after 1956, when travel between East and West Germany was heavily restricted, and even more so when the erection of the Berlin Wall in 1961 made it impossible or highly dangerous for V-men to move from one part of the city to the other. Radio Free Europe and the other "private" stations in Germany were widely and successfully used for transmitting coded, or even musical, signals to agents operating behing the Iron Curtain. Gehlen already had, of course, a powerful transmitter at Pullach; another was later erected at Stocking near Munich, and eventually a third was operated by the Frankfurt-Cologne regional branch of the "Org". However, Soviet and East German counter-espionage had perfected the interception of clandestine radio transmitters in their territories, using advanced types of mobile D/Fing (direction-finding) devices which led to the uncovering of many of Gehlen's operators. Signals were picked up and, at times, Pullach had to order radio silence. D/Fing worked, of course, both ways and many more Soviet spies were trapped by the superior electronic devices supplied to CIC and Pullach by the US Federal Communications Commission.

Berlin Uprising Directed by Radio

Gehlen's radio system, though then still in a fledgeling state, came into its own particularly during the Berlin revolt of 1953. The uprising caused no surprise at Pullach. Indeed, Gehlen had been preparing "Operation Juno" for several months previously, although later accusations by the Soviet government that the revolt was actually planned by Gehlen and the CIA must be taken with a grain of salt.

During the winter of 1952/3 the political and economic situation in East Germany had badly deteriorated. Many foodstuffs were in short supply, and the population was close to the starvation level. Desperate men tried to save their families by fleeing to the West. The flood of refugees to West Berlin alone reached an average of five thousand a week, despite brutal measures to halt it. Even the East German rulers could no longer disguise the utter misery of the population. But the measures taken to relieve it seemed to consist only of firing the minister of supply and the secretary of state at the food ministry, and blaming them for the food shortages. Unrest among the workers was blamed—in a Soviet note delivered on December 31, 1952, to the United States, British and French high commissioners—on "anti-communist propaganda and plots in the Western zones aimed at aggression against the German Democratic Republic".

Eventually the ministry of state security resorted to oppressive measures. Some ten thousand men and women were rounded up, accused of sabotage against the Five-Year Economy Plan and put in prison. For a time it seemed that the communists would succeed in bringing about a measure of economic recovery. Steel production went up to about 1,700,000 tons a year, electric power output increased by fifty per cent in two years, new coal mines were opened. But this was achieved through working conditions which were hardly different from the forced labour of Hitler's Germany. Many industries had been taken over by the Russians as part of reparations payments. At the uranium pits near Gera the Russian managers paid a weekly wage of 150 East Marks (about twelve dollars), and these miners were considered well paid. At the Agfa photographic plant also taken over by the Russians, a woman worker earned 1.50 East Marks per hour (about eight cents); she was compelled to work ten hours a day and produce eight hundred units.

When new "norms" were introduced, the output was set at 880 units, an impossibly high figure, whilst the wage remained the same.

Not only had people too little money, there was not enough food to go round. Yet there should have been no need for the East Germans to go hungry. The rich agricultural area they lived in, which had always shown surpluses before the war, could have been made self-sufficient. But the agricultural programme broke down, partly because the communist managers had created hundreds of thousands of unwilling, embittered workmen.

The new "norms" announced in the early summer of 1953 meant harder work, longer hours and higher productivity while wages remained frozen. Indeed, if a bricklayer's output fell below the inexorably increased "norm quota" his wages went down. On June 15, building workers in East Berlin downed tools in protest against the exploiters. They came into the streets, demonstrating and demanding better conditions, more political freedom, free elections, and the release of political prisoners. The frightened communist authorities released four thousand workers who had been imprisoned for "economic sabotage".

But it was too late. Spontaneous strikes began in Berlin, Magdeburg, Frankfurt on Oder and other cities. Students, workers and housewives demonstrated in the streets, and in some districts the demonstrations escalated into riots and attacks on the police. These strikes and demonstrations were led by the very people whom the communists claimed to represent. It was a revolt of the proletariat against the "dictatorship of the proletariat".

One cannot pretend that the many anti-communist organisations in West Berlin stood idly watching the eruption of this revolt. Tens of thousands of refugees had left their parents, brothers and sisters behind and, with millions of West Germans, they hoped the uprising would bring liberation and reunion. Many exiles hurried across the sector border to assist in the fight. Arms and explosives were smuggled to the rebels. Gehlen never confirmed nor denied reports that some of his West Berlin *Filiale* leaders and HV-men were involved in this assistance. But it is a fact that he ordered V-men already inside East Berlin, and others in West Berlin, to establish radio communications, and he received hour-to-hour situation reports. It is also a fact that some of his subordinates in West Berlin broadcast directions to V-men informing them of Soviet troop movements and advising a retreat to one part of the city, or an advance to another. At one time, when the blood of the many killed and wounded was flowing in the streets, the situation became grave; the US and British military governors alerted their troops. Across the border, Allied tanks and armoured cars faced the Soviet troops, whose guns were trained on West Berlin. The city had become a powder keg. One detonation could have caused an armed clash between Allied and Soviet troops, with horrifying consequences.

The revolt was quelled by Soviet tanks and guns; mass arrests and executions followed. The state of emergency and martial law were not lifted until the end of June. But the communists failed to break the spirit of the Berliners. In an effort to remedy the misery in East Berlin, a million food parcels were prepared by the West Berlin authorities and Allied military stores. But only a part of them could be distributed. East German police stopped all traffic to and from the Soviet sector and confiscated parcels already brought in. An offer by the United States government, to supply large quantities of food and commodities was refused by the Soviet commandant, who dismissed it as "capitalist propaganda".

"Operation Juno"

For several months before the Berlin revolt, Gehlen had warned the Americans and the Federal government of the coming eruption. He also predicted its bloody suppression and the danger which would arise should the Soviet government decide—on the pretext that the revolt had been incited by anti-communist organisations in the West—to renew its attempts to oust the Allies from West Berlin, or to send troops across the zonal border "to deal with terrorists and diversionists in West Berlin". This did not happen because of the precautions the Allies took after Gehlen's warnings. The show of force by American and British tanks, poised along the border, had impressed Soviet commanders.

During 1952/3 Gehlen had redoubled his efforts to obtain information about the strength and deployment of Soviet troops. He anticipated a closure of the border and stoppage of traffic and he knew that he would have to rely on radio signals rather than on couriers to maintain communications with his agents. Thus "Operation Juno" was devised. It aimed to train a large number of radio operators equipped with small and easily workable transmitters. Although the Americans supplied Gehlen with modern W/T sets, he had to use small transmitters with low output because these were more easily smuggled and concealed by the operators. Most of the operators had received only elementary training, a few had been brought to West Berlin for instruction and a handful of skilled W/T telegraphists had been sent to East Berlin after the outbreak of the revolt. Nevertheless, Gehlen's stations in West Berlin, Munich (an emergency receiver tuned to the prearranged wave lengths was also installed at Radio Free Europe) and Pullach received a flow of signals.

210

Obviously, no official figures about the employment of radio operators have ever been disclosed by Gehlen. But estimates published by the East German ministry of state security were not entirely inaccurate. Some were based on Gehlen's own documents, which his former agents Wolfgang Paul Höher[9] and Hans Joachim Geyer, who defected in 1953, handed over to the communists. Thus in 1952 there was one W/T operator maintaining communications for eleven or more agents; by 1953 the ratio was improved to one to seven. In 1963 an East German writer (whose publication was, of course, approved by the Ministry for State Security), gave the following interesting estimate of the percentage of Gehlen's W/T operators in proportion to the number of agents apprehended by the East German authorities.[10]

	1953–1955 (org. Gehlen)	1956–1963 (BND)
East Berlin	17	40
Magdeburg	—	40
Karl-Marx-Standt (formerly Chemnitz)	17	20
Leipzig	32	18

He listed only large cities, and gave for two others percentages for the whole period of 1953-1963, namely nine per cent for Frankfurt on Oder and Erfurt.

From the wealth of my material concerning Gehlen's radio networks, only cases which subsequently became known to Soviet counter-espionage can be quoted here. But even these selected instances provide a comprehensive picture of their wide ramifications. The turning point in the organisation of clandestine radio posts can be set at about the middle of 1952. At that time there was a great increase in the establishment of P-sources; many new agents were recruited and set up. With the deterioration of the situation in the Soviet zone and the increased tempo of activities among anti-communist organisations in West Berlin—and not least the improvement in radio propaganda—Gehlen anticipated an early outbreak of disaffection in East Berlin and other towns. This was almost a year before the June uprising, but Gehlen's measures were taken not a day too soon.

To ensure that communications with his agents were maintained should courier traffic become difficult or impossible, a number of new radio posts were established; until then W/T operators had been infiltrated somewhat haphazardly. Gehlen did not want to burden his P-, R- and S-sources with the risk of operating transmitters in addition to collecting information. He introduced an efficient system of TBK's (dead letter-boxes) where V-men might deposit their reports. A courier would then empty several of the caches and take the reports to one W/T operator, who would signal the contents in code. The system relied on the quickness of the couriers and the skill of the operators; otherwise even the most valuable information would have not reached Pullach. Gehlen's "collectors" and instructors, particularly "Hochberg" and "Paulberg" (code names) found a number of able men and women for this task. Some were experienced W/T telegraphists, others underwent instruction.

One was forty-one-year-old Hans Joachim Koch, a former NCO in the SS Prinz Eugen Division and a trained W/T operator and cypher expert. He was given a small transmitter and he set up the radio post at the house of his parents in an East Berlin suburb. For a while he sent trial signals and listened to "blind" broadcasts from Gehlen's station at Stocking. Eventually Hochberg supplied him with two more modern sets; one was a portable American twelve-watt transmitter with HF oscillation, which could be tuned both to the Stocking and Frankfurt receiving stations. Its frequency range went up to sixteen megacycles per second and despite the smallness of this tranceipt (transmitter-cum-receiver), it gave fairly strong signals over a long range. One disadvantage was that it required a long aerial, but Koch overcame this by disguising it as a washing line which he fixed in the yard.

Koch laid out a number of TBK's in the Burger Park and the Castle Park at Pankow and collected many reports about Soviet tank and troop movement during the June uprising. He maintained a constant link with the receiving stations for several weeks during the critical period. He was ordered by Gehlen not to participate in any demonstrations and stay at home as much as possible. This, incidentally, earned him jeers from his neighbours, critical of his apparently unenthusiastic attitude to the revolt.

Considering his excellent work and the risks he took, the bonus of 150 Marks he got for his radio operations during the June days appears not very generous. Koch worked until March 1955; in 1954 he sent valuable reports about the Soviet air bases at Werneuchen and in Upper Barnim, north-east of Berlin. On March 9, 1955, on another visit to Werneuchen, he was arrested by a VOPO patrol for loitering near the base. When his home was searched, his three transmitters were found and this sealed his fate. After a trial before the Supreme Court on June 15, 1955, he was sentenced to death and—there being no right of appeal—executed a few days later.

At the end of 1952 the Americans put a man who had been recruited by a CIC agent in touch with the Gehlen Organisation. He was Wilhelm Lehmann, who had escaped from East Berlin a few months earlier. During the June rising Lehmann supplied reports about Soviet troop movements between Wuhlheide, and Arnswalder Platz and the deployment of VOPO units. Posing as a stationery salesman, he visited over a long period twenty-five barracks of the VOPO and the People's Army, and also Soviet Army establishments, and made friends amongst officers and NCO's. He probably held the record for crossing the zonal border: during the three years 1953 to 1955 he made sixty-eight visits to West Berlin to confer with his superiors. Amongst his reports were more than forty descriptions of Soviet airfields.

Lehmann's work as a radio organiser began at the end of 1954, when his instructor, "Muller", brought him together with two other agents, Erich Eich and Martin Schneising. The three set up a clandestine radio network, code-named "North-East". Eich, a wartime W/T operator, became the chief telegraphist, while Schneising, a photographer, acted as courier for the TBK's which Lehmann laid out. Their code names were selected with a sense of humour: Lehmann was "Schnabel" (Beak), Eich "Schreck" (Fright) and Schneising "Schnell" (Quick).

Within a few weeks radio posts were operating south of Stralsund, at Rothemühle on the Polish frontier, not far from Stettin, at Frankfurt on Oder, and at Krien. They had powerful American transceivers, which later prompted the East German counter-espionage chiefs to claim that the team had been sending signals to NATO Intelligence headquarters in Paris and Copenhagen. The trio was well paid—at their trial they stated that Lehmann received 15,000 Marks, Eich 28,000 Marks and Schneising 12,000 Marks. Schneising supplied two hundred photographs of new railway installations, bridges, locomotive sheds, turntables and signal points in the Oder-Neisse region, built to improve strategic rail communications between the Soviet Union, Poland and East Germany.

In the spring of 1955 they were, one by one, discovered and arrested. Tried before the Supreme Court, Lehmann was sentenced to death, Eich to life imprisonment and Schneising to twelve years. But several of their radio operators continued working; indeed, some of the W/T posts they established are still in operation in 1971.

Another important radio network was established by Manfred Naumann and his assistants Peter Blank, Heinz Hollberg and Werner Knoll, a former Waffen SS telegraphist. Their posts operated from the forester's lodge at Eggersroder near Blankenburg, and from a quarry north-east of Berlin. They were issued with new American transmitters built into Thermos flasks. Eventually, through betrayal, they too were caught and given long terms of imprisonment.

A successful W/T post was set up in 1952 by twenty-seven-year-old Karl Heinz Schmidt. He was a former U-boat sailor, trained in 1943 as a radio operator at the famous U-boat school at Pillay. After his return from a British POW camp, he worked as a diesel engine mechanic at Luckenwalde and eventually joined the Gehlen Organisation. From his post, condenamed "Sirene", he also conveyed many signals before, during and after the June uprising. Working alone, he suggested to his instructor, Trettner, that his wife should be trained in West Berlin as his assistant. But on their return from one of their visits there, the couple was followed by SSD agents, and the trail led to their clandestine radio post. At his trial Schmidt was sentenced to life imprisonment and his wife to eight years.

Between 1953 and 1956 Gehlen carried out a carefully planned system of radio posts and operators. One of his most successful recruiting officers and instructors in this field was the former Abwehr officer "Paulberg". Under his guidance W/T posts were set up by Helmut Schwenk, a thirty-year-old teacher at Burgstadt in Saxony, by Karl Rudert at Erfurt, by Armin Zopf at Tennstedt in Thuringia, and by agents in Magdeburg and Karl-Marx-Stadt (Chemnitz), thirty miles from the Czechoslovak frontier. There were many more across the length and breadth of East Germany. A map secretly circulated in 1956 by the Ministry for State Security to high party officials, showed forty-seven places where radio posts of the Gehlen Organisation and its successor, the BND, had either been located or were believed to operate. Even at that time quite a few more escaped the attention of communist counter-espionage, and the number increased in the following years.

Operators were equipped with modernised American "rapid" automatic transmitters with a maximum transmission time of forty-five seconds and capable of emanating up to 5,400 signs per minute by electronic compression. The great advantage of these transmitters is that the operator needs only very simple instruction, which may take no more than one or two days. Training operators on older manual apparatus with an output of only eighty Morse signs per minute used to require up to eight weeks. Since the take-over of the "Org" and its transformation into the BND, the Federal government has invested about five hundred thousand Marks annually in replacing and replenishing the radio equipment of its V-men operators. American and West German radio manufacturers have more recently constructed prototypes of automatic soundless transmitters, which can be worked by remote control, enabling the operator to hide the apparatus, for instance, in a tree, and work it from inside a building several hundred yards away. Even if D/Fing located the transmitter, the operator could remain undetected or make a quick getaway.

Whilst the above-mentioned instances of the work of Gehlen's W/T operators concern agents in East Germany, similar tactics, if on a limited scale, applied to "deep-penetration" operators inside the Soviet Union and other communist countries.

XVI

The Right Man
In The Right Place

The four years between 1953 and 1957 saw the culmination of Reinhard Gehlen's career as the spy-master of the Cold War in Europe. At the start of this period a series of momentous events had drastically changed the concept of international politics. In the United States the war in Korea had created a deep crisis of confidence. In a state of barely concealed panic most Americans had come to believe that communism had passed beyond the use of subversion to conquer independent nations and was prepared to resort to armed aggression. Shades of Pearl Harbour were seen everywhere. Stalin, attacking by proxy, had entrapped the armed forces of the US—which had dwindled from eight million at the end of the Second World War to a puny half-million—in a far-away theatre of war, while keeping his own ready in Europe. Would he now turn upon Berlin, West Germany, indeed Western Europe?

General Eisenhower's overwhelming victory at the polls in 1952 had been won in no small measure on the election plank of foreign policy prepared by John Foster Dulles, who had promised that the new Republican administration would "end the negative, futile, and immoral policy of containment towards communism, which abandons countless human beings to despotism and God-less terrorism, which in turn enables the communist rulers to forge their captives into a weapon of our destruction". In their policy statements in 1953, both Eisenhower and, particularly, Dulles, who had virtually assumed the direction of United States policy, pledged "a policy of boldness" by which the Soviet Union rather than the United States would find herself on the defensive. Dulles proclaimed a "spiritual crusade for the liberation of the captive peoples of Eastern Europe", leaving it open as to whether this crusade might not one day escalate into the use of military force.

By 1953, Senator Joseph McCarthy, backed for a considerable time by a majority of American public opinion, had painted a most fearful picture of the global communist conspiracy: "Stalin is Satan, supreme in his craft and power, an adversary fit to grapple with God

216

himself, and perhaps to triumph.''[1] Stalin's emissaries were everywhere, corrupting Western civilisation and sawing away at the very foundations of American life and freedom. McCarthy had gained considerable influence over the administration, if only because Congress had made it possible for him to gain control over various parts of the executive and to place his henchmen in several departments.[2]

All this was music to Gehlen's ears. With the advent of the Eisenhower-Dulles administration, his sponsor, Allen Welsh Dulles, had become not only director of CIA, but also director of Central Intelligence, a newly created position which carried with it a seat at the National Security Council, next to the President, Vice-President Nixon, the secretary of state—his brother—and the chiefs of staff. For practical purposes, Allen Dulles had assumed control of all American Intelligence activities; soon he was being described as "the third most powerful man in the world".

The death of Stalin and the ensuing struggle for power in the Kremlin, culminating in the downfall and execution of Lavrenti Beria and many of his supporters, had temporarily weakened the Soviet espionage machine; this was compounded by the bitter setback Moscow suffered through the disclosures of the defector Vladimir Petrov in Australia.

In October 1954 the German Federal Republic joined NATO and Chancellor Adenauer subsequently put the new German armed forces under the command of the Supreme Allied Commander in Europe. Until 1955, despite the advent of Khrushchev, no significant change in Moscow's objectives had taken place; the Soviet leaders after Stalin, despite variations in their conduct, were still pursuing with unalterable determination their conspiratorial purpose: the overthrow of capitalism. From the middle of 1955, however, when Khrushchev ordered the withdrawal of Soviet troops from Austria, returned the naval base of Porkkala to Finland, agreed with Tito that socialist states had the right to follow their own path to socialism and, above all, recognised the German Federal Republic and offered negotiations on disarmament, new hopes for peace and coexistence were kindled. But the ruthless suppression of the Hungarian uprising in 1956 by Soviet tanks showed Moscow in its true light and dashed Western hopes of an abatement in the Cold War.

From the German point of view, indeed, the situation had worsened. Whatever the Geneva Summit in July 1955 might have promised, the foreign ministers' conference in October displayed to the full the unbridgeable differences between the West and Moscow on Germany's future. The Russians violently objected to West Germany's adherence to NATO, demanded her "neutralisation" and rejected reunification as totally unacceptable. The establishment of the sovereign Federal Republic was countered by the signing of the Warsaw Pact by the eight communist states and the setting up of a unified command of their armed forces under Soviet leadership. In 1958, Moscow was to make yet another major assault on the freedom of West Berlin, in a further attempt to oust the Allies from the city.

During the mid-fifties Gehlen's status and power within Germany increased enormously; he also exerted a not inconsiderable influence on international affairs through his involvement with NATO. Through his close relations with Secretary of State Dr. Hans Globke, Chancellor Adenauer's *éminence grise* for ten years, Gehlen had become the overlord of all Federal intelligence departments, placing his nominees in positions of control in military intelligence and in the internal counter-espionage department. Some seventy per cent of all intelligence material obtained by NATO's military committee and SHAPE on the Soviet Union, the Warsaw Pact countries and, indeed, on many other parts of Europe and the world came in those years from Pullach.

Moreover, at CIA, Wisner and Richard M. Bissell, the new deputy director of Plans and Operations,[3] continued to rely on Gehlen—even after the "Org" had been officially transferred to the Federal government and renamed *Bundesnachrichtendienst* in July 1955.

Meanwhile, across the borders of the two divided Germanies the Cold War never abated. It was said that in those years, twenty-two different countries maintained spy centres in West Berlin. A multitude of anti-communist organisations and agencies, many run on an entirely mercenary basis, pitted themselves against the enormous communist espionage machine across the zonal border. In scores of clubs, coffee-houses and night-dives the buying and selling of "secret" information developed into a way of life for thousands of freelance "agents". They were nicknamed *Hundert Mark Jungen* (Hundred-Mark Boys), and they offered to lay bare the innermost workings of the Kremlin, the Pentagon, Whitehall or the Quai d'Orsay for the price of a good dinner.

There were and, of course, still are scores of important espionage and propaganda centres in West Berlin. Neutral observers in the late 1950s estimated that there were at least seven thousand agents, spies and informers in Berlin, of whom perhaps two to three thousand held official assignments from the intelligence services of the United States, Great Britain, France and the Soviet Union, while the rest consisted of dubious individuals and gangs making a dishonest living on the fringes of that sordid game.

218

In more recent years cloak-and-dagger activities, in a literal sense, have moved from Berlin to the cities of the Federal Republic. Every "local" war or rebellion anywhere in the world brings a crop of agents, exiles and hangers-on to Munich, Hamburg or Frankfurt. Urban guerillas regard them as favourite venues, Croats kill Croats in the streets of German towns, Arab sky-jackers and saboteurs attack Israeli airliners on German airfields; hardly a month passes without the discovery of yet another Soviet, Polish or Czech spy ring.

In the mid-1950s it was West Berlin, a convenient observation post for East-West intrigues, arms deals and propaganda. Scores of "research institutes", seemingly genuine public relations services, economic consultants, cultural societies operated there—and still do—from respectably conducted offices many of which are entirely devoted to espionage, offering information to the highest bidder, while many more combine dubious activities for either side with genuine business on behalf of East-West trade relations.

On the surface both halves of Berlin, one prosperous and flashy, the other then still shabby and subdued, might just have seemed over-populated, bustling cities; but, underneath, the witches' brew of intrigue, venality, conspiracy, spying and black propaganda was always boiling and bubbling away. Moreover, Berlin remained a powder-keg; a single match might have turned an explosion into a world-wide conflagration.

Wollweber

Only in this peculiar climate could a man such as Ernst Friedrich Wollweber have developed his talents, which all his life he had devoted to villainy. After the Berlin riots he had succeeded Wilhelm Zaisser[4] as minister for state security and head of East German espionage. Zaisser had been fired for not having prevented the uprising and, even more, for having failed to deal with Gehlen's successful infiltration of spies, agitators and radio operators. Wollweber was expected by his Soviet masters to put things right. He inherited a large and fairly efficient espionage apparatus, created and still chiefly controlled by the Russians.

Soon after the occupation of East Germany, the MGB had established its German HQ at the buildings of the Sankt Antonius Hospital at Karlshorst. General Ivan Serov, Beria's successor, came to supervise the organisation of a political police system which divided the Soviet zone into districts (*Bezirke*) and circuits (*Kreise*), each with a Soviet police chief. Parallel to this an elaborate Soviet espionage network covered both East and West Germany. German Communist Party officials, many of whom had returned from Russia where they had spent their exile during the Hitler regime were

219

attached to these Soviet regional and local offices, but held no executive power.

During the second phase of Soviet occupation, which began on August 17, 1947, with the issue of Order No.201 by the Soviet military governor, a German political police force was created which also took over some espionage and counter-espionage functions. Its headquarters, known as "*Kommissariat 5*", or K-5, was attached to the Soviet MGB at Karlshorst; Zaisser was made its head, with Erich Mielke[5] as his deputy. Eventually, in February 1950, K-5 became the ministry for state security. Its executive organ, particularly in the espionage field, was the *Staats Sicherheits-Dienst* (SSD—initials reminiscent of Himmler's and Heydrich's notorious SD).

Zaisser and Mielke, though themselves old and trained "Chekists", had an "adviser" in Major-General Trukhanov, one of the MGB chiefs. This middle-aged trio was joined in 1951 by a brilliant young man, Markus Johannes Wolf. In 1933, as a schoolboy, he had gone into exile in Moscow with his father,[6] where he graduated from the Karl Liebknecht academy and the Comintern college for advanced spy training at Kushnarenkovo, later perfecting his knowledge in diplomatic posts. At the age of twenty-eight, with the rank of major-general, Wolf became the real boss of the SSD at the huge, grim block of the security ministry in Normannenstrasse in Berlin-Lichtenberg.

These were the men with whom Gehlen had been conducting a battle of wits before Ernst Wollweber, one of the Kremlin's most formidable hatchet men, arrived on the scene. For the following four years he was Gehlen's most dangerous opponent, often excelling his Soviet masters. He was born in 1898 in Hannoversch-Munden in Hesse, the son of a miner, and as a boy he went to sea. In 1917, while serving in the Imperial Navy as a stoker in the battleship *Helgoland* he was one of the leaders of the mutiny in the Third Fleet at Kiel on October 28, 1918, which heralded the Revolution and the downfall of the Kaiser's Reich. As a member of the first Workers' and Soldiers' Council he led a group of mutineers in storming the Bremen town hall where they disarmed the police and hoisted the Red Flag. Ernst Wollweber and the new German Communist Party grew up together. His greatest ambition was to go to Moscow to be trained as a political organiser. With a handful of comrades he boarded a trawler at Bremerhaven and out at sea they overwhelmed the skipper and crew and ordered them to sail to Murmansk. Thence he reached Moscow, where he was received as a hero of the German revolution and met Lenin and Zinoviev, the chairman of the newly created Comintern. Soon he was an assiduous student at the military-political college which had then begun to train Comintern agents. He graduated as a fully-fledged agent earmarked for high office.

Lenin's hopes and Zinoviev's predictions that the German revolution would culminate in the establishment of a Soviet Germany were frustrated. But during the early 1920s, while the Weimar Republic strove to establish a democratic regime but was rent by recurrent rebellions from both right and left, Moscow never ceased to plan and prepare for a take-over. The Agitprop department of the Comintern, with Trotsky's war commissariat and the GPU (the present-day KGB), had drawn up detailed battle tactics. Germany was divided into six "military-revolutionary" districts, each headed by a German communist leader and more powerful Russian "advisers".

At the peak of the great conspiracy there were several hundred Soviet agents in Germany in command of an army of agitators, informers and organisers supplied by the strong German Communist Party. Centres were set up in Berlin and all cities and larger towns, and organised on military lines. Wollweber was one of its most energetic organisers, working mainly amongst the sailors, dockers and shipyard workers in northern ports.

At that time Reinhard Gehlen, five years younger than Wollweber, had entered the Hanover military school and was receiving his first training in the craft of intelligence. He was already preoccupied with gathering knowledge about communism, the Soviet Union, its espionage and the work of spies and agitators in Germany, but it is most unlikely that he had heard of Wollweber. Yet this young man was rising rapidly in the German communist hierarchy. During one of his several visits to Moscow he had met Stalin, who took a liking to him and for the next thirty years, during which most of the communist leaders were "purged", remained Wollweber's protector.

Wollweber soon moved into the international field of communist activities. In the 1930s a host of "fronts" was established by the Comintern, such as the League of Peace and Democracy, the International Workers' Aid, the World Federation of Democratic Youth, the Womens' International Federation, the World Association of Scientific Workers, innumerable "friendship societies" for cultural relations with the Soviet Union and, particularly, associations designed to infiltrate trade unions throughout the world. In this field the communists were particularly successful: The World Federation of Trade Unions, founded in 1913 and including the British T.U.C. and the American A.F.L., eventually fell completely under communist domination and the great British, American and French organisations were compelled to leave it.

One of the "fronts" built up by Ernst Wollweber was the International Seamen Union (ISH). Outwardly, it was a thoroughly respectable body, looking after the working conditions and welfare of seamen and founding many sailors' hostels and clubs in large ports; it had its headquarters at Hamburg, where a German Social Democrat, Albert Walter, was its secretary general. In fact, however, Wollweber was the real power behind the scenes. He organised branches in twenty-two countries and fifteen British and French colonies, which were regularly visited by his fifty "welfare officers" and travelling "supervisors", all communist agents. Membership dues and payments for hostel accommodation, food and drink at the canteens were ridiculously low, being lavishly subsidised by the maritime section of the Comintern to the tune of eight hundred thousand dollars a year. The ISH had, of course, very special tasks to fulfil. It could effectively prevent the transportation by sea of troops and arms, which might be used against the Soviet Union, provide agents and couriers in every harbour and naval port, and use blackmail against governments by threatening dock strikes. Above all, its specially trained members could be employed on even more sinister tasks: the sabotage of ships and of port and dock installations.

The Great Ship Saboteur

In this field Ernst Wollweber became an unrivalled expert. A big strong man of rugged appearance—only later did he grow fat and flabby from good living and acquire the nickname *Pfannkuchen auf Beine* (Pancake on legs)—he had inexhaustible energy and a penchant for organising elaborate outrages. In order to acquire respectability, he got himself elected as a member of the Prussian Diet in 1928, and in 1932 became a member of the German parliament, which gave him at least temporary immunity from arrest.

By 1928 Wollweber was already engaged in sabotage actions against Western shipping. The first attempts were directed against Germany and France, the two countries "most ripe for revolution". Dock strikes were staged at Hamburg, Bremen, Bordeaux and Marseilles. In the latter port the newly built cargo boat *Paul Legat* was burnt out by arson when still in the dock; next came the *Paris*, a luxury liner at Le Havre. Then the fine new German liner *Europa* was destroyed by a fire which twelve hundred firemen were unable to extinguish, and the French *Asie* burnt out shortly before she was to sail to the Red Sea. In the United States Wollweber had established an effective cell where the notorious Comintern agents George Mink and Thomas Ray were active; James Ford, the Negro agitator who later became a communist-sponsored candidate in a presidential election, was one of their collaborators. The FBI was able to prevent more serious sabotage actions, but Wollweber's men succeeded in destroying the USS *City of Honolulu*, which burnt out soon after leaving Hawaii.

By the early thirties Wollweber began the biggest ship sabotage campaign the world had ever known; within three years the London insurance market had to pay out more than £7,000,000 (at that time about thirty-five million dollars) for ships damaged or destroyed, mainly by fire. This campaign reflected the international policy of the Comintern and the Soviet government: support for the civil disobedience movement in India, accentuated by Gandhi's imprisonment and his threatened "fast unto death"; support for the uprising against the French in Tonkin and other parts of Indo-China; support for the nationalist revolt in Siam; support for Mao Tse-tung against the reactionary Nanking government of the Kuomintang; defiance of Japanese aspirations in China and the occupation of Manchuria and so on.

Hence, between 1930 and 1933, Wollweber's fire-raisers were mainly directed against British and French shipping. The catalogue of ships destroyed, damaged or crippled during that period is very long: the *Lamartine* at Marseilles, the *André Lebon*, the *Azay-le-Rideau*, the *Fontainebleu*, the great liner *France*, the *Ile de France*, and eventually the forty-two-thousand-ton luxury liner *L'Atlantique* and the seventeen-thousand-ton *George Philippar*—all French and some carrying troops and arms to Indo-China; and amongst British ships the *Bermuda*, first set on fire at Hamilton (Bermuda) and, after refitting at the Workman Clark Yards in Belfast, once more sabotaged and burnt out; a new Nelson Line cargo ship under construction in the Harland & Woolf shipyards in Belfast; the *Duke of Lancaster* destroyed by fire at Heysham harbour; and several more fired at Liverpool, Bristol, Hull and Newcastle. At that time Wollweber even had contacts with IRA saboteurs, whose actions against the British were prompted by very different motives.

The arson aboard the big Dutch ship *Moldanger* in Rotterdam port caused damaged worth £1,000,000; a few months later another Dutch cargo ship *Pieter Hooft* under steam from the Far East was destroyed in port; a third, *Dempo*, was burnt out, also in Rotterdam. One of the largest Japanese cargo boats, the *Biao*, exploded soon after leaving a European port with a load of arms for Japanese troops in Manchuria. The same fate overtook the *Tajima Maru*, sailing from Rotterdam on a similar passage.

To this catalogue could be added an even longer list of German ships destroyed or damaged in port or on the high seas. In addition to the *Europa*, which was to have been the queen of the German merchant navy, the *Munich* went up in flames, and a whole fleet of smaller vessels were blown up or badly damaged. Nor was American shipping overlooked; its main loss was the *Segovia*, destroyed by fire when nearing completion at Newport News, Va.

In all these cases sabotage was established as the cause and in most officials of the British MI5 and Naval Intelligence, and the French Sûreté found debris of time bombs. Official inquiries were held and dossiers exchanged between the British, French, German and Dutch secret services, but the perpetrators were never apprehended, though the trail usually led to Wollweber and his ISH. A Lloyds underwriter, whose insurance syndicate had suffered enormous losses, stated after returning from a secret conference with the French special commissioner, Charles Calen, in Paris: "Quite apart from helping their communist friends by destroying ships, which may carry arms and ammunition, the Russians have another interest in these sabotage actions. Under their Five Year Plan they are building a large new merchant fleet. It could well be that Stalin has decided to dispose of at least some ships of the capitalist countries and thus secure a larger slice of the world's maritime traffic for Russia at some future date. In any case, destruction of ships and dockyards would be just another piece in the communist repertoire, like the extermination of men whose survival has become inconvenient to the Stalin regime."

Wollweber Becomes Britain's Ally

After the nazis came to power in Germany Wollweber went underground and eventually had to flee. He went to Moscow and in 1935 emerged in Copenhagen, where he set up a shipping firm under the name of Adolf Seelo & Co. It became the centre of elaborately devised sabotage operations against the shipping of nazi Germany. Scandinavian ports were soon unsafe for any German and Italian vessel. Between 1937 and the outbreak of the war nine hundred German ships were destroyed or damaged in German and foreign ports and at sea, despite strict security measures and special guards provided by the Gestapo and the SS.

During the last year of peace, Wollweber established four "cells" of saboteurs in Stockholm, Kiruna, Lulea and Porjus in Sweden. Some of these ports were of particular importance because Swedish ore was shipped from them to Germany for the manufacture of tanks and armaments. In all these ports there were mysterious explosions, and outrages were stepped up after the outbreak of war. Indeed Wollweber had somewhat unwittingly become a British ally. Despite the Molotov-Ribbentrop "friendship pact", Moscow was determined to weaken Hitler's war potential and, particularly, to deprive the Ruhr armaments industry of supplies of Swedish ore. To the British this was one of the top priorities of economic warfare. In December

1939 the D-department of the British Secret Intelligence Service had devised a plan to blow up the port installations at Oxeloesung and Nykoping, the main Swedish iron ore ports. William Stephenson,[7] a Canadian millionaire and chairman of the Pressed Steel Company, who had good contacts in Sweden, volunteered to supervise the sabotage plan. A team headed by SIS agent Alfred Frederick Rickman was sent to Stockholm, but the Swedish police intercepted a letter to Rickman and discovered the plot; he and several of his British and Swedish helpers were arrested. In June 1940 Rickman was sentenced to eight years, his assistant Ernest Biggs to five, and two other British agents to three years each; their sentences were subsequently curtailed and they were deported.[8]

Wollweber was not discouraged by the British setback. A series of sabotage actions wrecked ore warehouses at Lulea, damaged quay installations and loading ramps, and for several weeks stopped the ore shipments to Germany. More sabotage actions were carried out at Kiruna and attacks on ships in German and Swedish ports continued unabated. On May 8, 1940, one of Wollweber's agents, Richard Krebs, placed time bombs aboard the transport *Marion* at Bremerhaven; she was carrying four thousand German troops to Norway where, after the German invasion in April, British forces were holding Narvik. Eight minutes after reaching a fjord, the *Marion* was blown skyhigh; there were no survivors.

The Swedish government, under German pressure and threats of invasion and seeing its ports in danger of destruction, turned upon the Wollweber group. Several of his agents were arrested and Wollweber himself taken into custody on a charge of having entered the country with a forged passport. While he was under arrest, sabotage actions continued with even greater ferocity. His deputy, Jacob Liebersohn, organised attempts at Krylbool, Lulea and Luossa; at Krylbool twenty freight trains were blown up. Eventually Liebersohn and several saboteurs were arrested and sentenced to terms up to eight years' imprisonment. The German government demanded Wollweber's extradition. But he was able to prove to the Swedes that he had been deprived by the nazis of his German citizenship in 1933, and was a stateless person. He asked to be deported to the Soviet Union and he arrived there shortly after the German attack on Russia, greeted as a hero.

Until the end of the war he remained in Moscow, a member of a group of exiled German communists who included the later first president of the German Democratic Republic, Wilhelm Pieck, the future premier, Walter Ulbricht, Zaisser and Mielke. They prepared their plans for victory, even when it seemed far away and when large territories of the Soviet Union were conquered by Hitler's armies.

Wollweber could present to his Soviet masters an impressive balance of his sabotage activities during the first years of the war: at least seventy German, Italian and Japanese ships had been sunk in ports in Germany and nazi-occupied Europe, in neutral countries and on the high seas; in addition many neutral ships, which carried supplies for Germany, were also destroyed. At least a hundred more had suffered heavy damage, and innumerable harbour installations, docks, ship-yards and railway track had been sabotaged.

Back in East Germany in 1945, the Russians gave Wollweber the obvious job: "Commissioner for Transport and Shipping", later promoted to ministerial rank when the DDR puppet government came into being in 1949. One of his first measures was to open a school for saboteurs at Wustrow on the Baltic Sea, where two hundred men were soon being trained. During the following years a large number of sabotage acts occurred in German ports in the US-British bi-zone, in Hamburg, Luebeck and Bremerhaven, directed against ships bringing supplies under the Marshal Plan. Explosions also took place at the French ports of Le Harve and Brest.

Gehlen Warns Britain

Gehlen was asked to assist the American CIC in investigating the outrages—he was able to provide information because, as we shall see, he had succeeded in placing an agent in Wollweber's own "shipping ministry". A report from Gehlen, passed by CIA somewhat belatedly to Sir Percy Sillitoe, director general of the British Security Service (the former MI5) in November 1952, warned that ninety-six British and Commonwealth seamen and eighteen dockers, all avowed communists, had been trained at Wollweber's schools and sent home with dangerous assignments. By then British counter-espionage was faced by a series of unsolved outrages. In 1947 and 1948 thirty ships had been damaged in British ports, causing insurance losses to the tune of £10,000,000. Among seriously damaged liners was the *Monarch of Bermuda* in the Tyne; there were twelve mysterious fires on the Clyde, and by 1950 fire-raisers had inflicted grievous harm on British shipping. There was a huge blaze at Pembroke Docks, and at the Kingswood Ordnance factory nearby ammunition exploded for twenty-four hours. The *Indian Enterprise*, carrying arms for British troops in the Middle East, was blown up; sabotage acts had damaged the Royal Navy aircraft carriers *Vengeance, Theseus* and *Glory*, all bound for the war in Korea; the armament ship *Bedenham* was blown up in Gibraltar Dockyard; and there was sabotage of machinery in the destroyer *Cavendish* at Rosyth and the cutting of cables in the submarine *Tabard* in Malta.

Although after Gehlen's warnings the Admiralty, Naval Intelligence, the Directorate of Security and the Special Branch of Scotland Yard redoubled their combined efforts, sabotage actions against British ships persisted throughout 1952 and 1953: the *Empress of Canada* was destroyed by a mysterious fire at Liverpool; three days later a fire badly damaged the *Queen Elizabeth* at Southampton; the *Ribera* was burning at Hull. Sabotage was particularly directed against British, Danish, Norwegian, Italian and Turkish men-of-war serving under NATO command. The damage caused in the aircraft carriers *Indomitable* (23,500 tons), *Centaur* (20,330 tons), *Warrior* and *Triumph* (both 13,350 tons), the destroyer *Duchess* and several other ships remained officially unexplained. A number of NATO ships, including several of the US Navy, such as the aircraft carrier *Bennington*, also suffered serious damage and were put out of commission for many months.

Brutus

In a frantic attempt to discover the saboteurs before they could inflict further harm, Gehlen had ordered the infiltration of more *T-Quellen* and *U-Quellen* agents into Wollweber's sabotage training establishments, which by 1952 had spread to Labedow near Greifswald and Bogensee. V-men were also sent to Hamburg, Bremen and Luebeck to mix with dock workers and sailors suspected of being Wollweber's men. Above all, Gehlen relied on the reports he was receiving from a man who was sitting in a room two doors away from Wollweber's, at the operational centre of the sabotage conspiracy, the shipping ministry in East Berlin.

This man was Walter Gramsch, a former official of the German seamen's union and a member of the Social Democrat Party before 1933. In 1939 Gramsch, who like many trade unionists had been active in anti-nazi resistance and was held for two or three years in a concentration camp, was called up for service in the merchant navy and in 1940 taken prisoner by the British aboard a German cargo boat off Norway. He spent most of the war in British POW camps and in 1946 returned to his home town in East Germany. Although he had never been a communist, he knew Wollweber from pre-Hitler days. When he heard that the former IHS leader had risen to great heights in the new regime, he paid him a visit. In fact, this call was made on Gehlen's instructions. Gramsch had been approached by one of the Pullach "collectors" and recruited for the "Org".

Wollweber welcomed his old colleague with open arms; he did not doubt that the ex-Resistance fighter had by now embraced the communist creed, and Gramsch left him in this belief. Within months Gramsch climbed the ladder of officialdom at Wollweber's "shipping centre". He became head of the Planning Department concerned with the build-up of a new East German merchant navy and the restoration of harbours and docks. Eventually he was put in charge of the department for shipping and ports. From the start of his new career at the ministry, Gramsch was sending a flood of reports to Gehlen. He had himself chosen his code name: "Brutus".

To protect him, Gehlen had devised an elaborate system of communications with "Brutus". As a high official of Wollweber's ministry, Gramsch had frequent if "unofficial" dealings with the Federal government in Bonn, which did not recognise the East German regime. West German businessmen were eager to supply goods to East Germany and by 1951 exports had reached a total of 145 million Marks; this figure was nearly doubled two years later. Reports from "Brutus" reached Pullach by the way of private and even official cover addresses. Couriers also carried them between East and West Berlin, after "cut-out" agents at both ends had made sure that the messages were conveyed by several stages in order to obliterate the trail.

At that time strict restrictions had been imposed by the United States on trading with the East; there was a long list of goods which could not be exported to communist countries, and it included almost all industrial production. The Federal government was bound by this embargo, to the chagrin of many West German manufacturers. Gehlen was asked by CIA to watch this illicit traffic, which was conducted by the use of forged documents, fake certificates of origin, and by exporting goods, mainly machinery and spare parts, via Scandinavia to Baltic ports. "Brutus" provided Gehlen with inside information about these machinations which were, in fact, promoted by his own department. Thus Gehlen was enabled to conceive "Operation Vulcan", which exploded a ring of East German agents involved in illicit trade and espionage.

The East German "fronts" were the "Institute for Economic Research" and a number of trading firms in Hamburg, Frankfurt and West Berlin. An interesting sidelight was that several East German communist leaders and their families, including Wilhelm Zaisser, the minister for state security, the daughter of the DDR President Wilhelm Pieck, and probably also Wollweber, had financial interest in the dealings. Eventually, thirty-five people were arrested; the number included several agents who conducted espionage besides their "economic" assignments. The court imposed lenient sentences, perhaps because respectable West German manufacturers and traders were involved on the business side of this affair.

Gramsch provided all the relevant information in this complex case, but he also kept Pullach informed about political events, the military presence of Soviet troops in East German ports and plans

228

Block-Nr.: Y333 000   Absendedatum: 23.5.58

Betreff:

Forschung BAPTIST

Sachgebiet: III/66

Land: Polen

Quellen-Nr.: 18148/DOU DE DOMONT

Feststellungsort: eigen

Bezug: Y 330 498 v.28.3.58

Anlagen:

1 PU der UQU (4 x)

Fest. Zeit: 20.3.-16.5.58

Feststel. Zeit: wie vor

Vorausgemeldet durch:

MELDEWEG: Treff mit Quelle am 16.5.58

Dauer: Nächst. Tr. m. Qu.

GT-Meldung abgefaßt am:

Poststempel Ort:

Eing. West:

STEINMANN   Käthe   HAMBURG
Hohe Weide 50 oder 52
Ehefrau des Erich Steinmann

2 Kinder

verheiratet

ca. 1914   Kassel

Vorgesehen zum Einbau als Putzfrau bei
einem Verdächtigen. Die St. ist zuverlässig, schlagfertig, hat Mutterwitz,
kerndeutsch. Ehemann war Tapferkeitsoffizier, Leutnant, Ritterkreuz,
getippt: durch V-16601, in dessen Haus die St. früher wohnte.

A data sheet of an agent of the *Bundesnachrichtendienst*

It concerns a female agent, Frau Käthe Steinmann, recommended by "tipper" V-16601, and investigated and trained by *Forschung Baptist* of Gehlen's counter-espionage Group III between March 20 and May 16, 1958. Her eventual enlistment, dated May 23, 1958, was for her use as "a domestic help in the home of a suspect". She is described as "reliable, alert, possessing common-sense and truly German". Her husband is mentioned as a "brave officer, formerly a Wehrmacht lieutenant, awarded the Knight Cross of the Iron Cross."

and progress in improving road, rail and water transport; he also gave details on East German agents, which led to the breaking up of several other networks inside the Federal Republic.

Whilst "Brutus" gave extremely valuable service, Gehlen had several other agents "in the right place". His "collectors" had succeeded in ensnaring the personal secretary of the East German prime minister, Otto Grotewohl. Her name was Ella Bartschatis, a spinster of forty-two, definitely beyond her first bloom. Through "Brutus" Gehlen had learnt that she had become besotted with a man who had at one time worked in Grotewohl's office as a legal adviser, Dr. Karl Laurenz.

Geblen's V-men soon found out that Laurenz, a former Social Democratic Party official, had fallen foul of his masters. He was discreetly approached, offered a high reward and the result was that his "fiancée", Fraulein Bartschatis, became Pullach's informer. For many months copies of top-secret documents from the prime minister's desk were thus finding their way to Pullach. Fraulein Bartschatis, blessed with excellent memory and an accomplished shorthand expert, produced near-verbatim reports on Grotewohl's conference with the Soviet high commissioner, General Vladimir Semyonov, and on cabinet meetings of the East German government.*

Betrayed Cabinet Secrets

Gehlen had yet another right man in the right place amongst his amazing team of informers in the corridors of power in East Germany. He was Professor Hermann Kastner, the leader of the Liberal Democratic Party, which the communists had left in existence after 1948. The formation of non-communist party organisations was encouraged by Moscow after the establishment of the "independent" German Democratic Republic to uphold a pretence of true democracy in East Germany. Besides the Liberal Democratic Party there was a Christian Democratic Party, in theory identical to that of Dr. Adenauer in West Germany. In fact, both these parties were a sham. Their leaders, eager to play some part in political life and deriving many personal advantages from this role, had thrown in their lot with the communists. Their "parties" were factions of the so-called National Front, completely dominated by the Socialist Unity Party of Grotewohl and Ulbricht. Votes in elections had to be cast for National Front candidates, and were then apportioned by the communist bosses to their servile partners. In this way there were a few "Liberal" and "Christian Democratic" ministers presiding over the least important departments, and supervised by their communist secretaries of state.

* See page 273

One of these politicians supplying the required window-dressing for the East German regime was Herr Kastner; he acted first as minister of justice, and later as deputy prime minister "without portfolio". Well aware of his precarious position, Kastner hedged his bets by establishing contact with Gehlen, appearing in the Pullach files under the rather disrespectful code label "S-Quelle Helwig". As will be recalled, S-Quelle meant *Spitze*, or top source, but it still only described a V-man.

Kastner's reports, Gehlen decided, could not be entrusted to even the most reliable courier. Not only was "Helwig" far too valuable an informer to put in jeopardy, his discovery by the East German security service would have led to a drastic tightening of surveillance in all government offices and endangered all his other informers placed there. Kastner therefore took his wife into his confidence and she proved a most excellent courier. Like all members of the East German *élite*, the Kastners enjoyed many privileges denied to ordinary comrades. Frau Kastner, who either genuinely suffered from some ailment, or pretended to do so, expressed a desire to receive medical treatment from specialists in West Berlin. She had, of course, no difficulty in obtaining the necessary passes, and once a week was driven in her husband's official limousine across the sector border to the St. Franciscus Clinic in West Berlin. The VOPO-men smartly saluted the "Frau Minister" and she hardly troubled to conceal the sheafs of papers she carried. At the hospital one of Gehlen's assistants from Group III/F was waiting, in a white coat and with a stethoscope hanging from his neck. To this pseudo-doctor Frau Kastner handed the papers, which every week included a copy of the minutes of cabinet meetings, and notes of documents exchanged between the East German government and Moscow and other communist capitals.*

Yet another important *S-Quelle* informer was sitting pretty at the East German ministry for state security. This agent was a sophisticated lady who by a lucky chance had been enlisted as early as 1950. She was Frau Doktor Hilde Halm, born in 1923 at Ober-Barnim, north of Berlin. During the war she had served as a youthful secretary in the Wehrmacht quartermaster general's office. In 1945, during the Soviet bombardment of the city, she had saved some important files from his blazing office and was probably the last of the few German women to be awarded the Iron Cross for bravery. If she had been a good nazi, this did not hinder her from becoming an ardent communist soon after. In 1946 she was behind a desk in the office of *Kommissariat 5*, the Soviet-German security and espionage headquarters at Karlshorst.

* See page 272

In 1950 she went to West Berlin on a nostalgic errand—to find her old teacher. This visit brought her to a Frau Thum, who happened to be one of Gehlen's "collectors", and looking for a bright damsel from across the border. It did not take much persuasion to make Fraulein Halm change her allegiance once again. She became V-Frau "Queck", provided with the alias "Elizabeth Span", and advised to find a post inside the newly established ministry for state security. She did not succeed at once and for a time Gehlen had to be satisfied with *her* job at the ministry of finance. For four years she produced excellent information and with her previous experience as a secretary in the police department, she proved herself useful during the Berlin uprising in June 1953, reporting on the arrests of rebels and V-men and about their interrogations and secret trials.

By 1954 she finally succeeded in getting herself transferred to the ministry of state security, of which Wollweber had become the head. But to Gehlen's chagrin, her stay there lasted only eighteen months. She must have slipped up, for in April 1956 she was arrested, tried for treason and espionage, and sentenced to life imprisonment. However, Fraulein Halm had recruited two other officials at the ministry for state security, of which Wollweber had become the head. they continued to supply Pullach with reports long after the prison doors had closed behind their sponsor.[9]

If Gehlen had every reason to be satisfied with the right people he had put into right places, Wollweber had not been idle either. He had done exactly the same as his hated adversary: he had planted two of his superior spies in the nerve-centre of the Gehlen Organisation, one at the Pullach HQ, another in the most important West Berlin branch. Years went by before Gehlen made the terrifying discovery that one of his trusted officers was a communist double agent.

Gehlen Finds and Loses Martin Bormann

In his memoirs Gehlen states that only now—in the autumn of 1971—he can "break the long silence and provide the key to one of the most mysterious cases of our century". After this fulsome fanfare he goes on to say that Admiral Canaris told him during the war that he had reason to suspect Martin Bormann, Hitler's deputy, of being a Soviet agent in touch with Moscow by a clandestine radio link. Gehlen gives no hint as to when and where Canaris told him this besides saying that "Canaris described to me his grounds for suspicion or supposition and his evidence for the motives of Bormann's treachery" (whatever this tortuous phrase means).

Gehlen adds that only in 1946 he could undertake investigations into "Bormann's mysterious disappearance". Any imprudent move during the Hitler regime "would have meant our end". In exactly five lines on page 48 of the German edition of his memoirs he goes on to state that "two reliable informers in the 1950s convinced me that Martin Bormann was then alive in the Soviet Union, where he was kept incommunicado, having crossed to the Russians when the Red Army occupied Berlin; he later died in Russia."

This is "the key" Herr Gehlen provides in his much advertised memoirs to the Bormann mystery. But his new statement is in complete contrast to several reports which Gehlen made over the years to Dulles and CIA officials, when requested to assist them in the search for Bormann.

In January 1953 Dulles approached Gehlen after CIA had received a curious piece of information from the British Secret Service. On January 12, 1953, seven former nazi officials, had been arrested in the British zone by order of the British High Commissioner, Sir Ivone Kirkpatrick, suspected of trying to revive a secret neo-nazi organisation. They were taken to the British military prison at Werl near Dortmund. Amongst them was forty-eight-year-old Dr. Werner Naumann, former secretary of state in Goebbels' propaganda ministry. After his release from Allied detention in 1946, Naumann— barred from legal practice—had been working as manager of a Dusseldorf chemical works. During his interrogations in January 1953 he denied any neo-nazi activities. He said he had lost any nazi enthusiasm he might have had already during the war when he—and other members of Goebbels' staff—had discovered that Bormann "was a Soviet agent". Goebbels knew about it, too, but neither he nor anyone else dared to tell Hitler about it.

Naumann described to the British Intelligence officers how he left the Chancellery bunker on May 1, 1945 when Hitler and Goebbels had committed suicide. Naumann was in a group which included Bormann and several nazi party officials.[10] They ran across the Tiergarten towards the Lehrter Station. There they were caught in the cross-fire between Red Army and SS units who were still entrenched near the station. There was nothing new about this. What was new in Naumann's statement in 1953 was his almost casual statement: "Bormann was rescued by the Russians. He was a Soviet spy and he must have arranged beforehand where to meet the Red Army advance units. We had to run for our lives; one of us, Dr. Stumpfegger was killed by shrapnel . . ." And he added: "Bormann now lives in Moscow."

Neither the British Intelligence officers nor CIA, who were informed of Naumann's depositions, attached much credence to Naumann's story. He and the other former nazi officials were eventually released. Gehlen was told of Naumann's strange testimony and this is, probably, the real source of the statement in his memoirs about Bormann. For eighteen years he made no use of it.

At this time of Naumann's deposition, Allen Dulles asked Gehlen to produce a report about the likelihood or otherwise of the Bormann rumour. This Gehlen did—though he avoids mention of it in his memoirs—and he handed it over to a CIA agent, James McGovern. In this report Gehlen stated that neither of the various rumours about Bormann's fate were true and that there was hardly any doubt that Bormann had been killed on May 1, 1945.

The disappearance of the Fuhrer's deputy, the only one of the nazi leaders who had never been caught and was sentenced to death at the Nuremberg Trial *in absentia,* had remained an unsolved puzzle for many years. At least four versions about his fate were in circulation, each more fantastic than the last. First, it was rumoured that he had been a British agent since before the war and had talked Rudolf Hess into his flight to Scotland in 1941. After his escape from the Chancellery he had gone to Ploen in Holstein, by then occupied by British troops; thence he was taken to England, where he became a foreign office consultant on German affairs, and then lived happily ever after as a British pensioner. A second theory was that he had reached the Baltic coast, was taken aboard a waiting U-boat, sailed to the Argentine, and became adviser to the dictator Juan Peron. (Simon Wiesenthal, head of the Jewish Documentation Centre, who tracked Adolf Eichmann in 1960 in Buenos Aires from where he was abducted by two Israeli agents, firmly believes that Bormann, now seventy-one, is still living in South America. In May 1967 an elderly carpenter in Guatemala, named Juan Martinez, enjoyed a brief notoriety when held by the police as the elusive Bormann; but it was a case of mistaken identity.)

A third version echoed Dr. Naumann's statement, that Bormann, a Soviet agent secretly connected with the famous "Red Orchestra" espionage network during the war,* had arranged by radio a meeting with Russian officers of General Vasili Chuikov's 8th Guards Army, whose advance elements had arrived on May 1 in the vicinity of Hitler's Chancellery. He was collected near the Lehrter railway station, taken to Chuikov's HQ, and then to Moscow, where he became a high official of Soviet Intelligence, eventually returning to East Germany after having undergone facial plastic surgery; there he probably died as an elderly man in the 1960s.

The last, and the most likely, story of Bormann's fate is the simplest and one for which Gehlen ultimately produced rational evidence. Bormann was neither a British nor a Soviet agent (although

* See page 81

234

Gehlen did not exclude the possibility that, like Himmler, Goering, Schellenberg and other nazi leaders, he might have made secret contacts with either the western Allies, or the Russians, or both, hoping to save his neck). After leaving the Chancellery with the four other officials, he and Dr. Stumpfegger, Hitler's SS doctor, were killed during the bombardment of the city. The neighbourhood of the Lehrter Station, Invalidenstrasse, Hannoverschestrasse, Luisenstrasse and the square in front of the Charité Hospital were strewn with the bodies of men, women and children killed in the cross-fire which ravaged the district north of the Tiergarten. Two days after the surrender of the capital by General Hans Krebs to General Chuikov, the Russians collected a number of Germans and ordered them to bury the bodies in three mass graves in the park near the station.

Two years later Gehlen could tell the CIA official McGovern that one of his V-men had seen photographs of Bormann's diary, which Russian soldiers had found on his body. The corpses had been searched before being buried in order to identify them and Bormann's identity thus established. Gehlen came to the conclusion that the Russians had then removed his body but that Bormann was not buried with the other people. One reason why the Soviet authorities never made an announcement of Bormann's death might have been that Moscow officials learnt of the exact circumstances of Bormann's death only after the Nuremberg Trial and found it embarassing that a dead man had been sentenced to death. Or, as James McGovern put it in his CIA report, Stalin's idea of leaving the world guessing about Bormann was not bad at all; it was a constant reminder of the nazi atrocities, in which Hitler's deputy had his full share.

The Jewish Documentation Centre in Vienna, however, continued its own investigations. Then, in 1965, Gehlen produced a new and startling sequel to his investigations as a confirmation of his own theory that Bormann had been dead and buried for twenty years. According to the report handed to CIA, one of Gehlen's branch managers in West Berlin had come across a retired sixty-eight-year-old postman, named Albert Krumnow, who had been one of the men ordered in May 1945 by Russian officers to bury the bodies. The man stated that he had recognised Bormann and buried him in the park near the Lehrter Station. Gehlen arranged with the West Berlin police that the park should be dug up. This was done on July 20 and 21, 1965 in the presence of Pullach and CIA officials. A large quantity of bones and a few well-preserved skeletons were found. Skulls were taken to a police laboratory, in the hope that if one of them was Martin Bormann's he might be identified by the characteristics of his teeth. But neither the dentist who treated him nor his dental chart were found and no further investigations took place afterwards.

This then is the real story of the search for Bormann, in which Gehlen had taken part and about which he had produced reports which he omits mentioning in his memoirs. Confronted with all this evidence in contradiction of Gehlen's new story, one can only deplore Gehlen's attempt to excite interest in his forthcoming book with his "disclosure". It is a pity that he should have stooped to sensationalism of this kind, which can only detract from the credibility of any other statements in his memoirs.

XVII

By Parachute Into Russia

The activities of the Gehlen Organisation were originally divided into *Nah-Aufklärung*—near reconnaissance—and *Tiefen-Aufklärung*—reconnaissance "in depth". The first, limited to the Soviet zone of East Germany and East Berlin, was producing satisfactory results. But espionage "in depth", aimed at penetration of the communist countries had, until 1951, developed very slowly. Successes had been achieved in Czechoslovakia and Poland, but early high expectations that the R-Net and the rebel groups* would secure a permanent foothold in the Soviet Union soon faded out.

By 1950, American pressure on Gehlen to provide factual information from the Soviet Union, rather than producing hearsay reports such as those from returning prisoners of war, had greatly increased. There were several weighty reasons why the Americans wanted Gehlen to redouble his efforts and deliver the goods. In Washington the CIA had undergone drastic and far-reaching changes. The euphoria of the Hillenkoetter era had come to the end. President Truman had recalled General Walter Bedell Smith from his post as ambassador to Moscow and appointed him director of CIA. Smith had gone to Moscow in 1946 confident that he would succeed in helping to cement a peaceful coexistence between East and West. He came back a deeply disillusioned man and, on taking over CIA, he quickly realised that the agency had but scanty knowledge of what was going on in the Soviet Union and hardly any information on Stalin's political and military plans and intentions. Indeed, he found the system of gathering foreign intelligence in a deplorable state: CIA relied to a very large degree on Gehlen to provide information on the whole of Eastern Europe.

One of his first steps was to turn to an old friend, Major-General (later Sir) Kenneth Strong, who had been chief of intelligence at Eisenhower's SHAEF during the war, when Smith was chief of staff. He asked Strong to become his deputy in the CIA and take charge of

* See page 146

all foreign intelligence. General Strong had become head of the Political Intelligence Department of the foreign office after the war and in 1948 head of the newly created Joint Intelligence Bureau at the ministry of defence. The offer was certainly tempting. But it presupposed that he would give up his British citizenship and become a naturalised American. Strong declined the offer, as he says, first because of his fundamental reluctance to cease being British; and secondly, because he felt it would have been difficult for a "foreigner" to work in CIA.

Smith was greatly disappointed by Strong's refusal; he found it difficult to choose a substitute and eventually appointed William H. Jackson, a New York investment banker and wartime intelligence officer under Strong at SHAEF, to the post of deputy director. Jackson had been on the small committee which Truman appointed in 1949 to report on the working of the CIA under Hillenkoetter and of which Allen Welsh Dulles was chairman. Jackson accepted the CIA post reluctantly; after the war he had become managing director of the banking house of J. H. Whitney & Co.[1] and joining CIA meant a great financial sacrifice; moreover he did not feel that he was up to the task Smith had envisaged for him.

On June 24, 1950, the North Korean communists invaded South Korea with a well-equipped army of seventy thousand men, spearheaded by one hundred Soviet tanks. Neither CIA nor Army G-2 Intelligence had information, in the words of Lyman B. Kirkpatrick, the CIA's inspector general, as to "when the attack was going to take place nor under what conditions".[2] The conflict in the Far East was another factor which convinced Smith of the urgent need to reorganise CIA's collection of foreign intelligence. Thus, as his third best choice, he turned to Allen Welsh Dulles, who after submitting his report had expected that Truman would call upon him to succeed Hillenkoetter; bypassed by Smith's appointment, he had returned deeply offended to his legal practice in New York. When Dulles arrived at the dingy CIA offices in the old Government Printing Office buildings in Washington's Foggy Bottom district, Smith offered him the post of deputy director with these words: "Now that you've written this damn report, it's up to you to put it into effect."[3]

The Advent of Allen Dulles

Dulles eagerly accepted the No.2 position, which comprised the directorship of the Plans and Operations Division. Measured by American standards, Dulles was undoubtedly a foremost intelligence expert, seasoned in two World Wars, and a man who understood international and, particularly, European affairs. He brought to

CIA a Pandora's box of brilliant ideas on how to combat communism and defend the free world; he released from it all the mythological "evils which spread throughout the world". Many years later ex-President Truman sought to divest himself of responsibility for some of the more outrageous CIA operations during his tenure of office: "I had never thought that it would be injected into peacetime cloak-and-dagger operations . . . that it would be so far removed from its intended role and interpreted as a symbol of sinister and mysterious foreign intrigue."[4]

In fairness to Dulles, this criticism was not entirely valid. CIA would have had to develop aggressively even without him, after Stalin had destroyed the Potsdam agreement, turned the nations of Eastern Europe into slavish satellites, staged open aggression in Berlin and fomented the Korean War, compelling the United States and several of her allies to engage their armed forces whilst keeping his own uncommitted. Thanks to the Soviet espionage conducted by the Canadian Spy Ring and the atom spies, such as the Rosenbergs, Klaus Fuchs and Allan Nunn-May, the West's trump card—the nuclear bomb—was soon matched by the Soviets' own nuclear power. Behind this threat Moscow could expand her influence into South East Asia, the Middle East, Africa and, by 1961, place atomic missiles on America's doorstep in Cuba.

In those early days, when Moscow's ruthless world-wide confrontation began to develop, even the most loyal admirers of Bedell Smith could not claim that he had the breadth of vision or sense of intrigue needed to direct the operations of the young CIA. He was a plain and honest soldier, the only American four-star general who had not graduated from West Point and the War Academy. Yet to him must go the palm for laying the real foundation of CIA's efficiency and organisation; the meticulous training of its agents, and the setting up of a world-wide network of "stations".

The reorganisation also brought a decisive change in the status of the Gehlen "Org". Hitherto Gehlen had still been responsible to the interdepartmental Office of Special Operations, in which CIA shared control with the State Department and the Pentagon. One of Smith's first actions had been to obtain Truman's approval for a merger of this body with the Office of Policy Co-ordination (the ten-slash-two creation of the National Security Council) headed by Frank G. Wisner, the titular deputy assistant secretary of state. After the merger CIA obtained exclusive control over both these, which were incorporated into the Plans and Operations Division under Dulles with Wisner as his deputy. The change of name made little difference: it remained known as the "office of dirty tricks".

Soon after taking up his new appointment, Allen Dulles went to

239

Pullach to confer with Gehlen. Wisner had, as will be recalled, already paid visits there. On the agenda at this first Dulles-Gehlen meeting, which was followed by many more, was a plan for the immediate intensification of espionage against the Soviet Union. Dulles made it clear to Gehlen that he must without delay find agents willing to go to Russia and able to procure the vital intelligence required. Dulles promised that CIA would take care of their safe dispatch, either by air or by sea, since Gehlen did not regard the land route across East Germany and Poland as feasible. The two men, who had, of course, met four years earlier, understood each other. Indeed, a strange friendship developed between the tall, voluble, gregarious Dulles, who possessed undeniable charm, and the small, withdrawn, taciturn and ascetic Gehlen. Over the next eleven years their relationship grew from that of a sponsor with his protegé to a partnership, in which at times it was Gehlen who assumed the role of the senior partner.

Wisner Sets Up CIA's Private Army

Dulles had made it clear to Gehlen that top priority must be given to the selection and training of agents for work in Russia. Wisner had already discussed this with Gehlen the year before and also a plan to recruit men from amongst Eastern Europeans for hush-hush armed units to assist insurgents inside communist countries. The plan was not put into practice until 1952, when after his election President Eisenhower eased out General Bedell Smith from the CIA and made Allen Dulles its director; his brother, John Foster Dulles, had become secretary of state just before, and was embarking on his policy of brinkmanship. The Dulles brothers believed deeply that Stalin's captive nations would rise against communist oppression given a modicum of encouragement. A private mercenary force was to be established in Germany to be ready for such an emergency and to be employed without involving regular US forces.

Who else than Gehlen was the man to help in laying the foundations for such "Special Forces"? He and his former FHO and WALLI men, and also the SS officers who had served in the "Brandenburg" sabotage units and the *Jagdkommandos* against the Red Army and Soviet partisans had all the experience that was needed. There was no problem in finding enough volunteers among the many hundreds of thousands of displaced persons who still lived in misery in crowded camps. At the end of the war, Allied forces of occupation had found seven and a half million people who had been brought from a dozen countries for slave labour in Germany, as well as huge numbers of half-starved prisoners of war. Though within weeks more than three million French, Dutch, Belgian, Danish,

Norwegian and, with a few exceptions, Yugoslav citizens, as well as a good number of Poles, were repatriated—the Soviet authorities took care of their nationals in the Eastern zone—and many East Europeans who refused to go home were enabled to emigrate to the United States, Canada, South America and Australia, there were still several hundred thousand families in German camps when the funds of the International Refugee Organisations ran out in 1952. Many were unemployable, but the younger ones found lowly and poorly paid jobs on the land or as industrial labourers, clearing bomb rubble and working on the rebuilding of German cities. They provided a vast reservoir of potential recruits for the American-sponsored units, in which living conditions would be paradise compared with the utter misery of their present existence.

The Ukrainians, Byelorussians, Poles, Latvians, Estonians, Lithuanians and the motley crowd of Russo-Asian nationals who represented the remnants of Vlassov's 600,000-strong Army of Liberation attracted Wisner's and Gehlen's attention. In the space of two years about five thousand were enlisted, assembled in camps at Bad Wiessee, at Kaufbeuren in Bavaria and at the US Army Hammand Barracks near Mannheim, and trained by American officers and former German Wehrmacht and Waffen SS NCO's. At Kaufbeuren the commandant and chief instructor was Major Ronald Otto Bollenbach, former US assistant military attaché in Moscow.

These units became the nucleus of CIA's private army, later better known as the "Green Berets" in Vietnam. Some of them are today still stationed in West Germany: the 5th Special Reconnaissance Group, now entirely airborne, at Oberursel, and the 10th Special Group in Bavaria.

Nearly a hundred associations of these foreign nationals had sprung up in Germany, some confining themselves to charitable and social work, but most of them pursuing political aims. Munich had become "the capital of the DP's"; at one time in the 1950s there were no less than eighty such organisations with headquarters in the Bavarian capital, often competing with each other, and most of them financed from CIA funds. Later the Federal German government contributed substantial sums under the headings of welfare and educational assistance. In 1971 Bonn is still handing out a total of 5,400,000 Marks to organisations, which besides established bodies, such as the Ukrainian Central Committee, the Association of Polish Refugees, or the Baltic, Slovak, and Croat associations, include quaintly named associations such as the Kalmuk-Tibetan Defence Society, or the Free Ukrainian Committee of Byzantine Rite.

Gehlen alerted several of his assistants who had a thorough knowledge and first-hand experience of Eastern European countries and their people, and also approached an acknowledged expert on anything about the East, whom he had known and admired since his school-days in Breslau. He was Dr. Michael Achmeteli, born in 1887 in Borjom in the Caucasus, where his father amassed a great fortune when oil was discovered on his land by British and American mining engineers (amongst them the later president of the United States, Herbert Hoover). During the Revolution Achmeteli had fought with the White Armies against the bolsheviks and eventually came to Germany, becoming a lecturer in Slavonic Studies at Breslau University. He was a close friend of the Gehlen family; several of Achmeteli's books, in which he expounded Germany's mission of "civilising communist Russia", were published by Ferdinand Hirt & Son, of which Gehlen's father was manager. Achmeteli had been closely connected with Abwehr intelligence in its early days. The *Ost-Institute* he founded was, in fact, a "front" for espionage against Poland and the Soviet Union even before the nazi regime. Under Hitler he had become professor and head of the Institute for the study of communism and the USSR. As a friend of Hitler's chief theoretician of the nazi Aryan doctrine, Alfred Rosenberg,[5] his advice was needed at OKW, and he also acted as a "super analyst" for Gehlen's FHO. In 1945, Achmeteli went into hiding, afraid that the Allies might hand him over to the Soviets, but he later reappeared under the alias of "Dr. A. K. Michael" at Unterweilbach, a village in the shadow of the former Dachau concentration camp near Munich, where Gehlen obtained for him a villa paid for from CIA funds.

Professor Achmeteli went to work with two Pullach officers selected by Gehlen to form the first staff of the secret "Special Forces". One was another academic, Dr. Franz Alfred Six, ex-lecturer at Koenigsberg University, who had managed to combine his scholarly vocation with the service in the SS;[6] he had risen to the rank of SS Brigadefuhrer (equivalent to brigadier-general) and became head of Section VII at Himmler's RSHA. He had "dived under" after the collapse of the Third Reich, but Allied intelligence officers, searching out war criminals, found him after two years. In April 1948, Six came before a US military tribunal at Nuremberg, charged with having ordered the executions of civilians, including hundreds of Jews, when in command of a *Jagdkommando* in July and August 1941 at Smolensk. Judge Dixon sentenced him to twenty years' imprisonment.[7] However, four years later Six was free and busy advancing the fruition of the CIA-Gehlen project.

The third member of the triumvirate was Dr. Emil Augsburg, born in 1904 in Lodz in Poland, according to official Polish sources, of Jewish parentage—which, if true, did not hamper his ultimate admission to the SS[8] in which he rose to become Standartenfuhrer (colonel) heading a section attached to Adolf Eichmann's S-4 department, which handled the "Jewish problem", with "final results" that are well known. After the collapse, Augsburg fled, as did Eichmann, with the assistance of ODESSA[9] to Italy, where he found charitable aid from circles close to the Vatican which helped escaped nazis. After a year or two when he rightly assumed that enough grass had grown over the past, he returned to Germany as "Dr. Althaus" and was enrolled by Gehlen, working first as manager of the Karlsruhe branch "L", and then at Pullach. These three experts prepared the briefs for the would-be agents to be sent into Russia, assembling masses of topographical material, information about everyday life in Soviet towns and villages, and up-to-date regulations about travel, police registration, food distribution, etc., in order to make the agents' movements as safe as possible.

Several of Gehlen's assistants, under his personal supervision, were busily devising operational tactics. Amongst them were ex-Major Karl Edmund Gartenfeld—now using the aliases of "Schaffer", "Baumann", or "Erhard"—and Wilhelm Ahlrichs, who had a splendid record of infiltration of wartime spies into the United States. Both had been with the Abwehr Hamburg-Ast, Gartenfeld during the first two years of the war, when he commanded the Luftwaffe Staffel, which dropped seventeen German spies and saboteurs into England by parachute. His operations included "Lena", "Lobster I and II", "Fink", "Siegfried", "Hector" and others. Although forty-one years old at the beginning of the war, he personally piloted several of these dangerous sorties, for which the agents were dropped with rubber boats on the coasts of Banff, Kent and Essex. In 1942 the Gartenfeld squadron was moved to the eastern front and was again engaged on dropping spies behind Soviet lines. Gehlen had used the squadron on many occasions to dispatch his FHO spies.

Ahlrichs had a no less remarkable wartime service. He had organised, in cooperation with Captain Fritz Weidemann, chief of the German spy net in the United States, and Dr. Gerhard Westrich, the "commercial counsellor" in New York in 1940, a number of daring landing operations for spies and saboteurs on the east coast.[10]

NTS—"We Bring Death to Tyrants!"

Gehlen and Wisner, not entirely satisfied with the human material the Pullach "collectors" had found among the Eastern European DP's, approached several anti-communist refugee organisations to get really reliable and able-bodied men. They had a wide choice. The largest, oldest and most respected was NTS, whose Russian name, *Narodnyi Trudovoy Soyuz*, literally meant National Labour Council, but was usually mistranslated as "National Alliance of Solidarists".

Some of its members even paraphrased the initials as standing for *Nosim Smert Tiranom,* which means "we bring death to tyrants".

The NTS was founded back in the late 1920s in Belgrade by Socialist and Menshevik exiles, many of whom had taken part in the October Revolution of 1917, but had had to flee from bolshevik wrath. Politically, too, NTS was originally a left-of-centre group, though in the course of years many right-wing Russian exiles had joined it and it had acquired a strongly anti-communist character. From Belgrade its headquarters were first moved to Paris and later to Frankfurt on Main; it had enjoyed political and financial support from several European governments and from business concerns which had had investments and industrial plants in Tsarist Russia before the revolution, and never gave up hope that the Soviet rulers would one day be ousted. Amongst these NTS patrons were tycoons such as Sir Henry Deterding, chairman of Royal Dutch-Shell, Sir Basil Zaharoff, the mysterious armaments king, Henry Ford and Fritz Thyssen, head of the German steel trust, who later also financed Hitler.

The revered leader of the NTS was Vladimir Poremski, and important members of the national council were Dr. Georgi Okolovich and Dr. Alexander Truchnovich. During the war they and thousands of their members had collaborated with the Germans, providing teachers, instructors and interpreters, and had played an important part in the creation of Vlassov's Liberation Army. Many NTS members worked for Admiral Canaris' Abwehr and for Gehlen's FHO. But by 1943, the collaboration of many of them had turned to hostility towards the nazis because of the atrocities committed by SS *Jagdkommandos* in Russia. This was not the liberation from the communist yoke they had been dreaming of; rather it was another and in many aspects a much worse kind of slavery that the nazis had imposed upon their subjugated compatriots. More than sixty NTS leaders were rounded up by the Gestapo and sent to concentration camps, where twenty-eight perished. In 1945 Poremski and several other leaders were freed by the Americans and took up their activities again, receiving support from the US military government and various anti-communist business groups and committees in America.

Besides welfare work among the two and a half million Russian displaced persons and ex-prisoners of war, the NTS embarked upon an offensive against Moscow. A weekly newspaper and several journals, as well as many millions of leaflets, broadsheets and pamphlets, were distributed and special camps established for about a hundred thousand Russians who had refused to go home. A "secret operations committee" was set up, which established bureaux for espionage and subversion, internal security, economic planning and so forth. Branches and "militant groups" spread all over western Europe, the United States, South America, and as far as Japan and Chiang Kai-Shek's Formosa. Indeed, NTS had declared war on Moscow, and it succeeded in infiltrating agitators amongst the returning prisoners and repatriated forced-labour workers. Some of them, after reaching the Soviet Union, had remarkable success in spreading disaffection against the Stalin regime.

Over the past twenty years CIA had provided substantial funds for NTS activities. At present the NTS operates radio transmitters, broadcasting as Radio Free Russia in Germany and several countries bordering on the Soviet Union in the Far East; it publishes several weekly and monthly newspapers and journals, some designed to attract women and young people, and conducts many clandestine operations. Mr. Gerald Brooke, the London lecturer arrested in Moscow in 1965 and eventually released after a long imprisonment in exchange for the KGB's master spies Peter and Helen Kroger, has admitted that he carried subversive material for the NTS.

Amongst other organisations which began to cooperate with Gehlen in the early 1950s were the Monarchist Brotherhood of St. George, ROND (Russian National People's Movement), various smaller and shrinking right-wing groups composed of veterans of the White Armies, and above all the strong and flourishing organisations of Ukrainian and Polish exiles, such as the OUN, the OUNS, *Wolnosć i Niepodlegnosć* (Freedom and Independence), *Ocalenie Polski* (Save Poland), Latvian, Estonian and Lithuanian groups, and a host of others. For NTS recruits a special sabotage school was established at Bad Homburg; Ukrainians, whose leader, Stefan Bandera, had collaborated with the Germans since 1939, were trained in another camp near Oberursel.

The First Parachutists

By the end of 1951, Gehlen's foreign legionnaires were ready for action. Wisner had long since returned to Washington but he and Allen Dulles kept a protective arm over the enterprise, and, what was even more important, an open purse to satisfy Gehlen's ever-growing demands for funds. So elaborate were the preparations that some of the would-be agents were sent for final training to the US Air Force base at Fort Bragg, North Carolina.

The first two agents to go into action were F. K. Sarantzev, a twenty-six-year-old Red Army corporal[11] taken prisoner by the Germans in 1943, and A. I. Osmanov, twenty-three, a deserter who had served in the Vlassov Army. Their destination was Moldavia, the great, fertile area of vineyards and orchards, sheep and cattle farms between south-west Ukraine and Rumania. Wisner had arranged with Gehlen and Gartenfeld that the flight should take off from a US Air Force base in Greece, though the distance from Thessaloniki to the dropping area was about seven hundred miles; overflying Bulgaria and Rumania was regarded as being much safer than the route across Poland or Czechoslovakia. These two were dropped on August 18, 1951.

The parachutists were equipped with excellently forged papers and identity "legends". Sarantzev had become "Sergey Pavlovich Feodorov", working at the Java Tobacco factory near Moscow and on vacation in the Caucasus, which was to be his ultimate destination after landing. After completing his assignment, which it was estimated would take about three weeks, he was to cross the Soviet-Turkish frontier at Kars. In Turkey CIA agents would take care of him. Osmanov was to make his way right across the Ukraine and the Volga region to the Urals, also returning by way of Turkey.

Both carried miniature radio transmitters and collapsable bicycles of East German make (which were exported to the Soviet Union and generally available there) and German-manufactured machine pistols. Each was given five thousand roubles, a small bag of gold coins, and several watches; these were to buy favours from peasants whom the agents might have to ask for food and shelter.

Their stay inside the Soviet Union was brief. A few radio signals reached Gehlen's receiving stations, but then they suddenly stopped. Both parachutists were caught long before they were able to reach their destination; many months later a brief announcement on Moscow Radio, which did not mention their names or aliases, stated that "two American spies" had been apprehended, tried by the military collegium of the Supreme Court and "according to Article 58 of the Criminal Code" sentenced to death and executed.

Meanwhile, on September 25, a "solo agent" was dropped, on a trial flight from a US airfield near Wiesbaden across eastern Germany and Poland. This was twenty-five-year-old Ivan Alexandrovich Filistovich, dropped near his birthplace of Ilya near Molodetchno, north of Minsk in Byelorussia. Despite his youth he had had an adventurous past. At the age of seventeen when his home town was occupied by German troops in 1943, he volunteered—as did quite a number of Byelorussians—for the HIWI units; later he joined the 13th SS battalion and was sent to Italy, where he fought British and American troops in Forli. After the surrender he made his way to Czechoslovakia, and eventually in 1946 to France and Belgium, where he became a student at the Catholic University of Louvain. Then, hearing from a compatriot that the Americans were enlisting young Russians for special operations, he went to Germany and was trained at Bad Wörishofen for the Special Forces.

His stay in western Europe was used to provide him with a seemingly cast-iron "legend". He was to pose as a former forced-labour worker who had been deported from Russia and sent to work as a miner in Belgium during the war, had returned to Germany as a DP, and was now trying to reach his birthplace. Filistovich's main assignment was to seek out any of the "sleepers" in Byelorussia who might still have kept their old WALLI radio transmitters and to revive an R-Net cell. Failing this, he was to send letters in invisible ink to a cover address, pretending to be communicating with a fictitious friend, another forced-labour worker, who had remained in France. The cover address was "Joseph Vysotsky, 8 rue Gambetta, St. Quentin, Paris", an outpost used by the "Org".

Filistovich remained for quite a while in Byelorussia, and sent several letters to Paris which, because of the strict censorship in those days took three weeks to arrive; but he failed to locate any of Gehlen's or Baun's old agents. In the end, the Soviet police must have become suspicious and it must be assumed that the young man broke down under interrogations and made a confession. Nothing was heard of him again until two years later when a pamphlet issued by the Soviet ministry for state security (MGB) mentioned his name amongst other "fascist agents and counter-revolutionaries who had been rendered harmless".

On October 18 another dropping operation from a Greek airfield met with disaster because the American pilot missed the dropping target. On this occasion Gehlen had selected a mixed double— Konstantin Saplakan, a native of Soviet Armenia, and a German, Wilhelm Spender, whose family had lived for many years in Russia, where he was born. They, too, were to parachute into the Ukraine, to establish a link with nationalist groups in Charkov and Kiev who were in contact with NTS and OUN organisations in Germany. However, they were dropped in the Faragas district in Rumania and captured on landing.

Several other parachute drops which took place before the winter of 1951/2 were only partially successful. In the summer of 1952, however, the operations were stepped up and amongst the fairly frequent drops some are worth mentioning. On May 2, a team of three agents, L. K. Koshelev, a twenty-three-year-old native of Sebastopol, A. P. Kurochkin and I. N. Voloshanovsky, both twenty-six, landed near Tsuman in Volhynia. Kurochkin had been a corporal in the Soviet Occupation forces in Austria; he had deserted in 1948 and escaped to Bavaria, where he was enlisted by one of Gehlen's "collectors" and trained at Bad Wörishofen. The other two were deserters too, both from Soviet garrisons in the Caucasus, who had made their way to Iran. The US embassy in Teheran sent them to

Germany. After training they were taken back to Iran and flown from a US airfield over the Caucasus, where they were dropped in the oil-field region. Only Kurochkin got into radio contact with the "Org", by way of the Teheran outpost to which his transmitter was tuned. This link lasted for several months and Gehlen and his analysts at first had reason to assume that the brief reports the agent was signalling were genuine, but they soon came to the conclusion that he had been caught and that the Russians were conducting a radio game.

The confirmation of this came almost a year later, when the Moscow magazine *Ogonyok* published a long article disclosing "fascist espionage" and describing the activities of Alexander Kurochkin. It appeared that soon after his landing he had reported to the police telling them all about his mission. A picture published in the magazine showed a farmer's wife, who was alleged to have given shelter to the parachutist and persuaded him to give himself up. Details of Kurochkin's equipment, including his American-manufactured miniature radio, were also published.

After these setbacks Gehlen had better hopes for two operations in August. Evgeny G. Golubev was, at thirty, a more mature and better-trained agent. A native of Dhagestan, he too had deserted from the Soviet Army in Iran, after which he was brought to Germany and trained at Kaufbeuren by Major Bollenbach and by a "specialist", Captain Harold Fiedler, at one time a courier at the US embassy in Moscow. Golubev was regarded as highly promising and was sent for final training to CIA's West Pacific centre at Yokohama in Japan. He was dropped in the Vladivostok region—he was supposed to reconnoitre the Soviet Far East—but nothing was ever heard of him again. Ten days after Golubev's drop at the other end of the vast Soviet territory, a team of four agents, M. P. Artyushevsky, G. A. Kostyuk, T. A. Ostrikov and M. S. Kalnitzky, all former DP's taken from German camps, parachuted into Byelorussia in an area between Vitensk and Mogilev. They were told to take up residence and find work in industry, posing as returned forced-labour workers, and were provided with suitably forged papers and "legends". Ostrikov, however, betrayed the operation and his companions were arrested, one by one, soon after their arrival. Kalnitzky was killed, apparently resisting arrest, and the two others were tried and executed; but Ostrikov was amnestied, though he probably spent some years in a "rehabilitation" labour camp to repent of his crime.

From the long catalogue in the Pullach files of the parachute operations between 1951 and 1957, only a few cases can be mentioned as illustrations of how the drops were prepared and carried out. A few were successful, however, and provided information over a brief period of time.

Soviet Agent Gets Free Return Ticket

Gehlen had great expectations of two parachute operations in April 1953. Two teams were assembled, both of men selected by NTS leaders and carefully trained, first at the NTS-Gehlen school of Castle Amalienburg at Bad Wiessee and then at the special school for radio telegraphy, which Gehlen had opened at Stocking near Munich. Both teams were to be dropped from Greece. The first consisted of Alexander Vasilyevich Lakno, the team leader, Sergey Izginovich Gorbunov, Alexander Nicolaievich Makov and Danil Nicolaievich Remiga. The first three were all twenty-nine, and Remiga twenty-five; they had all been recruited back in 1950 from DP camps. They were dropped during the rainy night of April 25/26 in the black-earth region of the Ukraine.

Between them they carried forty-five thousand roubles in used notes, and each had a bag of gold coins; poison ampoules were sewn into their shirt collars, which they promised to use if caught. In all cases every precaution was taken by the Pullach experts to provide the parachutists with Russian-made clothes and boots; some of these were very old and worn, taken from DP's who had come to Germany many years earlier. The clothes were carefully mended and the agents were told to buy new ones in Russia; they were given genuine vouchers for this purpose.

This was the first team to carry radio-beacon devices in small, well concealed boxes, which were to be used for directing aircraft carrying other agents or conducting reconnaissance flights. Each had a small transmitter of the latest model then available. Their destination was Kiev and the Black Sea port of Odessa. All were Ukrainians[12] and they were carefully briefed by Pullach experts and members of NTS who were natives of the cities where the agents were supposed to settle. Makov who had been a sailor, was to report on shipping yards and harbour installations at Odessa, which were known to have been greatly expanded, and also on ship movements to and from this port.

Nothing was heard from them after they had dropped. On May 27, 1953, *Pravda* published a brief official announcement stating that four spies "trained by the American-German fascist espionage centre of the war-criminal Gehlen in Munich" had been apprehended at their landing place after parachuting from an American plane; and that "after making full confessions at their trial at Kiev, they were executed by a firing squad on May 20". This was a blow to Gehlen and to his assistants and advisers, who had so hopefully trained and briefed this important team, particularly as it became clear that the operation must have been betrayed by a double agent. Gehlen had for a long time suspected that NTS and some of the other refugee organisations had been infiltrated by Soviet agents, and he was soon to obtain evidence for this, as we shall see in the next chapter.

The blow was, however, softened by the apparently splendid success of the second team, dropped also from a Greek airfield three nights later, on April 29. It consisted of Konstantin Igorovich Khmelnitzky, Ivan Kudryavtzev, Alexander Mihailovich Novikov and Nicolai Ivanovich Yakuta. All were former Ukrainian DP's and all had been trained at Bad Wiessee. Novikov was the youngest; he had come to Germany in 1943 as a forced-labour deportee at the age of seventeen, and at the end of the war was in a group of youngsters selected by NTS for higher education. He later worked at the Munich office of the Indiana Food Corporation.

Yakuta had packed into his twenty-nine years of life of adventurous misery. Wounded and taken prisoner in 1942, he had spent three years in a POW camp and, having refused to return to Russia in 1945, was befriended in a DP camp by a White Russian aristocrat, Prince Boloselsky, who had lived in Germany for many years as an emigré. The prince told Yakuta that he would send him to his estates in South America, but instead he took him to Casablanca, where he worked for almost three years as a porter. There he met an NTS recruiter, Boldyrev, who sent him back to Germany to be trained, first at the NTS sabotage school at Bad Homburg, and then at Bad Wiessee; his advanced training lasted nine months. Khmelnitzky, the team leader, a former Red Army sergeant and a trained W/T operator, was particularly trusted by the NTS leaders and Gehlen's experts. Before the team was flown to Greece, Dr. Okolovitch, the deputy chairman of NTS, came to see them at Bad Wiessee and, as he put it, to "shake the hands of brave men".

After a successful drop near Minsk in Byelorussia, Khmelnitzky apparently succeeded in establishing radio contact without difficulty. He reported that, according to instructions, the team had split up and that he himself was covering the Minsk-Mogilev region, whilst one of his companions had gone to Smolensk. Nothing was heard from the other three, but Khmelnitzky continued to transmit a mass of information. His reports continued for almost three years; he seemed to be travelling all over the Soviet Union, making a number of friends and setting up "cells of disaffection". So good was the material he was transmitting that Dulles and Wisner congratulated Gehlen on this achievement. Gehlen himself, however, began fairly soon to be disillusioned about Khmelnitzky's splendid exploits: he was too old a hand at the game to believe that they could be true. By early 1955 he was treating Khmelnitzky's reports with the utmost caution and even stopped including them in his weekly summaries to CIA.

The bubble burst four years later. In February 1957, the head of the press division of the Soviet ministry for foreign affairs, Leonid F. Ilyichev—known to foreign correspondents as "Hitchcock", because of his startling resemblance to the portly film director—called a special press conference.

In the hall lit by glaring TV floodlights, and behind tables littered with the props of the cloak-and-dagger trade, including three American transmitters, revolvers, maps, bags of gold coins, and neatly folded parachutes, he introduced to two hundred foreign and Soviet newspapers four real live spies: Khmelnitzky, Yakuta, Novikov and Kudryavtzev. While three of them looked dejected and their pallor betrayed their long imprisonment, Khmelnitzky was the life and soul of this strange party. He proudly declared that he had been a Soviet counter-espionage agent since 1945, had mixed with DP's in order "to discover the fascist conspiracy against the Soviet motherland" and he told how the Americans and their "Gehlen-lackeys" had "encouraged drinking, gambling and bad language, and even took us to immoral houses in Munich" after they were recruited and trained as spies. Even the Soviet newspapermen chuckled at this bowdlerised version of Khmelnitzky's adventures; a word such as brothel could, of course, not be uttered in front of high officials of the Soviet government.

Khmelnitzky gave some details about his training—a few were accurate—and told of his assignment: "military and economic spying, stealing Soviet documents, spreading false rumours, drawing morally unstable Soviet citizens into the fascist net and compromising Soviet officials and party workers . . .". This was certainly more than Gehlen in his wildest dreams would have thought of assigning to him. Then Khmelnitzky made his most sensational disclosure: for almost four years he had been conducting a radio game with Pullach, transmitting material prepared by Soviet security. This had been so successful, he said, that the Soviet authorities were able completely to mislead the Americans on many important matters, and from instructions and enquiries sent back to him, were also in a position "to discover many secret plans of the fascist conspirators plotting aggression against the Soviet motherland".

Khmelnitzky, alas, was telling the truth, even if it was heavily embroidered and shaped into familiar propaganda. But by 1957, when these disclosures were made in Moscow, Gehlen had long since known that not only this but several other parachute operations and infiltration attempts had been betrayed by one or several Soviet double agents who had wormed their way into the command centres of NTS.

With the take-over of the "Org" by the Federal government

Gehlen had to stop directing parachute operations into the Soviet Union. Dr. Adenauer was anxious to avoid an international incident, in which the new German Republic might become heavily involved. CIA did, however, continue sporadic parachuting, with Gehlen's "unofficial" assistance. With the coming of the U-2 spy planes and vastly improved aerial reconnaissance, the parachute operations lost much of their former importance. Sporadically, Moscow reported the capture of parachutists, such as of an American team code-named Quadrat B-52, of a "solo" agent named Okhrimovich at Kiev in 1954, and another, named V. M. Slavnov, as late as 1960. It would be unwise to reveal to the KGB that there were many others, between 1952 and 1960, who remain undiscovered and who are providing genuine and often extremely valuable information for Gehlen and BND, as well as CIA.

Newspaper readers in the United States and Western Europe did learn something about the parachute operations, if only through sporadic Moscow announcements about the capture of some of the agents. But more remarkable operations, which Gehlen conducted with the assistance of the British Admiralty and the Secret Intelligence Service, using the sea route to Russia, remained completely unknown. In the next chapter some of them are revealed for the first time.

XVIII

British Boats for Gehlen's Infiltrators

Both the parachute drops organised by Gehlen and CIA and their use of NTS members as agents followed a pattern originally established by the British Secret Intelligence Service, which had maintained relations with White Russian and Ukrainian organisations over a much longer period than had the Americans. They went back to the time of the "Intervention" against the Bolshevik Revolution after the First World War, and many of the leading figures in the SIS operations of these years, such as Sir Robert Bruce Lockhart, Sir Rex Leeper, or Brigadier George Hill, were still active in 1945. In the mid-1930s the head of SIS, Admiral Sir Hugh "Quex" Sinclair, who had been the director of Naval Intelligence in the "Intervention" years, patronised Stefan Bandera, the leader of the Organisation of Ukrainian Nationalist Revolutionaries (OUNR), the most reactionary of the emigré groups. Bandera boasted that he had the largest following among anti-communist Ukrainians inside the Soviet Union, but a few attempts to infiltrate OUNR agents on behalf of SIS at the outbreak of the Russo-Finnish war in 1939 badly misfired. Bandera later threw in his lot with the nazis and during the war organised Ukrainian units within the Waffen SS.

After the war Bandera emerged in the British zone, re-established his old contacts with SIS, and, claiming with some justification that his followers had staged rebellions in the Ukraine, persuaded the British intelligence chiefs to organise parachute teams of his agents for dispatch into the Soviet Union. The first group of three was dropped from an RAF Canberra aircraft in the Kiev region in July 1949, and other Bandera groups followed during the next ten months; nothing was ever heard again of any of them. Later British parachute drops of Bandera's agents were made from aircraft taking off from Cyprus, since this route was regarded as much safer. Several teams of agents, their numbers ranging from four to six, parachuted into the Soviet-annexed areas of eastern Poland, between Lvov and Brody, near Tarnopol and between Kolomiya and Kamenets, where Ukrainian, Polish and Ruthenian insurgents were fighting the Soviet

Army.* But they produced hardly any results. One reason for this was that at that time Kim Philby was head of the SIS section concerned with espionage against the Soviet Union, and so was instrumental in organising the dispatch of these agents. In his memoirs[1] he remarks with undisguised sarcasm: "I do not know what happened to the parties . . . but I can make an informed guess."

But, with or without Philby, the betrayal of these operations was inevitable. Bandera's organisation in Germany had been infiltrated by Soviet double agents, as were NTS and all the other anti-communist organisations with which Gehlen and the CIA were playing. Gehlen himself had sad memories of the fratricidal strife between the leaders of the Vlassov Army and the Ukrainian HIWIS during the war; he was wary of using "White" emigrés, but found that he had little choice. He did, however, warn CIA to have nothing to do with Bandera; but the SIS chiefs kept pressing General Bedell Smith, the new CIA director, to accept the OUNR as the main weapon for combined operations inside the Soviet Union. Sir Stewart Menzies, the SIS chief, sent Henry Lambton Carr, then head of the SIS Northern Department,[2] to Washington to urge this course. But Gehlen's warnings prevailed, and the negotiations broke down. The British continued for a time to work with Bandera, but eventually realised their mistake.

The Soviet MGB had devised elaborate plans for both penetrating and splitting the emigré groups in West Germany. An instance of how successful the Moscow spy-masters were was the case of Nikita Khorunshy, a Ukrainian captain stationed with the Soviet Army in East Germany and. a schoolmaster in civilian life. In 1948 he arrived at a US military police post in West Berlin and asked for political asylum as a defector. Desertions from the Soviet Army were quite frequent at this time and Khorunshy was taken to a CIC centre, where he declared, apparently quite honestly, that his motives were not political but personal. In his home town of Kherson he had a wife and two children, but during his service in East Germany he had met a German woman, Elizabeth Werner, with whom he had fallen in love and whom he wanted to marry. When he had asked his superior officer to help him arrange a divorce and to allow him to marry his German girl friend, he had been threatened with court martial and ordered to return home. After this he had decided to defect to the American sector in the hope that Elizabeth would be able to join him there.

Thus Captain Khorunshy became an agent of US G-2 Army Intelligence at Griesheim, joined not one but several anti-communist

*See page 146

organisations[3] and became an instructor at Oberursel, where the Americans—after Gehlen's move to Pullach—still maintained the G-2 Intelligence centre. He also made contact with CIA groups which worked independently of Gehlen's "Org" and he came to be regarded as such an excellent instructor for newly recruited NTS agents that he was asked to arrange special courses at the "spy school" at Bad Homburg, and also lectured at the training camps at Kaufbeuren and Bad Wiessee. Even Gehlen considered him very useful.

In fact, Khorunshy was a Soviet agent and all the time he was sending reports to the MGB headquarters at Karlshorst. The Russians learnt all that was worth knowing about the spy schools in West Germany, the methods of training and infiltrating agents, their radio equipment and communications and, above all, the organisation and leaders of NTS, OUNR, ROND, and the other anti-communist emigré groups vying with each other for American and British support and finance.

In Moscow the MGB chiefs had long since put the names of the prominent emigrés collaborating with the CIA, Gehlen and the SIS on a "liquidations" list. In due course specially trained "travelling executioners" were dispatched to carry out the death sentences. Georgi Okolovich, the NTS leader, had attracted the particular hatred of the MGB chiefs because they held him responsible for the successful distribution of millions of anti-communist propaganda pamphlets and leaflets smuggled into the barracks of Soviet troops in East Germany and Austria.

Korunshy delivered to his masters at Karlshorst a detailed scheme for the murder of Okolovich, complete with a plan of his apartment, his offices at Frankfurt and Bad Homburg, his usual daily routine, and photographs of the NTS leader, one showing him with his wife and Khorunshy at a party. In February 1954 the executioners, MGB Captain Nicolai Kholkov and two German communist agents, arrived in Frankfurt to carry out their assignment. Kholkov, however, repented. Instead of killing Okolovich with the poison bullets he had been given, he confessed to his intended victim and gave himself up to the police. Khorunshy, betrayed by one of his couriers, had already been arrested some time before and in 1954 sentenced to fourteen years' imprisonment. Five years later he was one of the first Soviet spies to be secretly exchanged and returned to Russia and an uncertain future. Only belatedly did Gehlen realise that it was Khorunshy who had betrayed at least one of his parachute drops in 1952; the double agent had been one of the instructors who had trained the team comprised of Lakno, Gorbunov and Remiga.*

*See page 247

The stories of Kholkov's "Operation Rhine", the kidnappings of several NTS and OUNR leaders, the bloody feuds between the various emigré groups—which led to many killings—the murder of the head of the Azerbaijan section of Radio Free Europe, the assassination attempt on the NTS president Dr. Poremsky, and eventually of the murders of Stefan Bandera himself and Lev Rebet, another leader of the Ukrainians in Munich—none of these can come within the scope of this book. But it is worth mentioning these events in passing to illustrate the maze of intrigue, rivalry, betrayal and communist penetration which persisted for many years—and still exists—within and around these groups in West Germany.

Little wonder, therefore, that Gehlen was cagey about maintaining too close a contact with them and in later years severed it altogether. There was, however, one homogeneous group of refugees neither torn by internal feuds nor given to exaggerated claims or bizarre schemes —the Latvians and Estonians, whose once independent countries had been turned into Soviet provinces.

Gehlen Vies With the British For the Balts

Many refugees from these countries on the Baltic, who had fled during the last months of the war from the Soviet armies advancing into Germany, eventually reached Britain. Latvia and Estonia had maintained trade relations with the British for several centuries and the exiles received a friendly welcome. Amongst them SIS found a number of reliable volunteers ready to return to their native countries as British agents. One of the earliest teams of these volunteers was taken to Estonia by a British trawler in the spring of 1952. The team consisted of Zigurd Krumins and Janis Plos and by a strange twist of fate we know Krumins' story from Francis Gary Powers, the U-2 pilot, who from September 1960 to February 1962 shared a cell with him in the prison of Vladimir.[4]

When Latvia was occupied by the Russians in 1940, Krumins was thirteen years old. A year later Hitler attacked the Soviet Union and German troops drove the Soviet Army out of the Baltic countries. In 1944, when the Germans were on the retreat, Zigurd, who like most of his countrymen nurtured a hatred of the Russians, joined the German Army. The Germans had promised independence to his homeland and the seventeen-year-old boy knew little about politics nor had he even any idea that the Germans were losing the war. What followed was a continuous retreat until his unit, half-starved and totally demoralised, reached Germany.

In April 1945, still in German uniform, the boy found himself in a British prisoner of war camp, where a kindly British officer took pity on him and gave him a job as messenger at a British Army headquarters. There he was recruited for secret work, taken to England and trained to operate and repair radio transmitters. Eventually he volunteered to go to Latvia to work in the underground Resistance, with instructions to transmit messages by radio and assist in smuggling people out of the country to Sweden.

Krumins and his companion made contact with various groups of nationalists, who had for some years camped in the woods, making occasional sorties to carry out sabotage actions. Krumins told Powers that he succeeded in establishing radio contact with England and that he lived with the partisans for almost two years until his group was betrayed and they were all captured by the Soviet security police. In 1955 he was tried by a Soviet military tribunal in Riga and sentenced, as a traitor and spy, to fifteen years' imprisonment. For almost three years he was held in solitary confinement, and in 1958 transferred to the Vladimir prison, where life was easier. When Powers arrived there in 1960, they shared cell No.31 and became friends. Powers was exchanged for the Soviet master spy, Colonel Rudolf Abel, and in his memoirs he describes the touching parting from Krumins, who had another six years to serve before being sent for "rehabilitation" to a labour camp to complete his sentence.

There were other British-trained agents dispatched to Latvia and Estonia, usually by sea from England; a few were smuggled in through Finland, whither they were taken by commercial flights. Gehlen, from whom few Allied intelligence schemes remained hidden, had learnt of the British expeditions. He suggested to Allen Dulles that CIA should propose to the British that they combine forces for infiltrations in the Baltic area. Gehlen considered the Balts far more suitable for intelligence operations than the wretched, squabbling Ukrainians. In any case, Latvia and Estonia could provide excellent jumping-off points for agents to be infiltrated into the Leningrad region.

After protracted negotiations between Washington and London, with Gehlen himself putting in a word to promote his scheme with the SIS station head at West Berlin's Stadium Building, an arrangement was made whereby Gehlen was to train the agents, the British to provide sea transport, and any information obtained fairly shared. Within a few months Gehlen produced thirty Baltic agents from his spy schools. Some of the agents were recruited in Germany, others came from the Latvian, Estonian and Lithuanian communities in Britain.

Before this combined scheme came into being, Gehlen had dispatched one of his agents, Marius Ozolins, with a PH-6 radio transmitter via Finland to Estonia. For a time Ozolins sent regular signals, but one night he reported that he was being trailed by Soviet security men and asked to be extricated. This was the last Pullach heard from him. Gehlen, growing impatient with the slow progress of the British naval arrangements, decided to prepare a parachute operation. At Kaufbeuren he had a special instructor for the Latvians and Estonians, a man with a mysterious past, named Harry Bromberg; he was a Jew, born in Riga, and he never talked of how or why he had come to Germany. In the "Org" he used the alias "Anderson". He had trained Ozolins and he suggested that a team should be dropped into the area to attempt a rescue operation, asking to be allowed to lead if himself. Gehlen always showed a surprising concern for agents in real trouble and he agreed to the suggestion, though insisting on meticulous preparations. He sent Bromberg and two Estonians, Karl Kukk ("Taluots") and Henry Tomla ("Jarve"), for parachute training to Fort Bragg in North Carolina; later they also attended a course at the CIA intelligence school of Poolesville, at Fairfax near Washington D.C. The result of all this was an anticlimax. The three agents parachuted from a US Air Force plane near Parnu and were all caught within a few days of their arrival; they never found their missing friend. Gehlen heard of this from agents who were landed some time later, but of the fate of the rescue party he learnt only in 1962, when the KGB published a pamphlet which described the capture of twelve agents of the "fascist Gehlen gang" between 1952 and 1958.[5]

Boats Sail from Portsmouth

It took more than eight months for the British Admiralty to consent to support the SIS-CIA-Gehlen scheme. It seems that it took all the persuasive powers of Sir Stewart Menzies to win over the director of Naval Intelligence, Rear-Admiral Sir Anthony Buzzard, and his deputy, Captain D. C. Ingram. At last approval was obtained from their Lordships to use one minesweeper for the operation. The Royal Navy already provided several minesweepers and coastal craft as fishery protection ships for German trawlers in the Baltic, the fishermen having been molested on many occasions by Soviet patrol boats. But to employ Royal Navy ships on spy business was another kettle of fish, and the admirals did not like it. Moreover neither the Admiralty nor the Foreign Office[6] was prepared to allow these "Q-ships" to carry a Royal Navy crew.

Gehlen had, therefore, to recruit the captain and crew himself. He was fortunate in finding a skipper supremely qualified for such operations: ex-Lieutenant Commander Hans Klose, who during the war had commanded the small flotilla of German speedboats which conducted innumerable hit-and-run skirmishes with the Red Fleet, was said to know the Baltic like his own bath tub. He enlisted a

258

handful of his former petty officers and ratings, and the British minesweeper and two old German S-boats which had survived the scuttling of the remnants of Grand Admiral Doenitz's fleet were taken to Portsmouth for refitting. New powerful engines permitting greatly increased speed—needed in case of pursuit by Soviet patrol boats or destroyers—were fitted, and special radar equipment and a radio transmitter were installed, capable of maintaining communications with the home base as well as with agents after their landfall.

Meanwhile, Gehlen set up in Stockholm an outpost to whose secret radio station the portable sets of the agents were tuned. They were landed on a lonely stretch of the Estonian coast south of Parnu and on small islands in the Moon Sund. One of the first to come ashore was Endel Mumm. He was later caught when his radio signals to Stockholm were intercepted by Soviet direction-finding apparatus. He was followed by a team of three, Harri Vimm, Jan Maltis and Evald Hallisk. They established contact with the leader of the Estonian underground Resistance, Richard Saaliste, and his groups scattered over the country. Although Moscow later accused Britain and the United States of having "plotted with the help of the Gehlen spy gang to foment a revolution against the Soviet authorities in Estonia", the agents were explicitly ordered not to engage in any violent actions or carry out sabotage. They were instructed to collect information on Soviet coastal defences, port installations, and general intelligence about conditions in the country. Some were to proceed into Karelia and the Leningrad region, but their stay there was expected to be limited to a few months. They were to be collected by the same boats from which they had disembarked and taken back to Germany. Only those who volunteered for a second mission would be brought back, after debriefing and a period of rest. As it happened, some of the agents stayed two years and penetrated deep into Russian territory. About half of the infiltrators perished.

The Soviet accusations that Gehlen was sending "armed bandits" may have been prompted by an incident when two agents, Ustel Lembit and Aksel Ports, were confronted on landing by a posse of Soviet guards; in exchange of fire the latters' commander, Lieutenant Kozlov, was killed. The agents escaped unhurt and later joined another group which had landed some weeks earlier. Some of the infiltrators made one of Gehlen's dreams come true: they found an old "sleeper" of the forgotten R-Net, one Paul Lille, an ex-SS man, who had served in the wartime *Zeppelin* enterprise. Notes in the Pullach files, which refer briefly to him, do not say whether he was pleased at being re-activated, nor whether he was of any use.

The underground partisans in Estonia implored the agents for supplies of small arms. After this request was signalled to the Gehlen outpost in Stockholm and relayed to Pullach, Gehlen dispatched two agents, Werner Hayli and Anthony Kalviainen, with a few crates of revolvers, sub-machine guns and ammunition. The operations in the Baltic continued fairly regularly for several years, but in 1956 the British Admiralty terminated the permission to fly the British flag on the S-boats.

Of the fairly large number of agents landed in Estonia, Latvia, on the Memel coast and on the islands of Dago and Oesel apparently only thirteen were caught by the Russians after landing. In 1962 Moscow gave a garbled description of some of the operations, claiming that Soviet security forces had found on the captured spies American radio transmitters, tommy-guns, codes and cypher devices and two hundred thousand roubles, sixty gold coins, pieces of jewellery and six hundred watches. In 1960 the KGB circulated a pamphlet amongst its officials which contained a brief summary of instances of infiltration by American and Gehlen agents by land, sea and air. Apparently it was intended as instructional material for the security police and frontier guards, and the names of captured agents were given only as "Joe", "Ben", "Karl" and "Fin". One of the alleged cases was a romantic tale about three Gehlen spies arriving aboard a motor cutter off the coast of Eastland where they part company, one of them falling in love with a girl, Hilda. Torn between her affection for the spy and her patriotic duty to the Soviet motherland, she eventually decides to report her lover to the police. This cautionary tale was obviously a literary effusion on the part of a KGB official and, like most of the other stories mentioned before, was far removed from real events.

After the take-over of the "Org" by the Bonn government, Gehlen was instructed to discontinue infiltrations into the Soviet Union by sea and air. As a NATO member, Federal Germany had to avoid causing a major incident which would provide Moscow with propaganda ammunition against all the members of the North Atlantic Defence Treaty. But the use of air and sea transport for introducing V-men into East Germany was not disallowed. In 1966 the DDR ministry for state security published a summary of cases of alleged infringement of air space from 1960 to 1965, giving a total number of sixty-two overflights "in which spies, saboteurs, or propaganda material were dropped on the territory of the DDR". In a number of cases cited the type of the aircraft was mentioned, such as US Air Force T-39 or RB-66 planes, or F-84 fighters of the West German Bundeswehr. But even if one accepts these figures as correct, it appears that few agents were conveyed by air and parachuted compared with the number infiltrated by land routes.

Gehlen Pays a Debt to Britain

In 1958 Gehlen was able to reciprocate the help the British Secret Service had given him in arranging naval facilities for the Baltic runs. A German officer on a special NATO course in Britain had been discovered to be a Soviet spy. Gehlen sent urgent messages to Sir Dick White, chief of SIS,[7] and Major-General Sir Kenneth Strong, director of the Joint Intellignece Bureau at the ministry of defence, warning them that the spy might have passed British defence secrets to Soviet agents in London.

The officer, Lieutenant-Commander Horst Heinz Ludwig, was then still at his base in Scotland. His accomplices in Germany had been taken into custody, but the chief culprit was unaware of this. To get him back to Germany, his commanding officer ordered him to return home to discuss his future posting. The British authorities spread a shroud of secrecy over this affair; only a few of its startling details came to light at Ludwig's trial at the Federal Supreme Court at Karlsruhe in January, 1960, which was held almost entirely in secret sessions in the presence of British and American intelligence officers.

Ludwig, thirty-four at the time of his trial, began his military career as a young conscript in Hitler's Wehrmacht shortly before the end of the war. After his release from an American POW camp he went to the Soviet zone, where his parents lived, and in 1947 became an engineering student at Jena University, graduating in 1950. A year later he fled to West Germany and found employment with an American-controlled labour unit engaged on minesweeping in the port of Bremerhaven. There he met Fritz Briesemeier, a former petty officer, and they became friends. In 1955 Ludwig applied for entry into the new Federal Army, was commissioned and received initial training as an air force pilot. Under an agreement between the Bonn government and the US administration, many officers of the Bundeswehr were sent for advanced training to America, and so Ludwig went to the US Navy Air Station at Pensacola, Florida, for an eighteen-month flying course.

While attempting to land on the deck of an aircraft carrier he crashed into the sea and suffered serious injuries. However, he recovered and returned to Germany where he continued his service, attached to the fledgeling air arm of the German navy. He gained quick promotion and in the early summer of 1958 was sent to the Royal Navy station at Lossiemouth in Scotland to receive further training under a NATO scheme in de Havilland Sea Vixen aircraft, being also earmarked for training in the new British all-weather naval fighter, the Supermarine Scimitar, then on the secret list and expected to go into operational service at the end of the year.

Ludwig carried full NATO clearance and at Lossiemouth he was given classified handbooks and operational guides on the aircraft.

Meanwhile in Germany Gehlen had caught a really big fish in his net. In 1956 the deputy chief of the East German "Department for Co-ordination", in fact the section of the DDR ministry of defence concerned with military espionage against West Germany and NATO countries, had become one of Gehlen's *S-Quellen*. He was forty-year-old Lieutenant-Colonel Siegfried Dombrowski, who enjoyed the complete trust of his superior, General Albert Linke, and the Soviet GRU officers who exercised real control at the ministry. Dombrowski was, however, a lover of the good life and he cast envious glances across the border to the West. In the summer of 1956 he decided to spend his vacation incognito in a luxury hotel in the Black Forest, where comfort, good food and drink were not regarded as rarities.

There he met, by chance, a fellow-officer with whom he had served as a young lieutenant during the war. By another strange chance this man happened to be one of Gehlen's "collectors". Over a few glasses of Rhine wine they soon clinched a deal, though not before the "collector" had received Gehlen's approval by telephone. Dombrowski was to return to his office and carry on as usual; for supplying information he would be paid a retainer of nine hundred Marks a month, which was a good deal more than his pay at his department, despite his rank and the importance of his work. For almost two years Dombrowski sent information of superb value. Once again, as in the cases of the *S-Quellen* in the DDR Cabinet Office and the ministry for state security, Pullach came into possession of top secret material.

Among Dombrowski's reports in August 1958 was one disclosing the existence of a spy ring controlled by a Soviet agent, whose code name was "Schutz", and whose identity even Dombrowski did not know. It was concerned with espionage inside the Bundeswehr and "Schutz" had succeeded in ensnaring at least one officer who had access to important NATO armaments secrets. Gehlen, who at that time had already assumed overlordship of all German intelligence services, including the BfV counter-espionage department, put his sleuths to work. The first agent to be netted was Werner Jager, a photographer in Mannheim who also acted as the spy ring's courier. From Jager the trail led quickly to Lieutenant-Commander Ludwig, his brother-in-law. Next was Fritz Briesemeier, Ludwig's old friend from the minesweeping operations, who had joined the new Federal navy and was a chief petty officer. Jager's wife, Hanni, Ludwig's sister, was also arrested; she, too, had been undertaking courier service for the ring. But the mysterious "Schutz" and other members of the network, more experienced than their dupes, managed to escape.

The arrests were kept secret and Ludwig, at Lossiemouth, was probably not particularly worried to have no news from his friends for a week or so. The handsome German was very popular with his brother-officers at the British base, and even more with the local young ladies. He became secretly engaged to a former Scottish beauty queen, twenty-two-year-old June Gilbert. During his stay in Scotland he sent microfilmed photographs of installations at the Royal Navy base and of aircraft in flight and on the ground, as well as copies of training manuals and scripts used on his training course, to various cover addresses in West Germany and to his sister. Her husband did the photographic processing and the material was then passed to "Schutz" or his couriers by way of an array of dead letter-boxes in various towns of the Rhineland. At the same time Briesemeier was making his contribution by supplying material from his naval base at Kiel.

At the trial of Ludwig, Briesemeier and the Jagers, Captain Kurt Hitz, an officer from Pullach's III/F department, told the court that Commander Ludwig "had built up an amazing mosaic of British air and sea dispositions in NATO, passed on designs and photographs of classified aircraft and missiles, and by procuring the names and postings of British senior Royal Navy and RAF officers, including those serving with NATO and SHAPE, enabled the Soviet Intelligence service to calculate the reasons for appointments of specialists and to infer the purpose and nature of their secret work . . . . " What Captain Hitz stated during the secret sessions of the trial, however, was not disclosed.

Ludwig made a full confession and described how he had been drawn, by threats and offers of money, into the net of Soviet espionage. At the beginning of 1954, when he was still working on minesweeping at Bremerhaven, his father had come to visit him and told him that an East German had approached him and asked him to bring his son to a meeting in East Berlin; if he refused, his parents would be in trouble. Ludwig went to the meeting and met "Schutz", who warned him that if he disobeyed his orders his father and mother "would not remain free" and told him to volunteer for the Bundeswehr and apply for training as a pilot.

From then on he had done what he was told by his "controller". He was generously paid and seems to have found the combination of an interesting career with spying not disagreeable. Briesemeier cynically declared in court that he had become a traitor solely for money, stating that he had received a total of 7,850 Marks. The German court treated the accused leniently; Ludwig was sentenced to five years, Briesemeier to four, Jager to three and his wife to one year in prison. British naval and American Air Force security came worst out of the trial. Neither at the US base in Florida, nor at the Royal Navy base at Lossiemouth had security arrangements been sufficient to prevent such an inexperienced spy as Ludwig from gaining access to secret information, from taking photographs at will or even from using the photographic darkroom at the base for the preparation of his microfilms. After the trial the British naval attaché in Bonn, Captain B. D. O. MacIntyre, RN, sent a long report to the Admiralty on the secret parts of the trial. It must have provided food for thought for the British Naval Intelligence.

To Gehlen it was just a minor incident, "all in a day's work", as he used to say. He was preoccupied with much more ambitious activities, concerned with international affairs and the building up of the BND into an instrument of his personal power both in Germany and abroad.

XIX

The Telephone Sluices

For some time Gehlen had been contemplating an idea which, if it could successfully be put into practice, might solve many of his problems. In simplest terms, it was to splice telephone cables in East Berlin and, by installing connections to a secret switch room in one of his West Berlin branches, to overhear all incoming and outgoing telephone calls at Soviet and East German headquarters, ministries and other offices. By using suitable pre-selectors at the secret "exchange", this operation could also yield complete records of overland calls, for instance to and from Moscow, Warsaw and other cities in the East.

Tapping telephone and telegraph lines was, of course, nothing new in the history of espionage. But the installation of such permanent connections would have been a novel development which would have revolutionised the gathering of secret information. Gehlen must have been fascinated by the idea of eavesdropping on Grotewohl's or Ulbricht's conversations with Bulganin or Khrushchev or of overhearing Wollweber's calls to his KGB masters in Moscow. However, when he discussed the idea with a few of his most trusted assistants and heads of the technical department, they were doubtful of its technical feasibility, pointing out that the installation of the connections would require men who had both technical skill and courage. The work of splicing the East Berlin underground cables would have to be carried out under the noses of the VOPOs, who swarmed along the border of the East and West sectors by day and night. Nevertheless, Gehlen decided that it was worth trying.

Early in 1953 he believed he had found a man who could be entrusted with this difficult task. By one of his confidants at the *Amt Blank*, the office concerned with the preparations for establishing the Federal army, Gehlen learnt of an application received from a former Wehrmacht officer for an appointment in military security. He was thirty-eight-year-old Major Werner Haase, who had had a remarkable war service in an engineers' regiment and, after his release from a British POW camp, had graduated from a technical college; he was an expert on telecommunications. Gehlen thought that this man could be very useful, and arranged an interview at which his investigator learnt that Haase had served in the Wehrmacht since 1936, had passed through the military college at Munich and the infantry and signals school at Doberitz, was an accomplished expert in W/T and telephone technique and had been an instructor with the signal corps. He had fought in France and Russia and held the Iron Cross 1st and 2nd Class and the Gold Cross for Gallantry. After his post-war studies, unable to obtain an engineering job, he had become a customs official.

One of Gehlen's executives, Major Brenner, was told to enlist Haase at a monthly salary of four hundred Marks, and he was attached to the West Berlin branch 120-D. He had still to prove his complete reliability before being entrusted with the secret scheme. The branch manager, Schuster, sent good reports about Haase's work, and in September 1953 Gehlen decided to put him to work on his great enterprise. Haase was transferred to the West Berlin branch 120-B, headed by one of Gehlen's most efficient "managers", Major Waller, known as "Ahrend", and made his deputy. At the offices of the branch, suitably disguised as those of a firm of electrical contractors, a miniature telephone exchange was built from which underground cables were laid to a dug-out not far from the sector border, where Haase was supposed to establish the connection with the East Berlin telephone system. The work was done by operators posing as telephone engineers carrying out routine repairs and cable replacements.

Then came the uprising in East Berlin and the work was interrupted for several weeks. Hereafter, the execution of plan became even more important than before. After the suppression of the revolt the new East German minister for state security had ordered drastic measures against anyone suspected of having collaborated with West German agents during the riots. Ten thousand people, most of them completely innocent, were rounded up. But among the arrested were also several of Gehlen's best radio operators, such as Ernst Preuss, Armin Zopf, Hans Krause, Hans Siebenroth, Helmut Schwenk, and eventually also Hans Joachim Koch, the West Berlin chief radio operator, who had gone across the border during the uprising to co-ordinate radio transmissions by others.

These grievous losses had deprived Pullach of the regular flow of reports from V-men by radio. The telephone interception could more than repair the damage. Gehlen ordered that the project should go ahead without further delay. To assist Haase with the supply and transport of tools and cables he appointed the manager of branch 9592-X, ex-SS Sturmbannfuhrer Brandler.

Troll, The Thriller Writer

Brandler's deputy was one of Gehlen's most colourful operators. Under his pseudonym of Henry Troll he was well known to readers of pulp thrillers on crime and espionage. Troll had created a hero of the James Bond kind; he had named him "John Kling" and his imaginary adventures became popular with German addicts to this sort of literature long before Ian Fleming invented his 007. The author's real name was Hans Joachim Geyer. He had made a small fortune out of his writings—his thrillers were published in large paperback editions, serialised in popular magazines, and several had been turned into film scripts—and he lived in luxury in an elegant villa in the American sector. But, it seems, he had become so inspired by his hero's imaginary adventures that he wished to enact them in real life. In 1951 Geyer-Troll confided his desire to one of Gehlen's "collectors", who happened to be a friend of his, and joined the "Org".

A braggart and eager to win renown, Geyer volunteered to go to East Germany and work as a "collector" of V-men. This he did for several months with considerable success. But during his stay in East Berlin he also made some undesirable contacts: in brief, the thriller writer became an agent of the communist SSD. Whether the inducement was money, or whether he was blackmailed into submission after being tricked into a compromising situation by communist agents is not known. Whatever his reasons, Geyer became a double agent and, after his return and promotion to deputy manager of branch 9592-X he supplied his contacts at the East German ministry for state security with an output of information as prolific as his production of "whodunnit" stories.

In the autumn of 1953, preparations for Haase's operation, which was to add to both the German and English languages a new technical term—*Telephone Schleuse*, telephone sluice—were nearing completion. Geyer was not in on the scheme, but he discovered the secret soon enough. Rifling the filing cabinets at branch 9592-X, he must have found papers referring to the purchase of cables and electronic material, and his fertile brain put two and two together. He also copied a list of V-men.

At about that time Geyer, a confirmed skirt-chaser, had acquired a new girl friend. In his usual bragging manner Geyer told her that, besides writing thrillers, he was engaged on highly secret and most dangerous affairs. Although they would bring him great fortune as well as fame, he might be forced to flee, perhaps to South America, and he asked her whether she would come with him. The girl got it all wrong and became frightened. She suspected he was either planning a great bank robbery or was involved in white slave traffic—she had probably read some of Geyer's thrillers—and accordingly decided to seek advice from a cousin who was a police detective. He promised to investigate and one evening he called at Geyer's villa; Geyer was out, however, and, perhaps rashly, the visitor told the manservant that he was a policeman. When Geyer returned home and was told of the visit he panicked, assuming that his treachery had been discovered. He grabbed all the money, valuables, papers and notes he had at home, packed a suitcase, and made off for East Berlin. At midnight he arrived in a state of great agitation at the SSD office in Normannen Strasse, and told his colleagues that he had been discovered and had escaped by the skin of his teeth.

Ministry for State Security

For Gehlen the defection of this cheapjack could not have come at a worse moment. For he had just encountered, in Ernst Wollweber, the new minister for state security in East Germany, his most formidable adversary ever, a cloak-and-dagger expert who like himself knew how to use every weapon in the armoury of espionage, subversion and conspiracy. Their battle of wits developed into a protracted game of catch-as-catch-can, at which even the mighty CIA and KGB remained on the sidelines.

Under Zaisser, Wollweber's predecessor, an efficient organisation had already developed from the *Kommissariat 5*. Yet Wollweber created an espionage machine which within an astoundingly brief period employed, in proportion to the population of East Germany (sixteen million), more officials, agents and informers than either the United States or the Soviet Union. This might sound incredible, but if one accepts the fairly reliable estimate that CIA and its various subsidiaries at the peak of its world-wide activities employed one hundred thousand operators and doubles this figure to gauge the number of officials, agents and informers of the KGB and MVD, the population ratio would be one CIA operator in two thousand and one Soviet agent in 1,250. With about twenty thousand officials and full-time agents, some five thousand VOPO officers exclusively on security and counter-espionage duties, and at least five thousand spies and informers in West Germany alone—at one time the exaggerated figure of sixteen thousand communist spies in West Germany was given in a publication of the US State Department[1]— Wollweber's operators in the mid-1950s must have numbered at least one in every eight hundred men, women and children in the DDR. Statistics may be tedious, but they give an idea of the problems Gehlen had to face.

Wollweber's chief organiser at the ministry for state security, the young Major-General Wolf, a prototype of the KGB-trained *apparat-*

chik, is today, after over fifteen years, still in charge of HVA, the ministry's *élite* department. For the three main branches under Zaisser, the HVA expanded into fourteen Main Departments (*Haupt-Abteilungen*). We can disregard those concerned with administration, communications, cryptography, training, archives, finance and so on, which are needed by every secret service organisation, and consider only those peculiar to HVA. The system outlined below still prevails today.

Main Department I, with about twelve hundred officials, ensures the reliability of officers and men in the DDR armed forces. Some nine hundred of its officials are attached to all commands and staffs of the army, navy and air force. Officers are enlisted to act as "political commissars" within their units, and report their observations on the conduct of their fellow-officers and men.

Main Department II comprises the "positive" intelligence service against foreign countries and, in particular, against the Federal German Republic and NATO. Its many sections are geographically organised and include American, British and French sections, as well as sections dealing with countries of the Warsaw Pact, especially with neighbouring Czechoslovakia and Poland. (It was the extremely hostile intelligence produced by the Czechoslovakia section against the Dubĉek government which prompted Moscow into armed intervention there in 1968.) This department employs the largest number of officials and spies; several sections deal with the analysis and evalutation of their reports. Next to the KGB, it maintains the largest number of agents in the West. (It will be recalled how East German agents tried to ensnare Mr. James Owen, a British Member of Parliament.) A special section, which Wollweber added after leaving the ministry of shipping, deals with the West's shipping and has its own small flotilla of "spy ships" which watch NATO naval movements in the Baltic and the North Sea.

Main Department III is responsible for the surveillance of all economic activities in the DDR. It has agents in every large industrial and commercial concern, who not only spy on the managers and employees but also watch productivity. It has many sections, one of which, for instance, supervises food production, markets and provision shops.

Main Department IV is the counter-espionage service. Its officials, agents and an army of informers safeguard "State Security". A special "tourist section" watches over visitors from abroad and provides "guides"—many of them glamorous young women—to accompany businessmen, visitors to the Leipzig Fairs, newspaper correspondents and so on. It cooperates with Main Department V, which exercises surveillance over political, scientific and cultural

269

organisations and institutions. This includes censorship of mail and telecommunications, and the proffering of "advice" to the editors of newspapers and journals and to book publishers who, in any case, are expected to be loyal party members. Another section supervises universities and watches for any "deviation" among lecturers and students.

Main Department VI is responsible for the protection of the armaments and other heavy industries, particularly against industrial espionage. It is also concerned with the surveillance of all transport undertakings. Some of its tasks overlap with those of Main Department III.

This complex organisation includes a number of lesser departments, some subordinated to the main departments, others independent and responsible directly to the head of the MSS. On the outskirts of East Berlin in the Freienwalder Strasse a huge modern building houses the Technical Department, which looks after the paraphernalia of espionage. It produces, or orders the production of, radio transmitters, cameras, wire-tapping and microphone equipment, and an array of "bugs" which include, for instance, parabolic directional miniature microphones which enable the user to overhear conversations at distances of up to two hundred yards and minute tape-recorders which can be hidden in a watch, cuff links or a lump of sugar. The Documentation Department produces forged documents, passports, identity cards and so forth. Such "technical" activities are, of course, conducted by all secret services, and Gehlen also introduced elaborate novelties in this field to the "Org" and the BND. But it is significant that East Germany, with a population not much larger than that of the Netherlands, created a secret service that has never fallen behind those of the great powers.

The superstructure of the Main Departments is General Wolf's HVA, the *élite* intelligence department, whose eight hundred officials enjoy seniority, and which can be compared to CIA's Plans and Operations Division—a department of "dirty tricks". It also co-ordinates the activities of all other departments in relation to espionage abroad, is responsible for the selection, recruitment and training of agents, and for the establishment, maintenance and syllabuses of spy schools. East German espionage chiefs disdain the ominous terms of "V-man" and "V-Fuhrer" for their informers which Gehlen adopted from the Abwehr and the Gestapo. If HVA's comrade informers are equal, some are more equal than others. An East German V-man is a *Geheimer Informator* (GI), that is, a secret informant. Next in the hierarchy is the secret chief informant, or GHI, and at the top, equivalent to Gehlen's V-Fuhrer, is the *Geheimer Mitarbeiter* or secret cooperator, a title reminiscent of the old French Deuxième Bureau's more elegant "honourable correspondent".

270

There were a surprising number of similarities between the "Org" and HVA. Its secret informers were barred from the ministry's headquarters as were Gehlen's V-men from Pullach. Likewise, HVA set up fourteen regional branch offices,[2] whose principal officials were put in charge of the informers (with the exception of the Potsdam branch office for East Berlin which remained under direct HVA control).

SS Men As Loyal Comrades

Ulbricht, Wollweber and other East German leaders never tired of alleging against Gehlen that besides being "a tool of American capitalism and imperialism" and "a warmonger who aggravates the discord between East and West", he was also a neo-nazi, and had surrounded himself with SS and Gestapo officers, war criminals to a man. The accusation that Pullach and its many branches swarmed with ex-nazis was not in fact far from the truth, but the ministry for state security, too, had opened its doors to former henchmen of Hitler.

Amongst HVA's departmental chiefs were Major-General Rudolf Bamler and SS Obergruppenfuhrer Hans Rattengruber. Bamler had served in the old Reichswehr of General von Seeckt and in 1928, as a major, became head of counter-espionage, showing great energy and prowess in his work against Soviet Intelligence. Promoted to colonel in 1933, he was chief of the III/F division of the Abwehr under Admiral Canaris, and proved himself such an enthusiastic nazi, devoted to establishing friendly relations with RSHA and the Gestapo, that this became too much for his boss. On September 12, 1939, after Canaris warmly recommended him for promotion if this meant his removal from the Abwehr, he was appointed chief of staff to the army command Danzig-West Prussia; after June 1941, as a major-general, he commanded the 12th Infantry Division in Russia. On June 27, 1944, by then a lieutenant-general, Bamler was taken prisoner by the Russians in the battle of Mogilev. He professed to his captors his anti-nazi sentiments, made them believe he had been involved in plots against Hitler, joined Field-Marshal von Paulus' "National Committee for Free Germany", and, rightly or wrongly, accused his former superior, General Gotfried von Erdmannsdorf, of having ordered a massacre of Russian prisoners; the general was put before a Soviet court martial and executed.

In 1946 Bamler arrived in East Germany; soon after he became chief instructor at the new "security school" of *Kommissariat 5* at Glowen. In 1950 he returned to the Soviet Union to attend a staff college, and in 1952 joined the ministry for state security, where he was rapidly promoted to become head of a department.

Even more fantastic was the meandering career of SS General Rattengruber. An "old" nazi, he had before the war commanded Hitler's personal SS guard. As chief security officer he accompanied Ribbentrop to Moscow for the signing of the pact with Molotov, and during the war attained high rank in the SS, while fighting in Russia. After a brief spell in a prisoner of war camp, he was sent to East Germany and given the command of the new People's Police at Leipzig. In 1949 he was asked to assist in the reorganisation of the Czechoslovak intelligence service in Prague, and eventually came to East Berlin as a senior official of the ministry for state security, later heading a section of Main Department II and working at HVA.

There were—and probably still are—many other SS and Gestapo men in important HVA posts; some were well known to Gehlen and his assistants who had come from the same stable but had galloped in the opposite direction. SS Hauptsturmfuhrer Ludwig Hagmeister, formerly at the RSHA *Militaramt* under Schellenberg was put in charge of the HVA branch in Schwerin; SS Sturmfuhrer Stanitzer, ex-Gestapo chief in Vienna, obtained a similar post with HVA at Erfurt; but the most astounding appointment was given to the former head of RSHA section V-B, SS Sturmbannfuhrer Heidenreich; as a colonel in the SSD he became chief liaison officer of HVA to the Central Committee of the Communist Party of the DDR.

This then was the mighty organisation under Wollweber, which at the time of the final preparations for the telephone sluice operations and thriller writer Geyer's defection, had begun an all-out offensive against Gehlen's "Org". At first, Geyer's disappearance caused little concern at Pullach. His branch manager had reported, as a matter of routine, that V-Fuhrer "Grell"—this was Geyer's code name—had vanished, but he was inclined to assume that it was an escapade probably connected with some romantic affair, rather than anything more serious. Geyer's HVA masters kept his arrival secret for a while, but the arrests of sixty V-men in East Berlin, all under the control of branches 120-A and 9252-X, soon apprised Geyer's former superiors of his defection.

Gehlen issued a general alert and ordered the immediate withdrawal of his most important *S-Quelle* informers inside the East German ministries. In some cases this was probably a precautionary measure, since Geyer had no knowledge of these top agents. Some of the first to be withdrawn by urgent radio signals were Professor Kastner, the "Liberal" deputy prime minister, and his resourceful wife. They safely reached West Berlin, and so did "Brutus" Gramsch. But in neither case had Wollweber and his spy-catchers suspected such loyal and proven servants of the regime of any treacherous dealings with Gehlen.

Not so lucky were Gehlen's two leading women informers, Fraulein Ella Bartschatis, the trusted secretary of Prime Minister Grotewohl, and Fraulein Halm of the ministry for state security. The first was given a secret trial—obviously no publicity could be given to Gehlen's success in having infiltrated a spy into the prime minister's office. She was executed on the night of the trial. The newly appointed minister of justice, Frau Hilde Benjamin, who before attaining this office had made herself notorious as "Red Hilde, the Hanging Judge", had reintroduced executions by beheading for persons sentenced to death for the capital offence of high treason[3] and so poor Ella Bartschatis paid with her head for her infatuation with one of Gehlen's "collectors". Fraulein Halm was held in solitary confinement for many months and eventually, at a trial with several other V-men, sentenced to life imprisonment. Two of her co-defendants, Held and Rudert, were executed. As will be seen, several others suffered the supreme penalty, and many more were sent to prison for life or sentenced to long terms of imprisonment.

Telephone Sluices Ahoy!

On November 9, Wollweber produced Joachim Geyer at a press conference in East Berlin, at which the thriller writer volubly described "the terrible crimes of capitalist aggressors against the socialist democracies" in general, and those of "the fascist lackey of dollar imperialism Reinhard Gehlen" in particular. He also complained that the pay for V-men was very poor and that Gehlen was not accessible even to a man of such importance as himself: "If an agent did succeed in seeing the chief of this espionage organisation, he was told that he must not consider it as an insurance company, which would pay him an annuity for life. Whoever works here, he was told, must realise from the very first day of his activities that he may be caught one day . . . . " Finally, Herr Geyer added a publicity puff for his next book, which he was to write about his experiences as Gehlen's agent, entitled *At the Beginning was the End*.[4]

Until Geyer's public reappearance, the ministry had refrained from arresting the betrayed V-men. Surprisingly, Wollweber succeeded in lulling Gehlen into a feeling of false security. Gehlen had withdrawn most of the important *S-Quelle* informers, recalled full-time agents and "collectors", and also some radio operators and vulnerable HV-men; but he left most of the others where they were. After all, Geyer had only been conversant with one or two West Berlin branches and could not be expected to inflict too much harm. However, another senior agent, forty-two-year-old former Wehrmacht officer Wolfgang Paul Höher, whom Pullach had employed since 1950, and who had been put up to spy on the French Intelligence outpost in West Berlin, had also crossed to the East, and was talking.

In order to reassure V-men left in enemy territory, Gehlen issued in early November a secret circular to all branch managers. The gist of Directive No. 852 was as follows: "The publication in the newspapers of the Soviet zone of news about the Geyer affair must have caused much apprehension among our V-men and led them to ask whether such an incident could not happen within their own circuits. At future meetings with V-men in the East our liaison men must discuss this with them and give them every reassurance. We must preserve the trust of our collaborators and also ensure that they believe that they are being looked after and protected by us."

However, Gehlen was worried by the quiescence he had imposed on almost all his East German networks. He could not stomach a situation in which Pullach found itself without a regular flow of intelligence from the eastern zone. Meanwhile he impatiently awaited the installation of the telephone sluices. Two connections were to be established simultaneously; one cable was to start from the dug-out in West Berlin's Kiefholtz Strasse across the Heidekampgraben, the other across a seven-hundred-yard-long stretch of the Jungfern Lake near Sakrow, north of Potsdam. It was decided to sink water-tight cables into the canal and lake, since digging ditches and burying the cables underground in the eastern sector was, of course, out of the question.

An ingenious method was devised to get the cables across the waterways. Gehlen's technical department at Stuttgart supplied model boats with remote control which would tow the communication cable; it was to be spliced into the main cable by an assistant on the opposite shore.

On the rainy and foggy night of November 13, Haase assembled his fellow-conspirators—the branch manager, a technical expert from Pullach, and his assistant—at his apartment in Filander Strasse in the suburb of Steglitz. They discussed the final arrangements and checked their material. Haase had been given a new identity card in the name of "Wilhelm Heissler", issued by the Munich police and showing his occupation as "telephone engineer" and his residence as "Maximilian Strasse no. 4, Munich". He wore working clothes and a peaked cap, and if anything went wrong and he were stopped by a VOPO patrol, he was to explain that he was a telephone worker who had inadvertently strayed across the border while repairing a broken cable.

Hasse drove alone to the Heidekampgraben, parking at a bomb-site nearby and then carrying the suitcase containing the heavy coil, tools and the model boat to the selected point. He attached the link cable to the toy boat, launched it on the water and was operating the

Fake identity card of Captain Werner Haase in the name of Wilhelm Heisler. He was caught when trying to splice East Berlin telephone cables and was sentenced to life imprisonment.

American-made cable used by Gehlen's agents in the telephone sluice operations in East Berlin.

Two of Gehlen's star agents: Hans Joachim Koch, (*left*), former SS Scharführer directed radio operations during the East Berlin revolt; Hermann Lauterbacher, ex-Hitler Youth leader, was Gehlen's liaison officer to the German intelligence instructors working for President Nasser. (*Below*) A miniature radio transmitter found on a captured agent in Poland.

control box when a car suddenly roard over the rough ground and stopped with a screech of brakes. One can hardly imagine a more bizarre situation. In the middle of a dark winter night a grown-up man stood on the bank of a canal separating the East and West zones of embattled Berlin, quietly pushing a toy boat to the other shore. The district, heavily bombed during the war, was a desert of rubble and even in daylight there were few passers-by. Several men jumped from the car, and Haase was overwhelmed and dragged into it; they then speeded towards Potsdam. At the same time, the agent who had been waiting on the opposite shore of the canal was also seized.

The attempt at laying another cable across the Jungfern Lake was also foiled. The V-man who tackled this job, Christopher Komorek, was captured in the same manner as Haase's helper. Then Wollweber delivered the *coup de grâce*. Haase was put on trial before the Supreme Court of the DDR on December 21, 1953. A few days before and for many months after, scores of Gehlen's V-men were pulled in all over East Germany. Eventually, the ministry for state security announced that "all the gangs of fascist diversants in the pay of the fascist Gehlen Organisation have been rendered harmless. Five hundred and forty-six spies, saboteurs, and terrorist have been arrested"; all were to be tried for their crimes.

For Haase a big show trial was staged and, to make it more impressive, five other V-men,[5] completely unconnected with the telephone sluice operation, were tried together with him. Haase, after prolonged brainwashing, had been promised that he would not be executed if he made a public confession at the trial. But, though confronted at the trial with the defectors Geyer and Höher, and with evidence which could have only come from one of the few men familiar with the operation, he gave little away. The prosecutor made much of the fact that the cables, which were exhibited in the court room, were of American origin and bore the trade mark of the General Cable Corporation. The president of the court told Haase that the punishment he deserved, and which the prosecution had demanded, was death, but that the judges "realised that the chief culprits, Gehlen and his American paymasters, could not be brought to trial". The court, therefore, decided to exercise leniency and spare the accused's life; the sentence was life imprisonment. Two of the other co-defendants were also sent to prison for life, and three were given fifteen years' imprisonment. Haase was released in 1958 in exchange for BND agents.

A Man of Many Parts

After this *débâcle*, Gehlen realised that Geyer must have gained a much greater knowledge of the telephone sluices than had been suspected. He stopped all preparations for further attempts to splice East German cables, though he did not entirely abandon the idea. However, one of the many American Intelligence offices in West Berlin, which had learnt of Gehlen's misfired scheme through the publicity given in the communist newspapers to Haase's trial,[6] embarked on a similar enterprise without Gehlen's knowledge. There were at this time a number of American agencies in West Berlin which worked independently of CIA. As mentioned before, Army G-2 had set up a parallel organisation after losing Gehlen to the CIA; one of its espionage agencies became known as FOI (Field Operations Intelligence). There were also several other "independent" groups connected with G-2 and CIC in West Germany, for instance, an organisation in West Berlin which operated under the innocuous title "Information Bureau West".

In Berlin-Zehlendorf, an outgrowth of CIC was controlled by a brilliant young German who had become a naturalised American. He was Johnny von Walter, the son of a wealthy landed baron who during the war had run into trouble with the Gestapo because of his anti-nazi attitude. In 1945 Baron von Walter sent his son to the United States, where he graduated from a famous college and joined the US Army as a volunteer at the outbreak of the war in Korea. He fought there until 1952 and was promoted captain. After receiving intelligence training, G-2 sent him to Germany, where he was put in charge of the West Berlin CIC unit "for special operations". Walter cooperated with Colonel Brooks of FOI which had its headquarters in Berlin-Zehlendorf.

After the miscarriage of the Haase plan, CIA was looking for other means of telecommunications interception. Captain von Walter and one of his associates, Dr. Bender, began to study the possibilities. One day in the spring of 1954, a man appeared in Walter's office who seemed to be a suitable sort of fellow to embark on another telephone sluice venture. His name and activities have hitherto remained unknown. Neither the Americans and Gehlen, nor the Russians have been inclined to publicise them. Yet he was one of the most interesting figures in the battle of wits which raged between Western intelligence in Berlin and its communist opponents.

His name was Friedrich Weihe. He was nearly fifty when he first met Captain von Walter, and his life had been crowded with strange adventures. The son of a bank manager, he received a good education and in 1927 obtained a job with the patrician banking house of Delbruck, Schickler & Co. A year earlier he had joined the nazi party and when this became known to his employers he was dismissed. This made him an even more ardent nazi; he took part in many brawls and beer-cellar battles until, wanted by the police on a charge of grievous wounding, he escaped to Finland. There he began work for the German Abwehr against Russia. After Hitler came to power he returned to Germany, became a Gestapo officer, obtained high promotion and was known as a friend and confidant of SS General and Chief of Police Kurt Daluege, then second only to Himmler and his great rival.

Weihe was appointed head of the Gestapo's "vice department". Under the pretext of fighting immorality and homosexuality, he exercised terror, carried out mass arrests and blackmailed his victims. Himmler must have been impressed by his exploits, for in 1935 he took him on to his personal staff. When Weihe was involved in another blackmail case, Himmler got him a job as a director of the *Kraft durch Freude* (Strength through Joy) organisation, a post which he combined with espionage in Scandinavia, where he posed as a sports journalist. When enough grass had grown over his misdeeds, Weihe returned to the Gestapo and Himmler gave him a very special assignment: spying on the other nazi leaders, and particularly on Goering and Ribbentrop, with whom the Gestapo boss did not see eye to eye.

But Weihe went too far. Some of the nazi leaders confronted Hitler with bitter complaints that Weihe had tried to blackmail them. Himmler had to cover himself; he ordered Weihe's arrest, stripped him of his SS rank, and sent him to the concentration camp of Sachsenhausen. There Weihe became an *Oberkapo*[7] in charge of three thousand Jewish prisoners who feared him more than their SS guards. He remained at Sachsenhausen until the outbreak of the war, when he was released; he then had to earn his way back by serving in the SS Penal Battalion, first in France and later in Russia. In the fighting against Russian partisans he must have gained his superiors' approval, for he was first promoted to NCO and later given back his officer's rank. By 1943 he was an SS major. In 1944, back in Germany, he was one of the men who arrested the conspirators of the July attempt on Hitler's life, and in April 1945 he was a member of the execution squad at the concentration camp of Flossenburg, when several of the conspirators were hanged from butcher's hooks. For this he obtained his last promotion, to SS Obersturmbannfuhrer.

A few weeks later, with military papers showing him as an ex-army sergeant, Weihe surrendered to the Americans in Bavaria. His real identity was not discovered. He had removed the SS *Blutzeichen*, the tattooed emblem under his armpit, by exploding a blank cartridge there. It was painful, but the injury left a convenient scar over the tattoo. He was soon released from the POW camp, and went to Berlin where, true to his inclinations, he became a warder at the Tegel Prison, guarding nazi war criminals in American custody. In 1950 he had an unpleasant experience: the widow of a man whom he had denounced to the Gestapo and who had died at Sachsenhausen concentration camp recognised him; Weihe was charged before a US military tribunal but he managed to talk his way out. The sentence was a year in prison, of which he served only eight months. Eventually, in 1952, while working for a "detective agency", he met Captain von Walter and became his agent.

He proved himself versatile, being particularly successful as a "collector" of V-men, and became the leader of a group of first six and later ten agents and couriers. He established a number of TBK's (dead letter-boxes) in the East Berlin districts of Oranienburg, Velten and Bernau, and trained some good agents. One of them, Cholly Sengbeil, made fifteen successful sorties into the Soviet zone and one to Poland.

In the spring of 1954, Weihe became a section leader and was entrusted with setting up the new telephone sluices. The connections had to be made to the main cables, parts of which ran overhead because of damage to the underground cables during wartime air raids. Some of the cables had been laid under the many arms of the river Havel and crossed the widespread canal system. Connections could not be made to the branch cables since this would have reduced the circuit capacity and intensity of sound; the telephone authorities would suspect a fault and the ensuing examination of the cables would soon expose any such arrangement.

Weihe had experienced telecommunications mechanics amongst his helpers and, after much planning, they got to work. The first sluice was made at Frohnau in the French sector, but after a few days French military police noticed the digging and the French military governor forbade further work. The second sluice was made a Konradshohe, but at the final stage the rubber boat which towed the connection cable sank in the river Havel. A third sluice at Lubars near Blankenfelde to the north of Berlin was more successful; it worked for several months and yielded much information.

In mid-1955, Captain von Walter—by then cooperating with Gehlen's technical experts and sharing the yield with the "Org"— decided to continue the work under a better qualified manager. Weihe was sent to Mecklemburg in East Germany to set up a network for collecting information about Soviet troops stationed at Fursten-berg and Neustrelitz. He went there with three agents recommended by one of the leaders of the League of Victims of Stalinism (VOS), another small anti-communist agency. A woman, Frau Remmling, acted as their courier. In March 1956 Weihe and another group were sent to Cottbus, where there were large Soviet Army installations and his team did satisfactory work; later Weihe was called back to Berlin

278

and once again put in charge of a group building new telephone sluices.

By then, however, Gehlen had become head of the Federal Intelligence Service and on his demand Captain von Walter's agency was closed down by the Americans. Gehlen was disturbed about the various mushroom agencies, particularly those in Berlin, which endangered his own work. He took over many of their agents, but rejected Weihe's application. In order to impress Gehlen, Weihe went to Beeskow east of Berlin to ferret out some special information about a Soviet Army base; but he fell into a trap laid by SSD agents.

At about the same time a similar fate had overtaken his close collaborator, thirty-five-year-old Werner Chrobock, who had built up an impressive group of V-men.[8] They had penetrated deep into East Germany, setting up cells in Leipzig, Dresden, Erfurt, Karl-Marx-Stadt (formerly Chemnitz) and Brandenburg. One of the more eccentric ideas of the Walter group was to convey radio transmitters, arms, explosives and propaganda material to agents by miniature submarines under the rivers Spree and Havel and the waterways system which connects Berlin, through the Spree-Oder and the Plauer Canal, with East Germany. A prototype of a two-man U-boat was built, but there is no evidence that it was ever used. Chrobock was to have been in charge of this submarine traffic, and it was on one of his visits to reconnoitre landing places in East Germany that he was caught.

The Telephone Tunnel

Gehlen learnt of the misfortune that had overtaken Johnny von Walter's operations, but he was not particularly sorry about it. He was working on a much more elaborate scheme for the interception of communist telecommunications than towing cables by a toy boat across a lake. He had put an ambitious plan to Dulles and Wisner for building a tunnel from the American sector of West Berlin a few hundred yards across the border towards a main junction of telephone cables at Glienicke in East Berlin. Pullach technicians worked for many months using wartime diagrams of the Berlin telephone system, which had been greatly enlarged at that time in order to serve Wehrmacht and Luftwaffe establishments. They soon found out that most of these lines were still intact and now served the many Soviet and East German offices.

The tunnel would start just outside a new US Air Force radar station which was being built at the suburb of Rudow in West Berlin, partly to serve the American airfield at Buckow but mainly to watch the nearby Soviet airfield of Schoenefeld. Additional earth excavation work, Gehlen argued, would attract no more attention by the

Soviet authorities than the building of the radar station had already done. But the estimates for the construction and equipment of the tunnel, which was to house a secret telephone exchange, were very high. Pullach's technical experts believed that about one million dollars would be needed; in fact the tunnel cost more than four times that figure by the time it was completed. At first, Dulles was not at all enthusiastic; he did not believe that the tunnelling could be carried out without being discovered. Wisner was all for it, but he was at that time preoccupied with CIA operations in Guatemala designed to oust the left-wing President Jacobo Arbenz.[9] The Berlin tunnel scheme was, therefore, examined by Richard Mervin Bissell, who had become Wisner's deputy in the Plans and Operations Divisions.

Bissell was a graduate of Yale and the London School of Economics and during the war had acquired intelligence experience in the office of war shipping administration; he knew the European scene and conditions in Germany, having been deputy administrator of the Marshall Plan, and he had joined CIA from the Massachusetts Institute of Technology where he had taught economics. He consulted technical experts at the Institute and, after discreet inspections of the site, eventually persuaded Dulles to advance the substantial funds needed for the scheme.

Gehlen's technical service took over the general control. His branch managers in West Berlin selected the workmen; they were helped by men of the US Signals Corps in plain clothes. The extensive digging at Rudow could not be concealed from Soviet patrols and East German VOPO across the boundary, but they were bamboozled by the construction work for the new radar station. The communist observers resigned themselves to the fact that the station was being put up; it was a reasonable explanation for the work carried out on the surface.

The tunnel started in the then still deserted and bomb-scarred corner of Rudow. It ran for six hundred yards under the barbed-wire fence into East Berlin. Thousands of tons of earth had to be hauled up and a small side tunnel was built leading into the basement of the radar station; there the earth and clay was neatly packed in large wooden boxes labelled with inscriptions suggesting that they had contained electronic material for the radar station and were being taken away empty on American Army lorries. It took nearly three months to complete the tunnel. It was a solid structure, sunk twenty-four feet beneath street level. The gangways consisted of cast iron tubes each about seven feet in diameter, which were pushed into the tunnel under a tarpaulin cover and welded together underground. There gangways led through three large chambers, each secured by electrically operated steel doors.

The American radar station which was used to conceal the construction of the Berlin telephone tunnel.
(*Below left*) A Soviet photo of the tunnel.

"Entrance forbidden" sign near the tunnel purporting to have been put by order of the Soviet commander.

Wilhelm Zaisser and Erich
Mielke, two East German
Ministers for State Security;
the first preceded, the latter
succeeded Ernst Wollweber,
shown below in a police photo
taken during the war in
Sweden when he was arrested
for sabotage.

(*Bottom*) The East-German
Ministry for State Security
at Normannenstrasse in East
Berlin.

One of the chambers contained the air-conditioning unit, another a monitoring and recreation room, and the largest the "exchange" switchboard. Electricity supply came from the radar station, but there was a generator to provide lighting power for the electronic equipment and heating in an emergency. There were two "security areas", with piled-up sandbags and barbed-wire entanglements. The men who worked in the tunnel were warned that in case of a sudden raid from the far end of the tunnel they would have to "shoot out" their retreat to the radar station. Explosive devices were built in to blow up the apparatus in such an emergency. In fact, there was little danger of a sudden raid, as the VOPO would first have to open up an entrance and if this happened, the doors of the three compartments would automatically shut.

The secret switchboard, designed as the terminal of the wires connected to the junction of the local and trunk cables of the East Berlin telephone net under the Schoenefeld Chaussee, was supplied by the New Jersey Bell Telephone Corporation. The operation chambers and shelves along the walls of the gangways were crammed with a mass of transformers, amplifiers, selectors and contact banks, switchgear and fuse boxes, tape-recorders, teleprinters and microphones, seismographs and hygrometers. Much of this equipment was British made. Any water which seeped in despite the careful insulation, or resulted from condensation in the air-conditioning ducts, was pumped out through pipes leading to the radar station's basement.

For more than nine months the tunnel was in full operation,[10] manned by US Army Corps technicians seconded to CIA, by Gehlen's own men from the Technical Group and by his German-, Russian-, Polish- and Czech-speaking monitoring experts. The main cables tapped connected practically all the Soviet headquarters at Karlshorst and Pankow, the Soviet embassy on the corner of Unter den Linden and Friedrichstrasse, the ministry for state security at Normannen Strasse, other ministries and public buildings at Leipziger Strasse and Alexander Platz, and the main trunk lines to Warsaw and hence to Moscow, as well as those to Leipzig, connecting with Prague, Vienna, Budapest and other important centres. Special amplification devices were installed in order to maintain the quality of the impulses and prevent the East German telephone operators from becoming suspicious. Re-selector units could convey as many as 432 simultaneous tapped conversations to a similar number of magnetophone recorders at the radar station, where the main receiving rooms for the monitors were located.

There were some exciting incidents which caused near-panic in the tunnel. On one occasion the men inside heard the noise of the pneumatic drill overhead; it came from the East Berlin end, and everybody believed that discovery was imminent. Frantic telephone calls to the radar station, however, brought relief: workers at Schoenefelder Chaussee, some ten yards from the tunnel's roof, were digging a new sewer ditch along the wall of the Rudow Cemetery. During the winter of 1955/56 there was another and more serious scare, which Allen Dulles described many years later.[11] During a heavy fall of snow it was discovered that, even through a twenty-four-foot layer of clay, the heat rising from the tunnel was sufficient to cause the snow to melt. In no time a path appeared, nicely outlining the whole length of the tunnel from the radar station to the corner near the cemetery where it ended. The heating was switched off and for some weeks the operators had to work in heavy overcoats, warming themselves at small portable electrical heaters. A refrigeration system was then installed in the tunnel ceiling, which cooled the layers of earth above.

The results of the tapping are still "strictly classified"; they have, however, been described as highly satisfactory. No doubt Gehlen obtained a wealth of information. Years later a "leak" from CIA indicated that thousands of telephone conversations were recorded, transcribed, digested and filed away for cross-checking and that analysts had been kept busy for many months evaluating the information.

On April 22, 1956, the tunnel was discovered; on that morning Soviet Intelligence officers burst into the dug-out after VOPO-men had opened a deep hole at the Glienicke end. But the tunnel had an elaborate alarm system and having smashed the steel door at the end they found it deserted. On a table in the recreation chamber a coffee percolator was still bubbling; the operators had left in a hurry.

The discovery was not entirely unexpected. For almost two weeks the monitors had noticed that the Soviet and East German offices whose lines were tapped were observing what amounted to a "telephone silence". Not only had the vast number of their incoming and outgoing calls greatly decreased, but the conversations were conducted in such a guarded manner that it became clear to the uninvited listeners that the communist officials were aware of being overheard. They must have been forewarned by someone who knew of the tapping.

George Blake's Betrayal

Five years later an oblique reference was made at the trial of George Blake to the part he played in this drama. Blake was at the time of the tunnel operation a senior official of the British Secret Intelligence Service station at the Olympic Stadium Buildings in West

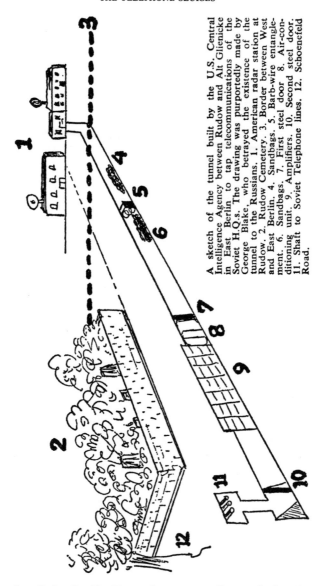

A sketch of the tunnel built by the U.S. Central Intelligence Agency between Rudow and Alt Glienicke in East Berlin to tap telecommunications of the Soviet H.Q.s. The drawing was purportedly made by George Blake, who betrayed the existence of the tunnel to the Russians. 1. American radar station at Rudow. 2. Rudow Cemetery. 3. Border between West and East Berlin. 4. Sandbags. 5. Barb-wire entanglement. 6. Sandbags. 7. First steel door 8. Air-conditioning unit. 9. Amplifiers. 10. Second steel door. 11. Shaft to Soviet Telephone lines. 12. Schoenefeld Road.

A sketch of the Berlin Tunnel purportedly made by George Blake in 1953 and passed to the KGB in East Berlin. It was reproduced in the Soviet publication *Caught red-handed.*

(1) American radar station at Rudow. (2) Rudow Cemetery. (3) Border between East and West Berlin. (4) Sandbags inside the tunnel. (5) Barb-wire entanglement. (6) Sandbags. (7) First steel door. (8) Air-conditioning unit. (9) Amplifiers. (10) Second steel door. (11) Shaft to the East German and Soviet telephone lines. (12) Schoenefeld Road.

Berlin, and had been a Soviet double agent for several years. He had betrayed many secrets and at least fifty British, American and Gehlen agents to the KGB, but at his trial at the Old Bailey in May 1961 there was no conclusive evidence that he had known about the tunnel. It was another nine years before the confirmation of this betrayal came from himself. After his escape from Wormwood Scrubs he vanished, and, although the British Secret Service fairly soon established that he was in Moscow, the Soviet authorities denied any knowledge of his whereabouts, still maintaining that he had never been their spy. Then in February 1970, it was officially announced in Moscow that Blake had been awarded the Order of Lenin, an honour ranking second only to the Gold Star of a Hero of the Soviet Union. The citation stated that "Comrade Blake had rendered eminent services over a long period of years and under perilous conditions, and had foiled the operations of the British Secret Service and other hostile organisations which were directed against the Soviet Union and other socialist countries."[12]

Blake then gave an interview to *Izvestia* which published it in a series of long articles. He stated that before his posting to Berlin in April 1955, he had been "deputy head" of the SIS Technical Operations Section, "whose agents' assignments included eavesdropping on representatives of the USSR and other socialist countries in various parts of the world". In Germany, he declared "the initiator of these operations was Mr. Peter Lunn, a senior SIS official" under whom he had worked in Berlin. "Such operations were conducted on a large scale and the British and Americans squandered on them vast resources." He then revealed that he had "spoilt" one of the biggest espionage *coups* of the past twenty years, attempted by the western intelligence services—" 'Operation Gold', the telecommunications tunnel in Berlin".[13]

Gehlen, at the time of Blake's disclosures already in retirement, could once again justifiably have bewailed the apparent lack of proper security arrangements by the Western Allies. Blake had deprived him of one of his greatest assets, which had cost CIA almost six million dollars. Blake was not in fact admitted to top-level conferences at the Olympic Stadium Buildings when the tunnel was discussed between British and American officials. But he did employ a former V-man of Gehlen's "Org", Horst Eitner, and it is probable that he obtained the first hint about the strange happenings at the Rudow-Glienicke corner from this man, a double agent like himself. At the SIS office, Blake had the opportunity to see confidential reports, some of which may have referred to information obtained as a result of the interception of telephone lines in the Soviet sector. He was fully conversant with such methods and he could easily have put two and two together. He must have made his discovery about a year after his arrival in Berlin, since he obviously did not warn his KGB masters about it before March 1956, when the tunnel had been operational for many months.

For two weeks after the warning the Russians held their hand, apparently waiting for the conclusion of the London visit of Khrushchev and Bulganin; they thus avoided an international incident during their talks with Sir Anthony Eden and Mr. Selwyn Lloyd, already marred by the Crabb incident.[14] This was the explanation for the temporary "phone silence". When they eventually pounced on April 22, the Soviet officers stopped at the last steel door of the tunnel, which bore the inscription: "YOU ARE ENTERING THE AMERICAN SECTOR". This was the short run of the tunnel under the approach to the radar station: the Russians strictly observed the warning.

After Soviet and East German Intelligence officers had gone through the chambers and gangways with a fine-tooth comb, and had removed the tape-recorders and monitoring equipment, they threw the tunnel open for inspection by the people of East Berlin, to show them "the diabolic extent to criminal spying against the socialist countries". Colonel Ivan Kotsiuba of the Karlshorst KGB, describing himself as the press chief of the Kommandantura, invited all the foreign correspondents and editors in both halves of the city to a press conference and led them to the tunnel. Truckloads of Soviet troops and VOPOs stood by, and humming mobile generators provided flood-lighting for the occasion, which was reminiscent of a Hollywood film location. The journalists were conducted in small groups underground and even the Soviet officers who went with them did not disguise their admiration for the perfect job of engineering, describing it as "admirable" and "most ingenious".

For six weeks the tunnel was the major tourist attraction of East Berlin. Some forty thousand members of "workers' delegations", not only from East Berlin, but from the whole of East Germany and even from the Soviet Union and Poland, were brought in coaches to Glienicke, and tens of thousands of schoolchildren were conducted there by their teachers and Soviet officers.

Immediately after the discovery, the Soviet government fired sharp protest notes to Washington, London and Bonn, complaining of violation of East German territory and demanding "severe punishment for those persons and secret organisations which had engaged in this subterranean espionage". But the State Department and the British Foreign Office would not admit to having known about the mysterious tunnel, nor would CIA or the Pentagon. Indeed, the first admission came from Allen Dulles years later, when he briefly referred to the exploit in a book published in 1963.[15] Stating that the tunnel had served its purpose, he wrote: "Most intelligence operations have a limited span of usefulness, a tunnel, a U-2, and the like. This is assumed when the project starts. The difficult decision is when to taper off and when to stop."

After the "tourist tours" of the tunnel were discontinued on June 9, 1956, the KGB published a collection of documents entitled *Caught Red-handed,*[16] which contained several photographs of the tunnel interior and equipment. The publication paid a handsome compliment to CIA's and Gehlen's ingenuity. The pamphlet also contained a list of other "criminal activities" of the Gehlen Organisation, stating that twenty-three of its agents had been caught between 1952 and 1956 in the territory of the Soviet Union and "rendered harmless". It described some of the equipment alleged to have been found in their possession. This included, besides American miniature radio transmitters, pencils that could write in luminous ink in the dark, fountain pen-pistols which fired poison-filled cartridges, and more such rather unlikely gadgets. Most of these agents, the pamphlet stated, had been landed from the air, but several had used more unusual means of entry. One had swum in a frogman's outfit to the beach of Sakhalin, the Soviet island neighbouring Japan.

After the "Org" became the official Intelligence Service of the Federal government in Bonn, and Gehlen its highest-ranking official, he was compelled to discontinue such operations as digging tunnels into the territory of another country. But his new status did not prevent him from engaging in many other undercover enterprises.

XX

President Gehlen

All Fools' Day, 1956, was a decisive landmark in Reinhard Gehlen's life. On that April 1, the Gehlen Organisation became the *Bundesnachrichtendienst* (BND), the official Intelligence Service of the Federal Republic of Germany. The director general of the "South German Industries Utilization Company Ltd." at Pullach was appointed a *Ministerial-Direktor*, a civil service rank equivalent to that of an assistant secretary of state in the government hierarchy of Great Britain or the United States; his "company", with all its subsidiaries, branches and district offices, was taken over lock, stock and barrel by the State. On his personal request Gehlen was granted the special title of President of the BND.

The gestation of the BND took exactly nine months; but it was preceded by several years of fierce infighting and secret intrigue. Dr. Adenauer's cabinet resolved on July 11, 1955, to "attach the Gehlen Organisation as a separate department to the Federal Chancellery, after which it is to be known as the *Bundesnachrichtendienst*". Its head was to be responsible to the federal chancellor through the secretary of state in charge of his office. This high official was none other than Gehlen's old friend and sponsor, Dr. Hans Globke. Together they had prepared the basis of the take-over and the future scope of the service. Its name had been conceived by Gehlen. It was not particularly original; the *Nachrichtendienst* had been the Kaiser's intelligence service and the designation *Abwehr* was, in Gehlen's eyes, tainted by both the Weimar Republic and Hitler's Reich.

The new BND was the final addition to the already existing nucleus of a Federal security and intelligence system. The "Org" had, of course, been fulfilling the unofficial function of a German espionage service for at least five or six years; since 1950 Dr. Adenauer had topped the vast sums provided by CIA with a modest annual contribution from his secret Chancellery funds. From now on the roles were reversed: the new department was to be financed by an appropriation voted annually by the German parliament; a secret arrangement was made with CIA to continue a reduced contribution in return "for a carbon copy of every report sent from Pullach to Bonn".[1]

Many months elapsed between the cabinet decision and the actual transfer. The two Opposition parties, the Social Democrats and the Free Democrats, pressed Dr. Adenauer to provide a legal basis for the new BND in the German constitutional "basic law". But the imperious "Old Man" successfully resisted all such demands, which would have subjected the new department to parliamentary control. All he conceded was that a "collegium" of three members of the Bundestag should have a nominal supervision; this in fact amounted to nothing more than the counter-signing of financial estimates which, in any case, never represented the true BND's true expenditure. Gehlen courteously but firmly debarred these three gentlemen from visiting Pullach. The terms of reference for the new BND announced by Dr. Adenauer were as brief as they were ambiguous: the new department was to collect "such information abroad as is of importance to the Federal government and will facilitate its policy decisions".

By 1956 Bonn had already two other secret service departments, one concerned with counter-espionage, the other with military intelligence; both had gone through a long series of crises and Gehlen had tried his best to get his fingers into both. The first was the clumsily named *Bundesamt für Verfassungsschutz* (BfV—Office for the Protection of the Constitution). The other, originally named *Sicherungsgruppe* (security group), was a small section of the department which in 1949 had begun to prepare for the re-establishment of the Federal armed forces.

Administrative responsibilities were gradually handed over to the Germans by the Allied military governments during 1946 and 1947. First in the British and then in the American and French zones, regional *Land* parliaments were elected and governments set up, each headed by a prime minister.[2] Following the London Conference in 1948, a parliamentary council for West Germany was elected by these regional diets, and a constitution promulgated on May 24, 1949. Dr. Theodore Heuss was elected Federal President, and on September 20, 1949, Dr. Konrad Adenauer became the Federal Chancellor and formed a coalition cabinet of members of his Christian Democrat Party and two smaller liberal parties. The new republic was not, however, given full sovereignty. Indeed the United States, Britain and France did not officially terminate "the state of war" with Germany until 1951. The new West German federal state had no armed forces, nor was it permitted to maintain embassies abroad or conclude treaties with foreign countries. For certain offences, such as espionage, Allied military tribunals still meted out sentences.

All that changed in the early 1950s. The Western Allies offered the Federal Republic membership in NATO and pressed for the creation of German armed forces which would share in the defence of the country. Public opinion in the United States and Britain clamoured for "bringing the boys home" and for a drastic reduction in the Allied forces of Occupation in Germany which, several years after the end of hostilities, still numbered six hundred thousand.

Amt Blank

Adenauer appointed a former head of the Christian trade unions federation, Theodore Blank, as the "Commissioner for Questions concerned with Allied troops and Matters of Defence". This was a cumbersome title, however, and the commissioner's office was popularly known as *Amt Blank*. Two former Wehrmacht generals, Hans Speidel and Adolf Heusinger, were called upon to organise the new *Bundeswehr*. Lieutenant-General Heusinger arrived from Pullach, where he had been working for Gehlen in an "honorary capacity". It will be remembered that he had been Gehlen's superior at Hitler's OKW Operations Department, which Gehlen joined in 1939.

At the rather ominous-sounding "Blank Office" was the embryonic section concerned with military intelligence, which another retired general, Count Gerhard von Schwerin, was to organise as Blank's "adviser on security". Schwerin needed someone to carry out this task and his choice fell on thirty-five-year-old Major Joachim Oster, son of the famous Abwehr General Oster.[3] During the war Major Oster had also served at the Abwehr office, but he had to leave it after his father's disgrace. Although an assertive young man he could hardly claim to be an intelligence expert up to the task of creating a service from scratch. He looked for a more experienced man as his deputy.

Thus Lieutenant-Colonel Friedrich Wilhelm Heinz joined *Amt Blank*. He set to work at his job with great zest, confident of his ability to accomplish it to perfection. Heinz had all the experience that Oster lacked. A member of the *Freikorps* in his youth, he later joined Roehm's SA; but he soon became disillusioned with nazism and as an Abwehr officer belonged to the circle of anti-Hitler conspirators around General Oster.[4] In 1940 he commanded the 1st Battalion of the Brandenburg regiment, handpicked to spearhead the invasion of England; a year later he was with the first units which swept into Russia. At Lvov some of the Ukrainian soldiers in his "Nightingale" battalion staged a terrible pogrom in which many thousands of men, women and children were massacred, but Heinz always rejected responsibility for this outrage. In 1942, fighting Yugoslav partisans in

Serbia, he concluded a pact with the royalist General Draga Mihailovic, thus turning the Cetniks against Tito's partisan army. In July 1944, arrested on charges of having participated in the attempt on Hitler's life, he was imprisoned and tortured at the Gestapo HQ in Prinz Albert Strasse in Berlin.

After the war, he had tried to emulate Gehlen in a modest way. Like the great Powers, the small liberated countries were trying to establish intelligence footholds in West Germany. The Dutch government sent a mission to Aix, one of whose officers was Major Jan Eland, an Amsterdam jeweller in civilian life and an ex-Resistance fighter. The Dutch intelligencers were mainly looking for Gestapo war criminals and they found in Colonel Heinz a willing helper. The Dutch mission was eventually recalled home, but Eland had become so enthusiastic about intelligence work that he stayed in Germany and went into partnership with Heinz. They ran one of the many independent "information bureaux" from an office at Lichter-felde in West Berlin, selling reports about the Soviet Army in East Germany to the Americans, British and French. Eland also approached the BfV with offers of information about communist agents. They did good business, Heinz being regarded, particularly by the French SDECE, as a great expert. Then came Oster's call to the *Amt Blank*, which Heinz accepted with alacrity. Eland was so cut up at losing his partner that he tried to commit suicide.

The Oster-Heinz combination had hardly any prospect of making their Security Group into anything remotely competitive with Pullach. Nevertheless, Gehlen viewed the goings on at *Amt Blank* with growing discomfiture. With even greater annoyance he watched the counter-espionage activities of the BfV which from its office at Cologne-Ehrenfeld was spreading out into a number of country offices.[5] Dealing with the menace of communist espionage as well as with attempts at reviving neo-nazism in the Western zones of Occupation had been the business of the Allied military govern-ments—in the American zone through CIC, in the British through officers seconded from MI5 and Scotland Yard's Special Branch. But with the coming of German sovereignty the BfV was supposed to take over many of these tasks.

The Americans were lukewarm about transferring any of them to this Federal government agency; CIA wanted Gehlen to look after counter-espionage. (It was on Dulles' instructions that he had set up his III/F department.) The British, on the other hand, viewed the American-run show at Pullach with a jaundiced eye. The Allied High Commissioners were entitled to approve or reject Adenauer's choice of the man who was to head the new BfV. Gehlen immediately produced a list of his own nominees, but they were rejected one after another by the British High Commissioner, Sir Ivone Kirkpatrick. Altogether Adenauer put thirteen names before the Allied representatives; none found favour with the British. Sir Stewart Menzies had alerted his friends at the Foreign Office, particularly Sir Donald Grainer, head of the German section; he objected to the appointment to this vital post of yet another of the ex-Abwehr or Gestapo men who already swarmed in Gehlen's office.

The pre-condition for the appointment was that the chief of BfV must not be tainted with a nazi past. At last, Adenauer's minister for all German affairs, the Christian Democrat trade union leader Jakob Kaiser,[6] proposed a man who had the required background, seemed to possess some of the qualifications needed and, above all, had every prospect of being acceptable to the reluctant British. He was Dr. Otto John, a lawyer of forty-one who had been a legal adviser to Lufthansa when Hitler came to power. A family friend of the notable anti-nazi Pastor Dietrich Bonhoeffer, he had joined a group of generals, conservative politicians and a few trade union leaders who were plotting the overthrow of Hitler and the replacement of the nazi regime by a "liberal monarchy" under Prince Louis Ferdinand, the second son of the ex-Crown Prince.[7] The prince was a close friend of John, who thus exercised some influence in the conspiracy. Since March 1942 John had maintained secret contacts with British and American Intelligence, being exempted from military service because of his work for Lufthansa, which also enabled him to travel freely between Berlin and Lisbon and Madrid. There he met Allied agents and kept them informed of the conspirators' plans. Early in 1944 the group of General Staff officers, led by Field-Marshal von Witzleben, General Beck and Colonel von Stauffenberg, was ready with its plan to assassinate Hitler. Several previous attempts had to be abandoned, but eventually, on July 20, Stauffenberg placed a bomb under the table at the Fuhrer's *Wolfschanze*. On the evening of that day, after the failure of the attempt and the arrests of the conspirators, Otto John decided to escape, thus saving his life. All the other conspirators, including his brother Hans, were executed after brutal tortures by the Gestapo.

The Man Gehlen Despised

In the confusion that followed the assassination attempt John managed to board a Lufthansa flight to Madrid; there he got in touch with British Intelligence officers and was taken to England. As "Oscar Jurgens" he worked during the remaining year of the war for the Psychological War Executive on its "Black Propaganda" radio service from Woburn Abbey, run by Richard Crossman[8] and Sefton Delmer, a former *Daily Express* correspondent in Berlin. After the war John became "re-education adviser" to the British Central Office of Germany and Austria, which dealt with the interrogations of prominent prisoners of war brought to the "cages" in England. He worked at the "cages" at Kensington and Bridgend near Bristol, and in 1949 assisted at the trial of Field-Marshal Erich von Manstein,[9] Gehlen's idol in his younger days. Although John did nothing more at that trial than act as an interpreter and translate documents Gehlen never forgave him.

John settled in London as an international lawyer and in 1948 married the well-known German opera singer Lucie Manèn who lived in England. He was greatly surprised when offered the position of head of the new BfV; but he accepted it after receiving encouragement from President Heuss, who had been a friend of his family in pre-Hitler days. Adenauer made this appointment with the utmost reluctance and only after being persuaded by his more liberal-minded cabinet ministers Kaiser and Dr. Lehr; the latter, as minister of the interior, became John's immediate superior.

Adenauer suffered from violent Anglophobia; he had never forgotten that, after a series of incidents in which he had behaved with the utmost arrogance, the British had in 1946 removed him from office as Burgomaster of Cologne. Besides, Gehlen had made strenuous efforts to dissuade Adenauer from signing John's appointment. He sent a stream of defamatory notes to Bonn by go-betweens (who included von Manstein's former chief of staff, General Busse, the man who when in command of the last remnants of the Oder army had told Goebbels on April 12, 1945, that a Russian breakthrough "was impossible"). John was described as a British agent, a communist, an alcoholic and a homosexual. However, president Heuss' recommendation, support from Adenauer's secretary of state, Dr. Lenz (Globke was not yet in charge), who had been a member of the anti-Hitler Resistance and had shared imprisonment with John's brother, and the intervention of Sir Ivone Kirkpatrick, eventually induced Adenauer to accept him.

At his new office John soon encountered difficulties. He was a charming and cultivated man, gregarious and somewhat volatile, and by nature quite unsuited to the jungle warfare of the spying game; nor had he any training or experience in intelligence work. He was told that the foremost task of BfV was to conduct research into organisations pursuing both extreme left-wing and ultra-nationalist aims, and he regarded his work as a sort of academic pursuit. The BfV had no executive powers; its officials and agents, who were called "observators", were not allowed to carry out arrests, conduct house searches, or seize seditious literature. Any reports of activities against the State which reached John's office had to be passed to the attorney general.

As an avowed anti-nazi he was determined not to employ former Gestapo men, but he was soon forced to compromise even on this point. He had to take onto his staff ex-police officers who had served with RSHA's security service—they were ironically called "the indispensables"—and then ask them to investigate the underground activities of former Werewolves or SS and SA members, with whom they sympathised. Nevertheless, he did some good work, uncovering several neo-nazi associations which in many ways constituted an even greater danger to the working of the newly established administration of the Federal Republic than the communists. Many years later Dr. John told the author that he had concentrated on conducting research and submitting reports to the government rather than on chasing conspirators and spies.

Gehlen saw to it that John's activities would interfere as little as possible with his own; he persuaded Adenauer to appoint one of his own men from Pullach as John's deputy: Colonel Albert Radke, a former Abwehr officer who had at one time been Canaris' liaison man to Himmler's RSHA. During the war Radke had been head of a security office in occupied Czechoslovakia and in 1944—with SS Standartenfuhrers Rattengruber and Panzinger—had been one of the investigators of anti-Hitler conspiracies in the Wehrmacht. But John had to put up with him—and with the fact that his office was soon permeated by other Gehlen nominees.

John's authority was flouted on several occasions, even by British and American counter-espionage. On January 15, 1953, Sir Ivone Kirkpatrick ordered over John's head a round-up of a secret neo-nazi organisation in the British zone. Among the leaders taken to the British military prison at Werl were Dr. Werner Naumann, former secretary of state at Goebbels' propaganda ministry, whom Hitler had nominated in his "testament" as Goebbels' successor, Karl Kaufmann, former Gauleiter of Hamburg, ex-SS General Paul Zimmermann, Dr. Gustav Sheel and Dr. Heinrich Haselmayer, both experts of Goebbels' broadcast propaganda machine, and several other former nazi officials.[10] For reasons of their own American Intelligence officers sometimes held a protective arm over ex-nazis whom John suspected of anti-State activities; some of them acted as V-men for US Army G-2 Intelligence. On one such occasion, when John was at loggerheads with the prime minister of Hesse, the G-2 chief at Frankfurt, General Lucien K. Truscott, intervened and arranged a compromise.

Having got a firm foothold inside BfV, Gehlen approached John in the guise of a friend, suggesting that in order to facilitate the other's work he should supply BfV with information about communist agents and right-wing extremists. John told the author that after 1952 he "left much of the intelligence work of this kind to the Gehlen Organisation" and that Gehlen did pass to him some important information. The old fox certainly knew how to manoeuvre men to his advantage and John fell innocently into the trap.

Gehlen was waiting for a chance to dispose of John. In 1953 his first priority was to remove Heinz and Oster from *Amt Blank* and to gain control of the military intelligence of the new army. Somehow he got hold of Heinz's dejected former partner, the Dutch agent Jan Eland. Eland was envious of Heinz' success, and proved more than ready to provide damaging material against him. Documents of very doubtful authenticity were produced which, by inference, showed that Heinz had at one stage supplied information to the East German minister for state security, Zaisser, and to the Karlshorst KGB office. Eland was then sent to John to whom he showed the papers and told a damaging story about Heinz. Although John was by no means convinced, he regarded it as his duty to make a report to his superiors at the ministry of the interior which was laid before the cabinet. John took pity on Eland, who was penniless and desperate. He gave him a small sum of money and advised him to leave Germany. Eventually Eland did so, went to Switzerland and a year later killed himself there. Fortune had always favoured Gehlen: Eland's death removed a potentially incriminating witness. Although Herr Blank defended Heinz and, more wisely than John, saw through Gehlen's scheme, Adenauer insisted on his dismissal. In October 1953 Colonel Heinz was "retired"; soon afterwards Major Oster also left, being given an appointment in the new Bundeswehr and later sent as military attaché to Madrid.

The field was now clear for Gehlen; two of his closest collaborators took over the organisation of the intelligence departments at the new ministry of defence. Colonel Gerhard Wessel was put in charge of Department II, which took over Oster's and Heinz' puny section and soon enlarged it into a fully-fledged military intelligence office. Subsequently Colonel Josef Selmayr, who for four years of the war had been head of Gehlen's FHO group for South East Europe, and since the creation of the "Org" had worked in a similar capacity at Oberursel and Pullach, became chief of the newly established MAD (*Militarischer Abschirm-Dienst*), the security and counter-espionage service at the ministry of defence. It was, of course, not exactly to Gehlen's disadvantage that at about the same time Lt.-General Adolf Heusinger became chief of the ministry's personnel department, responsible for assembling the new officer corps of the Bundeswehr. Gehlen could now turn his attention to the BfV chief.

The John Affair

Otto John relieved Gehlen from the need to administer the *coup de grâce*; he dug his grave himself. The story of Dr. John's mysterious disappearance in Berlin on July 20, 1954, is too well known to need more than a brief account. On that day, the tenth anniversary of the abortive attempt on Hitler's life, a distinguished audience assembled in a West Berlin hall in the presence of Federal President Professor Heuss to honour the memory of the men executed by the Gestapo after the discovery of the conspiracy. Dr. John was amongst the invited, not only because of his office but as the brother of one of the victims. In the evening he visited an old acquaintance, Dr. Wolfgang Wohlgemuth, a surgeon whom he had first met during the war when he was an assistant to the famous Professor Sauerbruch. They had coffee and all that John later recalled was that he felt drowsy, asked Wohlgemuth to take him to the hotel, and woke up in a house in East Berlin without his jacket and shoes, attended by a fat nurse and three Russians. He went through prolonged interrogations and eventually agreed to attend a press conference at which he read a statement which, he says, was prepared for him by Soviet officials. In it he criticised political conditions in West Germany, as he had done before publicly in Bonn and Cologne, saying that he resented the presence of ex-nazis and SS men in high positions, and that there was a risk of re-militarisation in the Federal Republic which would prevent the re-unification of all peace-loving Germans in East and West. He said: "I am here because I am deeply concerned for the fate of the German people and because I should never have had such a platform at my disposal in the West . . . the restoration of the forces which brought national socialism into power is too advanced in the Federal Republic for that to be possible."

He also made a broadcast on East Berlin radio, giving a further explanation of the reasons for his crossing to the East: "In Cologne I have been subjected to constant attacks by ex-nazis who are regaining influence in public life and within the Federal authorities. It was made impossible for me to entrust tasks . . . to men whose loyalty to the Federal Republic and the Constitution was beyond doubt. Thus it was impossible for me to continue in my office." He stayed for three weeks in East Berlin, always under guard, and was then flown to a villa at a resort on the Black Sea. Then he was taken to Moscow and finally, in December, back to East Berlin. He has said that all the time he planned to escape.

In East Berlin he was allowed to visit the Press Club, where he met a Danish journalist, Hendrick Bonde-Hendriksen, whom he had known in West Germany. He confided in him and on December 6 the journalist arranged his escape, driving John in his car across the border check-point to West Berlin. There John was arrested and taken to Bonn; later he was transferred to the prison of Pforzheim. He was kept in custody for eight months before being charged with treasonable activities, and was finally put on trial on November 22, 1956.

At his trial he insisted that he had been kidnapped by Wohlgemuth and taken against his will to East Berlin. He did not deny having made the statements, but explained that he had no choice if he wanted to regain some freedom of movement and prepare his escape. This is Dr. John's story. The star witness at his trial should have been Dr. Wohlgemuth, but he wrote a letter to the court from East Berlin excusing his non-attendance. He enclosed a written statement saying that John had told him on a previous occasion that he intended to defect to the East and, on the evening in question, had asked him to take him across the border. Wohlgemuth did not deny that he had contacts with East German officials; indeed, he lived in East Berlin, though he had a surgery in the American sector of the city.

The court found John guilty and sentenced him to four years' imprisonment. He was released after thirty-two months, the time he had spent in custody before his trial being taken into account. Ever since then he has fought for rehabilitation. At the time of writing these lines, in the summer of 1971, one of the chief prosecution witnesses is being tried in Frankfurt for perjury—after more than sixteen years.[11]

In 1968 John wrote a book in which he describes his case in great detail and argues that his affair centred around the British double agent Kim Philby. During the war when John supplied British Intelligence with secret information through Madrid, Philby was head of the Iberian section of SIS. After his arrival in London, John says, he discovered that Philby had stopped some of his reports from reaching the SIS chiefs. They described the plans of the anti-Hitler conspirators which, if successful, might have led to a separate peace with the West, but would also have produced an anti-Soviet pact between a new German government and the British and Americans. This Philby must have regarded as a danger to the Soviet Union, and so he blocked an understanding between anti-Hitler Germans and the West. Only after Philby was unmasked did John realise the double role he had played in 1943 and 1944 as a British SIS official and a Soviet agent. In East Berlin, John writes, he was again and again asked questions about Philby and about his work for the British Secret Service. At that time Philby was not yet unmasked, although after the flight of Guy Burgess and Donald MacLean he had been dismissed by SIS. John gained the impression that the Russians were not at all sure of Philby's loyalty. Indeed, John now ascribes his kidnapping to his wartime contact with Philby. After the book was published in Germany—its English translation is not yet available—Professor Trevor-Roper stated that "there was nothing implausible about John's claims".

Against John's defence there are the allegations of Wohlgemuth, an obvious East German agent, and statements by East German and Soviet officials to the effect that John was quite willing to cooperate. Different opinions are possible about the John affair. The fact that he returned at the first opportunity and faced his judges speaks for him. Kidnappings and brainwashing are, and were, particularly at the time in question, routine methods of KGB and its East German subsidiaries. As regards John's statements criticising the Adenauer government and the upsurge of nazi influence, he had never made a secret of his strong anti-nazi opinions and of the difficulties he had encountered as head of BfV. A man of stronger character might have given up his post and appealed to public opinion in West Germany and the free world. That John did not do so but instead got involved with Dr. Wohlgemuth was the cardinal mistake that ruined his life.

Whatever the truth about the strange affair of Otto John—Oscar Wilde said that "truth is rarely pure and never simple"—the only beneficiary of John's undoing was Gehlen. Without as much as lifting a finger, he had got rid of his only potential competitor. With two ex-Pullach men, Wessel and Sedlmayer, as chiefs of military intelligence, and with Radke in charge of BfV,[12] Gehlen had become the overlord of all the Federal Intelligence services. With much justification he now saw himself as the "German Dulles".

Reorganisation

The transfer was, in fact, a mere matter of form. On April 1, 1956, there was a little celebration in the main square of the Pullach compound, attended by more than a thousand of the employees of the *Suddeutsche Industrie* company and many of their wives, all nicely lined up in military fashion. They had become civil servants and had exchanged their humdrum titles of "director", "manager". "office supervisor" or "chief clerk" for much more high-sounding ones, such as higher government counsellor, government inspector, *Ober-Amtmann*, higher government assistant. Most of them, however, preferred to be addressed by their former ranks of major-general, colonel, or major.

The Stars and Stripes was solemnly lowered; though the dollars were still flowing in, only the black-red-gold flag of the Federal Republic was to be flown in future from the tall mast in front of the main building.

297

Gehlen made a little speech in his thin voice; he told his brigade that work would be carried on as usual and that their proven comradeship and loyalty would remain as firm as it had always been. A few familiar faces were missing, for Gehlen had had to bid farewell to some of his more notorious ex-SS and Gestapo men in order to make the new BND respectable. Gehlen had persuaded Dulles that the past services of these men must be suitably rewarded; he gave each of them a silver plaque inscribed *Für Treue Dienste* ("for loyal service") and an assurance that their occasional if discreet cooperation would still be appreciated in future.

The official roster of the new civil servants contained 1,245 names (quite a number were still aliases), arranged in three categories: 540 established officials, 641 clerical employees and sixty-four wage-earners, the latter including the "game-keepers", porters, electricians, stokers, messengers, cleaners and so on. In fact only about sixty per cent of the personnel were included in the list (No. 0404 of the Federal Chancellery's annual budget estimates). But obviously none of the full-time agents and V-men appeared anywhere in official documents. The annual appropriation for the new *Bundesnachrichtendienst*, as laid before the parliamentary finance committee, was 23,100,000 Marks. The real expenditure was very much higher, and within two years even the official figure was almost doubled to forty-three million Marks; even newspapers which supported Adenauer had expressed doubts as to the veracity of the original figures. At the Chancellery Dr. Globke had made suitable arrangements to provide Gehlen with additional income by inserting BND expenses under different headings in the budget. This was done quite legally, yet this clever book-keeping made it almost impossible for the parliamentary "collegium" to find out how much BND was really costing the taxpayer.

Only by laboriously ploughing through the Chancellery's complex appropriation lists could one extract some information. This was, in fact, attempted by a journalist; he found that, for instance, in 1957 the Chancellery paid for BND's "outside premises" (that is, for the still disguised "branches") rents amounting to 223,000 Marks; in addition, 278,000 Marks was spent on office maintenance, and about three-quarters of a million for the "acquisition of new premises and real estate". After the parting from CIA, Gehlen was being given a free run of the American "spy schools" and training camps, such as Oberammergau, Bad Toelz and Kaufbeuren, but BND was no longer dependent on the Americans; already the "Org" had established a number of permanent schools as well as temporary courses for visiting V-men. After the transfer a sum of 640,400 Marks was spent in a single year on improving the training facilities.

The Chancellery also made an annual contribution of 240,400 Marks for official motor cars and 150,000 Marks was refunded to Pullach executives for running their own cars. Other transport expenses amounted to 430,000 Marks, and for "extraordinary" telephone bills 150,400 Marks was paid by the Chancellery. All these figures related to the financial year 1956/7, immediately after the take-over of the "Org". In later years these payments doubled and trebled; by the mid-1960s it was estimated that the cost of BND to the German taxpayers exceeded one hundred million Marks annually.

During the first year the Federal government also advanced 495,500 Marks for the purchase of special radio transmitters for Gehlen's agents. Old models were replaced by the newest American and German (Grundig and Telefunken) miniature sets. Converters were supplied to V-men "in the field" in order to enable them to adjust medium-wave sets for HF short-wave transmissions of three to five mc. Eventually, Gehlen's dream of a computer came true; a Honeywell and a Control Data electronic brain were installed. They would have cost almost a million dollars, but it was whispered at Pullach that they had been presented to Gehlen by Dulles; apparently they were CIA's surplus. By 1962, Pullach also had its own "air force"; at first there were only two small sport-planes, to which later a Second World War Mustang fighter converted into a photo-reconnaissance aircraft was added. Eventually Pullach even boasted an American OV-1-Mohawk and a helicopter.

The transfer brought about changes in several of the chief executive posts at Pullach. The most important was the appointment in May 1957 of Colonel Hans-Heinrich Worgitzky as vice-president. It was preceded by a great deal of in-fighting, for after Wessel's departure to *Amt Blank* (the later ministry of defence), Gehlen had intended to make Major-General Wolfgang Langkau his deputy. Langkau, in charge of Pullach's Strategic Services section, was one of Gehlen's few personal friends. But he was unpopular with the majority of the officers and a palace revolution broke out when Gehlen sounded his chief assistants about Langkau's proposed promotion.

Colonel Worgitzky, whom Gehlen had known since his FHO days, when the other was chief of staff in charge of intelligence to General Henrici's army, was fifty when he became vice-president. He had joined the "Org" soon after its move from Oberursel to Pullach, and spent his first few years as "manager" of branch "N" at Bremen. After coming to Pullach he became the spokesman for a group of officers who wanted Gehlen to abandon or limit the casual infiltration of V-men into communist territories and replace them by fully trained agents of the *R-Quelle* type. Worgitzky also advocated a widening of the "Org's" scope by establishing resident agents in West European capitals. He was looking ahead to the role the Organisation would have to play when Germany joined NATO; he saw the *Bundesnachrichtendienst* becoming the intelligence service of a large, rearmed, economically sound Germany which would play its part in the councils of nations. The BND, in Worgitzky's vision, would soon have to fulfil tasks side by side with the great secret services of the United States, Britain and France. Gehlen agreed with Worgitzky's ambitious plans, but he did not dare to put them before Dulles; the CIA chiefs could hardly be expected to agree that their German subsidiary should become too independent and even organise outposts in friendly and neutral countries, in competition with CIA stations.

Once the "Org" became the Federal Intelligence Service, the road for Worgitzky's drive was clear. As we shall see in the next chapter, BND rapidly expanded in this direction. The reorganisation drastically affected the various *General-Vertretungen*, district offices and branches, whose number, by germination and self-propagation, had grown to over one hundred. Most of the main offices, still disguised as commercial businesses, remained intact, but many of the smaller branches were wound up or replaced by "inquiry agencies" in all the cities and many large towns.[13] With the expansion of BND activities on an international scale, a number of "residencies" were established in many capitals of Europe, Africa, Asia and South America, each headed by a full-time "resident" agent, using the convenient cover of a commercial representative or "cultural" delegate.

Another Pullach executive who moved into the top echelon was Lieutenant-Colonel (later Major-General) Horst Wendland. Forty-five at the time of the creation of BND, he had a brilliant military career in Hitler's army behind him; a gunner like Gehlen—they served at one point in the same artillery regiment—he had been at thirty-three the youngest ever chief of the OKW Operations Department, following in the footsteps of such men as Halder, Manstein and Heusinger. He, too, joined Gehlen in the early days of the "Org", later becoming head of its Administration Group and, after the transfer, Pullach's No.3. Worgitzky and Wendland were responsible for the internal reorganisation which took place between 1956 and 1958, and which resulted in a tightening up of the various groups, sub-divisions and sections which Gehlen had created, often for the sole purpose of promoting his yes-men. After the reorganisation there remained only four main groups, each of which was sub-divided into a number of departments.

The transformation of BND from an instrument of the Cold War into a secret service engaged on global activities kept pace with developments which gave the Federal German Republic a greatly enhanced status in international affairs.

Gehlen's NATO Aspirations

The admission of Germany to NATO was followed within a surprisingly brief period by the appointment of several Germans to high positions within this organisation. General Hans Speidel, who had been Adenauer's chief military delegate at the negotiations for Germany's adherence, became in 1957 commander-in-chief of AFCENT (Allied Forces Central Europe), the first German general to command American, British, French, Belgian, Dutch and Danish troops within the NATO set-up; he held this position until 1964. Admiral Friedrich Guggenberger joined the all-important NATO military committee in Washington; two years later General Adolf Heusinger (Gehlen's old chief at Hitler's Operations Department), became its chairman.

Gehlen was not slow in securing footholds in the NATO military councils and headquarters and at SHAPE, the Supreme Headquarters of Allied Powers in Europe. As soon as German officers began to be attached to these establishments, he managed to place within them several of his former collaborators. Amongst these was Colonel Hennig Strumpell, who like General Heusinger had been Gehlen's "honorary adviser" in the early days of Pullach and later joined *Amt Blank*. Strumpell became deputy to the British Major-General Charles Traver, the Assistant Chief of Staff (Intelligence) at SHAPE. Another ex-Pullach officer, Colonel Heinz Koller-Kraus, was made head of the logistics section at Speidel's AFCENT command. In later years posts were found at NATO for several other Gehlen men.

In 1957 Gehlen put out feelers to test the possibility of getting a NATO appointment for himself; he had nothing less in mind than to become chief of NATO intelligence. Aware that there would be strong opposition from many member countries, he prepared every move with the caution and perspicacity of a chess champion. Adenauer had asked General de Gaulle that the French representative at NATO should lend support for Gehlen's candidature; Gehlen himself made certain of Dulles' approval, which was willingly given. Above all, he needed the backing of the US Joint Chiefs of Staff and General Lauris Norstad, the Supreme Allied Commander in Europe. Dulles therefore arranged that Gehlen should visit Washington to meet American military leaders and intelligence chiefs.

This visit took place at the end of July. It was the only trip abroad which Gehlen had made since being taken to Washington in 1945, then virtually still a prisoner of war. This time the reception in Washington was very different. He attended several dinners and parties, though always pleading that invitations should be kept to a minimum and that neither politicians nor newspapermen should be amongst the guests. Dulles had asked Colonel Matthew Baird, the CIA's director of training, to be Gehlen's guide. They went on a tour of CIA and Army Intelligence spy schools and training establishments and Gehlen was introduced to many of the technological and electronic innovations with which American Intelligence agencies were then being equipped. He stayed for several days at the "spy college" at Monterey, California and, on his request, also visited the great collection of war documents of the Hoover Institution at Stanford University. There he had the strange experience of seeing many photostats and film prints of his own FHO archives, though most of his wartime reports on the Soviet Union were, at that time, still classified and not included.

After his return home, his appointment as chief of a combined NATO intelligence department with a seat at Fontainebleau near Paris was mooted to the military council by the American, French and, somewhat reluctantly, it was said, the German representatives. Gehlen's relations with most of the new Bundeswehr generals and even with his once loyal disciples, Colonels Wessel and Selmayr (now the heads of German military intelligence and military counter-espionage respectively) had become somewhat strained because of his constant encroachments on their preserves. A decision was postponed several times, due to opposition from the British, Canadian, Dutch, Danish and Norwegian council members who felt that Hitler's former intelligence chief was not the ideal paragon to defend Western values.

In Gehlen's favour were two remarkable exploits he had scored in 1956, besides the regular voluntary assistance Pullach had been rendering to NATO Intelligence.

Khrushchev's Denunciation of Stalin

In February 1956 Khrushchev had given his notable address to the 20th Communist Party Congress. In it he denounced Stalin and Stalinism in his most forceful manner. He also denounced the rule of the Soviet secret police and described Beria as a monster and a traitor. He called for a general liberalisation of government to give a greater scope to public debate and to the intellectual and creative pursuits in general. Even more sensational than the abuse which Khrushchev showered on Stalin was his abandonment of the concept that the Soviet leadership of the communist world movement was infallible. "The days of socialism in one country are over",

302

he said, "for now there are many socialist countries which must be permitted to devise their own brand of socialist society". For the first time for thirty years Moscow seemed to be abrogating her dictatorship over her satellites.

Khrushchev's address was given in a secret session and he emphasised that "we cannot let this matter go further than this Party Congress, especially not to the press, lest we give ammunition to the capitalist enemy; we must not wash our dirty linen before their eyes . . . ." An intimation of the gist of Khrushchev's speech nevertheless leaked out, mainly because of some comments made by the Italian communist leader Palmiro Togliatti in a communist newspaper after his return home. Obviously, Western intelligence services were instructed by their governments to make every effort to get hold of Khrushchev's full text.

But neither CIA nor Britain's SIS succeeded in doing so. It was Gehlen's German Intelligence service which procured the complete text within a few weeks. Gehlen passed it to Allen Dulles, who gave it to his brother. It was issued by the State Department on June 4, 1956, causing a sensation throughout the world. How Gehlen performed this extraordinary scoop has never been fully disclosed, but I can give here an authenticated clue.

In 1950 Gehlen had instituted one of his first "residencies" in Yugoslavia. His agent was a "Dr. Weber", who worked under the usual cover of a German businessman. In reality he was a former Abwehr officer, Captain Andreas Zitzelberger, who during the war had been attached to an Abwehr office in German-occupied Slovenia; in 1945 he had on Gehlen's instructions built up a few outposts of the R-Net* before returning to Germany, where he became a POW of the Americans. A year later Gehlen enlisted him for his "Org". In 1948 the breach between Tito and Stalin had become irreparable; the Yugoslav Communist Party was expelled from the Cominform and for several years Moscow Radio continued an aggressive propaganda campaign against Tito, whom Stalin had called a traitor to the communist cause who "must be liquidated". Soviet agents plotted anti-Tito rebellions in Serbia, Macedonia and Slovenia and on several occasions the Yugoslav ruler narrowly escaped assassination attempts engineered by Moscow's emissaries. A *Whitebook of Soviet Aggression against Yugoslavia* published in 1951, enumerated these conspiracies in 482 pages.[14]

Whilst Gehlen observed all this with barely disguised *Schadenfreude*, and Weber-Zitzelberger's V-men were busily spying on the Yugoslavs, he at the same time rendered assistance to Tito's secret

* See page 95

service[15] against Moscow; it was not, of course, in the interests of the West that Yugoslavia should fall victim to Stalin. In 1951, Gehlen probably saved Tito's life. One of Pullach's senior assistants at the Hungarian section, the former Major-General Paul Zako, of whom more later, had learnt from his V-men in Austria that a Soviet "executioner" was on his way from Vienna to assassinate the marshal. By an elaborate ruse a meeting between this Soviet agent and Zako was arranged in Klagenfurt, near the Yugoslav frontier; the Gehlen men offered him one thousand dollars and the would-be assassin happily defected. He was later employed by Gehlen.

In return for services rendered over a period of years, one of Tito's officials handed to "Dr. Weber" the full text of Khrushchev's speech in 1956. By then relations between Moscow and Belgrade had become much better and a Yugoslav Communist Party delegation had been invited to the Moscow Congress as observers; they were thus given the opportunity to hear Khrushchev's pronouncement of the new policy of liberalisation, and Gehlen was able to beat all the great intelligence agencies of the Western Powers by producing the text of the speech delivered behind locked doors.

The Hungarian Revolt

For a long time Gehlen had anticipated an anti-communist uprising in Budapest; indeed, it can be said that he had worked hard for several years to induce it. The Hungarians had probably suffered more under their ruthless communist rulers than had other satellite nations, for they tended to put their national views and interests more emphatically above their allegiance to Moscow than the others. This will for independence prevailed amongst many otherwise convinced communists in Hungary; faked trials, political purges and an oppressive police rule were the regime's retaliation.

Gehlen had set up a strong "Hungarian section" in 1950, headed by Colonel Isztvan Kolleny. Many of its members were former Hungarian Intelligence officers, such as General Zako, Colonel Ferenc Farkas and Count Bela Hadik. Clandestine anti-communist groups inside Hungary were supplied with propaganda material and arms by Gehlen's agents in Austria; from Radio Free Europe at Munich a broadcast barrage was maintained under the direction of the Hungarian-born journalist Ladislas Farago, alias "Colonel Bell", who during the war had served in US Naval Intelligence.

When during the first days of the revolt the Stalinist old guard was overthrown in Budapest and the "liberal" communist Imre Nagy (who had spent many years in prison as a "deviationist") emerged as the new leader, announced Hungary's withdrawal from the Warsaw Pact and demanded that Soviet troops leave the country, Gehlen strained all his resources to assist him. A large team of his Hungarian agents and officers who lived in exile in Germany and had been trained in emigré camps near Munich reached Budapest on the eve of the fighting. Dulles contributed a well-armed shock unit from CIA's "private army" in Germany.

This was the first time that Gehlen had crossed swords with Yuri Andropov, at that time the Soviet ambassador in Budapest and Hungary's overlord, who in 1967 was to become the head of KGB. Gehlen was unable to prevent the bloodbath in which the Hungarian revolt was destroyed by Soviet tanks. But he could prove the strength and preparedness of his organisation; he had informed NATO intelligence many months earlier of the imminent clash in Hungary.

These and other exploits could be advanced as testimonials for his ability to take charge of the intelligence side of NATO's "Strike Plan", the contingency plan against a Soviet attack on the West. Had his hopes of the NATO appointment not been dashed, he would have performed a remarkable hat-trick: from Hitler's intelligence chief to the head of the Federal German Intelligence, and thence to the control of NATO Intelligence. That he lost this chance which, despite opposition of some of the NATO partners, was almost within his grasp, was to a large degree his own fault. For once the cautious player had overreached himself.

Spying on the Allies

On July 16, 1958, a secret instruction from Pullach to Gehlen's newly appointed "residents" in London, Paris, Rome, Brussels and The Hague fell into the hands of French counter-espionage.[16] It revealed the startling fact that Gehlen's agents had been collecting information on Allied armaments, aircraft production, atomic developments and defence plans in general.

Diplomatic exchanges between Western capitals and Bonn and an investigation conducted by US General John Schweitzer at NATO were followed by profuse apologies from Adenauer. It looked as if Gehlen would emerge unscathed: it was all a terrible mistake by some of his over-zealous subordinates. But a French official leaked the story to the Paris newspaper *Liberation* which published a sensational report about Gehlen's "spying on Germany's allies". For obvious reasons little was said about Gehlen's operations in France, but the article featured the success of his agents in Turin in getting hold of secret blue-prints of the rocket-charging unit Fiat-G; of Gehlen's infiltration of agents into the Belgian flight-navigation school for NATO officers at Brusten near Liege; of his agents' curiosity concerning secret dam and dyke defences built by the

305

Dutch in the Zuidersee; and of his having placed agents in Britain.

Apart from the incomplete and partly inaccurate disclosures in the French newspaper not a word of Gehlen's activities in Britain reached the public. Yet his agents had been trying to find out about the development of the Thor intermediate-range ballistic missile launching sites in Norfolk and the Early Warning Station being built at Fylingdales Moor in Yorkshire, about the provision of berth facilities for a US Navy depot ship for the nuclear submarine Polaris in the Firth of Clyde, and about Royal Navy submarine stations in the Shetlands and Orkneys. There was extreme indignation in Whitehall, reflected in the demand by Social Democrat members of the defence committee of the German parliament that Adenauer should dismiss Gehlen and institute an investigation into the strange activities of his BND. But *"der Alte"* kept his protective arm over his "beloved general", and the affair was eventually hushed up. The NATO governments grudgingly agreed to forget, if not to forgive; after all Gehlen was producing a mass of valuable information from the Soviet complex. Nevertheless, his hopes of becoming NATO's intelligence chief had to be buried for good.

XXI

The Man Without a Private Life

For two decades the mere mention of Gehlen's name was enough to make senior government officials in Bonn clam up and assume the blankest expression they could muster. I experienced this phenomenon often enough when working as a foreign correspondent in Germany. Until 1956 they had the good excuse to offer that Gehlen—if he existed at all—was not a public servant; afterwards, following the announcement of his appointment as President of the Federal Intelligence Service, they explained that because of the nature of the service its head preferred as little publicity as possible and was not prepared to give interviews. Nor could any official visits to the Pullach headquarters be arranged. Newspapermen were politely advised to apply directly to *Herr President*; the inevitable result was that their letters remained unanswered. Those who somehow managed to discover the telephone number (68036), not of Pullach, but of Gehlen's only "official" office in Friedrich-Ebert Strasse at Bad Godesberg—the only address listed in the Official Handbook of Federal Authorities, but one which he hardly ever entered—were told by the switchboard operators that the President was not available, nor could one speak to any of his officials.

For many years Gehlen succeeded in keeping the residence of his family a secret. Since the move from Oberursel to Pullach in December 1947 he had lived above the office in a modest, three-room apartment in one of the larger buildings within the compound. He could, of course, have occupied one of the villas in the park. They had been used at the beginning of the war by the Fuhrer's deputy, Rudolf Hess, and his successor Martin Bormann; in 1945 Field-Marshal Albert Kesselring had also lived in one while in command of the Army Group G, charged with the defence of the mythical Alpine Fortress in the Bavarian mountains. But a detached villa standing in the park, even though protected by high walls, electrified fences and round the clock patrols, was apparently regarded as too exposed, if not to unlikely intruders, at least to the eyes of his own personnel.

At first Gehlen lived there alone, looked after by his three secretaries, the devoted "Alu", Frauleins Gaede and Janke, and a batman who brought him his meals from the compound canteen. His family remained at their wartime home in the Munich suburb of Schwabing, in a pleasant house with a fine view of the northern end of the Englischer Garten and the Isar river. Eventually his wife and four children, Katharina, Felix Christopher, Herta and Gretl (Margarethe), joined him at Pullach, where the family remained until 1956.

All his life Gehlen had been most frugal. He was a non-smoker, and only on rare occasions, when he attended an official function, would he indulge in half a glass of light wine; he never touched hard liquor. For many years he had been a vegetarian, and, although disciples of this diet had long since invested dishes which made chopped carrots look like a juicy steak, Gehlen remained satisfied with a meal of simple boiled vegetables. Members of his personal staff often wondered how he could maintain his extraordinary stamina on such a diet, and in fact it did not protect him from his later liver and stomach troubles.

This wonderment was shared by one of his frequent visitors, Henry Pleasants, the long-time station head of the CIA in Germany, to whom Allen Dulles had entrusted the discreet supervision of the "Org". Pleasants often stayed for many months at Pullach, preferring, however, more comfortable quarters in one of the villas which Gehlen had allocated to his group chiefs and most senior assistants. Pleasants, a distinguished music critic before he joined CIA who continued to write books and articles on music[1] and whose wife, Virginia, was a world-famous harpsichordist, tried to persuade Gehlen to change his withdrawn mode of life, and to convince him that, for the sake of his growing children at least, he should find a home where his family could entertain a few friends. But for years Gehlen waved aside such arguments.

A Gift From the CIA

Allen Dulles, the gregarious party-goer, also teased Gehlen about his "hermitage", and when the "Org" chief once remarked that he simply had not the money to acquire a private residence near enough to Pullach and yet suitably isolated from prying eyes, Dulles told him that this could be arranged.

The opportunity offered itself in 1955, when CIA transferred the Gehlen Organisation to the Federal German government. Dulles surprised Gehlen with the news that he was to receive a golden handshake in appreciation of the great work he had done for CIA; a gratuity of 250,000 Marks had been authorised. Dulles added the not entirely seriously meant condition that Gehlen should use the money to buy a fine house somewhere in the Bavarian mountains. Gehlen took it almost as an order. He bought a two-storey chalet of eight rooms, situated in about four acres of well-timbered grounds in the quiet village of Berg on Lake Starnberg, some ten miles south of Pullach, and easily accessible from his headquarters by a good road through the Forstenrieder Forest.

I have been to this house. It is a solid, square, rather ugly structure hidden behind tall firs. Its two upper floors, built of timber in the Alpine chalet style, rest on a stone foundation which extends over three arches to support a verandah at the back. Most of the windows are permanently shuttered; the rest are covered by skimpy chintz curtains, the sills adorned with tired-looking geraniums and fuchsias. Altogether the house is much less ostentatious than many of the villas belonging to well-to-do Munich businessmen which line the shores of the beautiful lake.

During the war and the long isolation which followed, Gehlen had been forced to abandon his favourite recreation, riding, in which he had excelled in his younger days. If he had hoped to take it up again after acquiring his country house he was disappointed; his security chief, General Langkau, alarmed at the danger of an assassin's bullet from the thick hedges flanking the lonely lanes of the Forstenrieder or Grunwalder forests, forbade it.

Gehlen took to motoring instead, and in his black Mercedes, with an armed bodyguard beside him, would drive to Pullach early in the morning and at breakneck speed, returning home after dark; but there were many nights which he spent at his office, catching up with a never-ending torrent of work.

His household at Berg was indistinguishable from that of any German businessman: an elderly cook, who had been for many years a trusted servant of his wife's family, the Seydlitz-Kurzbachs, looked after his culinary welfare; a maid and a gardener (who had been Gehlen's wartime orderly) were the only other servants. In addition there were three "gamekeepers" of the same kind as those at Pullach, who were detailed to guard the house and lived in a small lodge nearby. The house itself rarely saw any visitors.

Like those around Pullach, the people in the neighbourhood of Berg—a tiny village distinguished only by the chapel erected in memory of the demented King Ludwig II of Bavaria who drowned in the lake on June 13, 1886—hardly ever caught sight of their mysterious neighbour. Some swear that Gehlen drove to work in the morning wearing a black mask, but this is certainly an exaggeration prompted by the sensational stories in illustrated magazines.

Journalists made herculean efforts to get hold of a photograph of General Gehlen; they failed, however, to unearth any that had been taken more recently than 1943—the one showing him at his OKW headquarters at Mauerwald near Angerburg in East Prussia, surrounded by officers of his *Fremde Heere Ost* department. Since the end of the war, Gehlen had taken good care not to be photographed, a precaution which proved fully justified when in 1956 the East German ministry for state security was said to have offered a prize of one hundred thousand dollars for his assassination.[2] The only other photograph which ever leaked out was, on Gehlen's request, not published in Germany before his retirement; it was a snapshot taken without his knowledge in the mid-1960s when Gehlen, much against his rules, attended a regimental reunion of his old wartime comrades. Even after he had retired in 1968, he was reluctant to be photographed, though two snap-shots—one showing him with his youngest daughter in a boat and another swimming in Lake Starnberg—were published without his consent. These pictures were taken with a telescopic lens by a photographer who made a small fortune selling copies to newspapers and magazines all over the world.

Gehlen successfully preserved his anonymity for many years. His children were educated privately, later attending the Pullach staff school. But in 1951, when his eldest daughter was seventeen and decided to take a two-year course at the Munich College of Commerce and Business Management, she had to be registered in her real name, while her father was still using that of the mythical "Dr. Schneider", general manager of the *Süddeutsche Industrie Co.* In fact, however, it was around this time that Gehlen's name was first beginning to crop up in the German Press.

At college assembly, Katharina's professor, Dr. Jobst, made a critical remark about Prussian officers and their militarist spirit. Katharina jumped up and, defying the strict rules of a German college, exclaimed: "This is quite untrue, Herr Professor!" Dr. Jobst took this insubordination with good humour, but, suddenly realising that his student bore the same name as the chief of the mysterious spy organisation about which he had read in the newspapers, asked: "Are you by any chance the daughter of General Gehlen?", to which Katharina, well instructed by her father, replied that she was not, but that the general was related to her family.

The same Dr. Jobst later became director of the Starnberg grammar school, which Gehlen's only son, Christopher, attended. A little puzzled about the coincidence, he wrote to the pupil's father, inviting him to join the school's parents association, and also asking about his profession and circumstances—an enquiry which would hardly be made in America or Britain, but which is usual in caste-conscious Germany. Dr. Jobst's request met with a polite refusal. The explanation given was that his pupil's father had to travel a great deal on business and would be unable to attend meetings. Gehlen added that his job was that of a company director and that his firm was engaged on government contracts, which was a completely truthful answer.

Milk of Human Kindness

Gehlen has only once been seen with his family on a public occasion—at least as far as is recorded. This was at a Christmas party, and it may have been a gesture of defiance, for the outing took place a few months after the communists had described him as "a war criminal and a mass murderer", and had put a price on his head. With his wife and four children he visited the Munich *Lustspielhaus*, where the "famous Chinese conjurer Ka-lang" was performing at a children's matinée. Gehlen himself sat far back in the box, hidden in the shadow of a heavy velvet curtain. Ka-lang was performing the time-honoured trick of pouring liquids from one receptacle into another, changing them each time from water to wine, from wine to beer, from beer to coffee, or so it seemed by their changing colours. The conjurer then asked the audience to suggest yet another liquid.

"Milk . . . milk of human kindness, please!" cried out Christopher Gehlen, then a grade six student at the Starnberger high school and proud of his literary knowledge.[3] All eyes turned to the box, much to his father's embarrassment. There is no record that General Gehlen has ever since attended a public performance, although he is a music lover; in his younger days he went regularly to concerts and he has a large collection of classical gramophone records.

Frau Gehlen, a tall, distinguished-looking woman, now sixty-eight, must at times have tried to provide some social life for the family. She has not entirely shared her husband's seclusion; she often used to drive to Munich in her small blue Volkswagen, visiting friends and going with them to the theatre. The only boy, now married and himself a family man, used to speed on his motorbike through the lanes round the lake and to go swimming with a few carefully selected school-fellows. But his father, working sixteen hours a day, often seven days a week, discouraged social contacts for himself. Such visitors as the family entertained in those years were limited to a few senior officers from Pullach—and only a very few could claim this distinction—relatives and old friends. Amongst them would be Gehlen's brother, the publisher, his two step-brothers, one of whom, Dr. Johannes, had become chief medical officer at Pullach, and his cousin, Professor Arnold Gehlen, who was married to Baroness von Wolff. Professor Michael Achmeteli, a leading light of the German

East European Institute who had been Gehlen's adviser at FHO and later worked for the "Org", would pay an occasional visit. Frau Gehlen's elderly parents—both of whom have since died—were regular callers. Gehlen had assisted them in the purchase of a villa in the Waldstrasse nearby.

The Innocent Film Star

One of the Gehlen's house guests, however, did not follow this pattern. The surprising exception was Fraulein Ruth Leuwerik, the celebrated and beautiful film star, who had bought a large villa at Berg which adjoined Gehlen's estate. In the 1950s she was one of the most popular film actresses in Europe; the film *Auf Wiedersehen*, in which she starred with Carlos Thompson,[4] was a world-wide success. For a brief spell Miss Leuwerik seems to have been a fairly frequent visitor, much to the joy of the Gehlen children. Their usually forbidding father may himself have enjoyed occasional small talk about a world so far removed from his own. Then, one day, a German magazine published a story which Gehlen found extremely embarrassing. The feature described Gehlen's private life in sensational terms, obviously based on gossip; it told of how he pottered about his garden in an old camel-hair housecoat and slippers and ridiculed his habit of wearing out old clothes and uniform pants, and of fastening his tie to his collar with a steel safety-pin. The old tale that Gehlen wore a black mask when venturing outside his gate was repeated. Although Miss Leuwerik was completely innocent of the incident and had never talked to Press reporters about Gehlen, he decided after this to limit the circle of his acquaintances even more strictly than before.

The few people who have met Gehlen on official business, during his rare visits to Bonn or at the office of Dr. Hans Globke, the secretary of state at the Federal Chancellery, consider him a cold and humourless man, completely wrapped up in his work. But this is surely not the whole picture. Gehlen can be human and relaxed, even to the point of gaiety. One such occasion which outside observers have recorded was when he went to Hanover some years ago to attend a reunion of his old military college. It was a boisterous evening. While two bodyguards discreetly hovered in the background, Gehlen stayed right to the end, consuming two bottles of sparkling Rhine wine and exchanging reminiscences with a few of his old comrades. But he did not talk to men whom he knew only slightly, and one of these later complained that, although he had served with Gehlen twenty-five years earlier, the general would not recognise him, nor reciprocate his greetings. This officer told me, "At least Gehlen seemed relaxed, his face was flushed from the wine or the conversation; he moved his lips trying to take part in our gay singsong of old soldiers' *lieder*, and he even gesticulated with his hands . . . . " That Gehlen was not inhibited from gesticulating in public appeared to his old fellow-officer something so exceptional as to be worth recording.

Little wonder that comparatively few people could even give a reasonable description of what Gehlen looked like. Journalists, whose training might have enabled them to do so, had no chance of seeing him. Gehlen never in his life gave a Press interview or authorised the publication of a direct quotation. A few journalists and writers, like myself, did on rare occasions meet him; but any conversation remained distinctly one-sided. Nor was Gehlen more communicative when, very reluctantly, he was obliged to be presented by Chancellor Adenauer to a visiting statesman. He never attended official functions at Bonn's Palais Schaumburg, even while he was still Adenauer's "beloved general". But when General de Gaulle paid one of his visits to his friend Adenauer he expressed the wish to meet Gehlen, who had been maintaining discreet and fruitful contact with de Gaulle's secret service chief, General Paul Jacquier. Amongst the journalists accompanying the French President was Georges Penchenier, the distinguished foreign correspondent of *Le Monde*; but even such an astute newspaperman as he was unable to extract a few words from Gehlen and had to be satisfied with producing a brief pen-picture of the "mystery man": "A small man, pale, with thin lips, deep-set eyes, a high forehead . . . uttering hardly more than a courteous 'how d'you do' when the German Chancellor introduced him to the President of the French Republic."

After the transfer of the Gehlen Organisation to the Federal German government and the appointment of its chief to the office of President of the *Bundesnachrichtendienst*, it was, of course, inevitable that German journalists should rush into print with genuine or apocryphal memories of their meetings and interviews with Gehlen. None, alas, produced any tangible facts except such as concerned his appearance and clothes. The most interesting story was produced by the former Captain Walter Jacobi-Budissin, who had served in the air force counter-espionage section of the Abwehr; his observations, which he published under the *nom de guerre* of "Jaschka Jakow", went back to 1943, when he had met Gehlen at the height of the war. He wrote about it in a newspaper in January 1956:

"In the summer of 1943 I was told by the head of the Abwehr Luftwaffe counter-espionage group attached to the Messerschmitt aircraft concern, Captain Klein, to meet a senior officer of FHO at Regensburg in Bavaria. I was told to go to a room at the Park Hotel. That the officer I was to meet was Colonel Gehlen (then head of

FHO), I learnt only later; at the meeting he introduced himself as "Dr. Fritz Wendland". Relations between Abwehr-Luft and FHO were not very good and if a senior officer from FHO had asked for a meeting with one of our officers, that was of importance. The Messerschmitt factories employed many Soviet prisoners of war and civilian forced-labour workers.

"Gehlen received me in a darkened room, sitting behind a table in the corner on which stood a lamp with a large shade. He sat in the shadow, with a hat pulled low over his eyes and the collar of his leather overcoat up. He asked me to sit on a chair in the middle of the room, and briefly enquired about our work at Messerschmitts. His dislike of the Luftwaffe was well known; he had consented to cooperate with us only on explicit orders from Hitler.

"He said our counter-espionage work must be intensified and more vigorously conducted than hitherto. My task was to discover clandestine radio sets and to break any attempts at resistance amongst the Soviet prisoners and workers in the camps. He said: 'We cannot afford to be lax and flaccid any longer. Humanity and benevolence were nice things for men like Kant and Schopenhauer, for our work they are merely burdensome . . . . ' I saw Gehlen once again in the summer of 1944, this time at his private apartment at Pasing near Munich. With him were three FHO officers. We knew our colleagues only by their code names. On this occasion I was given instructions on what to do in case of an occupation of Germany by enemy forces. We [at Abwehr-Luft] later heard that Gehlen had similar meetings with intelligence officers in Munich, Hamburg, and Berlin at that time. After the 20th of July [the attempt on Hitler's life] Gehlen attached himself to the circle of officers who remained completely loyal to Hitler."[5]

"This Spooky Nazi Outfit!"

While negotiations for the take-over of the Gehlen Organisation by the German government were still dragging on, Gehlen received a bad press, particularly abroad. *Time* magazine described him as a "tight-lipped Prussian . . . with a fascination for tricky paraphernalia, obsolete codes and invisible inks" and remarked that some of Gehlen's agents were "ex-nazis . . . who served as German spies in World War II".[6] Sefton Delmer wrote in the *Daily Express* that Gehlen had realised the dreams of Himmler and Schellenberg and had continued to recreate an organisation patterned on Hitler's general staff as a basis for the rearmament of the new Germany. (Later Delmer revealed how after the appointment of Otto John as the head of the German counter-espionage service, Gehlen had arranged that "his own men should be introduced into key positions in the new service". The Austrian-born columnist Willi Frischauer wrote in a London Sunday paper: "As head of the Wehrmacht's Intelligence Gehlen cooperated closely with Himmler's security service of the SS Black Guards . . . . But much cleverer than most of his nazi thugs, he managed to impress his American captors . . . . "[7] The American writer Andrew Tully referred to Gehlen simply as "The CIA's Nazi".[8] French writers, such as Omer Neveux[9] and Gerard Sandoz,[10] declared that "Gehlen was one of the rare figures amongst German generals who had remained completely loyal to Hitler right until the surrender", and that he was "a good Hitlerite".

On top of all this unpleasant publicity an incident occurred which Gehlen took much more seriously. Indeed, for a while it seemed as if it might destroy his plans to become the chief of the Federal German Intelligence Service. At the secret meetings of the special committee of the German parliament appointed to debate the transfer, not only members of the Social Democratic opposition and the Free Democratic coalition party but even men within Dr. Adenauer's own ranks objected to Gehlen's appointment. Critical articles appeared in some leading German newspapers.

The most damaging attack came from America. During Adenauer's visit to Washington in October 1954 a reception at the White House was followed by a dinner at the German embassy in honour of President Eisenhower. The brothers Dulles and top-ranking American officials and generals were present, amongst them General Arthur G. Trudeau, who had succeeded General Strong as chief of G-2 Army Intelligence a year earlier. Suddenly, Trudeau approached Adenauer and told him that he did not like "that spooky nazi outfit at Pullach". He added that he doubted Gehlen's reliability and the advantage of having an intelligence service in Germany backed by America and headed by a former nazi officer. Trudeau told the German chancellor that, in view of the expected adherence of the Federal Republic to NATO, he should put his house in order. The American general had not forgotten that in 1942 Gehlen had temporarily been in charge of espionage against the United States, nor that in 1949 he had engaged as one of his assistants at Pullach Captain Wilhelm Ahlrichs ("Dr. Astor"), the former head of the *Abwehr Marine West* department who had dispatched two spy teams to America in 1942.* Chancellor Adenauer, visibly shaken, replied that these matters could not be discussed at a dinner reception and invited General Trudeau to come to the embassy next day. The chancellor wasted no time in telling Allen Dulles of Trudeau's words. Dulles was incensed; he regarded Trudeau's attack on Gehlen as a personal affront.

*See page 63

315

At first, it seemed that the incident would be forgotten; but, as usual, there was a "leak". John O'Donnell, the columnist of the New York *Daily News*, broke the news of the dispute. Dulles went to Eisenhower and demanded Trudeau's head. Trudeau had powerful allies and the secretary of defence, Charles E. Wilson, and the Joint Chiefs of Staff headed by Admiral Arthur W. Radford sprang to his defence; but the Dulles brothers finally triumphed. President Eisenhower removed General Trudeau from US Army Intelligence and sent him to the US Far East Command as deputy to General Lyman Lemnitzer. Back home Adenauer announced to the Bundestag Germany's pledge to Western defence and in an interview said that *mein lieber General Gehlen* ("my beloved General Gehlen") was the only man fit and trustworthy enough to head the new German Intelligence Service.

Buckets of Whitewash

Gehlen had circumnavigated a dangerous obstacle; nevertheless he decided that he would have to refute the recurrent charges aimed at his nazi past. Despite his abhorrence of the Press and newspapermen, he now made use of them for once, though in a typically secretive manner. Through a go-between he approached the Press magnate Axel Caesar Springer, whose papers pursue a nationalist-conservative policy, and the upshot was the appearance of a series of articles about the general. To make it as innocuous as possible, the man chosen to write them was not a member of the staff of one of Herr Springer's many newspapers, but a freelance writer, Heinz Bongartz, who wrote crime books under the name of Jurgen Thorwald. In his opening article for *Die Welt am Sonntage*[11] he told of his first meeting with Gehlen:

"Darkness was falling on that evening in Munich when a young man, very cultivated and polite, arrived and told me 'the doctor is waiting in his car in the street'. 'The doctor?' I asked. 'Yes, that's what we call our chief. Anyway, it's the person with whom you've arranged the rendezvous,' he said. We walked into Harthauserstrasse, where a modest Opel Kapitän saloon without lights and with curtains drawn at all the windows was parked under a tree. The young man knocked at the driver's window, the curtain was slightly raised and I was invited inside. At the wheel sat a man of slight build, in his fifties, and wearing a dark suit. He stretched out a gloved hand and said, 'Gehlen.' Then he started the engine and we drove towards the centre of the city. The young man followed us in my car, as I had arranged. We arrived at a villa in a side street of Schwabing which had been requisitioned by the Americans. At last in the light of the drawing-room I was able to take my first good look at Gehlen.

316

Nobody who did not know of his past would have taken him for a general. He was of medium size, thin, but fit-looking. His clothes were very simple—one might take him for an Englishman. He looked like an intellectual, absorbed in his work and caring little for his appearance. With his dark grey suit he wore a pullover of the same colour and shoes with crêpe rubber soles. His tie appeared to have been knotted in a hurry. There were no bulges in his pockets such as so often betray a hidden pistol. From his breast pocket projected a small notebook and a few ballpoint pens. His appearance was definitely harmless, and this impressed me most. Nor would his face attract any attention in a crowd: sparse greying fair hair, the skin pale, the moustache short and inelegant. But the impression of insignificance disappeared when one noticed his high forehead and his eyes, forceful and penetrating. Suddenly one realised that in this man there was an extraordinary mixture—high intellect, sensibility, the energy of a born organiser and the reserve of a diplomat . . . . "

After this intitial fanfare Herr Thorwald-Bongartz continued his eulogy for another three weeks in the Sunday paper, giving a pocket history of the war in the East ("lost mainly because Hitler had flouted Gehlen's advice"), and making the surprising admission that Gehlen had recruited and trained "young Russian anti-communists [from amongst prisoners of war] and sent them back to the Soviet Union", not as intelligence agents but in order to plant them on the Communist Party so that "in ten or, perhaps, fifteen years hence they may work for him".

Eventually, Herr Thorwald-Bongartz' effusion reached its real goal: to show that allegations of Gehlen's nazi allegiance or sympathies were quite unfounded. Indeed, he devoted almost the whole of one of his articles to showing that "General Gehlen desired the liquidation of Hitler as much as the conspirators of the 20th July . . . . I have reason to believe that in 1943 he shared in the hopes of the future martyrs . . . and that he maintained contacts with them."[12] In order to prove this surprising, though carefully worded, disclosure the writer produced the testimony of a "former colleague of Schellenberg" whom, however, he did not name. This anonymous informant was quoted as having told Herr Thorwald-Bongartz that "the SD would have caught up with Gehlen . . . had not events overtaken it". From this the writer inferred that Gehlen had, in fact, had a narrow escape from the Gestapo. Thus Gehlen, a most unlikely anti-Hitler conspirator, appeared invested with the aura of a "good German". Of his post-war activities the writer imparted very little, stating that as head of the "semi-private organisation at Pullach he was leading the life of a recluse".

Wisely, Herr Thorwald-Bongartz did not elaborate on his contention concerning Gehlen's anti-Hitler sentiments too heavily; he admitted, quoting the anonymous SD informant, that Gehlen "realising that the majority of young officers did not share the [anti-Hitler] ideas of the unpopular general staff officers, generals and forgotten politicians, decided to be wary of actually entering the circle of the conspirators amongst whom were many of his close friends".

General Halder, by then in his seventies, hurried to lend his support. In a Munich illustrated magazine he wrote, "Only an intellect as acute, a judgement as accurate, an ability to work as hard, and an energy as resolute, all married to the highest personal integrity, could ensure a career as extraordinary and indomitable as that of Reinhard Gehlen, who commands the admiration and friendship of us all."[13] Other writers, not inspired by Gehlen, were less charitable. George Andersen crisply stated that Gehlen was regarded as having been "one of the most forceful pioneers of Hitler's war of aggression",[14] and Alain Pujol expressed the opinion that "when Admiral Canaris had lost the confidence of Hitler and the nazi generals at the end of 1943, Gehlen rapidly managed to arrogate to himself the admiral's functions".[15]

Rather unkindly, Gehlen's adversaries played up his unprepossessing appearance, as if this had any bearing on his nature, or on his past and future activities. East German newspapers pounced on it with glee. The communist organ in East Berlin published a kind of "Wanted" police notice, quoting from the files of the Ministry for State Security his description: "Height: 1.70 metres. Build: slight. Face: oval, lean. Hair: mousy, sparse. Nose: pointed. Mouth: thin. Eyes: watery blue. Moustache: grey, Hitler-fashion (sic!). Resembles a bank clerk; usually wears Tyrolean felt hat with green band, rather worn and soiled, and an old sports coat or trench coat."

After his retirement little was heard of Gehlen. In 1967, despite opposition in the Bundestag and criticism in the Press, Chancellor Kiesinger had, on Gehlen's request, extended his service for another year beyond the normal retiring age of sixty-five. Gehlen was loth to leave Pullach and suggested to Kiesinger that he should be allowed to stay for yet another year. But with the elections fixed for September 1969, Kiesinger was anxious to avoid further controversy and told Gehlen that he would have to go. Gehlen still hoped to maintain his sway over BND after his retirement and he tried hard to get Major-General Horst Wendland appointed as his successor.[16] He failed, however, and General Wessel was made President of the BND.

Resentful of Wessel's hostile attitude since 1954, when the other had turned against him after becoming head of military intelligence, Gehlen all but severed his connections with the BND. In any case, the Social Democrats emerged from the elections as the ruling government party and Willi Brandt packed Pullach with his own nominees. After Wendland's mysterious suicide in October 1968, followed by a spate of speculation about his involvement in Admiral Luedke's alleged espionage activities, there was no opportunity left for Gehlen to act as an elder statesman and occasional adviser to the organisation which he had created and built up for almost a quarter of a century. Gehlen had the humiliating experience of being summoned before an investigation committee, headed by Secretary of State Reinhold Mercker, and questioned about his alleged nepotism during the final period of his presidency when he had put ten of his relatives, including his son, two brothers, two sons-in-law and several cousins into senior positions.

Today, on the threshold of three score years and ten, General Reinhard Gehlen has found a surprising new field of activities. He has become an evangelist. With still unimpaired energy he has taken over the direction of a campaign for building new churches and schools for the Evangelical Church in Catholic Bavaria. After a life of seclusion he frequently attends meetings all over the province at which appeals for new funds are launched; on occasion he does not disdain to visit members of his religious community in order to encourage the enterprise and to pass the begging bowl. This shows both determination and courage, for in some of the rural districts of proverbially "Papist" Bavaria one conducts such campaigns at one's peril.

XXII

Double Agent in Pullach

When all the spy scandals and revelations of the past decade are assessed one comes to the conclusion that 1961 was a disastrous year for Western security. In Britain the arrests and trial of Gordon Lonsdale, Peter and Helen Kroger, and two Admiralty officials showed that Soviet spies had been obtaining secret defence documents and naval blue-prints with startling ease. A few weeks later the trial of George Blake, who for several years had been an official of the British Secret Intelligence Service in West Berlin, revealed that for nine years he had been able to conduct espionage at highly sensitive levels, betraying more than fifty British and American agents. These discoveries led to protracted investigations by inquiry commissions, which recommended drastic measures to strengthen security arrangements and to revitalise the Secret Service, which had never before in its long history suffered such a humiliating infiltration by enemy agents. Yet within a year another spy trial revealed that the same KGB "controller" who had conducted Blake was linked with the treachery of the Admiralty clerk William Vassall.

The United States had its own cup brimful of sorrows. Still smarting under Moscow's jibes after the shooting down of the U-2 "spy plane" and the sentence of its pilot, Gary Powers, to fifteen years' imprisonment, the American people were confronted with the disclosure that two Soviet spies, Melekh and Hirsch, had ferretted out Polaris and anti-submarine defence secrets, and learnt that the US diplomat Irvin C. Scarbeck had been sentenced to thirty years' jail for betraying secrets to the communists. The Bay of Pigs *débâcle* shook the Central Intelligence Agency to its foundations and resulted in the retirement of Allen Dulles and his chief assistants, Frank G. Wisner and Richard M. Bissell.

France was plagued by the revolt of her generals in Algeria; General de Gaulle's life was threatened by assassination plots, and it was alleged that Soviet spies had penetrated the president's inner

320

circle.[1] The great Paques spy ring was eventually smashed two years later.

The most terrifying disclosures, however, came from Germany. No sooner had disquiet died down over the failure of the German security services to uncover in time the treacherous activities of Alfred Frenzel, a member of the Federal parliament and its defence and foreign affairs committees who had betrayed NATO secrets, than a fresh major *coup* of the KGB was disclosed: a Soviet agent had been discovered at the headquarters of Gehlen's BND. He had been working for the "Org" since 1951, rising eventually to become head of counter-espionage against the Soviet Union; all the time, for more than ten years, he had been a double agent. The disclosure was a body blow for Gehlen; it almost destroyed him and his organisation.

Worse even than the discovery of a Soviet spy in the nerve-centre of German Intelligence was the fact that the treachery became known, not through the efficacy of either Gehlen's security division, which the BND chief never ceased to praise, nor through any effort of the BfV counter-espionage office of his friend Albert Radke, but through defectors from East German and Polish espionage offices. They were not particularly high officials, but they were able to provide the initial information which threw Pullach into turmoil and put Gehlen's life-work in jeopardy.

Old Nazis Just Fade Away

The man who had put the explosive charges beneath Pullach's seemingly indestructible bed-rock was Heinz Paul Johann Felfe, then forty-three years old, head of the Soviet Union section in Department III/F of the BND at Pullach, with the rank of a higher government counsellor. It will come as no surprise that Felfe had once held another high-sounding title: at the youthful age of twenty-five, he had been head of a section at Schellenberg's *Amt VI* of Himmler's RSHA, with the rank of an SS Obersturmfuhrer.

He was born in Dresden in 1918, the son of a policeman. When the nazis came to power he joined the Hitler Youth, transferring as soon as he was old enough to the storm-troopers. Within a year or two he was in command of the mobile units of the NSKK, which the nazi leader employed in the years before the war to intimidate the people and to carry out raids, particularly on Jewish homes and shops. SS and NSKK units spearheaded the pogroms which raged throughout Germany on November 10 and 11, 1938, after an official of the German embassy in Paris had been shot by a Jew. Significantly, Felfe managed to stay far away from the battlefields of the war; in 1939 he contrived a safe job for himself in the RSHA in Berlin. Most of his war service was concerned with protecting the safety of nazi leaders, as an officer in their SS bodyguards, rather than in intelligence work at *Amt VI*, but towards the end of the war he was put in charge of the SD "Swiss" section which had established a large network in Switzerland, and concerned itself with watching Allen Dulles' activities there.

Felfe later claimed to have penetrated the OSS office in Berne and to have obtained through his agents accurate information about the Allied leaders' conferences at Tehran and Yalta. This was probably a characteristic boast; years later at Pullach he established a reputation for claiming the credit for other people's achievements, or simply inventing imaginary exploits. In fact, during the last months before the Third Reich's collapse, he was busily engaged in arranging caches for the valuables and art treasures that his bosses had looted.

In March 1945 he fled from Berlin to the Rhineland, fearing capture by the Russians. He was less lucky than many of his SS friends, who had thrown away their uniforms and posed as humble Wehrmacht soldiers, or simply "dived under", when the British and American troops occupied the area. He was captured still wearing his SS uniform, and in May 1945 the British sent him with other suspected war criminals first to an interrogation "cage" at Kensington in London, then to Doncaster,[2] and eventually to Canada. Seventeen years later, at his treason trial, Felfe tried to explain his work for the communists by stating that ill-treatment in the British prison camps had made him hate the Anglo-Saxons; he remarked that, whilst working for Gehlen, he had secretly disapproved of the "Org's" involvement with the Americans. There may have been an understandable human reason for Felfe's deep hatred of the two nations who had been the enemies of his Fuhrer and had bombed his home town of Dresden to destruction: he had relatives among the casualties. But basically Felfe was apolitical. His actions were dictated by a desire to get on the winning side, to live the good life, make money and enjoy personal power. In his early life he had been a staunch nazi; later he eagerly seized an opportunity to work for British Intelligence, then took CIA pay, and eventually decided to throw in his lot with the Russians.

Released in 1946, he was sent with a transport of ex-prisoners to Germany where, as a former SS official, he had to go through the denazification procedure. He was cleared with the well-nigh incredible classification "Category Four, Uninvolved",[3] and soon afterwards contrived to find himself a job as an informer with the British Intelligence HQ at Münster, where he helped to round up former SS and Gestapo men wanted as war criminals.[4] Although his pay for betraying his former comrades was poor, he could at least scrounge from the British a few packets of cigarettes, some canned food, or an occasional pound of coffee and a bottle of whisky. Nevertheless, he went through a lean time, a lonely man, unable to risk reunion with his wife and mother who lived in Soviet-occupied East Germany. At last he got a job with the Federal Office for All-German Affairs, which looked after the millions of refugees from the East, supervised welfare schemes, and also conducted a bit of intelligence work on the side, employing V-men to unearth possible communist agents among the refugees. Felfe's work for this office consisted chiefly of informing his superiors of such suspects. To this end he joined left-wing groups in Bonn and Cologne.

One day in 1948 he met an old colleague. He was Erwin Max Tiebel, who had been a lawyer at Radberg near Dresden before the war, and later, with the lower rank of SS Scharfuhrer, had served under Felfe at the RSHA. Tiebel, a mild-mannered and rather timid man, had never achieved any advancement in the Nazi Party and the SS, but he had done much better than Felfe after the war. He was now a prosperous builders' merchant at Lendringhausen, a small town in Westphalia. He had acquired property, had a fine house, and invited Felfe to stay with him. He told him of the misfortune of a friend, whom they had both greatly admired in the glorious days of the Third Reich: SS Sturmbannfuhrer Hans Clemens.

Clemens had been a true paragon of the SS *élite*. A Dresdener, like Felfe and Tiebel, he had been an "old fighter" in the early days of the Nazi Party, which he joined in the 1920s. The son of a military band leader, he had studied music as a boy and for a while played the piano in beer halls, but he soon became a professional riot leader, breaking up the meetings of political opponents, and rising to the rank of district commander in the then illegal storm-troopers. He acquired the nickname of the "Terror of Pischen", the suburb of Dresden where he lived; this was sufficient qualification, when Hitler came to power in 1933, to get him appointed as the local police chief. A year later he was superintendent of the Dresden constabulary and quickly rose to the high rank of *Kriminalrat* and head of the Gestapo office. For thousands of Social Democrats, communists, trade unionists, Jews, Catholic priests and other "undesirables" there was only one destination after Herr *Kriminalrat* Clemens had concluded their interrogations: a concentration camp.[5]

No wonder that the Gestapo chiefs called this bull-necked bruiser to an even more important post at the RSHA in Berlin. There he worked on Heydrich's staff and, remembering his friends in Dresden, he brought both Felfe and Tiebel to the RSHA. As a high Gestapo official and aspiring to yet loftier heights, Clemens had shed some of his obvious vulgarity; Himmler demanded that his officers should appear respectable and *korrekt*. After temporarily heading an SD intelligence section, where he was Felfe's immediate superior, Clemens was sent in 1943 to Rome as "security attaché" and chief liaison officer of the Gestapo to Mussolini's OVRA. The Italian rebellion against the Germans gave Clemens an opportunity for active service that was much more to his liking: he took command of SS units appointed to teach the unstable Italians a sharp lesson. In raids on towns and villages in Lombardy he acquired the fearsome name of the "Tiger of Como". Captured with some of his thugs at the end of the war by the Americans, he was handed over to the Italian authorities and charged before a war crimes tribunal with having ordered the execution of 335 Italian hostages. Whilst Clemens was in prison in Italy, Felfe and Tiebel wrote comforting letters to him and sent him food parcels. After four years Clemens was released and arrived at Tiebel's home, where he was warmly welcomed by his two friends.

The trio discussed their future. Felfe was in a sullen mood; he despised his lowly job and had been rejected by the West German police for a post because of his SS past—this despite a recommendation from British Intelligence. Tiebel was quite happy to carry on in his business, but he would do anything Clemens should order. Clemens had a solution to all their problems. When he was still in prison in Italy, his wife, who had remained in Dresden, had written that she had become very friendly with "some important officials" who were prepared to give Clemens a well-paid job if he wanted to settle in West Germany. Although she did not say so in so many words, it was clear to her husband that her important friends were connected with the Soviet Army of Occupation. After his arrival at Tiebel's house the correspondence continued and Frau Clemens suggested a discreet meeting between her husband and her friends. In the spring of 1950, Clemens travelled to Walkenried, a village on the zonal border which was the suggested venue. There he met a man who told him he was a colonel in the Soviet Army, and who asked Clemens to call him "Max". The Russian told him that he knew everything about his "excellent work as an intelligence officer" and invited him to Dresden. Clemens was a little wary, but—as he stated at his trial ten years later—the Russian had "embraced and kissed me, and gave me one thousand Marks, saying that I wouldn't need to spend any of that money, since I was his guest". At Dresden, in a villa belonging to the KGB district commander, they clinched a deal. Clemens was to go back to West Germany, where he would try to get a job in either a Federal ministry or an American headquarters and start spying for the Russians. His wife kissed him good-bye, but told him she would remain in Dresden; it did not surprise Clemens to learn that she was Colonel Max's mistress.

Back in Westphalia, he put to Felfe and Tiebel a plan that would ensure a good income for the three of them, and also much of the heady excitement that their old Gestapo work had entailed: spying. Only, this time it would be for the Russians. Without hesitation Felfe agreed; Tiebel was less enthusiastic, but promised to go along with his two friends, if only for old time's sake. They had now to find the jobs "Max" had suggested, but this proved not as easy as Clemens had hoped, though the self-confidence and impertinence of the former "Terror of Pischen" seemed to have no limits. After his applications were rejected by several Federal offices, he asked for an interview with the minister of justice, Dr. Gustav Heinemann,[6] stating in his letter that he had to communicate "a matter of utmost importance concerning Soviet espionage". Puzzled by this, Dr. Heinemann agreed to see him; but Clemens told the minister a wild story about a communist conspiracy perpetrated by a Soviet spy ring and including a plan to assassinate Chancellor Adenauer. In return for revealing its details he demanded a post "suitable to his former rank", in the newly established counter-espionage department of the BfV. Heinemann, who had on his desk a police report on Clemens' past, did not believe a word of this story and, in any case, he wanted no truck with this notorious nazi thug. He showed him the door after listening to him for a few minutes.

After this, things did not look too good for Clemens and his friends. Colonel "Max" was paying him the promised retainer of 1,500 Marks a month, but he was growing impatient. Felfe had remained at the ministry for all-German affairs and fed his friend with every scrap of information he could use to forward to the Russians, but they were not able to produce much. They were almost at their wits' end when by a stroke of luck all their troubles suddenly came to an end.

In the spring of 1951, on a train from Cologne to Düsseldorf, Clemens ran into an old colleague who had done very well after the war: ex-SS Standartenfuhrer Willi Krichbaum. A former section head at Schellenberg's *Militaramt* of the RSHA, he had been chief liaison officer of the SD to Canaris' Abwehr. After a spell in a war criminals' "cage", he was released, "de-nazified", and had joined Gehlen's "Org" when it was still at Oberursel. Since then he had advanced to various senior positions, had been Gehlen's "manager" of a district office in Bavaria and, shortly before his chance meeting with Clemens, had become deputy chief of the personnel department at Pullach. Krichbaum was happy to help an old SS comrade and engaged Clemens as a *Forscher* ("chief collector") attached to the "Org's" district office at Karlsruhe, then disguised as the Venetian blinds firm of Zimmerle & Co.* At his trial Clemens stated that his main duty there was to look around and recruit other ex-SD and RSHA men for the Gehlen Organisation. Gehlen himself did not know of Clemens' engagement. His organisation at Pullach had grown from the handful of FHO officers at Oberursel to a formidable staff of more than twelve hundred and personnel matters were left to Krichbaum, who was supposed to report on important appointments. In Clemens' case there was no need to do so.

Clemens did so well at the Venetian blinds office that within a year Krichbaum, in all good faith, transferred him to Pullach. Even more important, Clemens got a job for his friend Felfe there within five months of his own appointment. Krichbaum had no great opinion of the blustering vulgarian Clemens, but he was impressed by Felfe's *korrekt* behaviour when Clemens introduced him, and even more by his obvious knowledge of intelligence work and his previous activities for the British. He recommended Felfe to the head of Pullach's III/F counter-espionage department. In November 1951 Felfe started work as as assistant investigator (*Sachbearbeiter*).

Double Agent at Source

From then on the respective relations of Clemens and Felfe with the KGB changed: Clemens maintained the contact—Colonel "Max" had arranged that reports should be conveyed directly to the KGB headquarters at Karlshorst—but Felfe was now the boss. At Pullach he had assumed the alias of "Dr. Friesen"; to the Russians he was "Paul" or agent P-33 (P probably stood for Pullach). Tiebel had been roped in too, in a modest job as a Pullach courier to the West Berlin branches. His posting was ideal for the traitors' scheme: he carried Felfe's reports to KGB "cut-out" men on the sector border and handed them over at stations on the S-railway, then still open for traffic between East and West Berlin. On other occasions Tiebel travelled to places on the Thuringian zonal frontier between East and West Germany and placed microfilmed copies of Pullach documents in dead letter-boxes from which they were duly collected by KGB couriers.

Soon rich dividends were being paid. Felfe was by then getting almost twice as much pay as Clemens from the Russians. Although he admitted at his trial to having received about 180,000 Marks during his activities, the prosecution estimated that he must in fact have been paid many times this amount. By 1957 he was able to buy a ten-room manor in several acres of grounds at Oberaue, not far from the famous alpine resort of Garmisch-Partenkirchen, south of Munich. He paid £12,000 for it, also acquiring a farm and a herd of

*See page 159

cattle. Strangely, this seigneurial mode of life remained unnoticed by his superiors at Pullach; yet Felfe could hardly have afforded it on his salary, which totalled about 1500 Marks a month.

In 1954, during the negotiations for the take-over of the "Org" by the Federal government, Gehlen interviewed all his officials in higher posts and took the precaution of weeding out a number of them whose Gestapo pasts were too notorious; they were given substantial "golden hand-shakes". Felfe, however, was not only left in his post, but Gehlen arranged with his prospective superior at the Bonn Chancellery, Secretary of State Dr. Hans Globke, that the expert on counter-espionage against the Soviet Union should become an established public servant and be promoted to the rank of a government counsellor (*Regierungsrat*).

Felfe's rise to a position of command in the "Org" was rapid, but fully justified by his excellent achievements and his devotion to duty. No one at Pullach seemed so adept at uncovering the identity of communist spies; no one seemed to have such reliable information on drops and couriers, and even on schemes and conspiracies being hatched at KGB headquarters. In several instances Felfe rendered great service to the Americans by informing Gehlen of KGB agents infiltrated into US Army and intelligence establishments in Germany.

In August 1952 he "unmasked" the fifty-two-year-old former US Intelligence captain, Michael R. Rothkrug, of Westport, Connecticut, who had a year earlier resigned and gone into business with a German partner, setting up an export-and-import company in West Berlin. In fact, Rothkrug had become one of the many "independent" mercenary spies, selling information to the highest bidder. At one time he supplied the KGB, British, and French Intelligence simultaneously with doubtful reports. Felfe somehow discovered Rothkrug's activities, suggested to his KGB masters that the American was "expendable" and reported the case to the American CIC. Felfe had no scruples about delivering such small fry to Western intelligence in order to strengthen his position in Pullach. He did so, of course, with the full approval of his KGB paymasters. In any case, Rothkrug was a Jew, a native of Poland and an American citizen by naturalization; in Felfe's opinion he simply got his deserts.

The case of the KGB agents Victor and Erika Schneider was far more significant. The man was an adventurer; in 1935, after a manslaughter in a brawl at Frankfurt he had escaped to join the French Foreign Legion. He fought in Indo-China, where he was taken prisoner by the Japanese, but was released on account of his German nationality; he then made a fantastic trek half around the world to get home. By 1942 he was an SS Sturmfuhrer working at the RSHA under the notorious "Gestapo-Muller" (SS General Heinrich Muller, second-in-command to Himmler) on investigations which led to the destruction of the "Red Orchestra", the vast Soviet wartime espionage network in Germany. His immediate superior was SS Standartenfuhrer Friedrich Panzinger, whom we shall find, a few pages on, filling a strange role in the Gehlen Organisation.

In 1944, Schneider must have fallen foul of his Gestapo bosses, for he was sent to the Sachsenhausen concentration camp; he was freed by Allied troops in 1945. In the British zone he committed several robberies and was sentenced by a military tribunal to four years' imprisonment. In 1949 he re-emerged as a book-keeper at the local office of Adenauer's Christian Democrat Party at Siegen, and did so well that he was soon promoted to a managerial post at the party's head office in Bonn. In 1953 Chancellor Adenauer presented him with a special "plaque of merit". By this time Schneider had been in the pay of the KGB for three years and was supplying Soviet and East German agents with copies of every document which passed through his hand at the Bonn office. Moreover, he had obtained for his wife, Erika, a post as secretary in the newly established ministry of defence. The KGB at Karlshorst was receiving interesting material from the couple and was paying well for it.

Meanwhile Panzinger had joined the Pullach headquarters and one day told Felfe of the background of Adenauer's party office manager. What interested Felfe most was Schneider's connection with the destruction of the "Red Orchestra", which the Russians had never forgiven. He duly informed the KGB on Schneider and suggested that he should be denounced to the Federal authorities. This would be Schneider's just punishment for his wartime work against the Soviet Union; much more important, his exposure would be a major feather in Felfe's cap. Again, the KGB chiefs agreed and Victor and Erika Schneider, to the intense embarrassment of Dr. Adenauer and his party officials, were arrested, put on trial and sentenced to long terms of imprisonment.

Gehlen congratulated Felfe on this excellent achievement. He also commented with amusement on another of Felfe's exploits, the "unmasking" of a forty-four-year-old maiden lady, Fraulein Irmgard Roemer, employed as a secretary at the Federal ministry of foreign affairs of Dr. Heinrich von Brentano. She was a spiritualist who had been ensnared by a Soviet agent, Carl Helfmann, a member of her spiritualist group. For passing on copies of top secret documents, the woman had been paid small sums ranging from £5 to £20; she had spent all the money on financing a fraudulent medium, the eighty-year-old "Sage", Wilhelm Altmüller.

Felfe "bust" this pathetic little group. At her trial the wretched woman insisted that "foreign spirits speaking in Russian" at séances

Former SS Standartenführer Panzinger, with whom Gehlen staged "Operation Waxwork"

Heinz Felfe, ex-SS Sturmführer and Gehlen's chief of counter-espionage at Pullach, was for ten years a Soviet double agent.

The US Army camp at Bad Toelz in Bavaria, where units of the "Special Forces" and Gehlen's agents were trained.

(*Above*) Alois Brunner, former SS Sturmführer and Gehlen's agent in Syria; he later worked in Cairo where Lotz sent him a parcel containing a bomb which killed him.

(*Left*) Wolfgang Lotz, the Israeli spy whom Gehlen infiltrated into Egypt. He claimed to have been an officer in Rommel's Africa Corps. Lotz ferreted out the secrets of Soviet missile sites on the Suez Canal.

Major-General Hans-Heinrich Worgitzky, Gehlen's deputy; he quarrelled with Gehlen over the Lotz affair in which Gehlen had involved his stepson, and he resigned as vice-president of the BND in 1967.

had commanded her to copy the documents. The court conceded her diminished responsibility and she got off with three years' imprisonment; her seducer Helfmann, however, did not escape so lightly and was sentenced to eight years.

The calculated loss of a few dupes such as these meant nothing to the KGB. The writing off of a handful of German men and women who could supply interesting material only occasionally was a splendid investment in Felfe's future. However, Gehlen expected his counter-espionage chief to produce a really major *coup* from time to time, which might unearth KGB officials controlling networks in Germany, rather than merely expose their German dupes. To this end, supplied by his masters at Karlshorst with the required information, Felfe "broke up" a network centred on Hamburg and controlled by the KGB's "resident director" Vasili Kudravtchev. Obviously, the "director" was informed in good time of the impending action of the German counter-espionage and made a leisurely exit, taking with him several agents and all relevant papers and equipment, but leaving behind carefully prepared fake notes, wrong code taps and two or three obsolete radio transmitters. The clandestine office of the Hamburg network was duly raided and the planted material found; but the birds had flown—all, that is, except one whom the KGB chiefs were prepared to sacrifice. He was a German journalist named Rolf Ingelmann, who earned a precarious livelihood as contributor to sports magazines, and acted as courier and informer for Kudravtchev on the side. Ingelmann had been ordered to strike up friendships with women employees at the US embassy in Bonn, and he had succeeded in the case of the not very attractive Fraulein Lilli H., who worked there as a typist and became infatuated with the good-looking journalist. The affair was blown up by Felfe into a major spy scandal; Ingelmann, written off by the KGB, was duly delivered to the American CIC, and Felfe got another feather in his cap. The Federal Supreme Court gave Ingelmann a lenient sentence of two and a half years' imprisonment.

In this way the KGB cemented Felfe's position at Pullach. When some of Gehlen's department heads, suspicious of Felfe's exploits and, particularly, of his claims that he had discovered major conspiracies and detailed plans of the Karlshorst KGB headquarters and the East German ministry for state security, conveyed their doubts to Gehlen, their chief reproached them for denigrating Felfe's excellent work out of jealousy. Strangely, this old fox of the espionage game was completely taken in. It must be said, however, that Felfe proved himself a virtuoso of deception. His KGB masters were always ready to help him in devising impressive cases and did not mind being made to look foolish on occasions.

329

The Atomic Expert

One of the great charades which Felfe produced, and which apparently greatly impressed Gehlen, was "Operation Uranus"[7] Felfe reported to his chief that he had succeeded in "turning round" an East German geologist who worked at the uranium mines at Aue in Erzgebirge on the Czechoslovak frontier. These mines, under Soviet control, belonged to the famous Joachimsthal uranium corporation, the only such group in Europe. The geologist, Felfe reported, had provided important information about the exploration of new deposits and had supplied details of the workings, production, statistics and quantities of uranium being transported to Russia for the manufacture of atomic weapons. Felfe told Gehlen that his V-men were regularly meeting the geologist. He concocted an elaborate and confusing story about a woman chief geologist, Tatyana Petchenina, who had been sent from Moscow to supervise the scientific work at the uranium mines, and who was involved in his scheme. A whole cast of *dramatis personae* appeared in his story: Colonel Ivan Sergeyevitch, Major Suchyumkin, and even the chief of security at Karlshorst, Colonel Ivan Sorokin, who was responsible for safe-guarding security at the mines. Glamour was represented by the colonel's pretty interpreter, Rita Volodina, whom Felfe in a flight of fancy described as a former star of the Moscow Bolshoi ballet. One of Felfe's V-men had become her lover and succeeded in obtaining a lot of secret information from her.

Felfe could not resist putting himself in the limelight. He told Gehlen he had discovered that the Russians were planning his kidnapping and even assassination. In order to obtain uranium samples, he said, he had ordered V-men who had established the contact with all these important KGB officers to tell them that he, Felfe, was prepared to defect to the East. As he could not risk meeting the Russians himself, he had instructed one of his V-men, a former Wehrmacht sapper who was knowledgeable about mining, to impersonate him. This poor fellow, Felfe told Gehlen, had only narrowly escaped abduction when he met KGB agents in West Berlin, and later in Vienna, who believed that he was the hated chief of the III/F counter-espionage department at Pullach.

The story got even more confusing, but Gehlen believed it. Felfe used "Operation Uranus" to pay several visits to East Berlin; there he conferred with his masters, who over caviare and champagne celebrated with him the excellent progress of his great deception. The operation dragged on for almost two years; eventually Felfe produced at Pullach genuine samples of Aue uranium, which his KGB friends had obligingly provided. All this time Gehlen was sending long reports to Chancellor Adenauer and Dr. Globke; he had also informed Allen Dulles. So pleased were CIA chiefs about the samples, which were fairly divided for analysis between German government laboratories and CIA, that as a mark of his gratitude Allen Dulles sent Gehlen an invitation to Washington; this was Gehlen's only journey abroad after the war.

Whilst Felfe was keeping Gehlen and the Americans happy and collecting kudos for himself, he was working very hard at his real job—passing information to the KGB. The amount of information and the number of Western agents—Gehlen's, American, British and French—that Felfe delivered to KGB will never be known with any certainty. At his trial it was stated that in the ten-year period of his work for the "Org" and BND he had passed at least fifteen thousand microfilm exposures to the KGB, each representing a secret document. These included several important operational plans made at Pullach, Gehlen's directives to branch managers, reports from V-men and their evaluations, as well as lists of agents with their code names, locations, cover stories and efficiency ratings. Obviously, Felfe also gave the KGB all relevant details of the counter-espionage plans and activities of his own III/F department.

Besides sending over the microfilmed material, Felfe had been using tape-recorders at his country residence at Oberaue. At his trial he admitted that he had passed to the Russians "thirty hours of tapes of the spoken word", containing reports he had made into his micro-phones. Both Felfe and Clemens had been supplied with A-3 radio transmitters which they frequently used for direct communications with the KGB Karlshorst headquarters. Felfe stated at his trial that he had met his KGB contacts "on less than twenty occasions"; Clemens confessed that he made "more than forty trips for such purposes", meeting KGB officials in Berlin, Vienna and Salzburg and during holidays in Switzerland and Italy.

Tiebel, their chief courier, regularly shuttled between the Federal Republic and East Germany; he could do this easily enough as an official Pullach courier. The Russians had given him a small suitcase with a built-in secret compartment, inside which was a panel to conceal twenty microfilm rolls and two tape recorders. On his journeys Tiebel removed the panel on reaching a car park near milestone 107 between the border checkpoint of Helmstedt and Magdeburg and put it into a TBK drop. The panel was then collected by a KGB courier and when Tiebel arrived in Berlin another courier handed the panel back to him.

Naturally, no evidence was given at Felfe's trial or in official press releases afterwards of the repercussions of the traitors' activities upon the Gehlen Organisation. A former BND official told me three years later that he estimated that ninety-five agents had been betrayed. The fact is that many of Gehlen's networks and cells in East Germany were destroyed and that a number of V-men in Poland and Czechoslovakia and a few inside the Soviet Union were also caught. The KGB proceeded with their "liquidation" step by step so as not to jeopardize Felfe's position. Once the trio had been unmasked and arrested, the communists began a general round-up of the men and women Felfe and Clemens had exposed. A few were able to escape to West Berlin, some succeeded in going into hiding; but most were captured.

Gehlen had suffered grievous losses. About three years prior to the discovery of Felfe's treachery, Gehlen began to suspect that there was a traitor inside his headquarters. Some carefully planned operations had gone wrong; several of his best HV-men had been caught, and it had become obvious that the East German HVA had obtained knowledge of a number of "safe houses" and drops. One of BND's HV-men Gross, had had a narrow escape after he took a tin labelled "Champignons" (mushrooms) to V-man Kindermann. It contained an American RS-6 miniature radio transmitter, the latest type supplied by CIA and given only to very trusted agents. The V-man was arrested the next day and at his trial the new transmitter was displayed. The V-man had been working for Gehlen since 1956, producing valuable economic intelligence on such things as East German exports of potash and chemicals to the Soviet Union, and also to Britain, Norway and Finland, and on East German imports of raw materials and steel. The Pullach files also contained more than four hundred reports from this V-man on the arrivals and departures of cargo boats in East German harbours. Several other V-agents, including Alfred and Elfriede Rader, Tietz, Schoenwetter, Quehl, Krause and Speckmann were "burnt"; safe houses to which V-men resident in East Germany used to be taken for sandwich courses in W/T instruction were discovered, and on the Autobahn Nuremberg-Berlin eleven TBK's were seized by the East German SSD.

The regularity with which these painful discoveries were made pointed to a traitor in one of the Pullach departments, but no suspicion fell upon Felfe. Indeed, in 1960, Gehlen arranged a small party in his office to celebrate the tenth anniversary of Felfe's service for the "Org" and the BND. In the presence of the departmental chiefs he presented the traitor with a silver plaque showing a carving of Saint George killing the dragon—representing the KGB—surrounded by a wreath of German oak leaves and inscribed *Für Treue Dienste*, "For Loyal Service".[8] The Russians gave Felfe a more mundane gift to celebrate his long and loyal service to the KGB—a present of twenty thousand Marks.

Operation Waxworks

For a long time Gehlen had been worried about the inexplicable successes of communist counter-espionage and he decided to set an elaborate trap for the traitor. He turned to Felfe, as the chief of his III/F counter-espionage department, to devise it. The idea was to put up a Pullach officer, or a senior agent connected with headquarters, as a "defector". He was to approach the East German HVA and, equipped with sufficiently credible *Spielmaterial*, to convince the communist espionage chiefs of his probity. Gehlen hoped that in the course of time this pseudo-defector would be able to find out who was HVA's informer in Pullach.

Gehlen named the scheme "Operation Panopticum". In German *panopticum* means waxworks of the Madame Tussaud variety; the *agent provocateur* was to be the dummy in this game. The most difficult part of the operation was to find a man whose motives for defection would appear plausible, and who was, moreover, a man of some standing at Pullach. Only thus could the communist espionage chiefs be expected to accept him as genuine.

Felfe produced just the sort of man Gehlen had in mind—none other than ex-SS Standartenfuhrer Friedrich Panzinger. After having worked in Pullach Panzinger had been dismissed when the "Org" became the BND and Gehlen had to rid himself of at least some of the most notorious former Gestapo men. After this he had done occasional freelance work and was eking out a living as a commercial salesman. He felt bitter about his removal from the BND but when Felfe offered him the new assignment, he took it eagerly; Felfe promised him a much higher reward than his previous salary. Panzinger was not unknown to the KGB chiefs. They knew that he and his RSHA colleague SS Obersturmbannfuhrer Koppkow had been instrumental in smashing the "Red Orchestra" in 1942 and in arresting its chiefs, Arvid Harnack and Harro Schulze-Boysen, and 118 of its members, most of whom ended on the scaffold. Panzinger had had the misfortune to be captured by the Russians during the last month of the war, having been ordered to exchange his comfortable chair at the RSHA for the command of a hurriedly assembled unit of SS and Gestapo office-workers sent to the battlefront on the Oder. In the Soviet prison camp he had made up to his captors; indeed David Dallin, the American expert on Soviet espionage, has expressed the opinion that "Panzinger . . . went over to the East".[9] In any case he was not treated as a war criminal and, although he was kept in prison for several years, he was eventually released and returned to Germany where he finally joined the "Org". It is quite possible that he had also been doing occasional work for KGB after his dismissal.

This then was the "dummy" for "Operation Waxworks". Felfe had, of course, informed his KGB masters of all its details. The Russians must have been highly amused at the choice of Panzinger as the pseudo-defector and they treated him accordingly. He brought them the *Spielmaterial* from Pullach and they gave him some nicely prepared information and faked documents to plant on Gehlen, but the whole enterprise—though it went on for more than a year—finally petered out. The material brought back by Panzinger was soon recognised for what it was. Although Felfe pretended to be enthusiastic about it, Gehlen's evaluators reported that it was an obvious plant; the chief of the Pullach security group, Major-General Wolfgang Langkau, urgently advised Gehlen to discontinue the operation; he also expressed his serious doubts about Felfe's conduct.

Felfe got wind of this and decided to get rid of Panzinger lest his own double game with the KGB might be discovered. He denounced the ex-SS leader to the German prosecutor investigating war crimes against Jews and, of course anonymously, sent evidence of Panzinger's actions during his service with RSHA, which the SS man had hitherto succeeded in concealing. Panzinger was arrested and committed suicide in his prison cell.

But Felfe's luck was running out. He had become smug, and confident of his safety he began to disregard security precautions.

XXIII

Arrest Gehlen!

The crunch came in the late summer of 1961, when Felfe was still preparing a follow-up to "Operation Waxworks" after the Panzinger scheme had misfired. He had suggested to Gehlen that another BND officer should be groomed as an impostor to be planted on the Karlshorst KGB chiefs. Felfe devised this new operation, of course, in full accord with his Soviet paymasters. They were only too eager to convey misleading information to Pullach in this way. But by this time a series of dramatic events was unrolling which was to lead to Felfe's downfall.

In June 1961 the head of the East German HVA's American section, Captain Gunther Maennel, defected to the West. His arrival at a CIA station was shrouded in the utmost secrecy for several weeks whilst he was "de-briefed" at Camp King near Frankfurt on Main. There were weighty reasons for the Americans' desire to keep HVA's chief, Major-General Marcus Wolf, in the dark about Maennel's disappearance from his office. Not only had Maennel brought explosive material with him, he had in fact been a CIA double agent for at least a year prior to his defection. He had been "turned round" by a Gehlen agent who resided in East Berlin and whose most important assignment, given to him by the CIA station head in Germany, Henry Pleasants, was to find a HVA official prepared to supply information whilst remaining at his post. Maennel had accepted this extremely perilous job after receiving a substantial bounty—reputedly twenty thousand dollars—and the promise that he would be pulled out and brought to the West should his situation become too precarious.

For a year or more Maennel provided valuable information but, it seems, he kept back some of his most important knowledge until his eventual flight to the West. At Camp King he produced evidence that a US Air Force officer, Captain Joseph P. Kauffman, had been supplying the HVA with information on American radar installations and Air Force establishments since 1960. He told of several secret visits Kauffman had paid to East Berlin on which he had met KGB and Soviet Air Force officers. Even after Kauffman's transfer to the US Air Force base at Sonderstroem in Greenland he had continued to send information, which included details of radar installations in the far north and on the American U-2 "spy planes" which took off from Greenland and Norwegian bases for reconnaissance flights over the Soviet Union. Maennel also told of another American, Harold N. Borger, who after leaving the army had set up as a businessman in Nuremberg, whence he conducted espionage for the East Germans and Russians.

He kept unpacking more startling revelations: there were two traitors at the Federal ministry of defence, both deeply involved in NATO Intelligence, who had for several years been passing information to the Soviet and East German espionage organisations. One was Colonel Carl-Otto von Hinckeldey, once a general staff officer at Hitler's OKW and now head of a department of the defence ministry; he had been given "cosmic clearance" by the Americans and was allowed access to all NATO documents exchanged between Bonn, Brussels, Washington and London. The other was Dr. Peter Fuhrmann, head of a counter-espionage section of MAD, the Federal military intelligence, and formerly chief assistant to Lieutenant-General Horst Wessel. A third Soviet agent, Major-General Karl Feuchtinger, a wartime Waffen SS officer, had been working with Colonel von Hinckeldey but had died a few months before Maennel's defection.

So flabbergasted were CIA operators and CIC officers by this information that at first they paid hardly any attention to Maennel's other disclosures. Among these other items was the revelation that there was a Soviet double agent at the BND headquarters at Pullach, whose real name Maennel did not know, but whose description and code name of "Paul" he was able to give. Maennel also told how one of his colleagues, Captain Armin Grosz, had in 1958 and 1959 set up a network in London, where he had worked with another agent, Eric Hills, alias "Halter", in the guise of trade mission officials and had been in contact with Lonsdale and Peter and Helen Kroger. (After the arrests of the Portland naval base spies in January 1961, both Grosz and Hills returned safely to East Berlin.)

Naturally, the Americans were preoccupied with the cases which most directly affected themselves. Captain Kauffman was arrested at Castle air force base in California, flown to Germany and confronted with Maennel. He made a qualified confession, and was eventually tried by a US court martial at Wiesbaden and sentenced to twenty years' imprisonment.[1] Borger was also arrested; both trials took place in April and May 1962 and the confrontations of the prisoners with Maennel before the trials were arranged with the greatest

The defector Günther Maennel and his East German identity card. He gave away several communist agents in West Germany, the United States and Britain.

(*Right*) The defector Lt.-Colonel Siegfried Dombrowski who helped to unmask the communist spy Horst Ludwig in Britain.

tape recording "bug" inside a square signet ring.

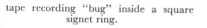

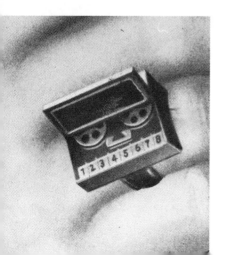

(*Left*) Hermann Kastner, East Germany's deputy Prime Minister, who betrayed cabinet secrets to Gehlen. (*Right*) Colonel Adolf Wicht, head of Gehlen's Hamburg branch, was arrested in the affair of *Der Spiegel*. (*Bottom left*) Colonel Heinz, head of German military intelligence, whom Gehlen ousted. (*Bottom right*) Sigurd Krumins, an agent landed from a British boat in Soviet Latvia.

secrecy. Meanwhile the gist of Maennel's depositions was communicated to the Federal government in Bonn. The British secret service was informed, rather belatedly, of Maennel's disclosures about the London spy ring. Colonel von Hinckeldey was taken into custody in Bonn, as was Dr. Peter Fuhrmann, but their arrests were at first kept secret. In due course Gehlen was informed of the mysterious "Paul", alleged to be at Pullach, but it took several weeks before the Americans eventually provided a description of this man.

Fuhrmann's case was a human tragedy; it revealed the sordid methods used by the communists to ensnare traitors. He was a lawyer and had been public prosecutor in West Berlin, where he became involved in several trials of Soviet and East German spies in the 1950s. Later he became head of the legal department of the Federal army command at Hanover and was subsequently promoted to high office at the ministry of defence in Bonn, with the rank of a higher government counsellor. In 1954, Fuhrmann, a married man and father of three children, became infatuated with a young woman. His mistress became pregnant and he persuaded her to have an illegal abortion for which he paid five hundred Marks. It seems probable that the love affair was arranged by communist agents and that the girl was their stool-pigeon. Within a week of the abortion a visitor arrived at the public prosecutor's house at Uhland Strasse in the Berlin suburb of Wilmersdorf. Fuhrmann was not at home and the stranger told Mrs. Gisela Fuhrmann that he was her husband's cousin, Helmut Weise, from East Berlin. He hinted at some very serious matters in which Fuhrmann was involved. Thus the long blackmail ordeal began.[2]

Asked by his cousin to meet some Soviet agents, Fuhrmann went to Hohenschönhausen, where he was introduced to KGB Colonel Balabanov. He was told that he was expected to supply secret information and that, in order to get the required materials, he should apply for a post at the defence ministry. If he disobeyed the West Berlin police would be told of the abortion; as an accessory he would face up to five years' imprisonment, as well as the ruin of his professional career, a public scandal and, most probably, the end of his marriage. Fuhrmann had hardly any choice.

He applied for transfer to the ministry of defence, which at that time was assembling its personnel. For the next seven years, during which he rose to positions of high authority in the ministry, he conducted his treacherous activities under the constant threat of being denounced for his old offence. Rarely had blackmail paid so handsome a dividend to the KGB.

The Cyanic Acid Murders

By October 1961 Gehlen and General Langkau, who was in charge of Pullach's security group, had a series of secret conferences. Gehlen had received the description of the mysterious "Paul" who, Maennel had stated, was the Soviet double agent at BND headquarters. Gehlen had little doubt that the description fitted one of his most trusted men: Higher Government Counsellor Heinz Paul Johann Felfe, head of the counter-espionage department and recipient of the Silver Plaque for loyal service.

It seems that Gehlen refused to believe this at first; if it were true this would be the most painful blow he had suffered in his long career as a spy-master. He had always prided himself on being a good judge of men and he could hardly bring himself to accept that he had been so disastrously deceived by Felfe over a period of many years. He realised that if Felfe were a traitor and this became public knowledge his own reputation would be irretrievably ruined. Yet he had to apprehend the traitor. He ordered Langkau to arrange for Felfe to be kept under round-the-clock surveillance.

Whilst Langkau's security men were trailing Felfe, intercepting his mail and watching his country house, another event took place that finally sealed his fate. On July 13, about a month after Maennel's defection and before Gehlen had received the description of "Paul" from CIA, a man and a woman came to the office of the West Berlin CID. The man produced papers in the name of Josef Lehmann and said the woman was his wife Inge, née Pohl, whom he had married in East Berlin a year before. He also asserted that his real name was Bogden Stashinsky and that he was a Ukrainian born in 1931 in a village near Lvov. Since 1951 he had been an agent of the KGB, and in 1955 he had infiltrated the Ukrainian anti-communist OUN in West Berlin.

After all this had been taken down by the policeman, Lehmann-Stashinsky made a startling deposition. He said that on October 10, 1957, he had killed Lev Rebet, one of the Ukrainian leaders, in the entrance to the offices of the newspaper *Ukrainski Samostnik* in Munich by firing from a gas pistol a phial containing five cc. of hydro-cyanic acid into Rebet's face. He then calmly added that two years later, October 15, 1959, he had murdered the leader of OUN, Stefan Bandera, in exactly the same manner. His KGB superiors had ordered him to return to Moscow from East Berlin, but he was afraid that he would have to carry out yet more of such assignments and had decided to give himself up.[3]

The German policemen who listened to this fantastic story believed not one word of it. They realised that the man was an East

European, probably a Ukrainian, and that his papers in the name of Lehmann were false. They knew of the sudden deaths of Rebet and Bandera in Munich, but in both cases investigations had resulted in a verdict of death by natural causes, though under strange circumstances. Rebet had been found lifeless in the entrance hall of his office in Munich's Karlsplatz, still clutching an attaché case. The doctors stated that he had died of heart failure. Bandera, the Ukrainian leader who had worked for the British SIS, then during the war for the nazis, and afterwards again for the British Secret Service and CIA in Germany, was found dead in front of the door of his apartment in Zeppelin Strasse in Munich. In his case protracted investigations were carried out, since it was accepted that he might have been murdered; but no injury of any kind was found, nor was poisoning established, and the pathologists pronounced death from natural causes, namely heart failure.

Stashinsky demanded to be handed over to American Intelligence and the German police chiefs gladly obliged. Investigations were conducted for several weeks by American CIC and Special Investigation Branch officers who distrusted Stashinsky's incredible confessions and suspected him of being a Soviet *agent provocateur*. Eventually he was handed over to the German police and BfV officers began to check his descriptions of his movements in 1957 and 1959; they found them to be accurate. Stashinsky also produced various documents including a diploma of the award of the Order of the Red Banner which, he said, he had been given for the murder of Bandera. Entries in his handwriting were found in the register of the Hotel Stachus in Munich where he had stayed before killing Lev Rebet, and he produced a broken key the wrenched part of which was found still embedded in the lock of the door of Bandera's apartment. He gave the investigators a description of the murder weapons, which catapulted glass phials filled with cyanic acid; he told them how he had swallowed anti-poison capsules, given him in Moscow, in order to immunise the effect of the deadly vapour by which his victims were killed. Experts confirmed that hydro-cyanic acid could cause immediate death if squirted at the victim's mouth and nostrils, and that after paralysing the heart it would leave no trace.

The investigations were conducted with the greatest secrecy and no announcement of Stashinsky's arrest and confessions was made. Early in October, however, a BfV official telephoned Felfe at Pullach, informing him of the amazing case and asking for his advice on some aspects of the prisoner's statements about KGB officials in Moscow who, Stashinsky said, had given him the instructions and the murder weapons. Felfe immediately informed the Karlshorst KGB office of Stashinsky's arrest and the progress of the investigations in Munich and Bonn. The Russians began preparations for a propaganda counter-offensive. On October 13, two days after the Federal ministry of the interior issued the first official announcement about the strange murders to which Stashinsky had confessed, the press officer of Prime Minister Grotewohl called a press conference in East Berlin to which West Berlin journalists and correspondents of American, British and other foreign newspapers were invited.

"Gehlen Ordered The Murders"

At the conference a former Gehlen agent, Stefan Lippolz, was produced. He was a German, he said, born in 1907 at Staraya Alexandrovska in Volhynia in Russia. In 1939 he had come to Germany, where he fought in Hitler's army and, because of his knowledge of the Russian language, was eventually posted to Schellenberg's *Militaramt* and became a liaison officer to the Vlassov Army. After the war he lived for a time in East Germany, then went to West Berlin and eventually joined the Gehlen Organisation, where he was ordered to recruit Ukrainians and Byelorussians for training as parachutists to be infiltrated into the Soviet Union. He told at length of his work for the "Org", and of how he became the landlord of the *Stephansklause Inn* in Munich, one of Gehlen's many "fronts" and the meeting place of the "Org's" agents and V-men. His superiors at Pullach were Roman Henlinger, formerly with Himmler's RSHA, and Jaroslav Sulima, á Ukrainian who was in charge of training the parachutists.

Lippolz stated that Gehlen had watched Bandera's activities on behalf of the British Secret Intelligence Service with misgivings. In 1956, Bandera and two of his aides, Vaskovich and Benzal, were training Ukrainian agents whom the British intended to infiltrate into the Soviet Union by the way of Austria. Gehlen, according to Lippolz, wanted to foil the British plans, for he regarded them as dangerous competition to his own activities for CIA. Lippolz was ordered to approach Bandera's two lieutenants and persuade them to relinquish their work for the SIS and join Gehlen's newly established BND; they were offered twice the pay they were receiving from the British.

In January 1957 an official from Pullach, whom Lippolz named as "Dr. Weber", met him in Munich and told him that Bandera must be "liquidated". Once the Ukrainian leader was out of the way, his aides could easily be persuaded to work for Gehlen. The Pullach official then offered Lippolz twenty thousand Marks for killing Bandera; they had several meetings and a plan was prepared to poison

340

him. He took his meals in the canteen at the office at 67 Zeppelin Strasse and Lippolz was given poison to put into his soup or a drink. The Pullach official gave him a fake passport in the name of Karl Lipnitzki and told him that immediately after completing the assignment he could go to Austria, where Gehlen's agents would look after him.[4]

Lippolz stated at the press conference that he had not been able to go through with the murder of Bandera, with whom his relations were friendly. Moreover, knowing of several killings amongst the members of rival factions, he was afraid that he might be discovered and become the victim of the vengeance of Bandera's supporters. Using the passport "Dr. Weber" had given him, he went to Austria and then to Italy. In Austria he heard from some Ukrainians opposed to Bandera that "the Gehlen people had hired another would-be assassin, one Dmitri Miskiv". In October 1959 he heard of Bandera's sudden death and realised that he must have been murdered by a hired assassin. He travelled across Europe to Norway and eventually, in 1961, decided to go to East Germany and ask for political asylum, although he had never been a communist; he had arrived in East Berlin a few weeks before the Stashinsky case was revealed in Bonn and had regarded it as his duty to inform the East German authorities of what he knew of Gehlen's efforts to "liquidate" Bandera two years earlier. Stashinsky's confession that he was a Soviet agent "was a tissue of lies contrived by the American CIA and Gehlen; he was a member of UPA and had been hired by Gehlen to dispose of the undesirable Ukrainian leader". There was not much factual evidence to support these enormous allegations. Nor was any better evidence supplied by another ex-Gehlen agent, Otto Freitag, who had also defected and was exhibited at a second press conference. The publication of their stories was conveniently timed to exonerate the KGB chiefs from the two murders and, at the same time, to discredit Gehlen and the CIA.[5]

Felfe probably had a hand in producing the two defectors. Certainly he was busily supplying the communists with material in order to keep the anti-Gehlen propaganda campaign going. During those weeks he exchanged frequent radio signals with Karlshorst, but by then he was under close surveillance. On October 27 a KGB radio signal to Felfe was intercepted by Gehlen's monitoring service at Stocking. It read: "Urgently require advice whether unmasking action against Gehlen should continue".

On November 6 the accumulated evidence against Felfe had become overwhelming. Gehlen had to take the unpalatable decision to order Felfe's arrest and risk a scandal of major proportions. On that morning Felfe was asked to come to General Langkau's office.

He came with a black attaché case which he put on Langkau's desk. During the discussion an official entered the room and gave Langkau yet another intercepted radio message and a note to the effect that during a search of Felfe's country house more damning evidence had been found. Langkau called in three officers and told Felfe that he was under arrest. He then took the attaché case and opened it. Inside were fourteen microfilms of secret Pullach documents and a tape he had prepared to forward to Karlshorst. It speaks for the nerve of this traitor that he took this material to his interview with Langkau, being confident that he would talk himself out of any suspicion Langkau might voice.

In the raid on his home were found three radio transmitters, more microfilms and tape recordings, and a mass of papers which left no doubt of his treachery. Clemens and Tiebel were also arrested and protracted interrogations of them began at Pullach. At first the arrests were kept secret and when they were eventually announced it was merely said that "two officials and a businessman were taken into custody under suspicion of treasonable activities on behalf of a foreign Power". Even when their names were later released their positions with the BND were not mentioned. Eventually, newspaper reporters got hold of the real story, but no details were forthcoming about the true extent of the trio's activities.

Messages To The KGB From Prison

The three men were transferred to the prison at Karlsruhe to await trial before the Federal Supreme Court. Gehlen took care that the trial should be postponed as long as possible. Meanwhile Felfe enjoyed agreeable privileges in prison. He shared a cell with Jurgen Ziebel, once a millionaire and "king" of the German delicatessen trade, who was facing trial for fraudulent bankruptcy. The two became great friends; despite his bankruptcy, money was no object to Ziebel. Exquisite bedding, carpets, crockery and cutlery were taken to the cell from Ziebel's home; meals were brought for the two remand prisoners from Karlsruhe's best restaurants. The two men spent their time playing chess.

German prisoners are put to "productive work" rather than sewing bags. At the Karlsruhe prison the inmates wrapped and addressed magazines for a local printing firm, and Felfe and Ziebel were put in charge of this work. It was quite easy for Felfe to address a few more labels to cover addresses and insert coded messages into the magazines. He was also allowed to write to his mother in Dresden. For many months he smuggled out messages to his KGB bosses keeping them informed of the progress of his interrogations, asking them to prepare a plan for his escape and, finally, when his spirits flagged, for a poison pill to be smuggled into the prison to enable him to commit suicide.

Only belatedly, after a released prisoner apparently envious of Felfe's special privileges informed the police of how the magazines were being used for getting out secret messages, was Felfe's game discovered. The East German regime, on KGB instructions, exerted all the political pressure at its disposal on the Bonn government in the hope that Felfe's trial would be abandoned. In East Berlin a mock trial was staged of Dr. Globke, Gehlen's immediate superior at Adenauer's Chancellery, on charges that he had between 1933 and 1945 committed crimes against humanity as an official of Goebbels' propaganda ministry, and that he was guilty of the deaths of millions of Jews. The charges against Globke filled 210 pages of allegations almost as sensational as those at the Eichmann trial, which took place at that time in Israel. Globke's trial was, of course, *in absentia*—he was securely sitting in his Bonn office—but it produced a great deal of compromising material.

At another East Berlin press conference in April 1962, the communists produced yet a further defector from the Gehlen Organisation, Ossip Werhun, a former officer in Skorzeny's *Jagdkommando*, who had worked with Gehlen during the war and afterwards became one of the "Org's" executives. He also accused Gehlen, repeating the charges that Stashinsky was an *agent provocateur* hired by Pullach, without producing any tangible evidence for it.

Stashinsky's trial began on October 8, 1962. He repeated his confession to the two murders and told of his long service with KGB. He was given a surprisingly lenient sentence of eight years' imprisonment and his pre-trial custody of fifteen months was deducted from the term he was to serve. This only produced more rumours that not everything was above board in this case. On September 24, 1962, the case of one of Felfe's minor accomplices, the hapless ex-state prosecutor Dr. Peter Fuhrmann, was disposed of, the trial taking place almost entirely behind locked doors. Fuhrmann was sentenced to ten years, the court accepting in mitigation his ordeal by blackmail.

But there was still no sign of judicial *dénouement* in the Felfe case. At last, after several postponements and one and a half years after their arrests, Felfe, Clemens and Tiebel were put on trial on July 8, 1963. Immediately after the reading of the indictment the court went into secret session; press reporters and the public were prohibited from attending until three days later. A cavalcade of long-faced Pullach officials, identified only by initials, passed through the court room as prosecution witnesses, but Gehlen was not among them. During his cross-examination in open session Felfe replied in monosyllables, but did not deny his treachery. He said his motives were ideological, he had come to the conclusion that Gehlen's alliance with the American CIA was "not in the interest of the German people" and that Adenauer's policy hindered the reunification of Germany.

When asked about his previous work for British Intelligence and the fact that, despite his service in the SS and Himmler's RSHA, he had been "de-nazified" and received the classification "uninvolved", he stated that this was done on the demand of British Intelligence officers, a remark that prompted the presiding judge to a loud exclamation of *"Donnerwetter!"* Light relief was provided by Clemens who frankly declared that his only motive in betraying the secrets to the Russians was "to make money". When the judge referred to his past as the "Terror of Pischen" and the "Tiger of Como", Clemens replied with a broad grin: "Yeah, I've never been a softy." He said that he was paid only eight hundred Marks a month by Pullach and got four times as much from the Russians, "plus handsome expenses". Telling of his meetings with KGB officials he said that they were really generous fellows and that "champagne flowed at our meetings". Felfe, as a higher government counsellor, received a BND salary of 1,680 Marks (then about £160) a month and he admitted to having received large payments from the Russians, which enabled him to acquire his country estate.

The prosecutor described the accused as the "most dangerous and unscrupulous traitors who have ever stood in a German dock", and said they had betrayed "very many agents and almost destroyed the entire system of German Intelligence". He asked the court to make an example of them. But shorter sentences than those demanded were eventually imposed. Felfe was sent to prison for fourteen years, Clemens for ten, and Tiebel, who played a pathetic role in the conspiracy, escaped with the lenient sentence of three years, his pre-trial custody of eighteen months being taken into account.

The trial caused a political furore in the Federal Republic, even though only a very small part of Felfe's activities had been disclosed. The sharpest attacks in the Press were directed against Gehlen. Leading newspapers, such as the *Süddeutsche Zeitung*, the *Frankfurter Rundschau* and *Die Zeit* asked how it was possible that former Gestapo men could occupy high positions in the German Intelligence Service, and they demanded Gehlen's dismissal. There was turmoil in parliament, where Opposition spokesmen echoed this demand. Gehlen had a worrying time and, at one moment it seemed that he would have to tender his resignation. But his old friend Dr. Globke hurried to his assistance. Adenauer's Chancellery announced that "only one per cent of *Bundesnachrichtendienst* employees were former members of the old SD of the Hitler regime, that they were experts difficult to replace, and that none of them occupied executive positions"—all of which was blatant untruth. Earlier Adenauer had tried to placate parliament and public opinion by creating, after the pattern of the United States National Security Council, a cabinet office, the *Bundes-Sicherheitsrat*, under a prominent Christian Democrat politician, Dr. Heinrich Krone, who had been imprisoned under the nazi regime. Krone, with the rank of minister, was to supervise BND and the other intelligence services and to initiate reforms.

Arrest Gehlen!

Even before the Felfe trial Gehlen had become one of the main figures in a great political scandal. With the trial coming up and expecting a bad press, he had searched for allies in the newspaper world. He had always been unpopular with editors and reporters, since he had prevented them from getting any stories from Pullach. In 1962 the leading German news magazine *Der Spiegel* was conducting a campaign against the minister of defence, the ebullient Herr Franz-Josef Strauss. After earlier accusations of corruption, the journal continued the attack on political grounds. For different reasons Gehlen was also at loggerheads with Strauss, who had greatly increased the scope of the military intelligence department at his ministry and resented Gehlen's interference. Strauss' animosity towards Gehlen was heartily reciprocated by the BND chief; on the other hand it also influenced Gehlen's relations with his former close assistants, Major-General Gerhard Wessel and Colonel Josef Selmayr, who had become chiefs of departments in Strauss' defence ministry. It was said that Wessel aspired to succeed Gehlen at Pullach and the situation in 1962 was such that he had every chance of doing so.

Gehlen sent the head of his Hamburg "branch". Colonel Adolf Wicht, to a secret meeting with the *Spiegel* editors, during which Wicht offered them information which could be used for an attack on Strauss. On October 10, 1962, the magazine published an article which exposed Strauss' policy in connection with the demand for atomic weapons. Some of the material used could be interpreted as being classified and emanating from secret government sources. After the article was published, Strauss alerted the BfV and the police. The proprietor of *Der Spiegel*, Rudolf Augstein, and several of his editors and managers were arrested on charges of treason. The offices of the magazine were raided by the police and lorry-loads of documents were seized and driven away. This police action was taken by Strauss

345

over the heads of the ministers of the interior and of justice. For a fortnight there were protracted negotiations to "localise" the affair. But Strauss was determined to destroy all his enemies at a stroke.

During the night of October 26/27 several ministers assembled at Adenauer's office. Strauss had demanded that Gehlen be summoned to explain how the secret documents had reached *Der Spiegel* through Colonel Wicht, who had already been arrested. Gehlen waited in another room while Strauss harangued the eighty-two-year-old Adenauer. He insisted that Gehlen was "an accomplice to the State treason" committed by Wicht and the magazine editors and must be arrested and charged. As leader of the Bavarian Christian Socialist Party which provided the chancellor with his majority in parliament, Strauss could exercise very strong political pressure. Adenauer, whose Christian Democrat Party had suffered serious setbacks in the general election in 1961, was hardly in a position to stand up to Strauss, who was, in addition, well known for his forceful volubility and rough manners.

Suddenly Adenauer turned to the minister of justice, Dr. Stammberger, and said: "Arrest Gehlen. We must get to the bottom of this intrigue." Stammberger replied that there was no legal evidence for the arrest of the head of the German Intelligence Service on a charge of treason and refused to accept the order. Nevertheless Gehlen was kept all night in a room at the Chancellery, with police detectives guarding the door.[6]

The outcome of the *Spiegel* affair was very different from what Strauss had expected. The five ministers who belonged to the Free Democrat Party, including the minister of justice, resigned, refusing to serve on with Strauss. All the arrested journalists were eventually released and the charges withdrawn. Ultimately Strauss himself was forced to resign; he has never since held a cabinet office. The *Spiegel* affair and, a few months later, the Felfe trial were contributory factors to Adenauer's downfall. A year after the abortive arrest of Gehlen and a few months after the Felfe trial Adenauer resigned; with him went Dr. Globke.[7]

Gehlen never fully recovered from the humiliation; he had also come to realise that his former friends Wessel and Selmayr had turned against him. His overlordship of the intelligence services had ended in *débâcle*. With the arrival of Dr. Ludwig Erhardt, the man who had accomplished the "economic miracle" of Germany's prosperity, as Adenauer's successor, his position as president of the BND was in jeopardy. Erhardt made no secret of the fact that he "despised the dirty game of espionage", and one of his first actions after he entered the Palais Schamumburg in Bonn was to order that the few BND officials who were Gehlen's liaison officers to the

Chancellery and occupied three rooms in the building should be "immediately removed". Dr. Erhardt was quoted as saying: "I could not stay with those fellows under the same roof!" His next actions were to make drastic cuts in the BND budget and to set up a commission to examine the whole structure of the Gehlen Organisation.

There is little doubt that Erhardt intended to retire Gehlen; but he was advised that there was no one who could replace him at that critical period. Germany's relations with her eastern neighbours had reached a dangerous point after the erection of the Berlin Wall. The international situation was extremely tense after the *débâcle* of the Paris Summit, culminating in the Cuban missile crisis; a month after Erhardt became chancellor, President Kennedy was assassinated. Erhardt's main reason for leaving Gehlen at his post was that the new defence minister, Kai-Uwe von Hassel, a former Abwehr officer, had told him that NATO Intelligence still relied to a large extent on information from Pullach and assured the new chancellor that Gehlen "would behave himself in the future".

The most resilient of men, Gehlen remained true to his family motto "Never give up". But for the first time in his long career he began to leave many day-to-day matters to his deputies, Worgitzky and Wendland, who got on better than he with ministry officials and the chiefs of the other intelligence services. About the cuts in the BND budget he was not particularly worried. Much earlier, when he was still Adenauer's "beloved general" and had the help of Dr. Globke, he had already made arrangements to tap other sources of finance. Leading banks and insurance companies, heavy industry concerns, steel and armaments corporations, shipbuilders, car manufacturers and large commercial firms were discreetly contributing funds. Gehlen had learnt this method of financing a government secret service by private enterprise from his friend Allen Dulles.

By the early 1960s, having weathered the storms which had nearly swept him away, with younger men at Pullach looking over his shoulder and waiting impatiently for his retirement, with his friend Dulles gone after the Bay of Pigs *débâcle* and with a chancellor who loved him not at all—Gehlen was still confidently looking forward to many years of busy activity.

XXIV

Global Alignment

Germany—and the *Bundesnachrichtendienst*—had progressed a long way since the early days of the Gehlen "Org", built from the rubble of the defeated, enemy-occupied, half-starved Third Reich. Now, in the 1960's, she enjoyed greater prosperity than any other nation in Western Europe; her industry was booming, her trade had expanded to every corner of the world and her currency was the envy of most other countries, plagued by recurrent economic crises. She also possessed the largest army of all European members of NATO.

Gehlen's role as the magician of the Cold War had greatly changed. Prompted by the growing disagreement with China, Khrushchev had stepped up his overtures to the West. After his visit with Bulganin to London he was the first Soviet prime minister to go to Washington. The honeymoon ended abruptly when, after the U-2 incident, Khrushchev broke up the Paris Summit meeting; nor was his appearance at the United Nations General Assembly in September 1960 conducive to a lasting *rapprochement*[1] and President Kennedy described his meeting with the Soviet chairman in June 1961 in Vienna as "sombre". Khrushchev's demand for the conclusion of a peace treaty with Germany, which would invoke the recognition of the East German regime by the West and thus put a stop to hopes for a German reunification, and above all his insistence on "transforming West Berlin into a demilitarized free city" was rejected by the Western Powers. Then came the erection of the Berlin Wall. It gave Gehlen another and the final opportunity for stepping up his activities against East Germany.

During the months after the erection of the Wall many human tragedies occurred in Berlin. People risked their lives by digging tunnels, by jumping from the Wall, or by running across through the few border checkpoints, with VOPO-men firing salvos after them. Once again organisations which had been conducting their private war against the East German authorities sprang into frantic activity in West Berlin. There existed several such "terrorist" groups which Gehlen had supported until the Federal German government had

348

ordered their dissolution in 1960 following a series of captures of their members and embarrassing trials in East Germany.

One of the oldest was the "KgU"—*Kampf gegen Unmenschlichkeit* (Fight against Inhumanity). Its founder was a young Berlin lawyer, Rainer Hildebrandt. Its members used to sneak into East Germany to guide escapees across the border or search for kidnap victims. Many on their own admission went there in order to carry out sabotage actions; quite a few had been employed as V-men by Gehlen. For years the East German ministry for state security was almost powerless to prevent or stop these terrorist actions, to which the KgU leaders proudly confessed. The communist authorities accused KgU members of having "poisoned wells, added soap and chalk to powdered milk stored for use in schools and hospitals", and of having poisoned cattle in the fields, and spread germs of hog-cholera (*bacillus suipestifer*) on farms, caused train derailments and committed innumerable crimes of arson and bomb outrages. Whilst some of the accusations were propaganda, others were valid and admitted by KgU and other groups.

Their members blew up the railway bridge at Erkner near Berlin just before the "Blue Express" for Warsaw and Moscow passed over it; the train, carrying Soviet officials and troops, narrowly escaped catastrophe. On other occasions a tunnel near Durrenbach and a railway bridge outside Weimar were blown up, a power station at Eberwalde was destroyed, several goods trains were derailed, and the radio station at Wusterhausen badly damaged by arson. The KgU and other groups, such as those led by Detlef Girrmann and Fritz Wagner—mainly composed of students of the West Berlin Free University—also conducted a skilful propaganda campaign by smuggling millions of anti-communist leaflets into East Germany. One of their devices particularly angered the East German rulers. On every bright spring and summer day tens of thousands of balloons were released, each bunch carrying a small parcel of leaflets which fluttered into towns and villages.

Over the years many millions of these balloons had floated across the border, despite repeated sharp protests by the Soviet military commandant in West Berlin and the Soviet ambassador in Bonn. It was no secret that the groups—at least as far as their propaganda activities were concerned—received generous finance from CIA, from Gehlen, and from various anti-communist and patriotic organisation in the Federal Republic.

Gehlen had maintained contact with the "terrorists" for a number of years. They provided him with many intelligent and daring V-men, but above all he had been impressed by the excellent propaganda material the KgU produced. They printed huge quantities of a

349

news-sheet, *Tarantel*, and a periodical, *Kleiner Telegraph*, which they smuggled into East Berlin and East Germany despite all the efforts of the DDR police to prevent it. In the early 1960s Gehlen eventually broke off regular contact with these groups because of the confessions of several members who had been captured and tried in East German courts. They were accused of murder, arson, and causing explosions whereby ordinary, innocent people, including women and children, were killed or maimed for life. Several of these terrorists, including Johann Burianek, Hans Muller, Gerhard Benkowitz and Hans-Dietrich Kogel were sentenced to death and hanged; many more were sent to prison for life or for terms of up to fifteen years' hard labour. Some admitted to having worked for Gehlen's BND.

When Dr. Erhardt became chancellor in succession to Adenauer he explicitly forbade Gehlen to have any truck with the terror groups, which were declared illegal. It was, of course, inadmissible for a government department such as the *Bundesnachrichtendienst* to support, finance, or encourage activities which endangered the lives of Germans who had the misfortune to live under communist rule. Gehlen accepted the Bonn order but, as we shall see, he later used some of the seasoned terrorists to help Pullach in its campaign against Algerian arms traffic. Above all, he made a take-over bid for the balloon propaganda enterprise. Pullach produced the leaflets and Gehlen made a deal—apparently behind the back of the Bonn government—with the Psychological Defence department of the Bundeswehr whereby the balloons were to be launched by soldiers from sites used by the army to send up weather balloons. Between 1961 and 1965 more than one hundred million leaflets were dispatched by balloons towards the East from three launching sites by Bundeswehr units from Münster and Ulm, trained at a special camp of the Psychological Defence department at Castle Alfter under the command of Colonel Trentzsch.

But times were rapidly changing. After Khrushchev's climb-down over the Cuban missile crisis, Moscow and Washington were on speaking terms again; another major step in the direction of a detente between East and West was made when in August 1963 the Great Powers signed the Nuclear Test Ban Treaty. The coalition government in Bonn, in which the Social Democratic leader and former West Berlin mayor, Willi Brandt, had become the foreign minister, was trying to attain some sort of coexistence with the communist-ruled "other Germany". This was not achieved until 1970, when after the Social Democrats formed their own government Brandt visited eastern capitals and exchanged visits with the DDR Prime Minister Willy Stoph. Eventually, the improvement in the relations between the two

German states made possible the agreement to ease movement between East and West Berlin which was signed in September 1971.

Global Orientation

Much earlier the long battle of wits which Gehlen had been conducting during the years of the Cold War had been replaced by a more subdued struggle of attrition. His old enemy Wollweber had long since disappeared; there was no armistice in espionage, however, and communist spies roaming West Germany were as numerous as ever. But Pullach's system· of V-men infiltration had been drastically curtailed. The photographic super-cameras of the "spy planes" and the electronic eyes of space satellites girdling the earth had in many ways rendered obsolete the laborious gathering of often piffling information on military camps, airfields and rocket launches by wretched V-men of doubtful reliability.

Gehlen and his even more "globally oriented" deputies, Worgitzky and Wendland, had found new inspiration meddling in the affairs of many nations. More and more "residencies" were established abroad. Hand in hand with German salesmen travelling the world came Pullach's agents; not infrequently they were identical. An elaborate radio communication system was constructed at Pullach and the receiving stations outside Munich and Frankfurt were extensively modernised. Masses of material were hoarded at the famous archives which were of hardly any use to the Bonn government. Indeed, Gehlen had begun to embark upon enterprises which were distinctly embarrassing and even damaging to the Federal cabinet. There were whispers amongst his assistants that "the chief" was getting old and growing even more eccentric. After the departure of his old friend Allen Dulles, they said, Gehlen had succumbed to a kind of megalomania, believing that he was running a second CIA.

True, some of the results of this new global espionage by BND were of value to NATO. Reports from far-flung "residents" told of the arrival of Chinese "advisers" in some East African republic or of Russian arms supplied to Vietnam, but such information was being gathered on a much larger scale by CIA and the British Secret Service and its relevance to problems directly concerning the Federal German Republic was extremely slight. It was said at Pullach that the intelligence produced there which was of interest to NATO formed a proportion of seventy per cent of the output, while less than one third was of use to the Bonn government.[2]

Some of Gehlen's old German colleagues at NATO headquarters were, of course, pleased to show off to the American, British and West European officers what a German Intelligence service could achieve. One wonders how much of this secret information which

351

Gehlen sent first to these German officers before officially conveying it to NATO's Intelligence Department, was seen by Admiral Hermann Luedke, who in 1968 committed suicide on the eve of his arrest as a suspected Soviet spy.

Gehlen's "global activities" did not, of course, begin over night. Some of his most fantastic involvements were in the Middle East and went back to the mid-1950's.

Friend of Egypt and Israel

When the British government decided to contract out of Egypt the United States, having taken on the thankless task of the world's policeman, moved in. In 1951 Allen Dulles had sent one of his leading Middle East experts to Cairo, Kermit "Kim" Roosevelt, a grandson of President "Teddy", the Rough Rider. Kim Roosevelt had already accomplished difficult assignments in Syria and Iran.[3] From Cairo he reported that King Farouk's situation was hopeless and, with Dulles' approval, he opened secret negotiations with the Free Officers Committee, led by a charming young colonel named Gamal Abdul Nasser, with whom he had "found a large area of agreement".[4] After "Black Saturday" in January 1952, when rioters went on the rampage in Cairo and Farouk was forced to abdicate, Nasser and Roosevelt agreed that the revolution should be carried out by easy stages. Farouk's infant son was proclaimed king, only to be replaced by the republic under the figurehead General Neguib. Within a year Colonel Nasser was in power.

Washington regarded him ·as a valuable ally, who would keep communism and the Russians out of the Middle East. At first everything seemed to go according to CIA's plans; Nasser's first measure was to suppress the Communist Party in Egypt and to imprison all its leaders. The grateful American government poured forty million dollars a year into Egypt's economy, which had been ruined by Farouk's extravagance and his ministers' corruption. Allen Dulles sent Nasser a "personal gift"—from President Eisenhower's unvouchered funds—of three million dollars, which Kim Roosevelt's colleague, Miles Copeland, conveyed to Nasser's secretary in two suitcases.[5] Next Nasser asked Roosevelt to help him reorganise Egypt's military intelligence and secret service in order to buttress his personal power. Political considerations meant that official employment of US officers and CIA agents by the Egyptian government was out of the question, however. Thus it came about that Dulles approached Gehlen for assistance.

At that time Gehlen was absorbed in his struggle with Wollweber, who had taken charge of the East German ministry for state security after the Berlin uprising. Nevertheless he obliged his friend by

352

recruiting a "military mission" of former officers of Hitler's army and the SS. This mission was dispatched to Egypt under ex-Waffen SS General Wilhelm Farnbacher; in time it grew to two hundred officers.

Besides the military mission, however, Nasser needed men to organise his secret service, directing espionage and training saboteurs against Israel, and also to advise on the surveillance of his many enemies inside Egypt, such as the powerful Moslem Brotherhood. Again his American advisers turned to Gehlen, asking him to recommend someone qualified to take on the task. During the secret negotiations which followed Gehlen thought at one stage of sending one of his own experts from Pullach; he had several men who had conducted espionage against the British during the war in Libya, Egypt and Iran. But he could not realistically spare one of sufficiently high rank to impress Nasser. He therefore suggested his old colleague, ex-SS Sturmbannfuhrer Otto Skorzeny of *Zeppelin* fame to take on the assignment in Egypt. After the war Skorzeny had spent three years in American captivity in Germany as a suspected war criminal; he had been released in July 1948, and was living in Spain, where he had established a prosperous engineering business. He was reluctant to accept; for one thing the Egyptians offered little financial inducement. He was promised that CIA would top up his salary from Nasser; Dulles and Gehlen also approached Skorzeny's father-in-law, Dr. Hjalmar Schacht, once Hitler's "financial wizard" who, after his acquittal at Nuremberg and the quashing of his eight years' sentence under the de-nazification laws, had become president of a bank in Düsseldorf. So, besieged from so many sides, Herr Skorzeny graciously agreed, on the condition that his stay in Cairo should be limited.

Skorzeny worked in Egypt for about a year and then left Nasser's secret service in the good hands of other SS and Gestapo men. He had recruited about fifty, of whom some had to be summoned from Argentina, Brazil, Paraguay and Spain, where they had found a safe haven from Allied prosecution as war criminals. Amongst his assistants was a high official of Goebbels' propaganda ministry and Himmler's RSHA, Franz Buensch; an "expert" on Jewish matters, he had worked with Eichmann on the "final solution" during the war, and had written a book entitled *Sexual Habits of the Jews* which was probably the most viciously pornographic document ever produced by the nazis.

These German intelligencers in Cairo looked to Gehlen for advice and he appointed a liaison officer to them, whom he sent from Germany. He was a bird of the same feather as they: an ex-SS officer and deputy Reich-leader of the Hitler Youth, Hermann Lauterbacher. The German-led Egyptian secret service achieved little against Israel, but it managed to foment much mischief in several Arab countries at that time strongly opposed to Nasser. This is not the place to enlarge on the complex intrigues which bedevilled the Middle East in the 1950s and which culminated in the Suez Crisis. It suffices to note that the Egyptian secret service engaged in subversion and intrigue in no fewer than six Arab countries during this period.[6]

After the Suez Crisis and Nasser's *volte-face* towards Moscow, relations between the United States and Egypt rapidly reached breaking point. Many CIA agents were withdrawn, American assistance ceased and, although the German agents remained, Gehlen washed his hands of the Egyptian secret service. Not that BND relinquished its interest in the Middle East. On the contrary, Gehlen established several residencies—the Pullach term for its foreign branches, equivalent to CIA's "stations"—in Arab capitals. In 1958 Gehlen was involved with some of Nasser's enemies, such as King Saud of Saudi Arabia, whose secret service he modernised and equipped with a radio communication system. For this the king gave him a jewel-encrusted sword, in addition to the agreed fees paid to Gehlen's emissaries.

To the Cairo residency of BND Gehlen sent one of his senior officers, thirty-five-year-old Gerhard Bauch, the stepson of Gehlen's vice-president, Major-General Hans-Heinrich Worgitzky. Bauch lived in Cairo under the cover of a representative of the Quandt Corporation, the German heavy industry concern. At Damascus the BND resident was ex-SS Hauptsturmfuhrer Alois Brunner, alias Georg Fischer, who posed as a director of the German-Syrian trading company OTRACO. Brunner later joined Buensch in Cairo; they were old colleagues, for they had both worked under Eichmann at the RSHA "Jewish department".

As Nasser became increasingly involved with Moscow, Gehlen's sympathy turned to Israel. Although he had employed in the past, and was still using in the 1960s, many rabid nazis, Gehlen himself had not been an anti-semite. His career had hardly ever brought him into contact with Jews and he certainly numbered none amongst his acquaintances. Like many middle-aged "good Germans" today he would say he knew nothing, or hardly anything, about the atrocities committed by the nazis; and like many of these Germans he felt occasional twinges of conscience about those terrible happenings. After the Suez war in 1956 he expressed his admiration for the amazing feats of the Israeli Army; his professional interest had been aroused too, by the efficiency of Israel's intelligence service. Though created by amateurs, it had soon proved itself far superior to anything that the Egyptians could muster even under the guidance of their German mercenaries.

Above all, by 1960, Gehlen had come to share CIA's belief that Israel was now a vital bulwark against Moscow's expansionist policy in the Middle East. Whenever and wherever communism appeared on the scene Gehlen saw red. The presence of Soviet advisers, military instructors and technicians in Egypt alone sufficed to predispose him in favour of lending a helpful hand to the Jewish state.

Through CIA agents in Jerusalem the chiefs of *Shin Beth*,[7] the Israeli National Security Office which also controls *Sheruth Modiin*, the military intelligence department, learnt of Gehlen's attitude, and in 1960 they secretly approached him with a strange suggestion. At that time *Shin Beth* had just suffered a painful setback: a high official of the defence ministry, Colonel Israel Baer, had been unmasked as a Soviet spy and sentenced to ten years' imprisonment. Baer had worked with Soviet agents in Egypt, and *Shin Beth* was anxious to follow up the trail. But a number of Jews had shortly before been arrested and executed in Cairo on charges of spying, and Israeli Intelligence was finding it increasingly difficult to infiltrate agents into Egypt.

The Pseudo-officer of Rommel's Army

The chiefs of *Shin Beth* suggested to Gehlen that one of their agents should be planted on the Egyptian authorities in the guise of a German, and an ex-Abwehr officer at that. Some of Gehlen's former superiors of the general staff would have rotated in their graves had they heard of such an impudent suggestion. Yet Gehlen immediately agreed, though making one condition: he should himself select the man from a list of candidates which the Israelis were to submit, and his chosen candidate should be trained at Pullach before embarking on his assignment. Thus the deal was clinched.

The man Gehlen approved was Major Ze'ev Lotz, the son of an "Aryan" German father and a Jewish mother, with whom he had emigrated to Israel in 1933 soon after Hitler had come to power. Born in 1921 in Mannheim and educated in German schools until he was thirteen, Lotz was a big, fair-haired man, having inherited from his father all the racial attributes which the nazis had most approved. Also, and perhaps this contributed something to Gehlen's favourable opinion of him, Lotz was an excellent horseman. During the Second World War he had fought in the British Palestine Legion composed of Jewish volunteers, serving for some time under the command of the British Major Aubrey Eban (born in Cardiff and now the Israeli foreign minister). Later transferred to the British Army, Lotz had spent four years in Egypt and spoke fluent Arabic. He later joined the Israeli Army and served as an intelligence officer during the Suez War in 1956. In the intervening years he had paid several visits to Germany, where some of his relatives lived.

He arrived in West Berlin as Wolfgang Lotz, an escapee from East Germany—this was arranged with the help of Gehlen's V-men—and went through the usual refugee procedure at the Marienfeld reception camp; he was then taken to Munich where he received instruction from Gehlen's training officers. An elaborate plan had been devised to equip Lotz with a cast-iron cover story. He was given a complete set of documents purporting to show that he had fought in Libya during the war as a lieutenant in the 15th Panzer Division of Rommel's Africa Corps. Gehlen arranged for Lotz' briefing by two former officers of that division and he memorised many stories, including one of how he had escaped after the New Zealanders captured General von Ravenstein at Tobruk in November 1941.

Early in 1961 Lotz was ready for his Cairo assignment; he arrived there well provided with money by *Shin Beth*. He was warmly welcomed by the German colony after he had dropped hints to the effect that he had spent many years abroad because of his Hitler Youth and nazi past, and had made a fortune in business in Austria. Soon he became a popular member of the Gezira Sporting Club, where on one occasion he met a former officer of Rommel's Africa Corps face to face. Lotz must have been an accomplished actor, for he stood his ground without a tremor. He told his new friends that he would turn his hobby into a business and establish a riding school. He bought several horses and his school, situated near an army depot at Heliopolis, soon flourished. Many Egyptian officers and members of Nasser's entourage became his pupils. Nobody found it strange that Herr Lotz had several radio transmitters and cameras—he explained that photography was his second favourite hobby and he liked to listen to German programmes. The charming and wealthy German had the engaging habit of sending crates of champagne to Egyptian officers whom he had met at parties.[8]

For four years Lotz and his attractive blonde German wife (with the Wagnerian first name of Waldtrude) lived in Cairo as a respected and well-liked couple. It has never been established whether the lady, whom he had brought with him from Germany, was also in the game and, perhaps, attached to him by courtesy of his Pullach instructors. All this time he was relaying reports to Jerusalem and Tel Aviv on a miniature transmitter. He gave his real compatriots invaluable information, establishing, for instance, that the first Egyptian emplacements of Soviet rockets in Sinai were not an immediate menace, since their guidance systems were still unreliable. His greatest exploit was to ascertain that the Shaloufa rocket site near

356

the Great Bitter Lake on the Suez Canal, manned by Soviet technicians, was at that time the only one which presented a real danger, for its range could reach all major cities in Israel.

One of Lotz' closest friends was General Fuad Osman, deputy chief of Egypt's military intelligence (since executed). He used to take Lotz with him on inspections of military establishments. Lotz was producing for *Shin Beth* a constant flow of intelligence of Egypt's military preparations and defences. He felt quite safe and had enlisted several Egyptians and two Moroccans as assistants. He became acquainted with Gehlen's "resident" Gerhard Bauch, and struck up a friendship with Alois Brunner and the German rocket expert, Dr. Adolf Pilz. Brunner used to boast about his wartime service with Eichmann, whose trial in Israel had been a regular topic of conversation among the Germans in Cairo. Pilz, too, made no bones about his loathing of Jews. This must have been too much for Lotz.[9]

On September 13, 1964, Brunner received a parcel at his home near the Ezbekye Park; when he unwrapped it a bomb exploded and he was killed. A few days later a parcel arrived at Dr. Pilz' villa; it was opened by his secretary and the explosives blinded her. No suspicion fell on Lotz. In February 1965 the East German Prime Minister, Walter Ulbricht, was due to pay a State visit to Nasser. By then Egypt, very much under Soviet influence, had concluded treaties with most of the Warsaw Pact countries and was receiving armament supplies from East Germany and Czechoslovakia.

The former nazis were still working for the Egyptian authorities and Police Minister Zaharia Mohieddin was worried that some of them might be planning some violent action against the leader of communist Germany. As a routine measure, therefore, the police visited the homes of several prominent West Germans. When they came to Lotz' villa in Heliopolis—he was absent from his home—they found after a perfunctory search a whole espionage armoury—three powerful transmitters, code pads, microfilms, files full of cyphered notes and all. Lotz was arrested the next morning, February 22, 1965, on his return from a visit to Suez. At the same time several Germans known to be his friends were held, including Gerhard Bauch, the representative of the Messerschmitt Aircraft Company, Franz Kiesow, and others quite uninvolved in Lotz' clandestine activities.

Lotz was put through rough interrogations, but even under torture he stuck to his "legend", admitting that he had worked for the Israeli intelligence service but insisting that he was a German and not a Jew. He claimed that Israeli agents in Austria had blackmailed him by threatening to disclose his nazi past and alleged war crimes. This was

357

believed and saved his life, in combination with one convincing detail: he was uncircumcised.

After his arrest Bauch firmly denied, probably truthfully, that he knew anything of Lotz' spying, but the Egyptians were convinced that he was an accomplice. Gehlen became greatly alarmed; the whole conspiracy was in danger of being exposed and causing a world scandal. Moreover, General Worgitzky was extremely angry with him, accusing him of having jeopardised the life of his stepson. He went to Cairo several times, doing a lot of explaining about Bauch and the other arrested Germans. Eventually, Worgitzky succeeded in having Bauch released; but the usefulness of Gehlen's "resident" had, of course, come to an end.

Lotz was sentenced to twenty-five years' imprisonment. Several of his accomplices and also a number of Egyptian officers, including Lt.-Colonel Abdel Rahman, a former military attaché in Beirut, were sentenced to death and executed. Kiesow was acquitted and expelled, as were several other Germans, including ex-nazi officers of Lotz' circle. Then came the Six-Day War in 1967. Its aftermath brought a purge within the Egyptian Army. Amongst one hundred and fifty officers tried for treason were many of Lotz' former friends. Field-Marshal Amer, who had been a frequent guest at Lotz' lavish parties, committed suicide under mysterious circumstances. A year later the Israeli government offered an exchange of prisoners. There were few Israelis in Egyptian hands, but many thousands of Egyptians including a score of generals were held in prisoner of war camps in Israel. First Frau Waldtrude Lotz was quietly exchanged, and then at the end of 1968, Lotz himself was freed in return for nine Egyptian generals and four thousand officers and men. He had served only three years of his sentence. He now lives happily in Tel Aviv; he has resumed his good Jewish name of Ze'ev and has been promoted colonel and awarded Israel's highest decoration for valour.

The affair had a series of repercussions at Pullach. Worgitzky openly accused Gehlen of deception; he had never been told of the Lotz deal with the Israeli Intelligence. After his return to Germany Gerhard Bauch resigned from BND and a few months later General Worgitzky also left Pullach. The ordeal had shattered his health; he had two heart attacks, and he died on December 13, 1969. The whole affair had engendered much animosity amongst Gehlen's staff.

For and Against de Gaulle

For another of the many strange affairs Gehlen never tired of engineering we must go back several years. The reciprocal admiration of the two Grand Old Men, Adenauer and General de Gaulle, led to a close cooperation between Gehlen and French Secret Service,

A rare photograph of General Gehlen taken unawares when he met an informer.
He looks the perfect spy-master, complete with slouch hat and dark glasses.

Lieutenant-General Gerhard Wessel, for ten years Gehlen's closest assistant and deputy at the wartime FHO department and then at Pullach. He succeeded Gehlen in 1968. In contrast to his former chief, Wessel is a gregarious and voluble man.

which began soon after de Gaulle returned to power in 1958. The Algerian fight for independence had exploded into open revolt against the French in the late 1950s, when the leaders of the Algerian FLN set up a "government in exile" in Cairo. The insurgents faced not only four hundred thousand French troops in Algeria but the *colons*, the French settlers determined to keep their economic rule of the colony and to destroy the liberation movement.

The Algerian leaders sent emissaries to Europe to buy arms for their guerilla forces. Most of their small arms supplies came from Germany or were shipped in small vessels from German ports. Officially the Bonn government had prohibited this clandestine arms traffic, but some German authorities connived at it; it was good business for German manufacturers, traders and shippers. The *colons*, with the assistance of the French Secret Service, set up a secret organisation which became known as the "Red Hand". Its avowed aim was to kill Algerian leaders in exile, dispose of their arms buyers and suppliers and blow up their stores and ships before they left port. Between 1957 and 1960 a large number of such murders and sabotage acts were carried out, mainly in Germany. How far Pullach was involved in it will never be ascertained, but it is a fact that amongst the mercenaries of the "Red Hand" were men who had previously been V-men of the Gehlen Organisation or members of some of the anti-communist terrorist groups. Gehlen might have explained the involvement of these men by saying that they were fighting communism, even though most of the Algerian nationalist leaders at that time were strongly opposed to it.

Much to the alarm of the Bonn government and the German police many cities became the scene of killings and outrages perpetrated by the "Red Hand". Hamburg, from where many arms shipments were made, became the "Red Hand's" main target. Bombs exploded in the warehouses of firms known to supply the Algerian nationalists; one of the German manufacturers, Otto Schlutter, narrowly escaped three attempts of assassination; his mother was killed and his daughter badly wounded in one of the bomb outrages. The cargo boat *Atlas*, loaded with arms in crates marked as motorcar spares, was blown sky high in the port. In Frankfurt, Munich and Bayreuth several Algerian exiles were murdered.

The French had found succour in Germany for several years in their fight against Algerian nationalists. But Gehlen turned against General de Gaulle after he executed a *volte-face* and offered independence to the Algerians. He regarded de Gaulle's decision as opening the door to communism in North Africa; ultimately Gehlen was right, for the present-day Algerian government of Colonel Boumedienne is undoubtedly under communist sway. Thus Gehlen sided with the French generals who staged the revolt against the French President. Gehlen was in full accord with the politicians such as Georges Bidault and Jacques Soustelle who had turned against de Gaulle and supported the OAS organisation, aimed at preventing the independence of Algeria. When Bidault and Soustelle and other OAS sought refuge in Germany from arrest by the French police, Gehlen advised Chancellor Kiesinger that there was no reason for refusing their request.

Gehlen had close contacts with the leaders of the anti-Gaullist rebellion. One June 15, 1961, General Raoul Salan had a secret meeting with Gehlen at a villa in Schwabing, used by BND for clandestine purposes. Earlier he had already met General Maurice Challe, the chief author of the generals' Putsch in Algiers. Two other OAS leaders, Joseph Ortiz and Pierre Lagaillarde, accused in Paris of having been involved in several attempts at the assassination of General de Gaulle also found a refuge in Germany—with Gehlen's help, according to subsequent disclosures in French newspapers. In supporting the OAS activities and protecting its fugitive leaders Gehlen had acted in direct opposition to Adenauer's avowed policy, which supported de Gaulle. An explanation for Gehlen's attitude was advanced in the French Press: General Salan and his fellow-conspirators had assured Gehlen that, after ousting de Gaulle, a military dictatorship in France under their leadership would offer West Germany important political and economic concessions. The French generals and the big business and finance tycoons who backed them regarded de Gaulle's attitude to the trade unions and left-wing movements as too conciliatory. France was plagued by recurrent strikes and riots; if de Gaulle failed there was, in their opinion, a real danger of a communist revolution. This must have been Gehlen's main reason for supporting the OAS. Eventually, de Gaulle made peace with the generals. Gehlen, however, continued to make sure that he received secret information from Paris.

When the question of his continuation in office was still being discussed by Chancellor Kiesinger and his social democratic coalition partners during the winter of 1967-8, another affair in which Gehlen was deeply involved burst into the newspaper headlines: a high official at the French ministry of the interior was arrested, accused of being an agent of a foreign power. He was sixty-one-year-old Maurice Picard, a former chief of the ministry's secret security department and later its civil defence director. At first it was believed that he had supplied information to Soviet agents, although he was known for his extreme right-wing views. Soon afterwards Paris newspapers revealed that the "foreign power" in question was the German Federal Republic and that Picard had been working for Gehlen for at least

Gehlen's house at Berg on Lake Starnberg, which he purchased in 1956 with money he received as a gift from CIA director Allen Dulles. (*Below*) Enjoying a swim in the lake after his retirement.

(*Left*) This picture was distributed during the past few years as that of Gehlen. He, however, denies in his memoirs that it represents him.

(*Below left*) General Gerhard Wessel as the new President of the *Bundesnachrichtendienst*.

(*Below right*) Dieter Bloetz, a former Social Democratic Party official, appointed vice-president in 1970.

eight years; indeed, he may already have been connected with Pullach when the disclosures of Gehlen's spying on Germany's allies were made in 1958.* What was even more disturbing was that Picard had been a "Pétainist" and had collaborated with the nazis during the war. In 1945 he succeeded in exonerating himself and eventually reached high rank in the government service.

The Picard affair ultimately sealed Gehlen's fate. Discussions were still going on in Bonn during the winter of 1967-8 whether Gehlen should continue in office for another year. One reason for the deferment of the retirement of the sixty-five-year-old BND president was that a feud had broken out amongst his senior officers at Pullach. Gehlen had recommended as his successor Major-General Wendland, but he had encountered strong opposition to his nominee. The majority of the Pullach officers wanted Lieutenant-General Gerhard Wessel, who had been strongly critical of Gehlen's strange adventures ever since leaving the "Org" to become Gehlen's chief competitor as head of the military intelligence department. Kiesinger's Social Democratic coalition partners, on the other hand, demanded a clean sweep at Pullach and the appointment of a government official of the younger generation, untainted by any nazi past. In this dilemma, Chancellor Kiesinger was inclined to leave Gehlen at his post until the general elections in 1970, which he hoped to win; this would have rid him of the uneasy coalition with the Social Democrats. The Picard affair changed all this and Gehlen was asked to retire in the spring of 1968, before the trial in Paris. Picard was sentenced to seven years' imprisonment in October 1968.

The Last Exploit

Assailed from every quarter, let down by his own colleagues with some of whom he had worked for nearly a quarter of a century, Gehlen remained true to his family motto of "never giving up".

His very last exploit was to predict in March 1968 that Moscow was determined to have a show-down with the "liberal" Dubcek regime in Prague. Gehlen still had his secret sources of information inside the Soviet Union. His reports to the Bonn Chancellery were, however, regarded with reluctance bordering on suspicion. The Social Democratic foreign minister, Willi Brandt, who had been waiting impatiently for Gehlen's departure, suspected that Gehlen's final effort was merely a product of the spy-master's obsessive hatred of Moscow. There was also the justified suspicion in Bonn that Gehlen was trying by this scare report to persuade the government to leave

*See page 303

him at his post. Gehlen then communicated his information to NATO, stating that Leonid Brezhnev was determined to use armed force in order to restore "hard-line" communism in Czechoslovakia. But this report received as little serious consideration at the NATO council in Brussels as it had in Bonn.

When a few months later Gehlen's warning proved uncannily correct and the Soviet tanks rolled into Prague, he was hurriedly summoned to Bonn, where NATO chiefs had arrived to confer with German ministers and military commanders about possible counter-measures. German, American and British troops were put on the alert and sent to the German-Czechoslovak frontier. By that time Gehlen, however reluctantly, had to agree that nothing could be done to save Czechoslovakia. Had his warning been taken more seriously at an earlier stage, a strong *démarche* by the Western Powers in Moscow, combined with a NATO alert, might, perhaps, have deterred the Soviet leaders from taking the decision to break the Dubcek regime by an invasion, or at least have raised doubts in their minds. Faced with the Soviet *fait accompli* the Western Powers at first did nothing and their subsequent protests to Moscow from the NATO council and through the United Nations only aroused the derision of the communist leaders.

Right to the very last day at Pullach Gehlen was still pursuing his own policy, caring little for the official line Bonn and its socialist foreign minister chose to adopt. An East German writer[11] took the trouble to trace the activities of BND during the final years of Gehlen's rule at Pullach. His table lists twenty European, nine African, seven Asian and five American countries where Gehlen pursued secret operations of one kind or another without the knowledge or approval of his government. Even if this evaluation is taken with a grain of salt, the facts of the arrests, trials and expulsions of Gehlen's "residents" and agents in these forty-one foreign countries are accurate. Indeed, more agents of the Gehlen Organisation got into trouble all the world over than did agents of the United States, Britain, France and other NATO members put together. German agents were expelled from seventeen countries during 1967-8, and the record for being an undesirable alien is undoubtedly held by Gehlen's agent Burkhard Funke, deported from Uganda after having been expelled in turn from Kenya, Tanzania and Zambia.

Gehlen even set up a number of "cells" in the United States. As early as 1963 the Senate Foreign Relations committee discussed the activities of the Julius Klein public relations company, which had established branches in Washington, New York and Los Angeles and also in Canada, employing a fairly numerous staff without apparently

Boating on Lake Starnberg with his youngest daughter.

(*Below*) Gehlen's last will, drawn up by the notary Otto Erhardt in Frankfurt on June 20, 1952 when the KGB and the East German Ministry for State Security offered a prize of 100,000 dollars for his assassination.

Gemeinschaftliches Teſtament **Erbvertrag vom** 20. Juni 1952				(Vom Standesamt auszufüllen)
Kom. Reg. 149 1952 des Notars Dr. Otto Erhardt in Frankfurt a.M.				Nr. 3461
Familienname des Erblaſſers: G e h l e n Bei Frauen auch Geburtsname aus früheren Ehen Vornamen: Reinhard Kräftig unterstreichen				
Geburtsangaben	Tag 3. Monat 4. Jahr 1902	Gemeinde Erfurt Straße und Nr. Verwaltungsbezirk Erfurt nur bei kleineren Orten	Stadtteil nur bei größeren Orten	Standesamt Register-Nr. 688 02
Stand (Beruf)		(bei Frauen:) Stand (Beruf) des Ehemannes Generalmajor		
Wohnort (mit Straße und Hausnummer)	B e r g b. Starnberg Obb. Nr. 68			Staatsangehörigkeit deutsch
Des Vaters Vor- und Familienname:	Walther Gehlen			
Der Mutter Vor- und Geburtsname: nur bei Sammelnamen angeben	Katharine geb. v. Kaernawyk			
(Vom Standesamt auszufüllen:) Sterbefallanzeige abgesandt an				am

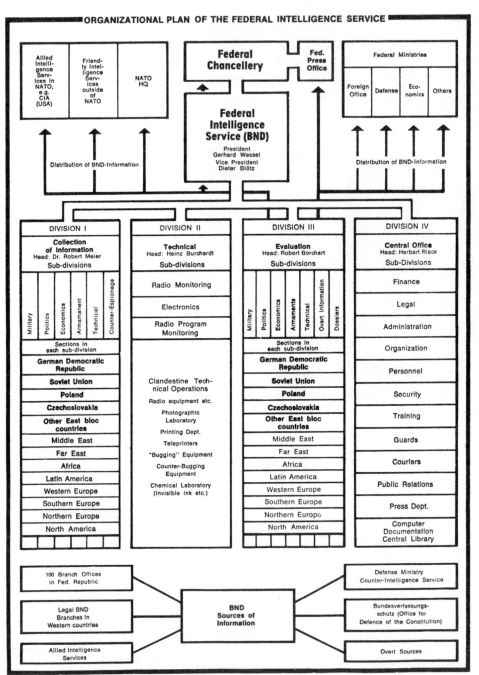

ORGANIZATIONAL PLAN OF THE FEDERAL INTELLIGENCE SERVICE

From *German Politics*

engaging on any publicity business. From this firm the trail led to the Association of American Citizens of German Origin, which was receiving large subsidies from an unspecified Federal German government department—the *Bundesnachrichtendienst*, it was later established. This foreign subsidy amounted to the handsome sum of 280,000 dollars in 1964 and was increased in later years. At first the FBI suspected that the firm and the association were clandestine East German "fronts" but then they discovered that they were run and financed by the secret service of a friendly NATO country.

The explanation Gehlen willingly gave to J. Edgar Hoover was that these organisations were engaged on "supervising German business-men, tourists and, particularly, students and officers of the Bundes-wehr sent to America for studies or specialised military and air force training". The FBI happily closed its file on this subject. Not so satisfactory at first were the explanations of Gehlen's connections with the large organisations of Ukrainians, Poles, Lithuanians, Latvians and other East European immigrants in the United States, which received finance and advice from three "registered" BND agents—Roman Henlinger, alias "Dr. Grau", Victor Salemann and Alexander Wieber. The American authorities were, however, pacified when they were told that from these organisations V-men were being recruited to be infiltrated into the communist orbit. Whatever Gehlen's "global" activities, he never entirely abandoned the time-honoured system of sending his V-men across the eastern frontiers. In recent years show trials have become rare in the Soviet Union; those of Penkovsky and Wynne, and of Gerald Brooke, were exceptions rather than the rule. Instead, captured spies are tried in secret and quietly rendered harmless. In Leningrad in 1967 four of Gehlen's agents were sentenced to terms ranging up to fifteen years; they included Ignati Ogutsov, described as a specialist in Tibetan studies. Usually it is only on the occasions of spy exchanges, which regularly take place between West Germany and East Germany and the Soviet Union, that one learns of Pullach spies caught and imprisoned in the East. Nearly all these cases go back two or three years, when Gehlen was still holding the reins of BND.

After Gehlen's retirement in May 1968 the *Bundesnachrich-tendienst* was gradually reorganised by his successor, General Gerhard Wessel, whose appointment Gehlen had failed to prevent. When the Social Democrats and their Liberal coalition partners took over the government after the 1970 election, another sweep followed at Pullach. Almost without exception the former SS and Gestapo men were eliminated; several officials of the Social Democrat Party were put into high posts, such as Herr Dieter Bloetz, forty-year-old manager of the party's Hamburg office, who was appointed vice-president to General Wessel. All the heads of Pullach's groups were also replaced; the most important Group I, concerned with the collection of intelligence and in control of all "residencies" and agents, was put under Dr. Richard Meier, hitherto head of the counter-espionage department of the Office for the Protection of the Constitution. The administrative group, which controls training, communications, security, and also Gehlen's famous archives, was put under another social democrat, a former director of the Hamburg higher education authority. The most interesting appointment was that of Herr Robert Borchardt as head of Group III, Evaluation of Intelligence. As a young man before the war he had studied botany and, although according to nazi racial laws he was half-Jewish, he was called up for service in Hitler's army, given a commission and awarded the Iron Cross for gallantry in the campaign in Russia. After the end of the war he became a journalist on a Munich newspaper and later an official in the foreign ministry, serving as press attaché at the embassy in Washington and finally becoming head of the press section of the foreign ministry in Bonn.

Gehlen must have swallowed hard when he heard of the men who had succeeded his old guard of former Abwehr and SS colleagues. For three years following his retirement he observed a Trappist's silence, rarely leaving his villa for a swim in the lake or a visit to a concert in Munich. He had almost fallen into oblivion when suddenly, in the autumn of 1971, a German publisher announced that he had acquired the world rights of General Gehlen's memoirs and offered the translation rights, as it were, for auction.

A short while later it was announced that an American publisher had offered one million dollars for the world right. What had made Gehlen change his vow that his memoirs would not be published before twenty-five years after his death was obviously the tempting offer of a fortune. Another reason might have been that after his retirement articles appeared in German newspapers and magazines containing strong criticism of his past activities. Perhaps he felt that he ought to produce a reply. One wonders whether he achieved this purpose. His memoirs are remarkable by the paucity of detail and total absence of documentation.

All his life Reinhard Gehlen had found his inspiration in the dark corridors of intrigue and subversion. The spying game with all its sordid aspects was his element. It is doubtful if he ever thought much about transcendental values and democratic freedoms. But it is difficult not to feel at least grudging admiration for the single-mindedness and shrewdness of this grey, secret man behind the scenes, whose motive force was his almost paranoic hatred of communism.

Whether we like it or not, Western democracy must be prepared in times of danger to accept such strange allies as Reinhard Gehlen in its defence against totalitarianism.

Notes

The main documentary sources are mentioned in DOCUMEN-
TATION AND SELECT BIBLIOGRAPHY on p. 384 Abbreviations
used in NOTES below: Documents of the *Trial of Major War
Criminals before the International Military Tribunals at Nuremburg*:
IMT, followed by the number of volume and page; documents of
Trials of War Criminals: TWC, with numbers of volume and page;
quotations from *Nazi Conspiracy and Aggressions*, 1946: NCA, with
numbers of volume and page; quotations from *Documents on
German Foreign Policy, 1918-1945*: DGFP, with numbers of volume
and page.

Chapter I: SPY OF THE CENTURY

[1] Blackstock, P.W., *The Secret Road to World War II: Soviet versus Western Intelligence*, Chicago, Quadrangle, 1939, p.330.
[2] Cf. Ransom, H.H., *The Intelligence Establishment*, Cambridge, Mass., Harvard U.P., pp.13,235f.
[3] Frank G. Wisner, first assistant director of the Office of Policy Co-ordination, later and until 1962 deputy director for plans and operations and, at one time, head of the CIA London station. He shot himself in 1965.
[4] In an article in the *Washington Post* on December 22, 1963.
[5] Truman, H.S., *Memoirs*, Vol. I, *Year of Decision*, New York Doubleday, 1955, p.226.
[6] President Kennedy's "Report to the Nation" delivered from the White House by television and radio on July 25, 1961.
[7] In 1919 Nicolai faded out but he never gave up intelligence work. For years he remained an "honorary adviser" to General von Seeckt's *Truppenamt* and later, rejected by Admiral Canaris, to Ribbentrop's foreign political espionage and various nazi party espionage organisations set up by Martin Bormann, Heydrich and Schellenberg. His ultimate fate is shrouded in mystery. According to Dr. Gert Buchheit (in *Der Deutsche Geheimdienst*, Munich, 1966, p.31) he was captured by the Russians in 1945. He was then seventy-two and he probably died in a Soviet prison camp.
[8] Leverkeuhn, P., *Der Geheime Nachrichtendienst*, Frankfurt, 1957, p.192.
[9] Actual security ratings were in descending order: Cosmic Top Secret, Top

Secret, Secret, Confidential, Restricted, and For Official Use Only. The acronym COSMIC stands for "Co-ordination of security measures in International Command" (i.e. NATO).

Chapter II: NEVER GIVE UP

[1] Dorpalen, A., *Hindenburg and the Weimar Republic*, Princeton, 1964, p.39f.

[2] He fled to Sweden disguised with a false beard and glasses but returned in summer 1919, saying to his wife: "It was the greatest stupidity by the revolutionaries to allow us all to remain alive, if ever I come to power again, there will be no pardon. With an easy conscience I would have Ebert and company hanged and watch them dangle.' (Cf. Godspeed, D.J., *Ludendorff*, Boston, 1966, p.280f.) He became the exponent of the Dolchstoss ("Stab-in-the-back") legend, soon joined Hitler and in 1925 was the nazi party's candidate for Reich President. Cf. his memoirs *Auf dem Weg zur Feldherrnhalle*, Munich, 1937.

[3] Cf. Carsten, F.L., *The Reichswehr and Politics*, Oxford, 1966: Wheeler-Bennett, J., *Hindenburg, the Wooden Titan*, London, 1936.

[4] Seeckt Papers in *Institut für Zeitgeschichte*, Munich (File 15, Roll 212).

[5] *Truppenamt* memorandum of July 26, 1920, in Fritsch Papers, *Bundesarchiv-Militärarchiv*, Freiburg, H-08/33-1.

[6] *Geschichte für höhere Schulen*, Ferdinand Hirt Verlag, Breslau, 1928.

[7] *E.von Seydlitz'sche Geographie für höhere Lehranstalten*, Ferdinand Hirt Verlag, Breslau, 1928-33.

[8] Comprehensive descriptions of the CHEKA are in Dallin, D.J., *Soviet Espionage*, New Haven, Yale U.P., 1955; Lewytzkyj, B., *Die Rote Inquisition*, Frankfurt Societäts Verlag, 1967; Cookridge, E.H., *Soviet Spy Net*, London, Muller, 1955.

[9] The talks were conducted in great secrecy in the private apartment of Major von Schleicher at a time when the British-French attitude in the Upper Silesian question had caused strong anti-Western feelings in Germany. Cf. Carsten, F.L., op. cit., p.136f.

[10] The contract is in the papers of one of the Reichswehr negotiators, Colonel Wolfgang Mentzel, *Bundesarchiv-Militärarchiv*, Mentzel, V,63.

[11] Carsten, op. cit., p.221; also cf. Records of Heereswaffenamt, Wi/I/F 5/518 in *Bundesarchiv-Militärarchiv*.

[12] Canaris succeeded in concluding an agreement with the Spanish industrialist Ecchevarrieta for the building of new torpedo works at Cartagena. Canaris' reports are in the files of Marineleitung PG-48903 (Spanien) at the *Militärgeschichtliches Forschungsamt*, Freiburg.

[13] Admiral Domvile later became an ardent admirer of Hitler, was vice-president of the Anglo-German "Link", a council member of other pro-nazi clubs in London, a regular dinner guest at Ribbentrop's embassy and, in 1936, one of Hitler's guests of honour at the Nuremberg Party Rally at which he was accompanied by his secretary Guy Burgess, then already a communist double agent. In May 1940 he was arrested with Sir Oswald Mosley, interned under the 18B-regulations and detained until the end of 1943.

[14] Abwehr Archives, *Geheime Kommandosache* 240/1930; also cf. Carsten, op. cit., p.406.

Chapter III: A WELCOME FOR THE FUHRER

[1] Originally an organisation of German ex-servicemen (like the British Legion

or the American Legion and Veteran organisations) it became a uniform-wearing, para-military organisation of the German National Party, absorbed in 1934 into the nazi SA.

2   Born 1904, he became in 1934 a lecturer in the University of Leipzig and eventually professor at the Technical College at Aachen. Wrote *Mensch und Natur, Urmensch und Spätkultur.*

3   Geyr von Schweppenburg, Baron L., *Erinnerungen eines Militärattachés*, Stuttgart, 1949, passim.

4   Geyr, op. cit., p.89.

5   German records of discussions between Hitler and Lord Halifax on November 19, 1937, Archives of the *Institut für Europäische Geschichte*, vol.21.

6   Chamberlain's speech at Birmingham on March 15, 1939.

7   Hitler's statement to the commanders-in-chief of the Wehrmacht and other military leaders on May 23 1939. A near-verbatim record was taken by his ADC, Colonel Rudolf Schmundt; it is quoted in NCA VII, pp.847f. The original German text is in ITM XXXVII, pp.546f.

8   Heusinger was born in 1897, served in the First World War from 1915, from 1920 on in the Reichswehr, after 1930 in the General Staff, 1937 head of a section and 1940 chief of the Operations Department; 1943, lt.-general and deputy chief of staff of the Army General Staff at OKW. He was badly wounded in Stauffenberg's attempt on Hitler's life on July 20, 1944. After the war he worked for about two years as an "honorary adviser" to the Gehlen Organisation in Pullach, then joined *Amt Blank* and in 1957 became the first inspector general of the new Bundeswehr. 1961-4, chairman of the military council of NATO in Washington. Retired 1965.

Chapter IV: THE RUSSIAN EXPERT

1   The construction of the West Wall fortifications began early in 1935. When Hitler made a tour of them in August 1938 he was told by General Wilhelm Adam that the West Wall could not be held against a French attack for more than three weeks. Work was greatly speeded up afterwards as a top priority for the Organisation Todt.

2   Halder, F., *Hitler als Feldheer*, Munich, Dom Verlag, 1949, p.36f.

3   The best English translation of the directives is Trevor-Roper, H.R., *Hitler's War Directives 1939-45*, New York, Holt-Rinehart, 1964.

4   Halder's Diary, excerpts in NCA, Suppl.B, pp.1537ff.

5   Rundstedt interrogations cited in *War Office Intelligence Review*; cf. Shulman, M., *Defeat in the West*, London, 1947.

6   Trevor-Roper, op. cit., pp.93-8.

7   Stieff, later a major-general, "the youngest and smallest general" (he was a hunchback), was involved in several attempts on Hitler's life; eventually arrested after the attempt on July 20, 1944, he was hanged with Field-Marshal von Witzleben and seven other officers on August 8, 1944; they were the first victims of the great army purge.

8   On Gehlen's card in OKH Personnel file 201, dated April 1, 1942.

9   There are two versions of this order, one to Army Group North, the other to Army Group South. The texts are in NCA III, pp.637f. and in NCA VI, pp.872f. This order and the "Commissars' Order"(see note 10) are also quoted in IMT C-50.

10   Halder's affidavit of November 22, 1945 in NCA, VIII, pp.645-66. It was followed on June 6, 1941, by the more explicit "Commissars' Order,"

OKW/Ops. 44822 Top Secret, which stated: "Political commissars have initiated barbaric Asiatic methods of warfare. Consequently they will be dealt with immediately and with maximum severity . . . they will be shot at once whether captured during operations or otherwise."

[11] NCA VI, p.876, IMT C-52.

[12] Goering's directive of May 23, 1941, NCA VII p.300, IMT EC-126. Cf. Strik-Strikfeldt, W., *Against Stalin and Hitler*, London, Macmillan, 1970, p.40.

[13] *The Goebbels Diaries, 1942-43* (ed. L.P. Lochner), New York, 1948.

[14] The British supplied nearly twenty thousand rifles, 650 machine guns, twenty-five million cartridges and enough artillery to equip two divisions. British political agents dealt with Latvian officers encouraging them to a war of liberation against the Germans. Cf. Watt, R.M., *The Kings Depart*, London, 1969, p.388.

[15] Rosenberg's East Ministry files were captured almost intact. Much of the material used here is in NCA III, IMT 1058-PS. Cf. Strik-Strikfeldt, op. cit., pp.39-42, 57f.

[16] He had great experience in irregular warfare as the commander of a clandestine unit of Sudetenland Germans in Czechoslovakia in 1938 and of a unit which undertook raids in Poland in August 1939. He was killed by Soviet partisans in the summer of 1943.

[17] As a major-general he accompanied Admiral Hans-Georg von Friedeburg, Rear-Admiral Gerhard Wagner, Colonel Poleck, and other officers to Field-Marshal Montgomery's headquarters on Lueneburg Heath where on May 4, 1945, they signed the document providing for the surrender of all German forces in north-west Germany, Holland and Denmark. On May 7, he went with General Jodl and Admiral von Friedeburg to General Eisenhower's headquarters at Rheims, where they signed the Armistice instrument providing for the unconditional surrender of all German forces on all fronts. Shortly afterwards both Kinzel and von Friedeburg committed suicide.

[18] Stauffenberg returned in 1943 from Tunis to execute his famous attempt on July 20, 1944. He was shot the same night in the General Staff building in Berlin. Von Tresckow evaded arrest and killed himself by pulling the pin off a hand-grenade; it blew his head off.

[19] Lindemann later became chief of the Ordnance Office, was involved in anti-Hitler conspiracies, and was executed by the Gestapo after the attempt of July 20.

[20] In 1945 Müller vanished; it is almost certain that he went over to the Russians. In his memoirs Schellenberg insisted that Müller had been in contact with Soviet Intelligence since the "Red Orchestra" investigations. Several people claim to have seen him as a Soviet official in East Germany after the war; it is believed that he died in Moscow in 1949.

[21] Dated June 1, 1942, FHO archives, Nr.3820/42.

Chapter V: CHIEF OF INTELLIGENCE

[1] Rittberg, like Roenne, was a member of the Kreisauer Circle, a group of anti-Hitler conspirators headed by Count Helmut James von Moltke; amongst them were several Social Democratic and trade union leaders and Catholic priests. Rittberg was arrested in 1943 suspected of illegal activities, but Gehlen got him released and Rittberg was sent to the Eastern front. In 1945 he was again arrested and executed with Count Moltke and other "Kreisauers" on January 23, 1945.

2 Roenne was put before an army's "court of honour," presided over by Field-Marshal Gert von Rundstedt, to inquire into his involvement into the attempt on Hitler's life on July 20, 1944. On August 24, the "court" pronounced Roenne's "dishonourable discharge"; he was immediately arrested by the Gestapo and executed on October 12 at the Ploetzensee prison.

3 Cf. the Soviet records on "Soviet Organs of State Security" (listed in the Documentation and Select Bibliography) p.21f.

4 On Gehlen's card in OKH Personnel file 201, dated May 1, 1942.

5 Most of them are preserved in the FHO archives, headed *Merkblat, Geheim,* with prefaces signed by Gehlen.

6 FHO Archives H3/63,173 pages, H3/68, six parts.

7 FHO Archives, H3/158, June 22, 1941, to December 1942 and H3/159 covering the year 1943.

8 Schlabrendorff, F.von, *They Almost Killed Hitler,* New York, 1947, pp.51 ff.

9 Schlabrendorff, op. cit., and Pechel, R., *Deutscher Widerstand,* Zurich, Erlenbach, 1947. A well-illustrated history of the German Resistance movements is *Illustrierte Geschichte des Widerstandes in Deutschland 1933-45,* edited by Kurt Zentner, Munich, Südwest Verlag, 1969.

10 Amongst them were General Jodl, Gehlen's friend Lieutenant-General Adolf Heusinger, and General Karl Bodenschatz, Goering's chief of staff.

Chapter VI: STALIN'S SECRETS

1 FHO Archives 572/40-I.L.

2 Marshal Boris M. Shaposhnikov, chief of staff of the Red Army.

3 FHO Archives, file 27-Ia/42.

4 Halder's Diary, NCA, Suppl.B.

5 Leverkuehn, op. cit., p.192f.

6 Manstein, E.von, *Verlorene Siege,* Bonn, 1955 (Engl. edition, *Lost Victories,* London, 1958.)

7 FHO Archives, Amt Ausland/Abwehr, WALLI III report dated August 8, 1943, in file 27-Ia/43.

8 Abel, the Soviet spy arrested in New York in 1957, sentenced to thirty years and exchanged in 1962 for Francis Gary Powers, the U-2 pilot, stated that during the war he had infiltrated the Abwehr and as a German Intelligence officer had conveyed radio signals to Soviet military intelligence (See also note 9 below).

9 Gordon Lonsdale, *recte* Colonel Konon Molody, arrested with Peter and Helen Kroger in 1961 in London after the discovery of the Portland naval spy ring, stated in his memoirs (*Spy,* London, Spearman, 1965) that he served under Abel in Germany. The story of their strange claims is told in Cookridge, E.H., *Spy Trade,* London, Hodder and Stoughton, 1971.

10 Buchheit, G., op. cit., p.358; this author's estimate is based on information he received from Colonel Schmalschläger, the former WALLI III commander.

11 *Sovietskye Organy* (Soviet Central State Archives), op. cit., pp.24-28.

12 Ibid., pp.31-3.

13 Strik-Strikfeldt, op. cit., Appendix III, p,256.

14 *Sovietskye Organy* op. cit., pp.35-36.

Chapter VII: THE WEREWOLVES

[1] Manteuffel, quoted in Freidin S. and W. Richardson (eds.), *The Fatal Decisions*, London, 1956, p.266.

[2] When the remnants of his army were eventually trapped in the Ruhr in April and 325,000 men including thirty generals surrendered, Field-Marshal Model committed suicide by firing a bullet into his head.

[3] FHO Archives, *Lageberichte Ost*, Nr.1410/45.

[4] Guderian, H., *Erinnerungen eines Soldaten*, Heidelberg, 1951; Engl. edition, *Panzer Leader*, London 1952, p.315f.

[5] Winter was also OKW liaison officer to the RSHA. He was the last Chief of Operations Staff South from April 24 to May 7, 1945.

[6] Burgdorf, a rabid nazi, was the officer who took poison to Rommel and forced him to commit suicide on October 14, 1944. He stayed with Hitler in Berlin until the end and shot himself in the bunker of the Reich Chancellery.

[7] FHO Archives. The original teleprinter message is SSD/HOE-03136, dated January 20, 1945, 1445 hours.

[8] Guderian, op. cit., pp.305f.

[9] OKW (Operations Staff) Fuhrer's Directive No. 68, dated January 21, 1945. The complete text is in *Hitler's Weisungen für die Kriegsführung* (ed. Dr. Walter Hubatsch), Frankfurt, 1962. The quoted Engl. translation is from the American document collection *Führer Directives*, 2 vols., Washington, DC, 1948. Also cf. Trevor-Roper, op. cit., pp.289-90.

[10] Depositions by Lt.-General Georg von Hengl (*Report on the Alpine Fortress*, April 1946, Office of Chief of Military History, US Army Dept., B-459), Lt.-General Alfred Jacob (*Report Concerning the Alpine Redoubt*, April 1946, OCMH B-188), Major-General Marcinkiewitz (Report on the *Alpenfestung*, June 1946, OCMH B-187).

[11] Trevor-Roper, H.R., *The Last Days of Hitler*, London, Macmillan, 1947.

[12] FHO Archives, FHO Group I, Nr.3/45, dated February 6, 1945, marked *Geheime Kommandosache* (Secret Command Matter) and *Chefsache* ("for chiefs only"). It gives a detailed plan for the Werewolves organisation and stresses the necessity of close cooperation of *Werwolf* units with SS *Jagdkommando* front reconnaissance groups and SS *Streifkommandos* (raiding parties) behind the enemy lines. (A microfilm copy is in US National Archives, T-78, Roll 458.)

[13] Pétan was taken to Sigmaringen on August 20, 1944, under SS guard. Laval later fled, was arrested in Austria, handed over to the French, tried for treason, and shot after trying to poison himself in prison.

[14] Skorzeny, born in Austria in 1908, was involved in illegal nazi activities from 1934 against Chancellor Dollfus and after the latter's assassination went to Germany. From 1939 to 1942 he was an officer in the SS Leibstandarte (Hitler's bodyguard). Later he was in charge of special SS units in Belgium, France, Holland and Yugoslavia. In September 1943 he rescued Mussolini, landing with his parachutists near the Duce's mountain prison on Gran Sasso. After the war he was imprisoned by the Americans, released in 1948 and went to Spain. For his involvement with Gehlen and his work for President Nasser see p.351. He recounted his adventures in *Geheimhommando Skorzeny*, Hamburg, Hansa Verlag, 1950; Engl. edition *Skorzen's Secret Memoirs*, New York, 1950.

[15] Speer, A., *Inside the Third Reich*, New York, Macmillan, 1970, pp.468f.

Chapter VIII: FAREWELL TO HITLER

[1] Hoettl served under Schellenberg in RSHA's *Amt VI*, being mainly concerned with subversive activities against Czechoslovakia, Yugoslavia, Hungary and Rumania. Later he operated in Italy. In his book *The Secret Front* London, Weidenfeld, 1953, originally published under the psuedonym of "Walter Hagen" as *Die Geheime Front*, Vienna, Nibelungen Verlag, 1950, he skilfully papered over his own activities and had little good to say of his closest comrades, such as Kaltenbrunner, Schellenberg and Skorzeny. In 1947 he began to work for Gehlen in Austria.

[2] There are many hundreds of dossiers in the FHO files relating to the *Funkspiel*. An interesting summary is in FHO-IIb Nr. 1945/45 to 1953/45. There are several volumes with tables of contents, enumerating the signals conveyed and received by the fake radio posts, also monthly reports under FHO-Ib Nr.1268/45.

[3] There is a complete dossier in FHO Archives on Colonel Hoyer, including a long report of FHO Group I-b of February 24, 1945, and correspondence between Gehlen and RSHA (OKH Nr.40/45, marked *Geheime Kommandosache, Chefsache*).

[4] FHO/Ib-856/45.

[5] FHO/Ib-1661/45, dated March 22, 1945, 2100 hours.

[6] There were several important survivors of the great network and there remained its French and Swiss groups. Indeed, after the Allied occupation of West Germany, American, British, French, Belgian and Dutch Intelligence officers began to conduct secret investigations into the "Red Orchestra" where the Gestapo had left off.

[7] Campbell, A., *Guerillas*, London, Barker, 1967, p.85. So unbiased a writer as the former Abwehr officer Dr. Gert Buchheit (in his *Der Deutsche Geheimdienst*) states that the four SS "Action Groups" massacred within two months one million men, women and children in Russia and that, for instance, Action Group C killed on two days—September 29 and 30, 1941—33,770 Jews. These examples could, of course, be multiplied. FHO corporation with these groups can be traced in many documents, for instance H/3-191, dated November 25, 1942.

[8] Campbell, op. cit., p.87.

[9] Worgitzky joined Gehlen at Oberursel as early as 1946; after 1951 he was the manager of the Bremen *Generalvertretung* of the Gehlen Organisation, and in 1957 became Gehlen's deputy and vice-president of the BND.

[10] FHO-Ib/H-3/655/45. The transfer of Scherhorn from Gehlen's control to that of Himmler's RSHA is in FHO-Ib Nr.1536/45.

[11] RSHA teletyped message to Gehlen Nr.6369, dated March 6, 1945.

[12] Schellenberg, W., *The Labyrinth*, London, 1956.

[13] Guderian, op. cit., pp.341-3.

[14] FHO-Ib/Nr.1740/45.

[15] FHO-Ib/Nr.1817/45.

[16] NARS, OKH-FHO T-78 Roll 486.

[17] He remained with Hitler to the very last day. On May 1, 1945, he came under the flag of truce to the command post of the Soviet Eighth Army where he informed General Chuikov of Hitler's suicide and offered the surrender of Berlin. Cf. Chuikov, V.I., *The End of the Third Reich*, London, Macgibbon & Kee, 1967.

Chapter IX: SURRENDER AT MISERY MEADOW

[1] OKW/Ops. Staff, Fuhrer's Directive No. 71, dated March 20, 1945.

[2] Originally a small local paper named *Miesbacher Beobachter*, which Hitler and Max Axmann bought for sixty thousand Marks, given to them by General von Epp, the commanding general of the Reichswehr in Bavaria.

[3] Minott, R.G., *The Fortress That Never Was*, London, Longmans, 1965, pp.88-9.

[4] Kesselring delayed the capitulation of his First and Nineteenth Armies until May 5. His death sentence for war crimes was commuted and he was released in 1952.

[5] Speer, op. cit., pp.464-5.

[6] Born 1907, he was G-2 officer to the VI Corps, 1937-8, and to the Seventh Army during the war. Director Strategic Service Unit, 1946-7; in Korea in 1950-2; O.C. 9th Inf. Div. in Germany, 1953-5; Deputy Director, Defence Intelligence 1961-4; O.C. Seventh Army in Germany, 1964-6.

[7] Dulles received much intelligence about it at his OSS office in Berne and during his secret negotiations with SS General Karl Wolff.

[8] Dulles, A.W., *The Secret Surrender*, New York, Harper, 1966.

[9] On May 3, 1945, he saw Himmler and Doenitz for the last time in Flensburg and then went to Sweden, still trying to negotiate terms for the surrender with Count Bernadotte. Cf. his *Memoirs*, loc. cit., p.380.

Chapter X: THE DEAL WITH THE AMERICANS

[1] General Weeks retired in 1946 and was succeeded by Air Marshal Sir Sholto Douglas, probably the only high-ranking British officer who was a registered member of the Labour Party.

[2] Murphy, R.D., *Diplomat Among Warriors*, New York, 1964.

[3] Which had been formed from the special operations sections of OSS prior to the establishment of the Central Intelligence Group (later CIA).

[4] Dulles, A.W., *The Craft of Intelligence*, op. cit., p.12.

[5] Ford, C., *Donovan of OSS*, Boston, Little Brown, 1970.

[6] Ibid, pp.262f.

[7] Wise, D., and T.B. Ross, op. cit., pp.98-101.

[8] In 1959 Donovan defended the Soviet spy Rudolf Abel, subsequently arrange his exchange, and was instrumental in many other spy barters with Moscow, East Berlin and Cuba. Cf. Cookridge, E.H., *Spy Trade*, London, Hodder and Stoughton, 1971.

[9] Quoted in Tully, A., *Central Intelligence, The Inside Story*, London, 1962, p.16.

Chapter XI: ORGANISATION GEHLEN

[1] With the coming of the new CIA, General Strong was determined to streamline the army intelligence establishment in Germany. Although CIC remained under separate command, General Sibert supervised it, as well as the other groups, such as the Field Operations Intelligence.

[2] Also "Claus Thomas", "Wilhelm Thorwald", "Helmut Fricke", "Dr. Walther". His Nazi Party membership card was No. 938.997, and his SS No. 308.171.

[3] Sommer's activities in Paris are described in Guérin, A., *Le Général Gris*,

Paris, Jouillard, 1968, in Delarue, J., *Histoire de la Gestapo*, Paris, Fayard, 1962 (Engl. edition *The History of the Gestapo*, London, Macdonald, 1964, pp.118-230). Both his superiors, SS Obergruppenfuhrer Karl Oberg and SS Standartenfuhrer Helmuth Knochen, were sentenced to death by the French after the war; their sentences were commuted and they were released from prison in 1960.

4 General von Mellethin went to South Africa in 1960 and became a director of the Trek Airways Company. His name was mentioned in arms deals between West Germany and South Africa.

5 Colonel Oscar Reile was a seasoned Abwehr officer since 1933. Born in 1897, he served as a young volunteer in the First World War, later became a policeman and by 1932 was chief of the CID in Danzig. Before the war he was chief of Abwehr Ast Trier, concerned with espionage against France. In June 1940 he was appointed chief of Abwehr III/F in Paris. At his headquarters in the Hotel Lutetia worked Sergeant Hugo Bleicher who was instrumental in the destruction of the main Paris network of the British SOE. Reile succeeded in capturing many British agents sent as instructors to the French Resistance, and also a large number of Resistance and Maquis leaders.

6 Cf. Report by General Ignacy Blum in *Wojskowy Przeglad Historyczny*, Warsaw, 1959. He mentioned a figure of 12,556 killed and estimated the number of sabotage acts carried out in Poland by the anti-communist bands and Werewolves at 29,970.

7 Kirkpatrick, L.B., *The Real CIA*, New York, Macmillan, 1968.

8 He wrote *The Goose Step is Verboten, The German Army Today*, New York, 1964.

9 He described his activities in *Saturday at M19*, London, Hodder and Stoughton, 1969.

10 As a lieutenant-colonel in the Intelligence Corps he was appointed British liaison officer to the German local authorities at München-Gladbach near Düsseldorf. He retired in 1966 and was presented by the burgomaster with the Golden Ring of the town.

11 According to Guérin, op. cit., pp.214-15 and 450-7, Hoettl was invited to join the Gehlen Organisation by Gehlen's branch leader in Linz in Austria, Harry Mast, alias "Count Bobby".

12 A comprehensive description of CIA functions as laid down by the National Security Act of 1947 is in Ransom, H.H., *The Intelligence Establishment*, Cambridge, Mass., Harvard U.P., 1970, pp.82-100.

Chapter XII: PULLACH

1 In 1969 the photographer who visited the Pullach compound with me was arrested; he was released only after frantic telephone calls to government offices in Bonn and London.

2 Many organisations in the United States and West Germany which closely cooperated with Gehlen were supported by private contributions. Some instances are given in Chapter XV.

3 Other such "commercial" fronts were Erwin Bender & Co., Export and Import, in Berlin; Wachsmuth & Co., in Stuttgart; Handelsgesellschaft AGRO in Hamburg; Ernst Meissner & Co., Ceramics Export, in Karlsruhe; Altoelverwertung Gesellschaft in Bremen, etc. Many branches were disguised as secretarial offices, typing, duplicating and copying services, photographic studios, and so forth. In articles in German newspapers it was said that

Gehlen maintained more than one hundred such "fronts" and that, even after the "Org" became a government department, there remained several scores of such covert enterprises working for BND in all large cities and many towns.

4 Instruction for the Organisation Section II at Pullach, Nr.833/An-a, dated November 2, 1953.

5 This figure was mentioned by several defectors from the Gehlen "Org" and at trials of Gehlen's agents captured in East Germany. Even if it is taken with a grain of salt it cannot be far off. Publications by the East German Public Prosecutor's Office (for instance in the official journal *Neue Justiz*, vol.XI, No. 19 and vol.XX, Nos. 9 and 17) gives the exact location of the schools and the names of some of the principals and instructors.

Chapter XIII: V-MEN

1 All recruits had to sign a solemn "Declaration of Loyalty" and to affirm it by a handshake with a senior officer or HV-man. They promised never to disclose to anybody anything about the "Org" and their work. They also had to accept a peculiar condition that they "would be severely punished for any infringement of secrecy". As the "Org" was a private organisation it could not inflict punishment in the legal sense. The condition was thus both ambiguous and and ominous.

2 After Dr. John's disappearance in 1954, he became, on Gehlen's recommendation, acting president of the BfV, the Federal counter-espionage office, until 1955.

3 "Dead drops"—in British Intelligence jargon DLBs, dead letter-boxes—caches for clandestine messages, were widely used by the Gehlen "Org" and referred to as TBK's, *Tote Briefkasten*. In Russian slang they are known as *dybok*, which literally means a small oak tree.

4 One of the members of the Free Jurists, Dr. Gunther Nollau, joined the BfV in 1960 and became its vice-president in 1967. He was one of the candidates for Gehlen's successor in 1968.

5 Knobloch was caught in March 1953 when burgling a shop in West Berlin, tried for the kidnapping and sentenced to eight years. He failed in his attempt to commit suicide by slashing his wrists in his prison cell.

6 Wagner held the eulogy at a memorial gathering of former Abwehr officers at the former concentration camp of Flossenbürg on April 9. 1965, the twentieth anniversary of Admiral Canaris' execution.

7 As Abwehr chief in Bulgaria during the war, Colonel Wagner used the alias "Dr. Delius". He worked there with the chief of the Bulgarian secret service, General Nicola Kostov, who escaped to Germany from the Red Army and eventually became head of the "Bulgarian section" under Wagner in Pullach.

8 Trial before the Supreme Court of the DDR, Zst-1/2/53.

Chapter XIV: OPERATION BOHEMIA

1 Rohleder was a pupil of Colonel Nicolai. He had spent more than twenty years in the intelligence service when in 1938 he became head of the III/F counter-espionage department of the Abwehr. In 1940 Canaris asked him to investigate the alleged leak of the German plan to attack Holland and Belgium. He discovered that the trail led to the anti-Hitler conspirators at the Abwehr headquarters, led by Major-General Hans Oster. On Canaris' instructions the discovery was kept secret and the conspirators survived for some years. In 1944 Rohleder was arrested by the Gestapo, but survived. He

joined Gehlen at Oberursel, later headed Gehlen's Munich office and was eventually replaced by a younger man.

2 Gehlen passed the information to General Sibert; it resulted in the replacement of several American officers.

3 Salgovič rose to become deputy minister for state security. Whilst serving under Prime Minister Dubček in 1968 he conveyed secret information to Moscow and prompted the Soviet invasion of Czechoslovakia. Gehlen had informers in Salgovič's office amongst the officers serving under Colonel Josef Hruby, loyal to Dubček. This enabled the BND to give a timely warning of the impending Soviet invasion; the warning was, however, disregarded by Western intelligence.

4 One wonders whether Kowalski had already worked in London during the war when he was General Sikorski's adjutant for Soviet Intelligence.

5 In October 1950 Adenauer appointed the CDU member of the Bundestag, Theodore Blank, as Federal Commissioner for Questions Related to the Strengthening of Allied Forces in Germany. This clumsy and ambiguous name for the office was abbreviated into Amt Blank. Its real purpose was to prepare the establishment of the new Federal armed forces, the Bundeswehr. Amongst Blank's earliest "advisers" who began this work was General Adolf Heusinger; he gave up his "honorary consultancy" at Pullach but remained in close touch with Gehlen.

Chapter XV: WAR OF THE RADIO WAVES

1 Cf. Perrault, G., L'Orchestre Rouge, Paris, Fayard, 1967. Engl. edition The Red Orchestra, London, Barker, 1968 (also a Mayflower Paperback, London, 1970).

2 On Rado cf. Dallin, D.J., op. cit., pp.201-33. On "Lucy" (Rössler) cf. Dallin, D.J., op. cit., pp.191-228, 326-9; Foote, A., Handbook for Spies, London, Museum Press, 1956.

3 Philby, H.A.R., My Silent War, London, Macgibbon & Kee, 1968.

4 Ibid, p.114.

5 Cf. Cookridge, E.H., Soviet Spy Net, London, Muller, 1955, pp.217-25.

6 Dulles, William H. Jackson, a former OSS officer, Mathias F. Correa, former assistant to James Forrestal, the secretary of the navy.

7 The Crusade for Freedom, which launched the money collection, became the Radio Free Europe Fund. The Free Europe Committee pursues many other activities and in addition to the radio stations has four other divisions: Communist Bloc Operations, Free World Operations, West European Operations and Exile Political Operations; it also publishes several periodicals. There are many other organisations in the United States devoted to anti-communist operations, such as the American Committee for the Liberation of the People of Russia, Asia Foundation, Congress for Cultural Freedom, Federation for Democratic Germany, Fund for International Social and Economic Development, etc. Radio Liberty is supported by the American Committee for Liberation, which also has an Institute for the Study of the USSR in Munich. The traffic is both ways. The CIA supports a large number of private organisations, foundations, university research centres, book and periodicals publishers, etc. In 1967 the disclosures about the CIA subsidies paid to such institutions and companies caused, in the words of Professor Ransom, the "greatest dismay and trauma". Cf. Ransom, H.H., The Intelligence Establishment, Harvard University Press, 1970.

8 Cookridge, E. H., *Inside SOE*, London, Barker, 1966; pp.401-7, 425-36, 450-91. (American edition *Set Europe Ablaze*, New York, Crowell, 1967.)

9 Höher's deposition at the trial of Haasse, *Strafsache Gegen Haase*, Berlin, VEB Deutscher Zentralverlag, 1954; pp.29-32, 55-6, Geyer's press conference arranged by the East German ministry for state security on November 9, 1953, articles in *Politik und Wirtschaft*, November 11-13, 1953.

10 Mader, J., *Nicht Länger Geheim*, Berlin, Deutscher Militärverlag, (first edition), 1966, p.260.

Chapter XVI: THE RIGHT MAN IN THE RIGHT PLACE

1 Halle, L.J., *The Cold War as History*, London, Chatto, 1967, p.238.

2 Ibid., p.239.

3 Bissell graduated from Yale University and the London School of Economics and in 1939 was a lecturer in economics at Yale and at the Massachusetts Institute of Technology. During the war he worked in the US War Shipping Administration, joined the Marshall Plan Organisation in 1948 and became acting administrator. He joined CIA in 1954 and in 1958 succeeded Wisner as deputy director for plans and operations. The present CIA director, Richard M. Helms, was then his deputy. Bissell directed the Cuba operations in 1961 and left CIA the following year.

4 Zaisser was a veteran of the Soviet intelligence service. He joined it in 1925 and had a remarkable career in China, the Middle East, and during the Civil War in Spain. (He worked there under the alias of "General Gomez"; cf. Thomas, H., *The Spanish Civil War*, London, Eyre & Spottiswoode, 1961, pp.379, 423, 494). From Spain he went to Russia where he spent the war years organising German prisoners of war. He returned to Germany with the Soviet Army of Occupation, was police chief in Leipzig, minister of interior of Saxony in 1948, and became the first East German minister for state security in 1950.

5 Mielke fled to Russia in 1931; when a young Communist Party official, he was accused of having shot two Berlin policemen in a street riot. He became Zaisser's deputy at the ministry for state security in 1950 and remained in this post under Wollweber (q.v.), succeeding him in 1956. A comprehensive description of the ministry and its espionage and subversion organisation is in Gerken, R., *Spione Unter Uns*, Donauwörth, Auer, 1965, pp.31-44.

6 Friedrich Wolf (1888-1953), a well-known German writer and literary critic of the pre-Hitler era.

7 Cf. Hyde, Montgomery H., *The Quiet Canadian*, London, Hamish Hamilton, 1962; Cookridge, E.H., *Inside SOE*, London, 1966, pp.40-2, 50.

8 The full story was never published in Britain. A German version is in Kern, E. (*recte* Kernmayer), *Verrat an Deutschland*, Göttingen Schütz, 1965, pp.111-20.

9 Transcript of trial before the Supreme Court of the DDR, 1/Zst, 1/56; cf. *Neue Justiz*, February 20, 1956, pp.99-104.

10 Arthur Axmann, the Reich Youth Leader, his adjutant, Weltzin, Dr. Ludwig Stumpfegger, Hitler's orthopaedic surgeon, and SS Hauptsturmfuhrer Gunther Schwaegermann, Goebbels' adjutant. Professor Trevor-Roper, who as a British Intelligence officer interrogated many of the people who had been with and around Hitler during the last days of April and on May 1, 1945, told a very full story of the events during the night from May 1st to 2nd in his *The Last Days of Hitler* published by Macmillan, London, 1947).

But his book was written several years before Naumann's arrest and depositions in 1953. Naumann's story has not been corroborated by any of the other survivors of the escape. On the contrary, several of them, particularly Erich Kempka, Hitler's chauffeur, who escaped from the Chancellery after having helped to burn the bodies of the Fuhrer and Eva Braun, always maintained that they had actually seen Bormann dead. Kempka was in the group in which were Bormann, Axmann, Naumann and the others mentioned above. In his own memoirs *Ich habe Adolf Hitler Verbrannt*, Munich, 1950, Kempka repeats his story of Bormann's death. In the introduction to the new and revised edition of his book, Professor Trevor-Roper states that "if we believe that Bormann is dead, it must be simply because no one has ever produced any acceptable evidence of his existence after May 1st, 1945."

Chapter XVII: BY PARACHUTE INTO RUSSIA

[1] The senior partner of the banking house, John Hay Whitney, was American ambassador in London from 1956 to 1961 and publisher of *New York Herald Tribune* from 1961 to 1966.

[2] Kirkpatrick, L.B., *Captains Without Eyes*, New York, Macmillan, 1969; p.157.

[3] Tully, A., *Central Intelligence Agency, the Inside Story*, New York, Morrow, 1962, p.45.

[4] In an article syndicated by the North American Newspaper Alliance and published on December 22, 1963.

[5] Achmeteli served under Rosenberg at the ministry for Eastern affairs.

[6] Six, born in 1909, joined the SD at RSHA in April 1935; he was an "old" Nazy Party member (Membership No. 245,670, SS No. 107.480), who became in 1939 head of *Amt II* of RSHA and was from 1941 to 1945 head of *Amt VII*. In 1940 Reinhard Heydrich appointed Six his "presumptive representative in Great Britain after the victorious invasion". He rose to the rank of SS Brigadefuhrer, commanding SD "Action groups" in Russia in 1941.

[7] He was released in 1952 and shortly afterwards joined Gehlen at Pullach.

[8] Applicants for admission had to prove "pure Aryan blood" in at least four generations of their forebears. His Nazi Party membership number was 5/518.734, SS No. 307.925. He was an SS Sturmfuhrer in 1938 and was promoted SS Sturmbannfuhrer in 1944.

[9] The acronym ODESSA stood for *Organisation der ehemaliger SS Angehörigen* (Organisation of former SS members). It was a secret organisation which assisted SS men in danger of arrest by Allied authorities and prosecution as war criminals to escape abroad. ODESSA helped a large number of SS men to reach Spain and South America.

[10] He was the organiser of "Operation Pastorius", the landing of two teams of Abwehr agents from U-boats on the coasts of Manhattan and Florida. See Chapter XXI.

[11] Sarantzev, a former Vlassov Army soldier, was at the end of the war a "displaced person" in a camp in Ingolstadt, where one of Gehlen's collectors enlisted him. He was trained at the Kaufbeuren camp of the Gehlen "Org".

[12] Other parachutists were recruited through the Russian emigré organisation NTS.

Chapter XVIII: BRITISH BOATS FOR GEHLEN'S INFILTRATORS

[1] Philby, op. cit., p.121.

[2] Philby, who was then SIS liaison officer to CIA, states in his book (op. cit., p.120) that "CIA proferred three objections to Bandera as an ally. His extreme Ukrainian nationalism with its fascist overtones was a handicap which would prejudice western dealings with the Great Russians; he was alleged to lack contacts with the new, more realistic emigration . . . and he was accused of being anti-American."

[3] Cf. Joesten J., "Just call me Muller" in *They Call It Intelligence*, New York, 1954; pp.261-8.

[4] Powers, F. G., *Operations Overflight*, New York, Holt, 1970, pp.204-19.

[5] *Polymany S Polichnim, Sbornik Faktom O Shpyonazhe Protiv SSSR (Caught Red-handed: A Collection of Facts about the Espionage against the USSR)*, Moscow, State Publishing House for Political Literature, 1963.

[6] There were protracted consultations between Sir Thomas Brimelow, Sir George Clutton, then political adviser to SIS, Rear-Admiral Sir Anthony Buzzard and Rear-Admiral Sir John Inglis, the directors of Naval Intelligence.

[7] He became chief of SIS in.1956, having been director of security (M15) since 1953. Sir Dick retired in 1969.

Chapter XIX: THE TELEPHONE SLUICES

[1] The document, running to twenty-one pages, was released by the US department of state on November 11, 1961. It stated that "from its headquarters in the Normannenstrasse in East Berlin, the MfSS carries out . . . activities through specialists amongst its sixteen thousand communist agents operating inside West Germany." It prompted a somewhat embarrassed statement from the Federal German government that there were not as many as sixteen thousand communist spies in Germany.

[2] In East Berlin, Chemnitz, Cottbus, Dresden, Erfurt, Frankfurt on Oder, Gera, Halle, Leipzig, Magdeburg, Neubrandenburg, Potsdam, Rostock, Schwerin, Suhl and Wismut. Each has several sub-branches in smaller towns. (Information to the author by BfV.)

[3] Hitherto there had been no capital punishment in the DDR. Frau Benjamin later became the President of the Supreme Court, which tried treason and espionage cases, but she eventually fell into disgrace in one of the recurring "purges" of high officials.

[4] Geyer, H.J., *Im Anfang Stand das Ende*, Berlin, Kongressverlag, 1954. It was the first book he published under his real name, having used the pseudonym of "Henry Troll" for his crime thrillers.

[5] Karl-Heinz Schmidt, Siegfried Altkrüger, Walter Rennert, Wolf-Wilhelm Oestereich, Helmut Schwenk and Walter Otto Schneider.

[6] The East Berlin newspaper *Neues Deutschland* carried many columns of the trial report and subsequently a book was published about it (*Strafsache Gegen Haase*), see note 9 in Chapter XV.

[7] A "Kapo" was a foreman in the Gestapo concentration camps, usually chosen from amongst "professional criminal" inmates.

[8] Amongst Chrobock's V-men were Alfred and Elfriede Rader, Speckmann,

Schönwetter, Karl Tietz, Krause, F. Kisewetter, Quel, and a man listed in Gehlen's files under the romantic code name of "Tannhäuser".

[9] Cf. Wise, D., and Ross, T.B., *The Invisible Government*, pp.165-83; Tully, op. cit., pp.64-71, 239-41.

[10] Cf. Tully, op. cit., pp.11-14. Also the Soviet publication *Caught Red-handed*, see note 5 in Chapter XVIII.

[11] Dulles, *The Craft of Intelligence* p.202.

[12] *Izvestia*, Moscow, 13 February, 1970, p.4.

[13] *Izvestia*, Moscow, 14 February, 1970, p.4.

[14] On April 19, 1956, SIS agent Lionel Crabb, a retired Royal Navy commander and wartime frogman, dived beneath the Soviet cruiser *Ordzhonikidze* in Stokes Bay, Portsmouth, which brought the Soviet statesmen to England. Apparently he intended to take some measurements. His action was discovered by the Russian crew and Khrushchev informed his British hosts about it. Crabb was never seen again and there were rumours that he had been taken aboard and "kidnapped". More probably he was drowned.

[15] Dulles, op. cit., p.202-3.

[16] It contained photographs of the Berlin tunnel and of American-made miniature radio transmitters found on captured agents of the Gehlen's agents. Some of these photographs are reproduced in this book.

Chapter XX: PRESIDENT GEHLEN

[1] Cf. Mader, J., *Die Graue Hand*, Berlin, Kongressverlag, 1961.

[2] In Baden-Württemberg, Bavaria, Bremen, Hamburg, Hesse, Lower Saxony, North Rhine-Westphalia, Rhineland-Palatinate and Schleswig-Holstein.

[3] General Hans Oster, head of Abwehr Central Department, was "retired" on June 19, 1943, by Hitler's order and on March 4, 1944, dismissed from the army. He was kept under Gestapo surveillance, was arrested after the attempt of July 20 and taken first to the Gestapo HQ in the Prinz Albrecht Strasse (where he was joined by Canaris) and on February 7, 1945, to the Flossenbürg concentration camp. There an improvised SS "court martial" sentenced him and Canaris to death; they were hanged at dawn. For Oster's anti-Hitler conspiracy cf. Colvin, I., *Hitler's Secret Enemy*, London, Gollancz, 1951; Bartz, K., *The Downfall of the German Secret Service*, London, Kimber, 1956; Bauer, F., *Oster und das Widerstandsrecht*, in *Politische Studien*, XV (1964) No. 154; Graml, H., *Der Fall Oster*, in *Viertell fahrshefte für Zeitgeschichte*, XIV (1966); Sandtner, K., *"Das Problem Oster"* in *Vollmacht des Gewissens*, vol.I., Frankfurt, 1960.

[4] As early as 1938, Heinz had suggested to Oster and Field-Marshal von Witzleben that Hitler should be ousted in a *coup* carried out by the 23rd Infantry Division garrisoned in Berlin, and if need be, killed. Heinz assembled a "raiding party" which was to capture Hitler. Most of its members were young titled officers, such as Count Hans von Blumenthal, County Haubold Einsiedel, Baron Treusch von Buttlar-Brandenfels and Count von der Recke, but it included also young socialist student leaders. The conspirators planned to proclaim Prince Wilhelm of Prussia, the eldest grandson of the ex-Kaiser, as "Reich Regent". Like all the other conspiracies this one petered out as soon as it was conceived.

[5] Each of the federated Lands established a *Landes-Bundesamt für Verfassungsschutz*.

[6] Kaiser had been a member of the Kreisauer Circle of Count von Moltke and

Stauffenberg. He became minister for all-German affairs in Adenauer's first cabinet and advocated an understanding with the East; this soon ended his political career.

7 His elder brother, who had been the conspirators' original candidate for "Reich Regent", died of wounds received in a battle with British troops in March 1940 in France.

8 Later Labour Member of Parliament for Coventry East and a cabinet minister in the Wilson government from 1964 to 1970.

9 Manstein was sentenced to eighteen years' imprisonment, but was released four years later. After his return to London John wrote a series of articles on the Hamburg trials of the generals in the *Army Quarterly Magazine*, stating that as the commander of the Army Group Don Manstein must have been aware of the atrocities committed in Russia and of the shooting of prisoners of war and civilian hostages. Nevertheless, John expressed the opinion that Manstein's sentence was too harsh. Gehlen was incensed about John's attitude; he later did all he could to prevent John's appointment.

10 It was on this occasion that Naumann made his depositions about Martin Bormann, mentioned in Chapter XVI.

11 The defendant was seventy-year-old Carl Albert Wittig, a former Gehlen and CIC agent, who had appeared as a prosecution witness in the John trial in 1956. He had testified that he had met John in 1955 in Weimar in East Germany and that John admitted to him that he had gone voluntarily to East Berlin. John firmly denied this. During the intervening period Wittig was arrested in East Germany and sentenced to fifteen years as a "Western spy"; he was released in 1969. When these lines are written the case against Wittig is still pending.

12 Colonel Albert Radke was in 1935-7 Abwehr's liaison officer to the RSHA; he later served in the "Protectorate" of Bohemia and joined Gehlen's "Org" in 1946, remaining at Pullach until his appointment as vice-president of BfV in 1951. He retired in 1964.

13 The various "commercial fronts" were transformed into official *Befragungsstellen*, i.e. enquiry offices.

14 Issued by the ministry of foreign affairs, Belgrade, 1952.

15 The discreet contact of Gehlen's "Org" was with the Yugoslav UDB, *Uprava Drzavne Bezbednosti*, state security office.

16 The compromising document was an instruction to Gehlen's agents marked "Top secret" MA/IV 63/1a.

Chapter XXI: THE MAN WITHOUT A PRIVATE LIFE

1 He was music critic of the *Philadelphia Evening Bulletin* and later of *New York Herald Tribune*. His book *Agony of Modern Music* (New York, Simon & Schuster, 1955) was strongly critical of modern composers.

2 Cf. *Revue*, Munich, October 1963; *Time*, July 11, 1960; Guérin, op. cit., pp.19-20.

3 Shakespeare, *Macbeth*, V.16.

4 Thompson, a film actor born in Argentina, was more recently involved in the controversy about Rolf Hochhuth's play *Soldiers* and he wrote *The Assassination of Winston Churchill*, countering the allegations that Churchill had been a party in the death of General Sikorski.

5 In *Berliner Zeitung*, January 1, 1956.

6 *Time*, New York, July 11, 1955.

[7] *Reynolds News*, London, August 10, 1952.

[8] Tully, op. cit., p.147.

[9] *Carrefour*, September 1, 1954.

[10] *Le Nouvel Observateur*, April 4, 1967.

[11] The series of articles in *Die Welt am Sonntag* was published on November 13, 20, 27 and December 4 and 11, 1955.

[12] *Die Welt am Sonntag*, November 27, 1955.

[13] In a letter published in *Münchner Illustrierte*, February 20, 1960.

[14] *Combat*, August 22, 1963.

[15] Pujol, A., *Dictionnaire de l'espion*, Paris, 1965.

[16] Wendland died in the mysterious wave of suicides among senior German officers and officials which started on October 8, 1968, when Rear-Admiral Hermann Luedke was found dead in a hunting preserve in the Eifel Mountains. Luedke, chief of the logistic section of SHAPE (Supreme Headquarters Allied Forces Europe), had "cosmic" clearance. He had knowledge of the location of some sixteen thousand tactical nuclear warheads and of all missile stockpiles for possible use in "Strike Plan", NATO's defence against a Soviet attack. The day after Luedke's death, Wendland shot himself at his Pullach office. On October 14, Hans Schenk, a high official of the ministry of economics, hanged himself in his Cologne home. On October 18, Colonel Johann Grimm, head of the alarm and mobilisation department of the ministry of defence, shot himself in his Bonn office; three days later Gerhard Boehm, a senior official of this ministry who was missing from his home for six days, was found drowned in the Rhine near Cologne. Several of the dead were connected with Admiral Luedke, who was one of General Wendland's close friends. The Federal government officially announced that all these suicides, except that of Admiral Luedke, "had nothing to do with security matters".

Chapter XXII: DOUBLE AGENT IN PULLACH

[1] Cf. *Memoirs* of Colonel Philippe Thyraud de Vosjoli, published in *Life* magazine in April 1968.

[2] Scotland, R., *The London Cage*, London, 1954.

[3] There were four categories of persons brought before German denazification tribunals: (1) Major offenders liable to be sentenced to imprisonment up to ten years, confiscation of property and permanent exclusion from public office; (2) Offenders, who could be imprisoned or fined and excluded from holding public office, but were allowed probation; (3) Lesser offenders and "nazi fellow-travellers" liable to fine but usually escaping with a warning; and (4) Uninvolved, the "good Germans", who could either prove that they did not belong to a nazi organisation, or had supported resistance against Hitler.

[4] British security officers led by Lt.-Colonel Leonard Burt and Captain Reginald Spooner (both were Scotland Yard detectives) were looking particularly for British traitors; Felfe was denouncing his own former comrades.

[5] After the German occupation of Czechoslovakia, Clemens was sent to the Sudetenland. In command of a SD "special unit" he rounded up hundreds of Czechs who were sent to concentration camps in Germany.

[6] Elected to the office of Federal President in July 1969.

[7] Cf. Gehlen's memoirs, pp.201-2.

8 Gehlen emulated Dulles who had created the CIA Intelligence Star, inscribed "For Valor".

9 Dallin, op. cit., pp.237, 253, 257.

Chapter XXIII: ARREST GEHLEN!

1 Maennel appeared at the trial wearing an auburn wig, a false moustache and thick, tinted glasses to prevent identification. He testified that he had met Kauffman four times in East Berlin and received from him important information.

2 Cf. Gerken, R., *Spion in Bonn*, Donauwörth, Auer, 1964, pp.18f. Bergh, H.van, *ABC der Spione*, Pfaffenhofen, Ilmgau Verlag, 1965, pp.370-80.

3 Cf. Anders, K., *Mord auf Befehl*, Tubingen, 1963 (A documentary report of the trial); Fedenko, P., *Pislya Procesu Stasinskogo*, Munich, 1963.

4 Lippolz' statement on "Gehlen's order to murder Bandera", *Neues Deutschland*, Berlin, October 14, 1961.

5 Freitag's statement on "Gehlen's torture cellars in the old Pioneer barracks at Berchtesgaden", *Neues Deutschland*, Berlin, November 11, 1961.

6 *Der Spiegel*, XVI, No. 46, November 14, 1962, pp.43-50.

7 *Der Spiegel*, XIX, No. 22, May 26, 1965, pp.4f.

Chapter XXIV: GLOBAL ALIGNMENT

1 Khrushchev made a personal attack on Secretary General Dag Hammarskjöld, demanding his resignation. His language was certainly unusual at such an assembly; on one occasion the chairman ordered that some of Khrushchev's remarks be expunged from the records, being "improper". Displeased with a speaker, Khrushchev took off one shoe, brandished it at the speaker, and then continuously banged his desk with it; in the turmoil that followed the chairman broke his gavel trying to restore order. Cf. Halle, op. cit., p.390.

2 Guérin, op. cit., p.554.

3 In 1949 he and another CIA agent, Stephen Meade, masterminded a revolt in Syria and set up General Zain as an American puppet. In Iran Roosevelt ousted Prime Minister Mossadegh and restored power to the Shah.

4 Copeland, M., *The Game of Nations*, New York, Schuster, 1968, p.53.

5 Ibid., pp.148-50. It is significant that in his eulogistic biography of Nasser, (published in the *Sunday Telegraph* in September 1971) his friend Mohammed Heikal tried to make out that this "gift" had been given by the Americans to General Neguib.

6 In 1958 Egyptian agents were instrumental in staging the revolution during which King Feisal, Emir Abdullah and Prime Minister Nuri were murdered. In Jordan they incited repeated attempts to overthrow and murder King Hussein. In Saudi Arabia the entire Egyptian mission was arrested in 1957 on charges of plotting to kill King Saud. Egyptian secret agents were involved in a bomb plot against the Lebanese president and were engaged on subversion in Libya and the Sudan.

7 Shin Beth are the initials of *Sheruth Bitachon*, National Security Council.

8 Cf. Lotz, W., *Ich War Spion für Israel*, Deutsche Nationalzeitung, XV (1965), Nr. 32.

9 Cf. Guérin, op. cit., p.464; on Brunner, pp.159, 210.

Documentation and Select Bibliography

A large part of the book is based on Gehlen's own FHO documents that he surrendered to the Americans in 1945, which were microfilmed and the copies lodged at the United States National Archives in Washington, D.C.: they include records of OKH (*Oberkommando des Heeres*, FH Ost, H3) listed under T-78, 458-504 and T-78, 548-591 and 670. Also on the records of OKW (*Oberkommando der Wehrmacht*, i.e. Hitler's Supreme Headquarters) referring particularly to *OKW/AMT Ausland Abwehr*, listed under T-77, 1434-1454, 1499-1506 with data sheets on T-176, 27-28, many of which contain "privileged material" of which the reproduction has been restricted. The author obtained access to these hitherto unpublished documents and was permitted to examine the originals at the *Bundesarchiv* (*Militärarchiv*) of the Federal German Government at Freiburg in Breisgau in April 1971. In addition microfilmed documents lodged at the US National Archives referring to OKW files listed under 77 OKW 202 ff, and 1483 ff. were examined by the author. In total these collections contain reproductions (many examined in original) running to 36,852 typescript pages.

Additional material was examined from the collection of the *Institut of Zeitgeschichte* in Munich (including the so-called Lahousen Diary), the Hoover Institution on War, Revolution and Peace at Stanford University, California, the Archives of Radio Free Europe, Munich, and from documents and publications issued by the Information Office of the Federal German Government, the *Bundesamt für Verfassungsschutz* (*Innere Sicherheit*), the *Bundesgerichtshof* and several other Federal German authorities. The author used information from a large number of Soviet, East German, Polish, Czechoslovak and other communist authorities, particularly the documents contained in the collection entitled *Sovietskiye Organy Gosudarstviennoy Bezopasnost* (Soviet Organ of State Security) in the Central State Archives of the USSR; the transcripts of trials before the military tribunals of the Supreme Court of the USSR and the Supreme Court of the German Democratic Republic (the relevant register numbers are mentioned in the Notes), and of trials held in other communist countries.

Over the period of more than four years the author conducted research in Germany and had several hundred interviews with former officers of the OKW, FHO, *Abwehr*, *Sicherheitsdienst* of the RSHA, Gestapo and with a number of former officers and agents of the Gehlen Organisation and its successor, the *Bundesnachrichtendienst*. In many cases tape-recordings of these interviews were made and affidavits obtained from the persons interviewed.

384

Among other documentary material the author consulted both unpublished and published sources, including:

Agenten und Spionagetätigkeit, Information der Bundesregierung, No. 59 ff., 1961-64;

Amerikanische Abhörzentrale auf dem Gebiete der DDR, Documentation H-119/1956 of the East German MfSS;

Anleitung für den Unterricht über Abwehr von Spionage und Sabotage, etc. OKW/3001/41g, 1941;

Anleitung für den Unterricht über Abwehr, Spionage und Zersetzung, WKB-80103/1942;

Bditelnost Nashe orushye (Vigilance is our defence), Voyenny Izdat, Moscow, 1959;

Der Soldat muss wachsam sein, Ministry of National Defence of DDR, Berlin, 1957;

Diversanti, Diverzantska sredstva; Yugoslav State Secretariat for National Defence, 1959;

Documents relating to the Eve of the Second World War, 2 vols., Foreign Language Publishing House, Moscow, 1948;

Documents on German Foreign Policy, 10 vols. US Department of State, Washington, D.C., 1957;

Documents on Soviet Foreign Policy, 3 vols., Royal Institute of International Affairs, London, 1951-53;

Documents on the Activities of American Agents in the Czechoslovak Socialist Republic, Ministry of Foreign Affairs, Prague, 1952;

Exposé of Soviet Espionage, prepared by the US Department of Justice, 86th Congress, 2nd session, Doc. No. 114, 1960;

Feindnachrichtendienst, Geheime Vorschriften der Wehrmacht, OKW/HpDv, g.89;

Geheime Lageberichte des SD 1939-44 (ed. H. Biberach), Berlin, 1965;

Geheime Dokumente des RSHA (ed. K.H. Peter), Stuttgart, 1961;

HICOG, Weekly Information Bulletins of the US High Commissioner in Germany;

History and Mission of US Counter-Intelligence Corps, C.I.C. School, N.Y., 1951;

Hochverrat und Staatsgefährdung, (trials before the Federal German Supreme Court at Karlsruhe, official transcripts, 1954-1958) ed. Dr. W. Wagner, Karlsruhe, 1958;

Internal Security Manual, US Govt. Printing Office, Washington, D.C., 1952;

Innere Sicherheit bulletins issued by the Federal German Ministry of Interior, Bonn;

Intelligence, a bibliography of its functions, methods and techniques, US Department of State, Washington, DC, 1949;

KGB, Komitet Gosudarstvennoy Bezopasnosti (a description of its functions), Institut po izucheniyu istoryi, Moscow, 1954;

Kontraobaveshtayna Slushba (Counter-espionage service), in Voyna Enc. Vol.4, Belgrade, 1961;

MAD, Der Militärische Abschirmdienst, (manual for the troops), Federal Ministry of Defence, H/10/1966;

Methoden kommunistischer Agenten, Security Group of the Federal Criminal Office, Bad Godesberg, 1965;

Murder and Kidnapping as an instrument of Soviet policy, US Senate report, Washington, D.C., 1965;

Nazi Conspiracy and Aggression, 10 vols., Washington, D.C., US Govt. Print. Office, 1946;

Operations against Guerilla Forces, US Department of the Navy, Manual FMFM-21, Washington, D.C., 1962;

OKW Amt Ausland-Abwehr, IMT, Nuremberg, Reg. Vol. 23/24, 1949;

ONI, Office of Naval Intelligence, reviews, 54th series, 1946;

Östliche Untergrundarbeit, memoranda of the West Berlin Senator for Internal Affairs, Berlin, 1959-1960;

Otvetstennost za imenu rodine i shpionash (The responsibility for treason and espionage), Moscow, 1964;

Poymanys polichnym, Zbornik faktom o shpionzhe, Soviet Information Bureau, Moscow, 1960;

Report of the Office of Intelligence Research, US Dept. of State, Washington, D.C., 1949;

Report on Soviet Espionage Activities, Investigation of un-American activities in the United States; House of Representatives 8th Congress, 2nd session, Washington, D.C., 1948;

Reports by Ernst Kaltenbrunner to Hitler and Bormann on the investigations of the attempt on July 20, 1944;

Spione, Verräter und Saboteure, a manual issued by the OKW and Reichsamt, Deutsches Volksbildungswerk, Berlin, 1938;

Spionage Unterrichtsbehelfe, issued by the Federal Ministry of Defence, Bonn, 1960;

Spionash i diversyi v arsenale agresorov, Voyenny Vestnik, Moscow, 1960;

Sicherheitsdienst, IMT, Reg. Vol. 23/24, Washington, D.C., 1949;

Staatssicherheitsdienst, manual issued by the Federal Ministry for All-German Questions, Bonn, 1962;

Strogo khranit voyennoyu taynu, Voyenizdat, Moscow, 1953;

Trial of the Major War Criminals before the International Military Tribunal in Nuremberg, 42 vols., published in Nuremberg, (referred in the Notes as IMT);

Trials of War Criminals before the Nuremberg Military Tribunals, 15 vols., Washington, D.C., 1951-2 (referred in the Notes as NMT);

US Congress, House Committee on the Judiciary, Registration of certain persons trained in foreign espionage systems, Washington, D.C., 1955;

West-Berliner Spionagezentralen, memorandum issued by the Ministry of State Security of the DDR, 1-Zst (I) 2/1959;

Zentrale Dienstvorschrift, Federal Ministry of Defence, ZDV-2/31 ff., Bonn, 1962-66;

Zionist Espionage in Egypt, memorandum issued by the Government of the United Arab Republic, Cairo, 1955.

Printed Sources, Books, Memoirs

Abshagen, K.H., *Canaris*, Stuttgart, 1949
Adamov, A. *Treff Cafe Schwalbe*, 1957
Alcorn, R.H., *No Bugles for Spies*, NY, McKay, 1962
Alsop S. and Braden, T. *Sub Rosa*, NY, Reynal, 1946
Anders, K., *Mord auf Befehl*, Tubingen, 1963
Anders, W., *Hitler's Defeat in Russia*, Chicago, 1953
Andreyev and Vladimirov, "*Imperialistichesky shpionsky konsortsyum*," *Mezdun. Zizhn*, No. 9, Moscow, 1964
Aronson, S., *Heydrich und die Anfänge des SD*, Berlin, 1967

Artemyev, V.P., *The Soviet Secret Police*, NY, 1957
Assmann, K., *Deutsche Schicksaljahre*, Wiesbaden, 1950
Augstein, R., and Ahlers, C., *"Zur Spiegel Affäre," Der Spiegel*, Vol. 19 (1965), Nos. 21, 22.

Baines, N. (ed.), *The Speeches of Adolf Hitler*, NY, 1942
Bakker, J.A., *"Wollweber, Koning der Saboteure," De Vliegende Hollander*, Vol. 9, 1953.
Bamler, R., *Der Deutsche Militärische Geheimdienst*, Berlin, 1958
Barclay, C.N., *Armistice*, London, 1968
Bardanne, J., *Le Colonel Nicolai, espion de génie*, Paris, 1947
Barth, K., *The Downfall of the German Secret Service*, London, 1956
Bauermeister, A., *Der Rote Marschall*, Berlin, 1939
Beaumont, F. (ed.), *The Third Reich*, NY, 1955
Bergh, H.van, *A B C der Spione*, Ilmenau, 1965
Bennecke, H., *Hitler und die SA*, Munich, 1962
Bernadotte, F., *The Fall of the Curtain*, London, 1945
Berthold, W., *Division Brandenburg*, Worishöfen, 1960
Bielicky, S.M., *Operativnaya Rozvyedka*, Moscow, 1949
Bols, P., *Mit Scheckbuch und Pistole (CIA)*, Berlin, 1965
Bor-Komorowski, T., *The Secret Army*, London, 1950
Bormann, M., *The Bormann Letters*, London, 1954
Boucard, R., *Les Déssous de l'Espionage 1939-1959*, Paris, 1959
Boveri, M., *Treason in the Twentieth Century*, London, 1962
Brockdorff, W., *Geheimkommandos im Zweiten Weltkrieg*, Munich, 1967
Buchdrucker, A., *Im Dunkel der Schwarzen Reichswehr*, Munich, 1931
Buchheim, M.H., *SS und Polizei im NS Staat*, Dusseldorf, 1964
Buchheim, M.H. and Broszat, M., Jacobsen, H.A., Krausnick, H., *Anatomy of the SS State*, London, 1968
Buchheit, G., *Sóldatentum und Rebellion*, Rastatt, 1961
        Der deutsche Geheimdienst Munich, 1966
        Die Anonyme Macht, Frankfurt/M., 1969
Buchner, A., *Kommando Unternehmen*, Bonn, 1965
Buckley, W. and Bozell, L.B., *McCarthy and his enemies*, Chicago, 1954
Bullock, A., *Hitler, A Study in Tyranny*, London, 1952
Buzek, A., "Diplomacy and Espionage in Czechoslovakia," *Mil. Review*, V.43, 1963

Carell, P., *Hitler's War on Russia*, London, 1964
Carsten, F.L., *The Reichswehr and Politics 1918-1933*, London, 1966
Chandler S. and Robb, R.W., "Front-line intelligence," *Wash. Infantry Journal*, 1946
Charisius, A. *"Spionage und Diversion . . . des Deutschen General Stabes," Zeitschrift für Militärpolitik*, Berlin, 1962
Chernov, F., *Lyubinets Kantslera* (The Chancellor's Favourite), Moscow, Gosudarst. Izdat Pol. Lit., 1962
Childs, D., *Germany since 1918*, London, 1971
Chuikov, V.I., *The End of the Third Reich*, London, 1967
Churchill, W.S., *The Second World War*, London, 1948-54
Clark, A., *Barbarossa*, London, 1965
Clay, L.D., *Decision in Germany*, NY, 1950
Collier, B., *The Lion and The Eagle*, London, 1971

Collins, R., "Army Counter-Intelligence Operations," *Army Inform. D.*, Vol. 19 (1964), No. 9

Colvin, I., *Chief of Intelligence*, London, 1951

Cookridge, E.H., *Soviet Spy Net*, London, 1956
    The Net That Covers The World, NY, 1956

Cooper, R.W., *The Nuremberg Trial*, London, 1947

Copeland, M., *The Game of Nations*, London, 1970

Craig, G.A., *The Politics of the Prussian Army, 1940-45*, London, 1955

Crankshaw, E.H., *The Gestapo*, London, 1956

Cutler, R., "The Development of the National Security Council," *Foreign Affairs*, Vol. 34, (1950), No. 3.

Dallin, A., *German Rule in Russia 1941-44*, London, 1957

Dallin, D.J., *Soviet Espionage*, New Haven, 1956

Datner, S., *Niemiecki okupacyjny aparat bezpieczenstwa*, Warsaw, 1965

Delarue, J., *Histoire de la Gestapo*, Fayard, Paris, 1962

Deriabin, P.S., *The Kremlin Espionage*, Washington, US Gvmt. Print. Off., 1959

Deriabin, P.S. and Gibney, F., *The Secret World*, NY, 1959

Diels, R., *Lucifer ante Portas*, Stuttgart, 1950
    Der Fall Otto John, Goettingen, 1954

Dulles, A.W., *Germany's Underground*, NY, 1947
    "The Role of Intelligence in the Cold War," in *Peace and War in the Modern Age* (ed. F.R. Barnett), NY, 1965
    The Craft of Intelligence, NY, 1962
    The Secret Surrender, NY, 1965

Dunajsky, M., *Niemecko dzungla spionaze* (German espionage jungle), Bratislava, 1968

Ebenstein, W., *The Nazi State*, NY, 1943

Edgar, J.H. and Armin, R.J., *Spionage in Deutschland*, Preetz, 1962

Edwards R., and Dunne, K., *A Study of a Master Spy* (Allen Dulles), London, 1961.

Emmet, C. and Muhlen, N., *The Vanishing Swastika*, Chicago, 1961

Erasmus, J., *Der Geheime Nachrichtendienst*, Goettingen, 1952

Eyck, E., *Bismarck and the German Empire*, London, 1950

Feiling, K., *The Life of Neville Chamberlain*, London, 1946

Feis, H., *From Trust to Terror, The Onset of the Cold War*, London, 1971

Fell, H.W., *Die Weltkriegsspionage*, Munich, 1931

Fishman, J., *The Seven Men of Spandau*, London, 1954

Flicke, W.F., *Die Rote Kapelle*, Hilden, 1949

Foerster, W., *Ein General kämpft gegen den Krieg* (General Beck), Munich, 1949

Foley, C., *Commando Extraordinary* (Skorzeny), London, 1946

Ford, C., *Cloak and Dagger*, NY, Random House, 1946

Freud, H., *"OKW-Amt Ausland-Abwehr,"* in *Feldgrau*, Vol. II (1964)

Frischauer, W., *Himmler, The Evil Genius of the Third Reich*, London, 1953
    The Man Who Came Back, London, 1958

Fuller, J.F.C., *The Second World War*, London, 1948

Gallacher, W., *US Spies in Socialist Countries*, London, 1953

Gaucher, R., *Les Terroristes* (OAS), Paris, 1965

Gerken, R., *Spion in Bonn*, Donauwoerth, 1964
    Spione unter uns, Donauwoerth, 1965

Geyr von Schweppenburg, L., *"Militär Attachés,"* in *Wehrwiss. Rundschau*, Vol. XI, 1961, pp 695-703
  Erinnerungen eines Militärattachés in London, 1933-37, Stuttgart, 1949
Gibney, F., *The Penkovsky Papers*, NY, 1965
  The Khrushchev Pattern, London, 1961
Gilbert, F., *Hitler Directs his War*, NY, 1950
Giskes, H., *Spione überspieled Spione*, Hamburg, 1959
Goerlitz, W., *History of the German General Staff*, NY, 1953
Gramont, S.de, *The Secret War*, London, 1962
Grosscurth, H., *Tagebücher eines Abwehr Offiziers*, Stuttgart, 1963
Grote, H.H., *Vorsicht, Feind hört mit!*, Dresden, 1956
Guderian, H., *Panzer Leader*, London, 1952
Guerin, A., *Le général gris*, Paris, 1968
Gunther, J., "Inside CIA," in *Look*, August 12, 1952

Haase, *Strafsache gegen* (Trial Transcript), *Deutscher Zentralverlag*, Berlin, 1954
Hagen, L., *The Secret War For Europe*, London, 1968
Hagen, W., (Hoettl, W.), *Die Geheime Front*, Vienna, 1950; Engl. Trans. *The Secret Front*, London, 1953
Halder, F., *Hitler als Feldherr*, Munich, 1949
Halifax, Lord, *Fullness of Days*, London, 1957
Halle, L. J., *The Cold War as History*, London, 1967
Hamsik, D., *Bomba pro Heydricha*, Prague, 1965
Hanfstaengel, E., *Hitler, The Missing Days*, London, 1957
Hegner, H.S., *Die Reichskanzelei 1933-45*, Frankfurt, 1964
Heiber, H. (ed.), *Hitler's Lagebesprechungen* (Fuhrer Conferences), Stuttgart, 1962
Heidenheimer, A.J., *Adenauer und die CDU*, The Hague, 1960
Heiman, L., "Israeli Military Intelligence," in *Military Review*, Vol. 43 (January 1963)
Henderson, N., *Failure of a Mission*, London, 1940
Herre, F., *Bibliographie zur Zeitgeschichte des Zweiten Weltkrieges*, Munich, 1955
Herz, P., *"Normannenstrasse—Agentenzentrale SSD,"* *Untersuchungsausschuss Freiheitl. Juristen*, Berlin, 1960
Heusinger, A., *Befehl im Widerstreit*, Stuttgart, 1950
Heydrich, R., *Aufgaben und Ausbau des SD in Dritten Reiche*, Munich, 1937
Higgins, T., *Hitler and Russia*, NY, 1966
Hilsman, R., "Intelligence and Policy-making in Foreign Affairs," in *World Politics*, Vol. 5 (1952), No. 11-45
Hirsch, R., *The Soviet Spies*, NY, 1947
Hitler's Table Talks 1941-44, London, 1953
Hoeher, W., *Agent 2996 enthüllt*, Berlin, Kongressverlag, 1954
Hornstein, E.von, *Staatsfeinde*, Cologne, 1963
Hynd, A., *Passport to Treason*, NY, 1943

Jacobsen, H.A., *Der Zweite Weltkrieg*, 3 vols., Munich, 1962
  Deutsche Kriegsführung 1939-45, Munich, 1961
Jentsch, A., *Agenten unter uns*, Dusseldorf, 1966
Joesten, J., *Im Dienste des Misstrauens*, Munich, 1964
  They Call it Intelligence, London, 1963

John, Otto, *Ich Waehlte Deutschland*, Berlin, 1954
    I Came Home Twice, London, 1971 (in manuscript)
Johnson, T.M., "C.I.C.—The Army's Spy Hunters" in *Reader's Digest*, 31, 1952
    "Battle Underground, The Work of the C.I.C." in *Combat Forces Journal* Vol. 3 (1953).
Jones, L.M., "G-2 Key to Nuclear Target Acquisition," in *Milit. Review*, Vol. 43 (1963)
Jong, L.de, *The German Fifth Column*, Chicago, 1956

Kahn, d., *The Code-Breakers*, NY, 1967
Kail, S.G., "Combat Intelligence and Counter-Intelligence" in *Milit. Review*, Vol. 36 (1956), No. 8
Karski, J., *Story of a Secret State*, London, Hodder, 1945
Kaufmann, W., *Case Barbarossa*, Cambridge, 1962
Kent, S., *Strategic Intelligence*, Princeton, 1949
Kern (Kernmayer), E., *Verrat and Deutschland*, Goettingen, 1963
Kersten, F., *Totenkopf und Treue*, Hamburg, 1953
Kesselring, A., *Memoirs*, London, 1953
Keitel, W., *Memoirs*, NY, 1966
Kiel, H., *Canaris zwischen den Fronten*, Bremerhaven, 1950
Kirkpatrick, L.B., *The Real CIA*, NY, 1968
    Captains Without Eyes, NY, 1969
Klein, J.K., "The Soviet Expionage System in Germany" in *Milit. Review*, Vols. 38 and 39, (1959).
Kleist, P., *Zwischen Hitler und Stalin*, Bonn, 1950
Kogon, E., *Der SS Staat*, Munich, 1946
Kohn, H., *The Mind of Germany*, NY, 1960
Konrat, G., *Assault from Within*, London, 1971
Kordt, E., *Nicht aus den Akten*, 1950
Kosthorst, *Die Deutsche Opposition gegen Hitler*, Bonn, 1954
Kotze, H.von, *"Hitler's Sicherheitsdienst (SD),"* in *Polit. Meinung*, Vol. VIII (1963), No. 86
Kozaczuk, J., *Bitwa o tajemnice*, (Struggle for secrets), Warsaw, 1967
Kriegsheim, H., *Getarnt, Getäuscht und doch Getreu*, Berlin, 1958
Krivitsky, W.G., *I Was Stalin's Agent*, London, 1939
Kuehne, H., *Kuriere, Spitzel, Spione*, Berlin, 1949

Lahousen, E., "Diary" in *Institut für Zeitgeschichte*, Munich.
Lauchner, F., *"Nachrichtenaufklärungswesen,"* in *Militärpolit. Forum*, II (1964)
Lenkavsky, S., *Sowjetrussische Morde* (Petlyura, Konowaletz, Bandera), Munich, 1962
Leverkuehn, P., *Der Geheime Nachrichtendienst*, Frankfurt/M., 1957; Engl. trans. *German Military Intelligence*, London, 1954
    Bilanz des Zweiten Weltkrieges, Oldenburg, Stalling, 1953
Lewitsky, B., *Vom Roten Terror zur Sozialistischer Gesetzlichkeit*, Munich, 1961
    Die Rote Inquisition, Frankfurt, 1967
Liss, U., *Erfahrungen im Feindesnachrichtendienst aus drei Armeen* in Wehrkunde, Vols. X (1961) and XI (1962)
    Der Wert der richtigen Feindbeurteilung in *Wehrkunde, Vol. VIII (1959)*
    Die Bearbeitung Fremder Heere im Generalstabe, Neckarsulm, 1959
Litan, J., *Bitteres Ende* (Zeppelin), Berlin, 1965

Lovell, S.P., *Of Spies and Stratagems*, NJ, 1963
Lueder, D.R., *Aerial Photographic Interpretation*, NY, 1959

McCamy, J.L., *The Administration of American Foreign Affairs*, NY, 1950
Mader, J., *Gangster in Aktion*, Berlin, 1961
    Die Killer lauern, Berlin, 1961
    Die Graue Hand, Berlin, 1961
    Jagd nach dem Narbengesicht (Skorzeny), Berlin, 1962
    Nicht Länger Geheim, Berlin, 1966
    Hitler's Spionage Generale Sagen Aus, Berlin, 1970
Mäkela, J.L., *Im Rucken des Feindes*, Frauenfeld, 1967
Mann, G., *Deutsche Geschichte*, Frankfurt, 1964
Manstein, E.von, *Verlorene Siege*, Bonn, 1955; Engl. Trans. *Lost Victories*, London, 1958
Manvell, R. and Fraenkel, H., *Himmler*, London, 1965
Melnikov, D.E. and Chernaya, L.B., *Dvulikiy Admiral Kanaris*, Moscow, 1965
Merten, K., *Die roten Maulwürfe*, Donauworth, 1964
Miksche, F.O., *Secret Forces*, London, 1950
Minayev, V., *Taynoye stanovtsya yavnim*, Voyenizdat, Moscow, 1960
Minott, R.G., *The Fortress That Never Was*, London, 1964
Morgan, F., *The OSS*, NY, 1957

Namier, J.P., *In the Nazi Era*, London, 1952
Nekrich, A.M., *V labirintakh taynoy voyny 1939-45*, in *Novaya Istoriya*, Moscow, 1966
Nettl, J.P., *The Eastern Zone and Soviet Policy in Germany, 1945-50*, Oxford, 1951
Nicolai, W., *Der Nachrichtendienst*, Berlin, 1920
Nikitinsky, *Kovorny metody*, Voyen. Izdat, Moscow, 1954
Nikulin, L., *Tukhachevsky*, Voyen. Izdat, Moscow, 1964

Orlov, A., *Handbook of Intelligence and Guerilla Warfare*, U. of Mich., 1963
Orb, H., *Nationalsozialismus*, Olten, 1945

Papen, Franz von, *Der Wahrheit eine Gasse* Munich, 1952; Engl. trans. *Memoirs*, London, 1952
Paget, R., *Manstein, Campaigns and Trial*, London, 1952
Peis, G., *The Man Who Started the War*, London, 1960
Perrault, G., *L'Orchéstre rouge*, Paris, Fayard, 1967
Peskov, E., "*Sociologya razvedka i shpionasha*," in *Kommunist* No. 11, 1960
Petrov and Chernyakovsky, *Razvedka SSA*, Moscow, 1964
Ploetz, K. (ed.) *Geschichte des Zweiten Weltkrieges*, Wurzburg, 1960
Powers, F.G., *Operation Overflight*, London, Hodder, 1970
Prittie, T., *Germany Divided*, Boston, 1960

Raimondi, G., "Capabilities and Vulnerabilities in the Evaluation of Military Information" in *Milit. Review*, Vol. 39 (1959)
Ranson, H.H., *Central Intelligence and National Security*, Cambridge, 1959
    Can American Democracy Survive the Cold War?, NY, 1963
Reile, O., *Geheime Ostfront*, Munich, 1963
    Macht und Ohnmacht der Geheimdienste, Munich, 1968
Reipert, F., *Kriegsmethoden und Kriegsverbrechen*, Berlin, 1941

Reitlinger, G., *Die SS*, Munich, 1957, Engl. *The SS, Alibi of a Nation*, London,
    The Final Solution, London, 1953
Rendulic, L., *Gekämpft, Gesiegt, Geschlagen*, Wels, 1952
Ribbentrop, J.von, *Zwischen London und Moskau*, Munich, 1953
Riess, C., *Total Espionage, Hitler's Secret Service*, NY, 1941
Roeder, M., *Die Rote Kapelle*, Hamburg, 1952
Rogge, O.J., *Nazi Penetration in the United States*, NY, 1961
Rosenthal, W., *Die Rote Gestapo* in *Digest des Ostens*, Vol. VIII (1965)
Rowan, R.W. and Deindorfer, R.D., *Secret Service*, NY, 1967
Royce H., *Wilhelm Canaris und der 20 Juli 1944*, Bonn, 1953

Sanger und Etterlin, F.M.von, *Die Feindlagebeurteilung* in *Wehrwissenschaftl.
    Rundschau*, Vol. 7 (1957), No.3
Schacht, H., *Accounts Settled*, London, 1949
Scharnhorst, G., *Spione in der Bundeswehr* Bayreuth, 1965
Schellenberg, W., *The Labyrinth*, London, 1956
                    (ed. Hagen L.,) Memoirs, 1956
Schlabrendorff, F.von, *They Almost Killed Hitler*, NY, 1947
Schmidt, P., *Statist auf diplomatischer Bühne*, Bonn, 1949 (the Engl. edition
    Hitler's Interpreter, London, 1951, is abridged)
Schreibershofen, M.von., *Das Deutsche Heer*, Berlin, 1933
Schofield, W.G., *Treason Trial, The Radio Traitors in WWII*, NY, 1964
Schramm, P.W., *Verrat in Zweiten Weltkriege*, Dusseldorf, 1967
Schroetter, H., *Stalingrad*, London, 1958
Schultz, J., *Die letzten dreissig Tage*, (OKW diary), Stuttgart, 1957
Schwarzwalder, J., *We Caught the Spies*, NY, 1946
Sendtner, K., *Vollmacht des Gewissens*, Frankfurt, 1960
Seifert, J., *Franz Josef Strauss*, Munich, 1963
Sheen, H.G., "The Disintergration of the German Intelligence Services" in *Milit.
    Review* Vol. 29 (1949).
Shirer, W.L., *The Rise and Fall of the Third Reich*, NY, 1959
                Berlin Diary, London, 1941
Skorzeny, O., *Secret Missions*, NY, 1950
                Geheimkommando Skorzeny, Hamburg, 1950
Shub, A., *An Empire Loses Hope*, London, 1971
Solberg, R., *God and Caesar in East Germany*, NY, 1961
Speich, H., "Fuhrerentschluss und Aufklärung," in *Schweiz. Militär. Zeitschrift*,
    Vol. 120 (1954), No. 8
Speidel, H., *We defended Normandy*, London, 1951
Steen, J.van, *Spionage in de tweede wereldoorlog*, Kampen, 1964
Steinhauer, G., *Der Detektiv des Kaisers*, Berlin, 1932
Strawson, J., *Hitler as Military Commander*, London, 1971
Strik-Strikfeldt, W., *Against Stalin and Hitler*, London, 1970

Telpuchovsky, B.S., *Die Sowjetische Geschichte des Grossen Vaterländischen
    Krieges*, (trans. from Russian), Fkft., 1961
Thomson, C.A.H., *Overseas Information Service of the US Government*,
    Washington, DC, 1948
Thorwald, J., *Das Ende an der Elbe*, Stuttgart, 1950
Trevor-Roper, H.R., *The Last Days of Hitler*, London, 1947
                    Hitler's War Directives 1939-45, London, 1964
Tully, A., *CIA, The Inside Story*, NY, 1962

Unna, W., "CIA—Who Watches the Watchman?" in *Harper's,* April, 1958

Vagts, A., *Defence and Diplomacy,* NY, 1958
Vogelsang, T., *Reichswehr, Staat-und NSDAP,* Stuttgart, 1962
Vosjoli, P., "The French Spy Scandal in Life," Vol. 44, No. 8

Waldman, E., *The Goose Step is Verboten,* NY, 1964
Wallich, H.C., *Mainsprings of the German Revival,* Yale, 1955
Waring, R., "Problems of Security within NATO," *Nato,* Vol. 8, 1963
Warlimont, W., *Inside Hitler's Headquarters,* London, 1964
Watt, R.M., *The Kings Depart,* London, 1968
Wechsler, J.A., *The Age of Suspicion,* NY, Random House, 1963
Wehner, W., *Geheim,* Munich, 1960
Weintal, E., and Bartlett, C., *Facing the Brink,* London, 1967
Weyl, N., *Treason,* Washington, D.C., 1950
Wheeler Bennett, J., *The Nemesis of Power,* London, 1948
Wighton, C., *Heydrich, Hitler's Most Evil Henchman,* London, 1962
          The World's Greatest Spies, London, 1963
Wilbrand, J., *Kommt Hitler Wieder?,* Donauworth, 1964
Wilson, J., "Moscow's Chief European Gangster" (Wollweber) in *Reader's Digest,*
    Vol. 71 (November, 1957)
Windsor, P., *Germany and the Management of Detente,* London, 1971
Wise, D. and Ross, T.B., *The Invisible Government,* NY, Random House, 1964
          The Espionage Establishment, NY, Random House, 1967
Wolff, Ilse (ed.), *Persecution and Resistance under the Nazis,* London, 1960
Wolin, S. (ed.) *The Soviet Secret Police,* NY, 1957

Zacharias, E.M., "The Inside Story of Yalta" in *U.N. World,* Vol. 3 (1949) No. 1
Zentner, K., *Geschichte des Zweiten Weltkrieges,* Munich, 1963
Zhukov, G.K., *Memoirs,* London, 1971
Zink, H., *The United States in Germany, 1944-1955,* NY, 1957
Zipfel, F., *Gestapo und Sicherheitsdienst,* Berlin, 1960

Index of Names